The Impact of Intervention

The Impact of Intervention

The Dominican Republic during
the U.S. Occupation of 1916–1924

BY BRUCE J. CALDER

 UNIVERSITY OF TEXAS PRESS, AUSTIN

First Paperback Printing, 1988

Requests for permission to reproduce material from this work
should be sent to Permissions, University of Texas Press,
Box 7819, Austin, Texas 78713-7819.

LIBRARY OF CONGRESS CATALOGING IN PUBLICATION DATA
Calder, Bruce J., 1940–
  The impact of intervention.
  Bibliography: p.
  Includes index.
  1. Dominican Republic—History—American occupation,
1916–1924.   I. Title.   II. Series.
F1938.45.C35   1984   972.93   83-23447
ISBN 0-292-73830-7
ISBN 0-292-73846-3 pbk.

Both the initial research and the publication of this work were made possible in part
through grants from the National Endowment for the Humanities, a federal agency
whose mission is to award grants to support education, scholarship, media program-
ming, libraries, and museums in order to bring the results of cultural activities to the
general public.

TO MY FATHER AND MOTHER
Jasper Allen Calder
Jean Johnson Calder
WITH GRATITUDE FOR ALL THEY HAVE GIVEN ME

Contents

Acknowledgments

Sitting down to write these acknowledgments stirs memories of those many persons who have helped me in one way or another with the long project I am now completing. Would that it were possible to mention them all. But editors and readers both would rebel at such a list! Therefore, with sincere apologies to those many persons omitted, let me be more selective.

The research and writing of this book were facilitated by major grants from the Fulbright-Hayes fellowship program and from the National Endowment for the Humanities. Also important were smaller awards from the Institute of Latin American Studies at the University of Texas at Austin and from the Research Board of the University of Illinois at Chicago, which also contributed toward the publication of this book. Finally, a partial sabbatical leave from the University of Illinois at Chicago afforded me the time necessary to bring this work to completion.

Among those many individuals who deserve my thanks for their help, none is more important than the late Thomas F. McGann, who served in a triple role as teacher, adviser, and friend. He first suggested the topic of this book and provided perceptive and critical advice during its writing. Richard N. Adams, Richard Graham, and Robert A. Divine also read and critiqued large parts of the manuscript at an early stage, while Susan Lince, Richard B. Lindley, Gail Malmgreen, and Elspeth Revere provided equally important advice and support over the years this project has continued. Among Dominicans I first want to mention Vetilio Alfau Durán, Francisco Elpidio Beras, the late Enriquillo Henríquez, Julio Peynado, and Emilio Rodríguez Demorizi. Their willingness to freely share their libraries, family papers, historical expertise, and personal memories has much enriched this book. Equally important have been the advice and support I have received from a younger generation of Dominicans, including Magdalena Acosta, Roberto Cassá, Emilio Cordero Michel, José del Castillo, Frank Moya Pons, and Nazre Sansur Tuma. And I want to thank my editors, including Scott Lubeck, Holly Carver, and Christina West, who deserve much credit for making this a better book.

As any researcher knows, the assistance of the directors and staffs of archives and libraries is critical to the success of one's labors. It is in this regard that I owe an immense debt to the many persons whose hard work, sound advice, and unfailing courtesy made fruitful the long hours I spent in the U.S. National Archives, the Archivo General de la Nación in Santo Domingo, the Marine Corps Historical Center, the Museo de Historia y Geografía in Santo Domingo, the Library of Congress, the New York Public Library, the Newberry Library, and the libraries of the University of Texas at Austin, the Universidad Autónoma de Santo Domingo, Indiana University, and the University of Illinois at Chicago.

If circumstances permitted, many other persons who provided significant support to my project would be noted here. They will know who they are; I hope they will also realize the gratitude I feel for their help. With all those named or unnamed I gladly share any credit which may come to this book. For its shortcomings I take full responsibility.

Introduction

The 1980s have seen the U.S. government deeply involved in the affairs of the Central American and Caribbean nations. Political meddling has twice led to military intervention, openly in Grenada and through surrogates in Nicaragua. To the historically minded, the situation is familiar, for the events unfolding now bear a serious resemblance to what has been going on between the great northern power and its weaker southern neighbors for decades. Indeed the scenarios of the 1980s, except for the names of individual actors and the specific content of the rhetoric, could be used to describe with remarkable accuracy many situations which took place twenty, thirty, sixty, or even eighty years ago. The events of today are reflections of an unequal relationship which has existed for almost a century.

The heyday of direct North American military intervention in the Caribbean lasted from 1898 to the mid 1930s. The subject of this book, the Dominican Republic during the U.S. occupation of 1916 to 1924, is a major chapter in the history of that period. Although the story of Washington's entanglement in the republic's affairs begins in the nineteenth century, the particular train of events which led to the invasion of 1916 commenced in a period of chronic political instability that followed the fall of a dictatorial government in 1899. From then until 1916, the United States steadily increased its involvement in and control over internal Dominican affairs. Facilitating this policy were political and financial manipulation, frequent threats and the occasional use of force, and the growing U.S. penetration of the private sector of the Dominican economy.

The Dominican Occupation: An Overview

In May 1916, in response to a revolution which threatened to topple yet another government, Washington intervened militarily. Although few U.S. officials envisioned a lengthy occupation at that time, it was late 1924 before the last of the invading forces left the island nation. During the eight years of the occupation, a military government attempted to bring a number of fundamental changes to the republic in the hope that its reforms by fiat would create a stable and friendly neighbor, and a reliable customer, to the south of the United States.

The most important immediate cause of the U.S. occupation of the Dominican Republic, aside from the logic of its ever increasing involvement in Dominican affairs, was strategic: the desire of the United States to protect the approaches to its southern coast and the Panama Canal against unfriendly powers, especially Germany. Also essential to this strategic concern was a larger economic consideration: to preserve U.S. hegemony over the entire circum-Caribbean region, which contained or was adjacent to areas of considerable importance to the U.S. economy. Of distinctly minor importance was the specific desire to protect U.S. control of the Dominican economy, of its trade and resources, which were insignificant relative to U.S. interests elsewhere. The republic had become a pawn in international sphere of influence politics by virtue of its location rather than its wealth.

The United States' aggressive intrusion into Dominican affairs in 1916 was not an isolated incident in the history of its Caribbean diplomacy. Though U.S. involvement in the area had generally been limited during the nineteenth century, this had changed in 1898 when, by virtue of the Spanish American War, Washington suddenly found itself in control of both Cuba and Puerto Rico. Thereafter, the U.S. presence in the Caribbean grew with each passing year. Washington maintained its hold over both Puerto Rico, turning it into a colony, and Cuba, instituting a protectorate with the Platt Amendment, and then embarked on a series of military interventions. The most important of these occurred in Panama in 1903, Nicaragua in 1909 and 1912, Mexico in 1914, Haiti in 1915, and Cuba several times. In addition, beginning in 1905 the United States had imposed customs receiverships to obtain financial and political control in the Dominican Republic, Nicaragua, and Haiti. It would have done the same in Honduras but was blocked by a negative vote in the U.S. Senate. The Dominican occupation of 1916 to 1924 was clearly part of a general pattern of expanding U.S. influence in the Caribbean after 1898. And increased U.S. activity in the Caribbean was but part of a growing U.S. presence in Latin America, the Pacific, and the Far East.

The U.S. occupation of the Dominican Republic was more, however, than a diplomatic incident on the northern nation's way to world power—it was an important episode in the history of the Dominican people. For six of the eight years of occupation, military officials tried to remake Dominican society, designing and implementing programs meant to change the republic's political, economic, and social life. In addition, occupation authorities continued the regular administrative activities of the government, in the process guiding the country through two periods of unusual economic stress, the first caused by World War I and the second by a severe worldwide depression which hit the republic in late 1920. The Dominican response to military government also lends significance to the occupation years. Depending on the issue, the place, and the time, this response ranged from enthusiastic cooperation to determined resistance. The latter included a five-and-a-half-year guerrilla war fought against U.S. Marines in the country's eastern region and a political-intellectual protest, conducted by nationalists both domestically and internationally.

Occupation officials implemented a wide range of programs and reforms by 1920, drawing on previous U.S. colonial experience, especially in Cuba, Puerto Rico, and the Philippines, on U.S. domestic models, and on previously existing Dominican laws and institutions. Among the most important programs were the creation of the country's first adequate road network, the implementation of other substantial public works projects, the rapid expansion and improvement of the republic's educational system, and the beginning of national public health and sanitation programs. Equally important was the reformation of the nation's military, with the establishment of an efficient, and theoretically apolitical, constabulary. Significant, but receiving less emphasis, were reforms of the Dominican treasury, the tax system, the courts and judiciary, the tariff structure, the land title system, the government agricultural service, and a host of other political, economic, and even social institutions.

This reform program was concentrated in the first four years of the occupation, from 1917 through 1920. After that, severe economic problems and a contemplated U.S. withdrawal forced military officials to concentrate on trying to maintain what they had already created and, in a few cases, on completing projects already in progress.

The programs of the military government left a double legacy to Dominican society. First was their immediate and intended impact. This in most cases was limited, either because the projects themselves were limited or because, in the case of the more ambitious efforts, they were only partially successful and then were crippled by the depression of the early 1920s or by the opposition of Dominican nationalists. Second was their eventual and unintended effect, which was often of greater significance than the first. Military officials, for instance, did not intend that the laws they promulgated concerning land and landholding, viewed as progressive at the time, would contribute to strengthening the system of plantation agriculture—thus creating an economic situation which condemned the republic's population to one of the lower standards of living in Latin America. Or, to cite a more famous case, neither did the designers of the new constabulary, the Guardia Nacional Dominicana, intend that it would serve as the primary vehicle for General Rafael Trujillo's thirty-one-year dictatorship.

Dominican resistance is as important to the history of the occupation as the record of the military government itself. Although it developed rather slowly, resistance eventually became quite strong, seriously hampering the work of the military regime and forcing the United States to move toward withdrawal.

In the east, peasants and sugar workers conducted a guerrilla insurgency from early 1917 until mid 1922, preventing the marines from controlling large areas of the region. Though unconnected with any other movement, the struggle was a nearly classical endeavor whose tactics might have come from a textbook on guerrilla warfare. The marines' advantages in weaponry and training were offset by the guerrillas' reliance on surprise, mobility, indigenous supply and intelligence networks, and an unsurpassed knowledge of the terrain. The Dominicans were masters of guerrilla war while the marines long failed to comprehend the nature either of their opponents or of the war they were fighting. This condemned them to make the same mistakes again and again. It also led to frustrations which caused some marines to brutalize Dominicans, both guerrilla opponents and ordinary citizens. This generated immense resentment against the marines, popular support and recruits for the guerrillas, and unfavorable publicity for the military government throughout Latin America and the United States. The war, debilitating to the military government and destructive to the east and its people, dragged on for five and a half years before the combined forces of marines and Dominican paramilitary auxiliaries finally began to put effective pressure on the guerrillas. This, combined with a pending agreement for the termination of the occupation, caused the insurgents to enter into negotiations and eventually lay down their arms in exchange for a nearly total amnesty.

In order to understand the guerrilla war for the purposes of this study, particularly why it occurred in just one area of the republic, it was necessary to look beyond the war itself at the society of the eastern region. Two phenomena which predated the war appeared to be of critical importance. One was the fact that the east was in the midst of an economic revolution, as it rapidly changed from an area dominated by traditional subsistence agriculture and grazing into a modern, capitalist, sugar-producing center. In the wake of this economic revolution came a social one, destroying the traditional way of life and leaving unsolved social problems, bitterness, and tension. The second factor was the east's political system. When the marines ventured outside of the important eastern city of San Pedro de Macorís, they encountered a relic of nineteenth-century Latin America, the caudillo system, whose power had survived precisely because the region had for so long remained undeveloped. Failing to understand this traditional political system and its deep roots in eastern culture, the marines challenged it, causing caudillo leaders to go to war. Once alight, the flames of war were fed by the east's volatile social conditions. The dispossessed, the unemployed, the exploited workers, and the threatened small landowners were easy marks for guerrilla recruiters. These Dominicans, along with the many alienated by the marines in their disastrous conduct of a war they did not understand, were more than enough to prolong the eastern conflagration for over five years.

The necessity of understanding the guerrilla war thus opened up new areas of inquiry, particularly those concerning the nature of eastern society and its political system. This in turn required a look at the history of sugar agriculture in the republic, insofar as information was available, especially at the expansion of the corporate sugar estates in the late nineteenth and early twentieth centuries. This led inevitably to the study of the Dominican and then the military government laws that had opened the door to investment capital, especially from the United States, and to corporate expansion into Dominican agriculture.

The sugar industry, by far the largest investment of U.S. capital in the Dominican Republic, serves as a paradigm for understanding the relationship between the military government and U.S. investors. Examination of the occupation legislation affecting the sugar industry reveals a surprisingly mixed situation. Some laws substantially favored U.S. interests; others did precisely the opposite. A variety of contradictory influences were behind this inconsistency, including the startling fact that military officials were often ambivalent or even negative about the use of foreign capital in the Dominican economy. In this as in other areas, it appears, some occupation officials acted not only as agents of imperialism but also as representatives of U.S. domestic political currents, particularly the then popular Progressive movement.

The second principal aspect of the Dominican opposition to the occupation, entirely unconnected to the warfare and socioeconomic change of the east, was the political-intellectual resistance. This movement originated among a small group of officials and supporters of Dominican President Francisco Henríquez y Carvajal, whom the United States had deposed in 1916. Consisting of staunch nationalists who were, however, moderate in their approach, the Henríquez-centered movement was later joined in its work by a more radical organization, the Unión Nacional Dominicana, which pushed confrontation with the military government and a hard line in dealing with Washington. Together these forces created a vigorous, broad-based protest movement within the republic by 1920.

The nationalists did not confine their campaign for liberation to Santo Domingo. They worked vigorously in the large cities of the United States, Latin America, and Europe, aided by diplomats, politicians, labor leaders, writers, editors, and other crusading intellectuals. Their cause was also furthered by the military government itself, which acted with such harshness in opposing the nationalist campaign in Santo Domingo that the occupation became a diplomatic cause célèbre and an immense embarrassment to the State Department in Washington. The publicity and protests soon led to investigations and eventually to meaningful negotiations for withdrawal.

The efforts to arrange a withdrawal are in themselves a complex story. As the result of the pressures created by the nationalist movement, the United States began to devise a withdrawal plan in late 1920. But the plan featured such restrictions to Dominican sovereignty that a wave of protest and rejection greeted its announcement. Further negotiations produced slight U.S. concessions and several more proposals, but each failed to receive approval from the politically diverse groups of Dominicans now loosely united under the umbrella of the radical nationalists. Eventually, after a stalemate of nearly a year caused by the mutual intransigence of the U.S. and nationalist camps, a compromise agreement emerged—known as the Hughes-Peynado Plan. This 1922 accord, by offering the prospect of a prompt withdrawal under terms which seemed reasonable to nonradicals, rapidly led to the disintegration of the larger nationalist movement. Though hard-core nationalists continued to fight the new plan, they could not prevent its implementation. In October 1922 a Dominican provisional government took over administration of the country, and in July 1924 a newly elected constitutional government assumed control.

The Dominican Occupation: Its Place in History

The guerrilla war, and to some degree the nationalist movement in general, raised a historiographical question. The papers of the military government, when examined at the beginning of this study, clearly demonstrated that the eastern conflict was a major event of the occupation period. Yet it was shrouded in historical obscurity. Neither North Americans nor Dominicans had written more than a few lines about the war. Those who did usually dismissed the guerrillas as bandits and the war as a short-lived affair.

The military government papers themselves revealed one reason for the disappearance of the guerrilla war from history. U.S. military officials sought to disguise the real nature of events in the east by labeling the rebels as bandits. The guerrilla resistance and the other forms of opposition to the occupation were embarrassing to the United States—such resistance tarnished the image of the United States in Latin America, making diplomacy there more difficult. And in Europe it called into question the goals, particularly the right of national self-determination, for which the United States claimed to struggle, first in World War I and then at the Versailles Conference.

Unfortunately, the guerrillas themselves were not very helpful to those who in later years might have tried to justify them and to disprove the myths which the military government had created. In general, these peasant fighters were inarticulate. They were nearly all illiterate, and their testament remained largely unwritten. They also lacked a singular leader, in the style of Sandino or Castro, someone whose charisma and connections might have attracted outside attention. Perhaps for this reason, no Carleton Beals or Herbert Matthews took the trouble to seek them out and advance their cause in the world press. Neither were the guerrillas always clearly patriotic, being a classic example of Eric Hobsbawm's "primitive rebels," whose motivations and actions sometimes cross the ill-defined line which separates the personal from the political.

Politically conscious and literate Dominicans of the time, even those irrevocably and actively opposed to the military government, generally accepted the banditry thesis if they paid any attention at all to the events in the east. Why did the Dominicans themselves adopt this paradoxical antinationalist position? First, they lacked information. News in the heavily censored press concerning the guerrilla struggle was scarce and usually reflected the views of marine and military government publicists. Second, Dominican society, split deeply into upper and lower sectors, put blinders on its elite. Their class orientation was away from the peasantry, whom they regarded as socially insignificant and politically backward. And the elite, at least the more intellectual stratum, were heavily influenced by the ideas of nineteenth-century liberalism and positivism, whose basic tenets of order and progress caused followers to look askance at popular social forces such as those represented by the guerrillas.

The Dominican historians writing immediately after the occupation were members of the liberal intellectual establishment. They, like other members of their social stratum, paid little attention to the guerrilla war; instead they devoted their energy to documenting the intellectual and political protest of their own class.[1] So, too, the North Americans who wrote extensively about the intervention, Sumner Welles and Melvin Knight, both failed to recognize the guerrilla war for what it was and all but ignored it.[2] Though their political predispositions toward the occupation were diametrically opposed, both took their cues about events in the east from Dominican intellectuals and discounted the guerrillas' importance. Welles, as a member of the State Department, was in addition defending U.S. policies and so endorsed the marines' banditry argument.

In Haiti—another country which saw its struggle against the United States denigrated as unimportant and criminal—national historians, such as Dantès Bellegarde, subsequently arose to clarify the record. But this failed to occur in the Dominican Republic because of the three-decade reign of General Rafael Trujillo, who made it clear to historians that it was best to ignore or gloss over the guerrilla war and the resistance in general. His motivation was obvious. The general owed his rise from humble origins to a position of great wealth and power to the opportunities afforded him by the military government and its institutions. In fact, Trujillo, a soldier in the U.S.-created and U.S.-controlled Guardia Nacional, had himself fought against the guerrillas.

Much the same fate befell the history of the elite's political-intellectual resistance and, indeed, the history of the entire occupation. Virtually all the histories of the period, usually in the form of document collections or personal memoirs, date from the 1920s (with the principal exception of Luis Mejía's *De Lilís a Trujillo*, published in Caracas in 1944). Afterward the severe repression of the Trujillo period assured that the occupation was rarely discussed in print. Similarly, in the United States, the occupation disappeared from view. After the decline of the radicalism of the 1920s and 1930s, U.S. historians seldom dealt extensively with any of the Caribbean occupations, particularly with such matters as anti-U.S. resistance movements. Behind their neglect were the general lack of interest in the usually quiet Caribbean of the postwar period, the fact that the Good Neighbor Policy and its aftermath invited the portrayal of the occupations as rather unimportant aberrations from the regular course of U.S. diplomacy, and the repressiveness of the McCarthy era, which discouraged thinking and writing on the subject. Only since the 1960s, after a series of events radically altered the situation in the United States, the Dominican Republic, and the Caribbean in general, have historians in both countries begun to analyze the events of 1916 to 1924.

This book, the first detailed examination of the Dominican occupation, joins a growing number of studies of U.S. intervention and occupation in the Caribbean area (and in the Philippines) between 1898 and 1935.[3] As a study of an episode in U.S. diplomatic history, this volume fits generally into the body of work produced by the "Wisconsin school" and by like-minded scholars. That is, it agrees with the concept of imperialism as a deep and ongoing phenomenon, often economically based, in the relationship of the United States with the non-European world. But, like other later writers of that general school, I am forced by the evidence to modify some of its original conclusions. I find particularly useful the work of Lloyd Gardner's student, Hans Schmidt, whose study of the Haitian occupation of 1915 to 1934 calls into question the applicability of the "open-door" concept to U.S.-Caribbean diplomacy. Also, Schmidt's dismissal of "liberal internationalism" as an element in U.S.-Haitian relations applies equally to the Dominican case. And his characterization of the occupation reform programs as "technocratic Progressive" in origin, which is to say Progressive without democratic political pretensions, is helpful in understanding the experience in Santo Domingo.

As a study of Dominican history, especially in its social and economic aspects, this work tends to support the general views of the dependency theorists. Their analyses of the process of modernization and development-underdevelopment are particularly useful in understanding the Dominican Republic's deepening involvement in the world capitalist economic system in the late nineteenth and early twentieth centuries. During the occupation period, the economy of the republic seems to have been moving between the two types of historical dependency situations described by Fernando Cardoso and Enzo Falleto: from a dependency situation in which the economy is more or less nationally controlled (as with tobacco and cacao) to a new situation where the entire process is owned and controlled by foreigners (as with sugar). This trend, depending on the cooperation of the generally foreign-oriented Dominican elite, was under way long before 1916, although some of the programs and legislation of the military government further advanced the process. Several contemporary Dominican historians have used the dependency theory as a means for understanding their nation's historical development. The most thorough analysis of the occupation period from this point of view is Wilfredo Lozano's *La dominación imperialista en la República Dominicana, 1900–1930*. I find myself in general agreement with Lozano's analysis, although the new data I have gathered here cause me to disagree with a number of the particular points of his argument.[4]

The increasingly numerous studies of U.S. intervention and occupation in the Caribbean area during the 1898 to 1935 period provide an inviting opportunity for a study in comparative history. As a group they provide ample material for a book-length study on intervention and its causes, on the nature of occupations and their programs, on the various forms of national resistance and/or adaptation, and on the complexities of withdrawal and the revival of national institutions. Unfortunately space limitations prevent the inclusion here of a detailed comparative essay on intervention and occupation. Briefly, however, I will note some of the important parallels and discontinuities which appear in this growing literature.

There has generally been a substantial difference between what North American and Latin American scholars have produced on the occupations. The North Americans, with relatively easy access to the most obvious original documents, have tended to write detailed monographs, often with a heavy emphasis on the process of policy formation. The Latin Americans, far from these documents and sometimes denied access to them by U.S. officials, have usually depended on secondary sources and have emphasized analytical and ideological concerns. The results are somewhat complementary— the Latin Americans compensating for the lack of analysis and of conscious ideology in the work of many U.S. authors. Similarly, the tendency of Latin American historians to emphasize the internal Latin American repercussions of occupation has counterbalanced the penchant of many U.S. writers to concentrate on the U.S. side of the matter.

The North American authors of studies on intervention have found a variety of forces shaping U.S. policy in the Caribbean (and elsewhere in the non-European world) beginning in the later nineteenth century. Monographs on specific incidents of intervention seem to agree in identifying strategic concerns as the most important, while broader studies, most notably David Healy's *U.S. Ex-*

pansionism, have identified other factors, economic, ideological-patriotic, and religious, as significant. Although the importance of some of these factors, such as the desire for empire and the "missionary impulse," seems to have been blunted by the difficult U.S. experience in the Philippines, they continued to operate. And, while economic forces appear increasingly obvious over time, they are much more influential in some cases than in others. They were less important, for example, in Haiti and the Dominican Republic, which featured small markets, few resources, and limited U.S. investments that were seldom if ever threatened. On the other hand, in Cuba and Mexico, where much more was at stake and U.S. interests were sometimes menaced, economic factors were more obviously significant. Important too is the fact that, even where economic factors seemed to have little direct impact on a given situation, they were still a critical background factor, heavily influential in overall policy considerations.

Some of the strongest parallels between the various occupations (but not the shorter interventions) can be drawn from their programs. In almost every case, beginning with Puerto Rico, Cuba, and the Philippines, U.S. officials set up programs to expand education, improve health and sanitation, create constabularies, build public works and communications, initiate judicial and penal reforms, take censuses, improve agriculture, and accomplish a wide range of other reforms. One reason for these parallels, besides the common needs exhibited by these societies, is clear. There was an extensive interchange of personnel between places occupied by the United States. The army and marine personnel who helped form policy in Cuba, Puerto Rico, and the Philippines also conducted the later occupations of Panama, Nicaragua, Haiti, and the Dominican Republic. Similarly, continuity was provided by the personnel of the State Department and the Bureau of Insular Affairs.

Inadequate or unclear policy often hampered the conduct of the interventions and occupations. Further complications arose from interdepartmental differences, usually between the State Department and the military but sometimes involving other agencies as well. The causes of these complications were differing departmental philosophies, interdepartmental competition, and political pressures which affected some departments, particularly the State Department, more than others. Haiti and the Dominican Republic stand as the worst examples of a lack of policy: after the marines had intervened, in both cases to end political turmoil, they were long left without clear guidelines. The reasons were that the onset of these occupations coincided with the increased involvement of the United

States in World War I and, more significant, that they affected two relatively unimportant small nations. Troubles in Mexico and Cuba, which occurred at the same time, received much greater direct attention.

Even the creation of a clear policy did not insure its implementation. On the contrary, a variety of factors often hindered the realization of occupation goals, resulting in changed, incomplete, and even failed programs and reforms. Among the problems were language difficulties, racism, cultural differences and misunderstandings, insufficiently trained personnel, and inadequate resources.

Important too was the matter of resistance. Perhaps only because the topic is so neglected in U.S. history, it is surprising to realize that nearly all the major U.S. interventions provoked resistance. In virtually every instance, portions of the elite mounted an intellectual-political resistance, though none was as successful as the Dominican campaign. Also common was armed guerrilla resistance, which occurred in the Philippines, the Dominican Republic, Haiti, Nicaragua, and, on several occasions, very nearly in Cuba. In response to these guerrilla wars, U.S. forces developed tactics, such as the use of concentration camps, which they employed in a number of occupations, usually with very limited success. U.S. forces also exhibited similar forms of behavior, most commonly demoralization and indiscriminate brutality, in response to the frustrations of irregular warfare.

Nearly every analyst notes that it is much easier to begin an intervention than to end it. It is a relatively simple matter to send in troops. But once they are there, having destroyed the normal political process or having become more deeply involved in it, the necessity of keeping them there grows day by day. In addition, there is the problem of fulfilling policy goals. These are usually ill-defined at first but tend to grow over time and are seldom easily accomplished, thus creating a further impediment to withdrawal. There is also a classic catch-22: if there is no pressure to end an intervention, it continues; but if there is pressure, the occupiers resist, not wanting to appear to withdraw because of the pressure.

Nearly all students of intervention and occupation, whatever their political point of view, come to the conclusion that these armed intrusions seldom accomplish more than the most limited goals and that they are one of the most expensive ways, both monetarily and politically, to carry out foreign policy. Indeed it was the realization of this fact which caused the State Department to begin experimenting with new forms of control over Latin America after 1920. The successful use of alternative methods led to the announce-

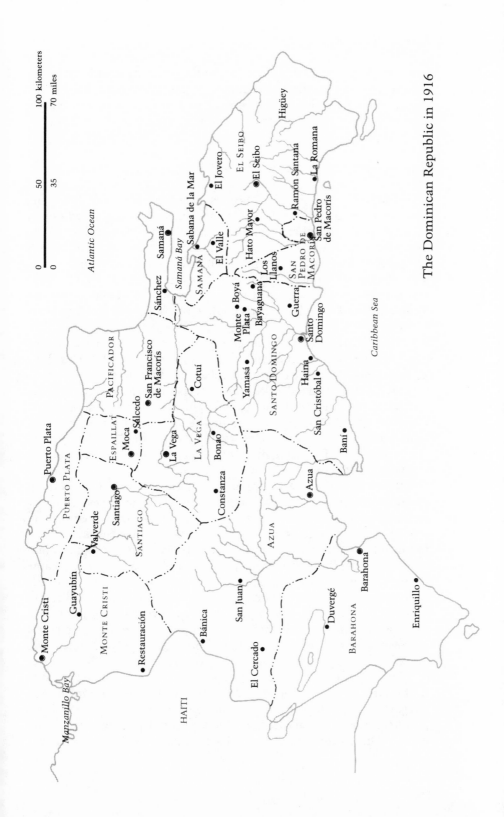

The Dominican Republic in 1916

ment of the Good Neighbor Policy, to the liquidation of most of the occupations (except for the Philippines and Puerto Rico) by the mid 1930s, and to an increased hesitancy to use direct armed intervention as an instrument of foreign policy.

The Dominican Republic in 1916

The republic which the U.S. Marines invaded in 1916 was a poor and underdeveloped country. Fewer than a million people, of whom 85 percent lived in rural areas and engaged in agriculture, inhabited its 19,129 square miles. The cities, though they were important centers of power and wealth, were small. The two largest were the capital, Santo Domingo, and Santiago, with an estimated 21,000 and 14,000 residents each. In all the rest of the republic, only Puerto Plata, La Vega, and San Pedro de Macorís could boast of populations in excess of 3,000.[5]

The wealth which supported these cities, and the nation, came almost entirely from the land in the form of agricultural exports. Three crops—sugar, cacao, and tobacco—dominated, making up 92 percent of the $21.5 million in exports in 1916. The total figure had mounted steadily as the result of the rapid expansion of the republic's commercial agriculture in the late nineteenth and early twentieth centuries; most important was the dramatic increase in the production of sugar, which by 1916 constituted more than half of the total exports.

The rest of the Dominican economy thus depended, directly or indirectly, on the prosperity of agriculture. The businesses of factors, exporters, and importers, whose earnings constituted a large share of the national income, were directly influenced by the success or failure of the annual crop and by the level of international commodity prices. Professional people, much of whose business came from the wealthy agricultural and business interests, were similarly dependent on the agricultural economy; ultimately, if less directly, so were shopkeepers, artisans, and laborers. Even the economic survival of the national government, which in 1916 drew 90 percent of its revenue from customs duties and other trade-related taxes, was directly connected to the success of export agriculture.

Imports, financed by expanding exports, had increased steadily in the early twentieth century; the dollar volume of $11.7 million in 1916 was more than quadruple the 1905 total. Imports consisted principally of manufactures and foodstuffs not produced in the republic. The United States had long dominated the Dominican import trade, competing particularly with Great Britain and Germany. But World War I had nearly eliminated competition from the latter nations, and by 1916 purchases from the republic's giant northern neighbor accounted for 90.4 percent of the dollar value of imports.

Most of the export-import business was in the hands of foreigners, with different nationalities dominating different aspects of the trade. Agricultural production, with the important exception of sugar, had tended to remain under Dominican control. But sugar, because it required ever larger amounts of capital and technology, was increasingly dominated by foreign owners.

Production, outside of agriculture, was left to a tiny group of industrialists, some of whom were hardly more than unusually enterprising artisans. Except for two cigar and cigarette factories owned by foreigners, most of these were small operations, financed with Dominican capital. They produced a variety of consumer goods, which generally supplied local needs only partially.

Despite the considerable economic activity of the above-mentioned groups, the overwhelming majority of Dominicans remained poor. This was owed to the fact that the benefits of the economy flowed almost entirely to elite Dominicans and foreigners. Also, much of the nation's potential wealth remained undeveloped or underdeveloped. A variety of factors contributed to this situation, including over three hundred years of colonial neglect as a backwater of the Spanish Empire, the chronic political disorders of the nineteenth century, and—in the twentieth century—continuing political turmoil, a relative scarcity of domestic capital, an unwillingness to invest it productively by most who possessed it, and a population too small to form an adequate market for many modern enterprises.

Another problem was the infrastructure, which was wholly inadequate despite the efforts of several Dominican governments to improve it. In typical colonial and neocolonial fashion, transportation and communication were not adequate to unite the country, each region remaining politically and economically isolated because such ties as did exist usually led abroad. Thus no road suitable for commerce connected the two largest cities, Santo Domingo and Santiago, and the two railroads which served the Cibao area, of which Santiago was the chief city, both led to seaports from which the products of the region were shipped abroad. Dominican ports were poorly developed, and seaborne domestic commerce was limited to a negligible coasting trade.

The Dominican social structure in 1916 both reflected the general underdevelopment of the country and acted as a further obstacle to creating something better. It was basically a society of two classes: a small upper class and a large lower class, separated from one another by a deep economic and social abyss.

Only in the cities and larger towns did one find much social differentiation. It was there rather than the countryside that most members of the upper class chose to live, and it was there that the economy afforded opportunities for a small middle sector to rise above the larger lower class. The rural areas, with neither a resident elite nor a middle group, were with few exceptions populated by the poor majority, peasants and agricultural laborers.

The upper class was divided into two strata by what is best described as a caste distinction. Those of the historically most important families, whose lineage society at large generally acknowledged, were the *gente de primera* (the elite, literally persons of first quality). They were followed by the *gente de segunda* (those of second quality, forming a sort of upper middle sector), persons of some substance, education, and culture who somehow lacked the credentials which would admit them into the highest society. The two strata were as one, however, relative to the masses.

A variety of factors other than lineage divided Dominicans from Dominicans. Some of the most important of these were occupation, wealth, race, and education; also significant were regional and urban-rural differences. Occupation and wealth were perhaps the most obvious distinguishing characteristics. Constituting the elite *gente de primera* were the owners of land and real estate, the leaders of commerce, professionals, and higher government officials. These pursuits generated large incomes which, in addition to wealth accumulated over the years, put the elite in a dominant economic position. The *gente de segunda* followed similar careers but as a group were slightly less wealthy than the elite.

In urban areas the remaining members of society fell into two groups. First there were the artisans, mechanics, small shopkeepers, clerks, and peddlers, who formed a lower middle sector. Beneath them was the lower class: common laborers, servants, a few factory workers, and the unemployed. Neither of these groups had significant incomes relative to the upper class, although important economic differences separated them. An inadequate number of steady jobs meant that there was tremendous competition for work; high unemployment and low wages were facts of life for lower-class Dominicans.

One substantial group, the immigrants, did not properly fit into any one social category, though they were found in fairly large numbers throughout the country. Sephardic Jews from Curaçao, Spaniards, Italians, Germans, English, North Americans, Chinese, Arabs, Canary Islanders, Cubans, Puerto Ricans, and other West Indians arrived in the late nineteenth and early twentieth centuries in noticeable numbers or in small numbers made visible by economic success. Many immigrants, mostly blacks from the West Indies, were imported as laborers for the cane plantations, and if they remained they often gravitated toward the rural lower class or the urban artisan group. Others, such as the Canary Islanders and Puerto Ricans, tended to join the lower middle sector, working as artisans and small merchants. Some, in particular the Chinese and Arabs, despite their considerable economic success as a group, stood somewhat apart from the rest of society, either by choice or because they encountered resistance to their assimilation. A few immigrants became part of the elite or at least solid members of the upper middle sector. These were generally Western Europeans, North Americans, and Sephardic Jews, all of whom were white and many of whom were financially successful.

The matter of race, whether one was white or black or where one fell on the scale in between, was an important factor in determining social status. Most Dominicans were of mixed ancestry racially, but generally the highest social strata were the lightest and the lowest were the darkest. This, plus several historical factors, established a clear bias in favor of whiteness. There were exceptions to the general pattern of white-black stratification, but the basic concept ruled. According to the loosely defined standards of the national census of 1920, the country was 25 percent white, 25.3 percent black, and 49.7 percent mulatto.

Regionalism was a strong divisive factor in Dominican life which cut somewhat across class lines. At its heart was the rivalry between the northern region (often called the Cibao), centered in Santiago, and the south, which focused around the city of Santo Domingo. The two areas had long had regional differences, augmented in the late nineteenth and early twentieth centuries by the extensive development of southern agriculture around sugar. Extensive sugar cultivation, especially to the east of the capital city, meant that Santo Domingo began a period of growth which resulted in its domination of the balance of economic power in the republic. Sugar also caused the growth of the south's black population, because of the numerous immigrants from Haiti and neighboring Caribbean islands, and a resulting *mulatización* of such integral aspects of life as language, food, and religion. Other parts of the republic also had their special flavors. The geography, the life-style, the customs, and the speech of the east, southwest, and northwest each exhibited uniqueness, and even within these regions there were strong contrasts.

Urban-rural differences, which correlated strongly with economic and racial patterns, were pronounced in the Dominican Republic. While urbanites were generally wealthier and lighter-skinned, rural residents tended to be poorer and darker. Within rural areas, the divisions which existed between people were based on their relationship to the land. Aside from a tiny minority of wealthier persons, most rural inhabitants were peasants, squatters, or the landless. A surprisingly large number owned land, most commonly as *pesos de terrenos comuneros* or shares of collectively held land. Some of these small proprietors led relatively comfortable if simple lives, although the primitive agriculture which they practiced generally offered no hope of substantial economic advance. Squatters lived in virtually the same way, but without title to their lands. However, members of either substratum might suddenly find themselves demoted to the third or landless group, put off their land by some large landowner or corporation. This happened with increasing frequency around 1916, owing especially to the expansion of the large sugar estates in the south.

A peasant without land had several options. One was to sharecrop, often for an absentee landlord who preferred life in town. A second option was to work as a laborer on an agricultural estate, often one of the large sugar corporations, thus becoming part of a rural proletariat. This difficult work was poorly paid, and most of it was seasonal. A third possibility for the landless was to move to an urban area such as Santo Domingo or San Pedro de Macorís, where they formed part of the lower class.

Urban residents, particularly the upper class, had a virtual monopoly over many aspects of Dominican life. Nearly all that was modern, scientific, or intellectual existed for their exclusive use. The educational facilities functioned almost entirely on their behalf, as did the republic's medical and legal systems. Most newspapers and magazines were written by and for the upper class, their contents often reflecting the elite's cultural orientation away from the Dominican Republic toward Europe and the United States.

The republic's urban areas also offered a more varied social life than the rural districts. At its center were the private social clubs, strictly segregated by social status, which served as gathering places for men and as the locations of a variety of cultural and recreational activities. There were also fraternal, ethnic, religious, and charitable organizations, theaters, a few cinemas, and the more common recreations provided by municipal bands, evening promenades, public

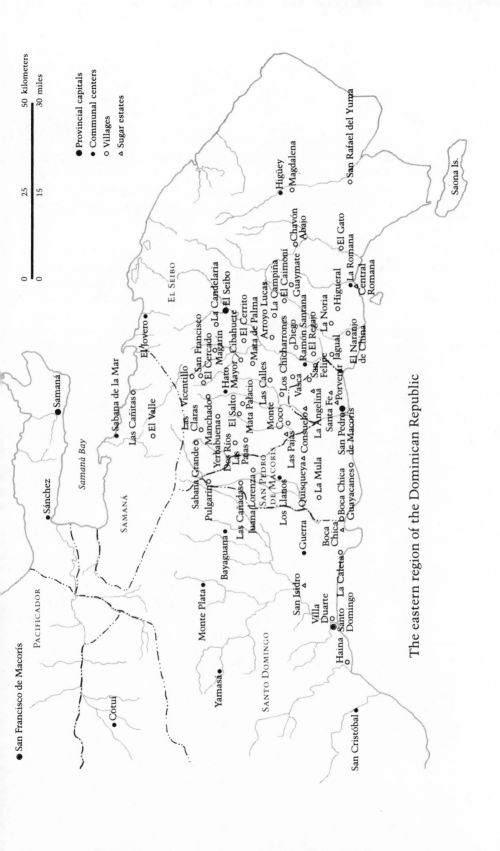

The eastern region of the Dominican Republic

dances, sports, and gambling. The rural areas, though hardly as diverse as the cities, had their own forms of entertainment. Undoubtedly the most popular were cockfights, gambling, dances, and folk religious ceremonies.

Catholicism exerted its influence in both urban and rural areas, although the church was less pervasive and powerful in the Dominican Republic than in the rest of Latin America. Religious observances varied widely by social stratum: the upper class, especially women, practiced a European sort of Catholicism while the lower class, particularly in rural areas, had created its own Afro-Catholic folk religion.

Deep cleavages thus divided Dominican society. First, a horizontal pattern of economic stratification divided the rich from the poor in both urban and rural areas, the upper stratum also being divided by caste differences. Second, a vertical division separated the city from the country. The distance across the whole scale was immense—from the wealthy and educated urbanite, living amid the technology of the twentieth century, to the poor rural inhabitant whose life was not appreciably different from a poor person's of the sixteenth century.

The deeply divided society and neocolonial economy provided a poor environment for the representative and democratic form of government instituted by Dominican lawmakers. Since the republic in 1916 had as essential elements such features as general economic underdevelopment, a poor distribution of income, widespread poverty, low social mobility, a backward transportation and communication network, and an inadequate educational system, it is not surprising that the government was in the hands of a few and tended to be weak, ineffective, and unstable.

The Dominican constitution in force in 1916, the nineteenth such document adopted since 1844, provided for a president, a Senate, and a Chamber of Deputies, all elected by universal male suffrage. The president chose the seven heads of the executive departments, selected the twelve provincial governors, who controlled most local officials, and commanded the armed forces. Thus the constitution gave the chief executive considerable power, but in fact he had to be an exceptionally strong and effective leader to use it—only three of the forty-three men who held the office between 1844 and 1916 completed their terms. An independent judiciary, appointed by the Senate, interpreted the nation's basic law (an adaptation of the Napoleonic code) as well as the laws of Congress and executive decrees.

Technically, a party system governed the competition for political office. But the political parties tended to be extremely personalistic, frequently named after their leaders, and difficult to distinguish ideologically. Often there was great rancor between the followers of one faction and another. In the years just preceding 1916, the two most important parties were the Jimenistas and the Horacistas, named after leaders Juan Isidro Jiménez and Horacio Vásquez and nicknamed *bolos* and *rabudos* after two kinds of fighting cocks. A third leader of note was Federico Velásquez, leader of the Velasquistas or Progresistas.

The constitutionally based party structure masked a deeper reality. Because of such factors as regionalism, allowed to flourish by the lack of adequate transportation and communication, the national government could not ordinarily monopolize power in the republic. Its survival depended on gaining the consent or temporary submission of popular regional leaders, the caudillos, whose authority ultimately rested on their military skills. However politically pragmatic this solution was, it was also unstable. There was continual competition, often in the form of revolution, between alliances of regional caudillo leaders, focused particularly around the rival aspirations of the elites of the Cibao and Santo Domingo City for control of the national government.

There was no shortage of grass-roots support for these revolutionary tendencies. In the relatively static economy and society of the Dominican Republic, rebellion had become one of the most promising means of upward social mobility. President Ulises Heureaux (1882–1899) and other important figures stood as permanent reminders of how much one might build from nothing with military skill, political acumen, and intrigue.

Revolution, or the threat of revolution, impaired development because it alienated investors and caused discontinuity between governments and programs. It was also costly: it paralyzed farming, dried up credit, and increased military expenditures to such a point that they absorbed the lion's share of the national budget. In 1903, for instance, the military accounted for 71.7 percent of the government's expenditures; in 1904, it accounted for 72.6 percent.

Money, or the lack of it, was always central to the problems of the Dominican government. Revenue was insufficient in part because, like most governments, that of the Dominicans ultimately depended on the nation's prosperity and, even in the best of times, the Dominican Republic was poor. Another defect was the inadequate tax structure, designed to spare the wealthy from having to support the cost of government. And the flow of revenue was irregular because when international economic factors brought a decline in prices for the republic's agricultural commodities there was an immediate drop in customs collections, which provided about 90 percent of the public income. At the same time, the shortcomings of the revenue system made necessary large foreign loans, which saddled the government with heavy interest payments.

Thus various forces conspired to keep the republic as it was, undeveloped and unstable. Indeed, the nation was caught in a perpetual cycle of weak and short-lived governments and an inadequately developed economy and society. The U.S. military government which Washington created late in 1916 resolved to change this state of affairs. Inspired with a confidence which sprang from a mixture of good intentions, misunderstandings, and a false sense of superiority, occupation officials would work long and hard to solve the republic's problems. But the occupiers, like previous Dominican reformers, would find that these problems were deeply rooted, that they often had international dimensions not subject to control from Santo Domingo, and that, ultimately, they were very resistant to change.

1

The Occupation Begins: 1916

The United States had a long record of involvement in the affairs of the Dominican Republic prior to 1916, beginning sporadically in the nineteenth century and continuing, with increasing regularity and intensity, into the first decade and a half of the twentieth century. Growing political and economic involvement gradually changed the relationship; indifference gradually gave way to constant interference and, finally, to the destruction of Dominican sovereignty in 1916. The Dominicans, almost as though they had come to accept the inevitability of this meddling, at first offered little resistance to their loss of independence.

A variety of forces brought the United States to the Dominican Republic. None of them, however, offered an adequate basis for an occupation policy and Washington, with its interest focused increasingly on Europe, failed to create one. Lacking an overall policy, it remained for occupation officials to piece together a program on an ad hoc basis. This they accomplished slowly, assembling it from a wide range of elements. Cooperating in the process were occupation military officers, the officials of various U.S. agencies, personnel from U.S. colonial possessions, and, as passions cooled, a number of Dominicans.

U.S.-Dominican Relations to 1890

The 1890s were a watershed in U.S.-Dominican relations as they were in the relations of the United States to other countries of the world. Before 1890, the Washington government was generally indifferent toward its Caribbean neighbor, a disposition reflected by the fact that North American officials waited until 1889 to create a permanent diplomatic mission to the Dominican Republic, having previously left official business to commercial agents and temporary special envoys.[1] Most of the impetus in diplomatic relations came from two sources, Dominican politicians and North American entrepreneur-adventurers.

The dominant political figures during the years from independence in 1844 to 1874 were Pedro Santana and Buenaventura Báez. Both worked hard to persuade the United States or a European power to establish some sort of protective relationship with the Dominican Republic, through either outright annexation or the establishment of a protectorate. The leading motivations for this unnationalistic behavior were fear of the neighboring Haitians, who often threatened to repeat their 1822 to 1844 takeover of the republic, and the Dominican leaders' desire to maintain their personal power, which the abundant money and arms of one of the great powers would make easier. The bait which Santana and Báez held out to interest other nations was the Bay of Samaná, which had great potential as a deepwater harbor and coaling station.

The Dominican leaders found surprisingly few takers. Except for a brief and tumultuous fiasco during the years 1861 to 1865, when Santana reconverted the republic into a colony of Spain, the European powers and the United States generally displayed a greater interest in preventing each other from usurping Dominican sovereignty than in actually taking over the country.

Not everyone, however, was deaf to the siren song of Santana and Báez. Two serious moves toward annexation were promoted by a U.S. citizen, General William L. Cazneau, an opportunistic veteran of the annexation of Texas. Cazneau saw the Dominican situation as a chance to obtain personal wealth and political power. His first attempt, which featured the cooperation of William L. Marcy, secretary of state (1853–1857) to President Franklin Pierce, and Dominican President Santana, was stillborn—owing especially to the strenuous opposition of France and Great Britain. During the second and more serious episode, Cazneau enlisted the services of Secretary of State William H. Seward (1861–1869) during the administrations of Presidents Andrew Johnson and Ulysses S. Grant. The expansionist Seward, who proposed to establish a West Indian naval base, found Dominican President Báez eager to accommodate him, first with the Bay of Samaná and then with the republic itself. But in 1871, with Yankee warships propping up Báez' failing regime, the treaty went down to defeat in the U.S. Senate.

Dominican-U.S. Relations after 1890

If the events associated with the attempted annexations were some-what extraordinary in the context of nineteenth-century U.S.-Dominican affairs, they would not have appeared so in the twentieth century. During the 1890s, for various reasons, government officials in Washington began to take a different view of the relationship with their southern neighbor. One reason for this was economic—a growing direct investment in the Dominican Republic, especially in sugar and, after 1892, in an operation known as the Santo Domingo Improvement Company.² Organized by a group of North American investors, one of them in the cabinet of then president Benjamin Harrison, the company bought up the extensive interests of a Dutch concern, and by the turn of the century it was worth $4.5 million. Its holdings included the national bank, one of the country's two railroads, and most of the national debt, the latter secured by a lien on Dominican customs revenues. Trade was also involved in the changing U.S.-Dominican relationship. The growing U.S. interest in Latin America and world trade during the 1890s found its reflection in Santo Domingo in a treaty of reciprocity signed between the two countries in 1891.

Strategic and political factors also contributed to these stepped-up relations. Some were timeworn, like the United States' desire, stated in the Monroe Doctrine, to keep the western hemisphere free of European control and its wish to protect its Gulf coast and the eastern approaches to the long-planned isthmian canal. The weight of these considerations increased tremendously, however, around the turn of the century. The U.S. attitude underwent considerable change as Puerto Rico and, to some degree, Cuba became part of the new North American empire, as a U.S.-dominated canal across Panama became a reality, as the government in Washington began to develop a global naval strategy, and as Germany began its rapid and successful commercial inroads into Latin America. The United States began to move to consolidate its political and military control over the Caribbean area.³

Hans Schmidt, a historian who has studied U.S. foreign policy in regard to Haiti in the early twentieth century, has noted that "the pattern of diplomacy in the Caribbean and the Pacific contrasted strongly with American diplomacy elsewhere in the world." Schmidt argues that "the framework of mutual respect which characterized United States relations with European nations" was absent from dealings with the nations of the Caribbean, because they were small and weak and because North Americans looked upon their people as inferiors. Furthermore, the liberal internationalism of the Open Door Policy on which Washington insisted in China, where its influence was limited, was forgotten in the Caribbean and in some areas of the Pacific, where it "exercised sufficient military power to enforce its own absolute hegemony." Interventions in particular, Schmidt writes, "were primary instruments of American control in the area."[4]

Schmidt's analysis is quite relevant to U.S.-Dominican relations, especially after 1899, when assassination ended the seventeen-year dictatorship of President Ulises Heureaux. The removal of this strongman plunged the republic into revolutionary turmoil which lasted on and off for the next six years and which further aggravated the financial condition of this poor and often insolvent country. Dominican financial straits resulted in heavy pressure from foreign creditors, represented by the German, French, Belgian, British, Dutch, Italian, Spanish, and U.S. governments. In response to this situation, as well as to the Anglo-German blockade of Venezuela from 1902 to 1903, President Theodore Roosevelt formulated his famous corollary to the Monroe Doctrine. This sought, in the case of the Dominican Republic, to eliminate the danger of another foreign government physically intervening to enforce the demands of its creditor-citizens by having the United States act as a collection agent.

To facilitate this plan, the United States began to pressure the Dominican Republic to allow North American agents to take over the collection of customs and thus control Dominican financial affairs. It justified the move as necessary to satisfy the claims of foreign bondholders, both European and North American. By 1905 this pressure led to the imposition of a modus vivendi by which the Dominican Customs Receivership, headed by an appointee of the president of the United States, would collect all customs, keeping 55 percent of the total revenues to pay off foreign claimants and remitting 45 percent to the Dominican government. In 1907 the parties agreed to modify the agreement by converting it into a treaty which preserved the original structure of the receivership, placing it under the administrative supervision of the U.S. Bureau of Insular Affairs. The treaty also included provisions for a loan of $20 million through a New York bank by which all outstanding legitimate claims would be paid immediately, thus making the United States the Dominican Republic's only foreign creditor.[5]

In the interim, by 1906, the Dominicans had elected a new president, Ramón Cáceres. Unlike previous administrations since that of Heureaux, Cáceres' regime proved both popular and stable. The new president was concerned with economic growth and thus began to modernize and develop the country, apparently with some success. In Washington the State Department was delighted with the stability and economic vitality of the Cáceres regime, conditions which U.S. officials attributed more to the beneficial effects of the Customs Receivership than to the abilities of Cáceres himself. In November of 1911, however, an assassin ended Cáceres' life, and from then until 1916 there ensued a period of almost constant revolution and, consequently, economic stagnation.

Creating a Diplomatic Cul-de-Sac, 1911–1916

Between 1911 and 1916 the United States, under the administrations of Presidents William H. Taft and Woodrow Wilson, sought constantly, though ineffectively, to reestablish stable government in the Dominican Republic. To this end, U.S. officials intervened in Dominican affairs more and more frequently, often on a daily basis, and with increasing belligerence, keeping up a steady pressure on the Dominicans to carry out various reforms—the implementation of which, it was supposed, would lead the republic back to normalcy. The United States used both diplomatic means and force or threats of force to persuade the Dominicans.[6] The republic was the object of numerous visits by North American warships sent to observe, to make shows of force against the government, to threaten revolutionaries, or to protect the lives and property of foreigners.[7] The result of this outside pressure and interference, combined with domestic political turmoil, was eight separate administrations in Santo Domingo in five years.[8]

After the death of President Cáceres in 1911, one of the main goals of the United States was to establish a stable, representative, and cooperative Dominican government. Among the more notable specific tactics it used to achieve that end was the sending of a special commission, accompanied by 750 marines, to Santo Domingo in 1912. The commission, by cutting off Customs Receivership funds to the republic and threatening to impose a military government, compelled the Dominican government to accept the U.S. fiat concerning the long-disputed border with Haiti, obliged Dominican officials to initiate certain reforms, forced the resignation of the constitutionally elected president, Eladio Victoria, who was besieged by revolutionaries, and, finally, imposed a new, interim president, Monsignor Adolfo A. Nouel, the archbishop of Santo Domingo.[9]

But disorder continued, which soon resulted in the resignation of President Nouel and prompted the United States to continue meddling throughout 1913. The State Department displayed an attitude of distinct hostility to the new chief of state, General José Bordas Valdez, once having U.S. gunboats fire on his forces while he besieged revolutionaries. On several other occasions Washington cut off government funds from the Customs Receivership to force Bordas to accept reforms; in August 1914, he was finally pushed from office.

The United States obtained Bordas' ouster through the work of a commission sent to Santo Domingo by President Woodrow Wilson. The commissioners' instructions formed the so-called Wilson Plan, which demanded that all revolutionaries lay down their arms, that a provisional president be selected in place of Bordas, whose legal right to the presidency Washington refused to recognize, and that open and fair elections, closely observed by U.S. officials, be held. Accompanying the delivery of these nonnegotiable demands was a "considerable show of force." Dominican compliance with the terms led to the inauguration of President Juan Isidro Jiménez in December 1914.

When, after endless interference and manipulation, the United States had achieved its goal of a representative democratic government under President Jiménez, it proceeded to put pressure on that government, which soon destroyed it. Since 1911 officials of the State Department had begun to formulate certain reforms which they believed would, in conjunction with the Customs Receivership, bring stability to the revolution-racked republic. The most important of these reforms was a plan to place two North American officials, appointed by the president of the United States, in strategic positions in the Dominican government, one as director of public works and one as a financial adviser. Both officials were to be above dismissal. The director of public works would govern all aspects of his office, awarding contracts and controlling the considerable patronage; the financial "adviser" was to draw up a budget for the national government and enforce it by requiring his personal authorization for each public expenditure. The Customs Receivership, moreover, was to expand its functions by collecting and controlling internal revenues, formerly the responsibility of the Dominicans themselves.

President Jiménez, though amenable to the proposed changes, met tremendous resistance. The Dominican Congress refused to cooperate, and there were soon threats of rebellion or impeachment. The response of the Wilson administration to Jiménez' predicament was not to withdraw its demands or to compromise but to threaten to send in a naval force to obtain them as well as to defeat any attempt, parliamentary or military, to unseat the president.

Pressed by the United States on the one hand and by the realities of Dominican political life on the other, President Jiménez was in an impossible position. And the situation grew worse as time passed. During 1915 the U.S. government escalated its original demands. State Department officials demanded greater powers for the financial adviser and added a new requirement, that the Dominican government disband its armed forces and replace them with a constabulary to be controlled by a nominee of the president of the United States. The terms of these demands, presented to the Dominican government in November 1915 by U.S. Minister William Russell in his Note No. 14, were such that no Dominican politician could have agreed to them and survived. Public opinion universally condemned them, and the Dominican government formally rejected the proposals as "an abdication of national sovereignty."[10] Increasingly, the State Department put itself into an untenable diplomatic position. Soon officials would have no alternative but to back down or to destroy Dominican sovereignty.

The Jiménez government was on its knees by early 1916. Armed revolutionists were in the field and impeachment proceedings appeared imminent in the Dominican Congress. And while the United States was willing to intervene militarily to maintain the government, a proposal which President Jiménez refused, it denied the president the opportunity to defend himself effectively. The State Department would not allow the receivership to release to the Dominican government the money it needed to station extra troops in potentially rebellious areas; such a policy reflected a willingness to let the Jiménez government fall despite official U.S. support, since its demise would justify an armed intervention and the imposition of U.S. demands, as had occurred in Haiti during 1915.

The United States had for some time considered full-scale military intervention. As early as September 1912, Minister Russell had contemplated the beneficial effects of "complete control by our Government,"[11] and U.S. officials had several times thereafter used the threat of military takeover as a diplomatic club. Finally, in mid July 1915, the United States had thrown down the gauntlet by publicly announcing that it would intervene militarily to preserve the Jiménez government and public order.

The Armed Intervention of 1916

In April and May of 1916, the Dominican political situation collapsed. When President Jiménez attempted to move against some of his insubordinate military officers, chief among them his minister of war, General Desiderio Arias, the general's followers in Congress carried out a resolution of impeachment against the president. Arias went into open rebellion and was soon in control of the capital. The United States faced a moment of truth: it had to forget its previous threats or to send in troops against the rebels. Minister Russell pressured President Jiménez to request the landing of U.S. Marines from the two warships which soon arrived at Santo Domingo, but, after some wavering, Jiménez asked only for weapons.[12]

Ignoring Jiménez' wishes, marines landed in Santo Domingo City, their announced purpose being to protect the U.S. legation. However, they also took possession of Fortaleza San Gerónimo on the western outskirts of the city, of the Haitian legation, where a group of foreigners had gathered, and of the offices of the Customs Receivership, fortuitously located "in a strategic position on the heights overlooking the city." Simultaneously U.S. warships proceeded to San Pedro de Macorís, Sánchez, and Puerto Plata, other important ports of the republic. President Jiménez thereupon resigned on 7 May 1916, refusing to exercise an office "regained with foreign bullets," thus leaving General Arias in control of the capital and the probable successor to the presidency. The State Department was, however, determined to humble Arias; on 13 May 1916, the commander of the U.S. forces, Rear Admiral W. B. Caperton of the navy, presented an ultimatum signed by himself and Minister Russell which threatened the occupation of the city and the forcible disarmament of the revolutionaries if Arias did not surrender by 15 May. Arias sidestepped a confrontation by evacuating his troops, and a U.S. force of six hundred men occupied the city peacefully.[13]

Government continued in Dominican hands. Jiménez' remaining cabinet ministers, threatened by Russell with a military government if they resigned, formed a Council of Ministers to carry on the business of state.[14] General Arias, meanwhile, announced from a safe distance in the countryside that he had not actually raised "a revolutionary banner," that his flag was that of the Dominican people, and that he would surrender his arms to any president selected by the Chamber of Deputies.[15] He clearly hoped that the new president would be himself.

U.S. warships were located off every major port city of the republic by late May; on the first day of June, combined forces of sailors and marines began to occupy the northern part of the country, ostensibly to support the constitutional authority against the revolutionaries. Although the northern cities had shown considerable anti-U.S. sentiment, military resistance was in general ineffective. Monte Cristi fell without opposition. At Puerto Plata, though the governor had vowed to fight a landing, the ayuntamiento or city council begged the citizens to be calm and not to aggravate the situation,[16] and the occupiers encountered only "a brief resistance" of "heavy but inaccurate small-arms fire." Santiago, the largest city of the north and the "stronghold of the Arias party," was the obvious target for the invaders, but Admiral Caperton awaited reinforcements before marching inland.[17]

In late June, a regiment of marines having arrived from San Diego, California, the U.S. forces, under the command of Colonel Joseph H. Pendleton, began a two-pronged march on Santiago from Monte Cristi and Puerto Plata. On both routes the invaders encountered considerable harassment and sniping, but the marines' vastly superior weapons made the fighting, and the casualties, very unequal. The Dominicans' major defensive effort occurred on the Monte Cristi road at Guayacanes,[18] where a small group of patriots, led by Máximo Cabral, heroically but futilely attempted to stop the marines' advance. On the Puerto Plata road, the leader of the Dominican resistance was Wenceslao Báez, a mere sergeant. He was mortally wounded and carried back to Santiago, where the Junta de Defensa Nacional ceremoniously rewarded him with the rank of brigadier general before he died.[19]

The leading citizens of Santiago who so honored Báez' heroism had also formed a peace commission to negotiate the surrender of the city. In telegraphic exchanges with Admiral Caperton, mediated by Archbishop Nouel, the commissioners were able to obtain few concessions. Caperton promised to guarantee life and property and the right of the ayuntamiento of Santiago to choose a new governor from among persons not aligned with Arias. In return, Arias and his men were to surrender their arms, for which they would each receive a payment of five dollars; any opposition, threatened Caperton, would be severely chastised. If there was no further opposition, neither Arias nor his men would be punished for bearing arms.[20]

On 5 July 1916, with the terms of the surrender already laid down, the peace commission and the new governor, Juan B. Pérez, went to meet with Colonel Pendleton. Together they made final arrangements; on 6 July, the marines moved into Santiago, occupying the Fortaleza San Luis and the Castillo, a fortified hill overlooking the city. After settling into Santiago, Colonel Pendleton and his staff began visiting the major towns of the surrounding Cibao region. In Moca, La Vega, and San Francisco de Macorís, Pendleton conferred with local officials and arranged for the marine occupation of those towns. Before the end of July, each had a marine garrison; only in San Francisco de Macorís, where a group of Dominican soldiers led by the governor of Pacificador Province occupied the local stronghold, was there even symbolic resistance.[21] With the garrisoning of the Cibao, the progress of the occupation stopped until 1917. Both the eastern and the western provinces, except for the northwestern port of Monte Cristi, were left unoccupied, though U.S. gunboats controlled access to the ports of every region.[22]

Why was the initial Dominican resistance to intervention so limited? In the first place, it was obvious to most Dominicans that the odds were overwhelming. No one was more opposed to the intervention than Dr. Américo Lugo, yet he wrote in 1916 that it would have been suicidal "to organize a resistance against the invaders . . . and to declare war against the United States." All the important leaders of political parties, as well as Archbishop Nouel, agreed with Lugo and said so publicly.[23] Propertied Dominicans, like the leaders of Santiago, also wished to prevent the possible destruction of their homes and businesses. Furthermore, no one, not even U.S. officials, realized in May and June of 1916 that the intervention would expand into a military government which would rule the Dominican people for the next eight years. The dominant impression in mid 1916 among the Dominican leaders, wrote Américo Lugo, was that "the Americans would remain in the country only as long as was necessary to guarantee 'free elections' in accord with the first Wilson Plan."[24]

Even as U.S. troops occupied their country, Dominican politicians continued their fratricidal struggles for power, particularly over control of the now vacant presidency.[25] Rather than uniting against the intervention, at least some opportunist political leaders tried to use the situation to their own advantage. General Arias' partisans, for instance, tried to convince intervention officials that the followers of Horacio Vásquez were about to rebel and suggested a preemptive U.S. strike against them.[26]

In late May 1916, a majority of the Dominican Congress agreed to support a compromise candidate, Federico Henríquez y Carvajal, the chief justice of the Supreme Court. The United States, however, was adamantly opposed to his election because he refused to make preelection promises to meet State Department demands for reform.

When, on 5 June 1916, a final vote of the Dominican Senate was about to confirm Henríquez' election, Minster Russell, in collusion with Federico Velásquez of the Council of Ministers, engineered a plan to arrest some of the pro-Henríquez senators. Though the scheme partially backfired by causing a tremendous public reaction, it accomplished its purpose. Henríquez was so disgusted with the "officious meddling" of the United States in Dominican electoral procedures that he withdrew his candidacy.[27]

A deadlock then developed in the Dominican Congress among the various political factions, including the followers of General Arias (whose selection U.S. officials refused to allow), of Horacio Vásquez, of expresident Jiménez, of Federico Velásquez, and of other lesser leaders. In late July 1916, however, with sessions about to expire by law, the legislators finally threw politics aside and hurriedly elected Dr. Francisco Henríquez y Caravajal, brother of Federico, to a five-month term as provisional president. In electing Dr. Henríquez, the Congress ignored U.S. demands for prior approval of the candidate. Nonetheless, Henríquez took the oath of office on 31 July 1916, cheered on by a large crowd in Santo Domingo. But, despite widespread public enthusiasm, the politicians nominally supporting his administration continued to fight among themselves over other issues throughout his term of office.[28]

Francisco Henríquez was an honest, intelligent, educated, capable, and patriotic man. With degrees in medicine from Paris and Havana, a degree in law, and experience as a physician, a university professor, and a diplomat, he was as well prepared as any Dominican to solve the problems which faced his nation in 1916. And, as he stated in his inaugural address, he was determined to do so.[29] But he confronted a nearly impossible situation. Minister Russell, without ever having dealt with the new president, judged him "not satisfactory" and recommended withholding recognition until he met the demands which the State Department had made upon previous administrations, especially those concerning financial control and a constabulary.[30]

Recognition was soon to be of critical importance to the Henríquez administration. After fewer than three weeks of its existence, U.S. officials, without warning, cut off all funds from the Customs Receivership. The receivership's public notice of 18 August 1916, nicknamed El Decreto de Hambre (The Decree of Hunger) by Dominicans, announced that the Dominican government would receive no further revenue until it had agreed to meet all the demands of the United States or, what amounted to the same thing, until the Washington government extended diplomatic recognition to the

Henríquez administration.[31] The financial stranglehold was all the more effective because of an earlier unilateral decision by Russell, in June, to extend the control of the receivership to all Dominican revenues, internal as well as external.[32]

Dr. Henríquez was a patriotic nationalist, but he was not intransigent. Because he wanted to carry out certain basic reforms and was willing to accept the help of the United States in doing so, he earnestly sought to negotiate with the representatives of the State Department. In fact the new president agreed, in essence, to permit U.S. control of all finances and of a new constabulary; however, he considered it constitutionally impossible to accede to the further demand that he bind future administrations to these arrangements without the consent of the Dominican Congress.[33] When it became apparent that Russell's instructions were to refuse anything less than total capitulation, the Dominican government attempted to break the deadlock by sending a cabinet minister, Francisco J. Peynado, to Washington to approach officials there directly. But this step was also rebuffed. U.S. officials consistently showed little inclination to negotiate. Instead, Minister Russell proposed to raise new demands in August concerning Samaná Bay and a new land title law (essential to the U.S.-owned sugar companies and other buyers of land), rather than compromise the original ones.[34]

The Initial Reaction to Intervention

Immediately after the seizure of Santo Domingo on 15 May, a strong wave of anti-U.S. sentiment swept the country, especially in Santo Domingo. This grew stronger each time some outrageous incident occurred, such as the seizure of the senators to prevent the election of Federico Henríquez or the cutoff of the revenues of the Dominican government.[35] Most of the anger and opposition generated by these events was expressed peacefully. Though the city of Santo Domingo had been riotous the night before the entry of U.S. troops, with people running about noisily and talking anxiously—some vowing to fight and making preparations to leave the city with General Arias—a call for receiving the invaders with a silent protest, a *duelo público* (public mourning), finally prevailed.[36]

When U.S. forces entered Santo Domingo in the early dawn hours of 15 May, they encountered deserted streets, closed doors, shuttered windows, and Dominican flags draped with black crepe. During the day scarcely anyone traversed the streets, while social centers, theaters, and other gathering places remained closed. On the second day of the occupation, however, the city came back to life. Newspapers greeted the invaders with condemnatory editorials, while ordinary citizens, officials, and organizations published protests.[37]

In the weeks following, the citizens of Santo Domingo, Santiago, and other towns of the republic formed *juntas patrióticas*. With the ayuntamientos, they sent delegations of "the most distinguished personalities" to protest to Admiral Caperton. In Santiago the Centro de Recreo, the most formidable redoubt of the city's elite, shut its doors in protest for the month of June, and its directors barred fiestas until the Christmas season of 1916. The masses expressed their feelings in a popular anti-Yankee song of many verses which appeared after the marines seized Puerto Plata.[38]

The resistance to the intervention, except for the few incidents which occurred in 1916 and the peasant struggle which developed in the east during and after 1917, was to be a war of words. It was waged by the republic's educated elite in the press, books, letters, and the theater and from the lecture platform and the soapbox. Newspapers, including some which sprang up for the purpose, became the principal means of expressing displeasure with the presence of the U.S. forces. Writers, prominent among them Fabio Fiallo, Enrique Deschamps, and Américo Lugo, often criticized policy or its implementation, and they were always anxious to publicize the incidents of friction which occurred with increasing regularity during 1916 between the general population and the armed intruders.[39] There was also a rash of self-criticism. While critical of the intervention, many writers looked inward to try to see what elements of the Dominican national character and experience had contributed to the state of affairs which brought about the intervention.[40]

The theater was another vehicle of protest in the first days of the occupation, although censorship caused it to diminish thereafter. During June and July an actors' group, the Cuadro Lírico, presented a series of original works by the playwright José Narciso Solá. *El intruso*, *No más yes*, and *Un matrimonio a lo yanqui*, as their titles suggest (*The Intrusion*, *No More Yes*, and *Marriage Yankee-Style*), were all concerned with the intervention. Among the plays of other writers, a comedy by Arturo Logroño and Rafael Damirón entitled *Los yanquis en Santo Domingo* presented a more self-critical view, caricaturing Dominican politics and politicians.[41]

Before long U.S. officials began to bring pressure to silence their critics, though it was difficult without the right of censorship. In one incident, a marine officer tried to force the civil governor of Santo Domingo Province to silence critics—this caused tremendous resentment. In a typical reaction, a Santo Domingo editor wrote sarcastically that the incident "shines out as a great triumph of Pan Americanism. In its beak the Yankee eagle carries liberty and justice to Spanish America." Nevertheless, the confrontation convinced the governor to warn editors "to think the matter over seriously." U.S. pressure was also responsible for the conviction by a Dominican judge of Miguel A. DuBreil, the editor of *El Loro*, a satirical weekly, for having insulted President Woodrow Wilson.[42]

In early October 1916, Dominican writers organized the Asociación de la Prensa to defend freedom of expression. This early nucleus of intellectual resistance included many notable Dominicans residing both in the republic and abroad, in Europe and the United States. One of their first actions, besides soliciting operating funds from theater owners, was to investigate the case of editor DuBreil. Minister Russell, in arguing for strict censorship in December 1916, paid a backhanded tribute to the effectiveness of one aspect of the association's work. It was, he wrote, founded "for the purpose of spreading anti-American propaganda throughout Latin America, and the effect of its work was beginning to be shown in the local press in the way of articles copied from newspapers of other countries, principally Cuba and Porto Rico."[43]

Not all encounters between Dominicans and the occupying forces were limited to words. The situation was, obviously, explosive and grew more so as time passed and pressures increased. Compounding the differences of language and customs which can cause friction between the people of any two cultures were other factors peculiar to the intervention, especially feelings of frustration and resentment on the part of the Dominicans and a sense of superiority and, on some occasions, belligerence on the part of the occupying forces. One concrete factor was that U.S. forces had assumed certain police powers, which brought the two sides into regular confrontations.

Disarmament and the enforcement of arms regulations were among the usurped police powers. Sporadic shooting, not aimed at anyone but productive of frayed nerves and general tension, had regularly occurred at night in Santo Domingo during the first months of the occupation.[44] Presumably to curb the shooting and to diminish chances of attacks on marine patrols, U.S. military officials on 14 September decreed the revocation of all permits to carry arms issued before 12 August 1916. The actions of North American troops attempting to enforce this decree led to confrontations and, in a number of cases, to violence. Military officials also determined that the order granted them the right to make forcible searches of homes for suspected weapons. These incidents led to bitter protests, especially in one case where marines allegedly threatened to torture a householder to make him reveal supposedly hidden weapons.[45]

Disarmament was only one problem. For a variety of reasons, a succession of violent incidents occurred in the occupied Dominican cities, especially Santo Domingo, between Dominicans and North Americans. During September, October, and November 1916, newspapers reported the following events in the capital city: a marine lieutenant shot and wounded a Dominican woman; a drunken U.S. soldier assaulted a schoolteacher and her mother in their own home, an outrage followed the next day by the beating of a North American soldier by Dominican men; a number of U.S. troops severely beat a man and killed another who had interfered; a group of Dominican girls and various spectators accused a number of North American troops of molesting them on the street; a marine patrol, thinking it heard shots from the direction of a café, charged it and shot to death a man crossing the street, a boy eating his dinner next door, and the sixty-seven-year-old owner of the establishment, who was also bayoneted in the abdomen as he attempted to close his door; and a marine shot to death a deaf-mute who failed to obey his command to halt. The worst outbreak of violence occurred in a Santo Domingo suburb, Villa Duarte, when a marine patrol went to arrest General Ramón Batista for an alleged offense which took place before the intervention. He and some relatives and friends fired on the marines, killing two and wounding others. The U.S. troops then returned with reinforcements, killed their attackers and an innocent woman in the neighborhood, and smashed and burned several houses. In the aftermath marines belligerently roamed the streets of Santo Domingo, killing two Dominicans and wounding or beating numerous others.[46]

The Villa Duarte incident finally moved the Dominican government to accuse the U.S. forces publicly of arbitrary and illegal actions, of various outrages and depredations including the use of the *ley fuga*—the shooting of prisoners while they "attempted to escape." Worst of all, the government complained, U.S. grievances against Dominicans resulted in prompt action, whereas all kinds of North American crimes and misdemeanors went unpunished. Despite the promise of U.S. officers to punish future depredators if exact information were provided, little changed.[47]

The Imposition of a Military Government

Continuing conflicts between U.S. military personnel and Dominicans gradually changed the attitude of ordinary citizens from one of
grudging acquiescence to one of nearly universal hostility. This fact
was a source of great discomfort to the government in Washington
and a strong inducement to resolve the situation. In addition, developments in internal Dominican politics were creating another pressure, the threat of a new, constitutionally elected president to replace the interim chief executive.

The same act of the Dominican Congress by which Dr. Henríquez y Carvajal had been chosen interim president had created a
constitutional assembly to write long-advocated reforms to the 1908
constitution, including a new system for electing the president of
the republic. Failing completion of the reform document within the
five months beginning 31 July 1916, elections were to be held according to the provisions of the old constitution.[48]

Quarrels between the various political parties prevented even
the opening of the constitutional assembly until 29 September 1916.
And thereafter factional debates continued to impede the delegates'
progress. When it became apparent in mid November that the constitutional reforms would probably not be completed in time, the
president issued a decree for the convocation of the provincial electoral colleges on 3 December. The colleges' task was critical, for
they were to elect both a new constitutional president and replacements for Dominican senators and deputies whose terms would expire on 29 November 1916.[49]

The impending convocation brought matters to a head. Because
Washington officials thought elections would result in control of the
Dominican government by General Arias, the State Department
moved to implement a previously conceived plan to create a military
government. This drastic step was necessary, according to the State
and Navy Department officials who originated the plan, because
there seemed no other way to obtain complete satisfaction of U.S.
demands for economic and military control, because of the growing
economic crisis in the republic, which had resulted from withholding receivership funds, and because of the continuing violence between North Americans and Dominicans. Also of concern were the
numerous protests regarding the Dominican situation which had arrived in Washington from all parts of the hemisphere. A confidential
message to President Henríquez in mid November concerning the
conference's decision brought no substantial change in the Dominican position.[50]

On 29 November 1916 Captain Harry S. Knapp, commander of the Atlantic Cruiser Force of the navy, proclaimed the establishment of a U.S. military government in the Dominican Republic. "This military occupation," the proclamation read, "is undertaken with no immediate or ulterior object of destroying the sovereignty of the Republic of Santo Domingo, but on the contrary, is designed to give aid to that country in returning to a condition of internal order that will enable it to observe the terms of the treaty [of 1907]." Dominican administrators were to remain in office under the guidance of military officials, Dominican law was to continue in effect as long as it did not conflict with the goals or regulations of the occupation, and the court system was to remain, but in conjunction with military tribunals which would deal with matters directly affecting the military government and its personnel. All revenues of the republic were to be collected by the receivership and paid to the military government, which would then meet the regular administrative expenses of the country as well as those of the occupation.[51]

On the day Captain Knapp announced the U.S. takeover, the Dominican constitutional assembly sought to meet the challenge by quickly adopting a new constitution. This was complete with special provisions which would have insured the continuity of constitutional government, pending a new election, by establishing a new interim president after Dr. Henríquez' mandate expired and by permitting senators and deputies whose terms were expiring to continue temporarily in office.[52] But the assembly's action was stillborn, a futile assertion of an independence which was already lost.

The proclamation of a military government appeared the next day in Dominican newspapers, along with orders establishing censorship of the press, of speech, and of radio and other telecommunications, abolishing all permits to keep and carry arms, and making arrangements for the payment of all past-due salaries. Reflecting a populist tendency often present in subsequent military legislation, officials directed the Customs Receivership to pay these wages in an elaborate way intended to prevent moneylenders from collecting usurious interest, rumored to be as high as 75 percent in some cases, on the unpaid government salaries which they had bought up.[53]

U.S. authorities had planned in advance for the possibility of a military government. In Santiago, for instance, when the marine commanding officer, Colonel Theodore P. Kane, received word of the proclamation a little after midnight on 29 November, he immediately canceled all liberty and sent out patrols to gather up individual marines from the city's bars and other places of recreation. The commander then strengthened marine patrols and put all his troops on alert. The next morning he appointed a censor, a provost marshal, and a provost judge, all officials who could act quickly to suppress any open manifestation of sentiment against the new government. After these preparations were complete, Colonel Kane summoned Santiago's ayuntamiento, the local judiciary, the chief of police, and other officials, announced the imposition of the military government, and asked the Dominicans to continue in their posts. Despite some obvious displeasure with the situation, all of them agreed, and Santiago remained tranquil. Similar episodes took place in other occupied cities.[54]

The laws of the military government, many of them destined to become part of the permanent law of the Dominican Republic, were called executive orders. The first one appeared on 4 December 1916, declaring Dominicans ineligible to hold the cabinet posts of Interior and Police and of War and the Navy, both positions which controlled portions of the Dominican military. Captain Knapp, now military governor, invited the other cabinet members to continue in charge of their portfolios, without pay or official recognition. By 8 December, however, all cabinet members had stated their refusal to serve under the military government, a fact recognized by Executive Order No. 4, which declared their offices vacant and designated U.S. military officers to replace them.[55]

The last remaining high official of the executive branch was President Henríquez himself. Unrecognized and overpowered, he continued to protest until no vestige of Dominican sovereignty remained. Finally, he left his country on 8 December, last setting foot on Dominican soil at the still unoccupied port of San Pedro de Macorís, where the people and the ayuntamiento of the city gave him a warm reception and presented him with a loan of two thousand dollars.[56]

The legislative branch of the Dominican government disappeared almost as quickly as the executive. Within a few days after the proclamation of 29 November, U.S. officials noted many members of the Congress leaving Santo Domingo City for their home-towns. In mid December Military Governor Knapp, on the advice of Minister Russell, decided that the new constitution voted by the constitutional assembly was itself illegal, thus disposing of those senators and deputies whose terms had expired in late November. On 26 December the military government ordered that no elections were to take place until further notice, making the elections of replacements impossible. Then, using as an excuse the lack of a quorum in the Dominican Congress, the military government suspended its sessions indefinitely on 2 January 1917.[57] Thus, within little more than a month, military officials had eliminated two of the three branches of representative, democratic government. Except for many lower officials and employees of the executive branch, only the judiciary remained. Most state governors and other provincial employees stayed at their posts. And, on the local level, the members of ayuntamientos or city councils remained in office, despite the expiration of their legal tenure, by fiat of the military government. Subsequently, military authorities reappointed or dismissed these formerly elected officials as they pleased.[58]

Adjusting to Military Rule

There was little show of resistance to the proclamation of a military government, much less, in fact, than there had been to the initial occupation earlier in 1916. Perhaps this was because the announcement of 29 November merely made de jure an already de facto situation. In any case, the only immediate military reaction was that of Governor Manuel de Jesús Pérez Sosa, nicknamed Lico, of Pacificador Province, who had earlier refused to surrender the stronghold at San Francisco de Macorís. Although this refusal was primarily symbolic, as the Dominicans made no attempt to use the building or its less than a dozen troops for any active military purpose, the marine commander considered the situation intolerable. When on 29 November a squad of marines successfully stormed the lightly defended fort, killing several Dominicans and wounding others, Governor Pérez and a group of fellow citizens angrily declared a rebellion. But, because the marines immediately sent reinforcements into the area and because many Dominicans worked to persuade the governor to avoid a bloody confrontation, the subsequent violence never escalated beyond occasional incidents of sniping. Nevertheless, Executive Order No. 3 declared Governor Pérez an outlaw in early December, replacing him with Juan Ramón de Lara, and in March 1917 Pérez surrendered to the military government.[59]

Another governor, Fidel Ferrer of the province of Samaná, apparently refused to continue to serve as a public official under the occupation. Executive Order No. 13, of 26 December 1916, stated that he had abandoned his office and replaced him with Volney Thomás Boisrond. Ferrer, a onetime schoolteacher and author of a textbook on Dominican history, later joined with peasant guerrillas fighting the marines in the east and was killed in 1918.[60]

However, the predominant reaction of Dominicans to the proclamation of 29 November was peaceful. "Notwithstanding the people's muffled murmur of protest," noted an eyewitness, "their inaction was as great as their stupor." Both members of government and leaders of the political parties had counseled the population not to resist, believing that an armed struggle would be useless.[61] The Henríquez government confined its reaction to the diplomatic front. The Dominican representative in Washington, Armando Pérez Perdomo, composed a strong formal protest to Secretary of State Robert Lansing against "the illegal actions of the intervening United States' forces in the territory of the Dominican Republic" and sent other legations a memorandum explaining the situation in detail. Similarly, before his ouster, the Dominican secretary of state, José María Cabral y Báez, sent a protest to Lansing.[62]

President Henríquez sought to confront U.S. officials personally, to convince them of the error of their policy or at least to obtain an assurance that the military government was only a temporary measure. Accompanied by his son, Dr. Max Henríquez Ureña, who officially served as secretary to the office of the president, Henríquez journeyed first to San Juan, Puerto Rico, where he received fervent expressions of sympathy from the beleaguered nationalists of that island, and then to New York and Washington. He found officials in Washington unwilling to discuss Dominican affairs. Only through the newspapers could he be heard, and the United States' approaching entry into World War I, which attracted most of the public's attention, rendered even that platform ineffective. Since a successful antioccupation campaign in the United States appeared at least temporarily impossible, Henríquez went south to Cuba. There, in Havana and Santiago, with the help of other Dominicans, he took the first steps in a nationalist campaign of publicity and agitation which would last until the withdrawal of U.S. troops in 1924.[63]

In the weeks following the proclamation, U.S. personnel wrote various dispatches commenting with pleasure on the situation throughout the country. Marine officials in various northern towns reported that all was quiet, with most citizens ignoring politics and going about their business and some sympathetic, friendly, and openly cooperative.[64] U.S. Minister Russell reported in a similar vein that "prominent citizens and former officials of Santo Domingo" had indicated to him "their opinion that present control by the United States was what the Dominican Republic needed and that petty politicians are the only people dissatisfied."[65]

Though Russell was stretching the truth to complement U.S. policy, it is certain that some Dominicans had been happy to see the crisis of 1916 resolved, especially because of the economic difficulties which the suspension of Customs Receivership payments had caused. An apparently common feeling was that, the deadlock having been broken, the United States would arrange matters as it wanted—perhaps for the better—hold new elections, and then leave.

Dominicans who opposed the military government found it difficult to make their views known. Owing to strict prior censorship, it was impossible to publish, in any form, any opinions "of a violent or inflammatory character, or which tend to encourage hostility or resistance to the military government" or are "unfavorable to the government of the United States of America or to the military government in Santo Domingo"; indeed, no material concerning the occupation or the policy of the U.S. government could be published which had not been submitted to and approved by the censor. When one editor, Dimas Frías, declared that he would not abide by the rules of the censors, the military authorities suppressed his newspaper, the *Heraldo Dominicano*. When the editor then published a handbill critical of censorship, he was imprisoned "for circulating literature against the American occupation." A military court found him guilty and imposed a fine.[66]

One of the ironies of censorship was that U.S. newspapers printed material concerning the military government which never appeared in the Dominican press. And U.S. or other publications which contained such material were frequently refused entry to the republic.

The Policy of the Military Government

Why had the United States intervened in the Dominican Republic and, having intervened, what did North American policymakers hope to accomplish? How did Washington organize the military regime to bring about the changes which it desired? And what were the principal endeavors of the military government?

The proclamation of the military government declared that the Dominicans had caused the intervention. They had allegedly violated article 3 of the 1907 U.S.-Dominican treaty by increasing their public debt without the required prior agreement of Washington officials. Because the debt was the result of expenses incurred quelling revolutions, the reasoning continued, the United States had intervened to reestablish domestic peace, to institute certain reforms to secure the continuance of peace, and thus to insure future compliance with the treaty.[67]

If the proclamation offered a somewhat superficial explanation of the rationale for the intervention, it was at least a statement of a legal and diplomatic position, and it was with this position that Dominicans did battle while the intervention continued. Nationalists argued that the occupation and the military government were illegal, that the Dominicans had not increased their public debt but had only done the short-term borrowing necessary to the daily operations of any government. They also noted that they had faithfully made every required payment on the $20 million loan established by the 1907 convention to liquidate the Dominican debt, repaying even more than the specified minimum amounts. Furthermore, even if the alleged increase of the debt had occurred, they argued correctly, there was nothing in the treaty or in the international law which would justify the destruction of a constitutional government and of Dominican sovereignty as a result. Finally, a military government, with dictatorial powers based on the laws of war, had no place in governing a people who were in no sense at war with the United States.[68]

Behind the reasons advanced as a legal justification for the occupation were other, unstated motives which did not have any legal weight but which were actually closer to the real causes of the intervention. These factors, which have been previously discussed in the context of preintervention Dominican-U.S. diplomacy, included the desire to protect U.S. interests in the Caribbean and Panama Canal region, especially against the possible encroachments of Germany;[69] the Wilson administration's "missionary impulse," the desire to set things right in the Latin American republics by imposing good leaders, democracy, and stability;[70] and the wish to protect North American economic interests in the Dominican Republic.[71] Because these goals appeared threatened by the republic's instability, the United States had tried to obtain economic, military, and thus political control over the country. When Dominican statesmen had found it impossible to cooperate, the State Department's diplomacy had become more and more belligerent, soon leading to the use of force. Thus the accrued weight of these actions themselves became a powerful factor leading to intervention.

A classic antiimperialist explanation of the intervention, such as that of Scott Nearing and Joseph Freeman, would argue that economic imperialism was the cause, that the primary purpose of Washington's Dominican policy was to protect established economic interests or to enhance investment opportunities or economic control in the future. In a narrow sense, this does not seem to have been of paramount importance. In terms of the U.S. economy or even of U.S. investments elsewhere, such as in Cuba or Mexico, the investment in Santo Domingo was tiny; besides, there was no threat to this investment in 1916. Nor did those in Washington generally view the republic—with its small population, wealth, and resources—as an important place for future investment. Moreover, Dominican governments had consistently acted to favor the interests of foreign investors. It is in the larger sense, in the context of U.S. hemispheric policy, that the concept of economic imperialism is a useful explanation. Control of the Dominican Republic was important to maintaining domination of the sea routes to the Panama Canal, which was vital to U.S. domestic and world trade, and to controlling the Caribbean area and South America, which harbored large investments, markets, and quantities of raw materials.

What were the goals of U.S. officials after they had assumed dictatorial powers in the Dominican Republic? The surprising answer to this question is that there were no clearly stated goals. "Although we maintained a military government in Santo Domingo for eight years," noted one critic, "neither we nor the Dominicans have ever received an authoritative statement of why we were there and what we were trying to accomplish."[72] Another writer, otherwise favorably disposed toward the intervention, complained in late 1921 that "there is no evidence that Washington had at the outset, or had developed since, any well-thought-out policy or program. . . . Seemingly Washington has drifted along in a hopeful attitude, settling problems as they have arisen but holding no clear vision of what it wants to do. The men on the ground have been left to their own devices."[73]

The "men on the ground" in Santo Domingo after 1916 were Military Governor Knapp and U.S. Minister Russell. These two, with Knapp in the more powerful position, would gradually work out and begin to implement a policy during the first year of the occupation. Though they looked to Washington for approval of major decisions, that approval was generally given with slight consideration because both the State and the Navy departments were becoming more and more involved in affairs in Europe. Washington failed to pay serious attention to its agents in the Dominican Republic until after World War I and the Versailles Conference, when the military government began to suffer internal problems and attacks from an increasingly vocal nationalist movement. But by then, in most cases, it was too late to make policy. U.S. officials had to devote all their energy to carrying out existing commitments and to negotiating a withdrawal.

Significant obstacles hampered the formulation of policy. Most important was the fact that three separate and coequal agencies of the U.S. government were involved in the Dominican Republic. The three were the Department of State, the Department of the Navy, and the Department of War, which controlled the Bureau of Insular Affairs, the parent agency of the Customs Receivership. The Bureau of Insular Affairs resolved part of the problem of divided authority almost immediately, in December 1916, when it ordered the receiver general of customs to "place yourself at the disposition of the Military Government,"[74] but relations between the State and Navy departments remained ambiguous. Minister Russell, who continued to represent the interests of the United States before the "Dominican" government of Captain Knapp (a diplomatic charade intended to demonstrate the unimpaired sovereignty of the republic), merely received instructions to consult and cooperate with the military governor.[75]

After early 1917 the State Department, though theoretically maintaining its control of policy, tended to leave Dominican matters to the Navy Department, which in turn granted the military government considerable freedom. Over time the pattern of Navy Department dominance in Dominican affairs became institutionalized, as the State Department discovered to its chagrin when it attempted, unsuccessfully, to reassert its control in early 1919. Thereafter the absence of a clear policy and the problem of overlapping authority caused increasing tension and at times open conflict between the two departments. But it was not until late 1920, after the military government had created an international cause célèbre over censorship, that the State Department, with support from the office of the president, managed to reclaim control.[76]

How did Knapp, Russell, and their aides establish the objectives of the military government? In the first place, they had to deal with obvious and immediate necessities resulting from the destruction of the Henríquez government. The occupiers had to organize the new military government, take up the operations of the old administration, and establish their authority throughout the republic. Captain Knapp, soon to be rear admiral, attacked the first major problem by appointing U.S. military officers to take over the various departments of the Dominican government.[77]

The structure of the new administration mimicked that of the executive branch of the former Dominican government except that, alongside the civil structure, there stood a parallel military one. At the head of both was the military governor, a powerful figure responsible only to the U.S. secretary of the navy. At the top of the military structure was the commander of the Second Provisional Brigade, later called the Second Brigade, of the U.S. Marine Corps. Under the brigade commander were two (later three) regimental commanders, each responsible for a large section of the country. Reporting to them were the commanding officers of the battalions and companies located in the various towns and villages of the republic. Other important officials were the provost marshals. Operating in conjunction with the provost courts, they were the top police and judicial officials of the military government.

Though many Dominican civilian officials continued in office, there was little doubt who held the real power. Henry C. Davis, a battalion commander in San Pedro de Macorís, made this abundantly clear in the course of lecturing a member of a citizens' group who hoped to change the personnel of the ayuntamiento there. Davis told the man that his proposal was presumptuous, warned him to stop his "political agitation," and "informed him in no uncertain manner that I was head of the Government as far as this Province is concerned and when I considered any changes desirable they would be made and not before."[78] Davis' conduct was apparently not unusual, prompting one observer to note the tendency of local military commanders to act "like little kings." The problem, commented Marine Colonel Rufus H. Lane, was that "military authorities . . . were inclined to be somewhat arbitrary and to apply military principles and discipline to the civilian population at large."[79]

Once the structure of the military government had been established, its cabinet-level officials, naval and marine officers under the direction of Military Governor Knapp, immediately set about continuing the daily operations of the former administration. This task they accomplished with the help of the Dominican employees who remained at their posts and the Dominican budget for 1916, which, though allegedly "ridiculous" in some of its provisions, was extended into 1917.[80]

The military government had to immediately establish its authority throughout the republic. To this end military officials enforced the newly instituted censorship rules, employed the military courts, and soon put to work a secret service. They considered disarmament a necessity for obtaining domestic peace—by mid 1917, they had collected 43,418 firearms and 187,720 rounds of ammunition.[81]

The military government proved much less quick to act on larger questions. No doubt these issues seemed less pressing; but they often involved large commitments of time and money, thus seeming to require careful planning. Furthermore, in the absence of any clearly stated policy, it was necessary for high officials of the occupation to formulate their own policy, based on what they understood of Washington's goals and the necessities of the Dominican Republic. The resulting policy, which emerged during 1917, was the work of the military governor and his advisers, Minister Russell, and to a lesser degree Clarence H. Baxter, the head of the receivership. They solicited ideas from the U.S. consul (who was also the representative of the United Fruit Company) in Puerto Plata and from many Dominicans—middle-rank bureaucrats who continued to work for the government as well as prominent citizens who conferred extraofficially with military administrators.[82]

Officials of the military government did have some reasonable bases for deciding upon the goals of their policy, despite the lack of clear direction from Washington. In the first place, the diplomatic struggle which preceded November 1916 had clearly identified several issues, namely, the U.S. government's desire to create a mechanism for financial control and its wish to establish a constabulary to replace the traditional armed forces of the republic. In addition, other matters had received attention in diplomatic correspondence from time to time, sometimes in the form of suggestions from Russell himself. These concerned strengthening U.S. authority over Dominican public works and extending it further to the state-owned railroad and the telephone and telegraph systems (measures contemplated to improve efficiency and to end graft), enacting a new land title law to facilitate taxation and the buying of real property by large North American corporations, and establishing a naval base in Samaná Bay. Military Governor Knapp, as he became more familiar with the Dominican situation, also noted aspects of Dominican life which he believed needed improvement, in particular education and transportation.[83]

From these various ideas, all of which either predated the military government or followed within several weeks, came the basic programs of the occupation. In addition to the daily business of administration and the surprisingly difficult task of subduing the east militarily, U.S. officials focused most of their energy on public works, particularly road and harbor construction and improvement, education, public health, the development of a constabulary, and a land survey program.[84] Other objects of preintervention diplomacy, such as financial control, followed automatically from the creation of the military government.

The vague demands and proposals for reform made by the State Department generally fell far short of concrete measures for their implementation. And so it was up to the military government to create the policies and the detailed plans which would effect them. As many critics within and without the military government have pointed out, the military officers in charge of the various departments of the government usually lacked any understanding of and experience with Dominican problems and did not have the training necessary to accomplish the technical aspects of their jobs. They had to turn to others, both North Americans and Dominicans, for help.[85]

The military government employed Dominicans in as many positions as possible, at least below the cabinet level. But it was difficult to find Dominicans with the special training needed for certain jobs and, in any case, antioccupation hostility made it almost impossible to persuade educated citizens to accept positions of responsibility within the military government, especially in the first months after November 1916. The problem had several solutions. One was the use of military officers in civilian positions. Though the Department of the Navy at first objected to this policy and Minister Russell persisted in his efforts to change it, Washington allowed the military government to continue the practice until the inauguration of the Dominican provisional government in 1922.[86]

A second solution to the shortage of qualified and cooperative Dominicans was to turn to what might be called the U.S. "colonial service." In 1917, occupation officials gratefully received from Brigadier General Frank McIntyre, the chief of the Bureau of Insular Affairs, a list of names of civilians who had previous experience in the U.S.-held Philippine Islands. Thereafter military officials often looked to former personnel of U.S. administrations in the Philippines, Puerto Rico, and Cuba and employed a number of men with this background.[87]

The military government borrowed information as well as officials from previous colonial experiences. In 1917, the author of a proposed reform of the prison system based his ideas on an earlier project in the Philippines, noting that "the work in the Philippines seems in many ways more like this in Santo Domingo than any other."[88] The writers of contemplated laws on labor and immigration ordered copies of Puerto Rican and Philippine as well as U.S. legislation on the subject before beginning their own drafts. "Information as to the experience in similar countries is most valuable," noted Military Governor Thomas Snowden, Knapp's successor, as he ordered copies of the *Reports of the Governor General of Cuba* as well as works by the earl of Cromer and Viscount Milner on the British administration of Egypt.[89]

Puerto Rico entered into the administration of the Dominican Republic in another way. The military government recruited and hired Puerto Ricans, usually for middle-status jobs of a kind which demanded native Spanish speakers but which few Dominicans could be persuaded to carry out, such as collecting the unpopular new taxes, spying, and interpreting. The nature of these jobs, the alleged superior air which Puerto Rican officials used in dealing with Dominicans, and the fact that some Dominicans viewed them as betrayers of the Hispanic people made them thoroughly disliked.[90] J. Luis Cintrón, a Puerto Rican deported because he sympathized with the Dominican nationalist position, revealed a popular conception of Puerto Ricans when he charged that the Puerto Rican Association in Santo Domingo was "nothing but a bunch of spies." Ironically, U.S. mainland personnel looked down upon their Puerto Rican fellow citizens working with them for the occupation.[91]

Eventually, Dominicans became involved in the military government and contributed to the policies of the occupation. Although U.S. officials had claimed from the first that many educated Dominicans supported the military administration, most qualified Dominicans had refused to take positions of responsibility in the new regime or to have any intimate association with it. But, as it became evident that the occupiers were planning to stay for some length of time, increasing numbers of persons began to come forward. Dominicans, especially members of the bourgeoisie, naturally began to see the military government as a patron—as a source of jobs, as a potential customer, as a possible sponsor for their favorite projects, or even as an ally in settling grudges against other Dominicans.[92] Some Dominicans, it must be added, aligned themselves with the occupation government with no ulterior motive but simply because they believed that it would effect benefits which no Dominican administration could achieve. Even some of the intervention's most active opponents, frustrated with the republic's traditional political life, hoped that this would be the case.

One of the first breaks in the wall of noninvolvement came as the result of the action of Félix María Nolasco, a chief clerk in the Ministry of Interior and Police, who had made himself known to his superiors as "from the beginning a warm friend of the military government." Nolasco and an associate presented officials with a whole list of names of persons they described as "friends of progress as well as sympathizers with the American occupation . . . , not politicians, but true and sensible people." From this list, which bore the names of several influential Dominican families, came the republic's new envoy to Washington, Manuel de Jesús Galván, and several other future appointees of the military government. In return for Nolasco's helpfulness, the military authorities looked favorably upon his desire to be named *síndico* of the ayuntamiento of Santo Domingo and later named him to an administrative board.[93] Other Dominican cooperators also received preferment for their support.

Beginning in March 1917, a number of very important Dominicans approached the military government, either to offer their support or to present advice to military officials. Mario Fermín Cabral, a ranking member of the oligarchy and president of the Senate before the intervention, offered Military Governor Knapp his wholehearted support, even giving speeches in favor of the new regime. Haim H. López-Penha, of a wealthy and socially important family, wrote a long memorandum concerning "Some Necessities of the Dominican People," and Francisco A. Herrera, an exchief of the Ministry of Treasury and Commerce, offered his support as well as a long list of problems and suggested reforms. Also volunteering advice to the military government were P. A. Ricart, vice-president of the Santo Domingo Chamber of Commerce, Industry, and Agriculture; Francisco J. Peynado, a prestigious lawyer, diplomat, and former cabinet official; and Dr. A. Fiallo Cabral, the superintendent general of public education.[94]

Particularly helpful to the military government were the overtures from the leaders of political parties. Horacio Vásquez visited Military Governor Knapp in March and publicly gave his support to the occupation's disarmament program. Luis F. Vidal did the same in a public announcement asking for the cooperation of his followers in the Legalista party. Federico Velásquez, a personal friend of Minister Russell who was considered sympathetic to U.S. policy, waited a respectable amount of time to present himself publicly to the new authorities, but he cashed in all the same. "Under the Military Government a large majority of offices were filled by members of this [Velásquez'] party," wrote Russell later.[95]

In April, Emilio Joubert, a high official of Horacio Vásquez' party, wrote a letter to party members announcing the chief's decision to back the occupation: "We have no just reasons to consider the American intervention as a covert and artful conquest and so has it been understood by the leader of the party, whose patriotism no one may doubt. [Vásquez], not only by his remonstrance but by his example, has shown that he wishes that the period of unfruitful civil warfare be ended and that efforts be made to hasten the termination of the present abnormal occupation by cooperating to suppress the obstacles which prolong it." Later that month, Joubert privately suggested that Vásquez' party was interested in coming to an accommodation with the United States over the demands of Russell's infamous Note No. 14 of November 1915.[96] Joubert himself early decided to associate with the military government by accepting paid positions on several advisory commissions; he later received a reward for his action, being named the Dominican representative in Washington. "I have always been willing to give myself, body and soul, to the task of helping the Military Government or the State Department in any endeavor tending to promote the good of the Dominican Republic," he wrote in 1922.[97]

These examples are from the largest cities of the republic. The same pattern asserted itself in other towns and regions. Some citizens remained aloof, many went about their business and ignored the intruders, and some fraternized. As the occupation became more established, the higher officials of the military government developed a coterie of Dominican individuals and organizations which they consulted regularly. On economic and business matters, for example, the military governor and his staff often approached the chambers of commerce in Santo Domingo and Santiago, even asking them to help in the drafting of certain laws. The communication was not one-way, as both individuals and organizations felt free to put their ideas before the military government, which sometimes responded by adopting them into its program.[98]

As military officials began to feel more familiar with circumstances in the Dominican Republic and as the political situation began to thaw, the military government began to appoint a series of commissions with Dominican, North American, and sometimes Puerto Rican members. These panels were to study and to make recommendations concerning public education, the Dominican diplomatic service, and the republic's "food situation" in light of the increasing world shortage of goods and transportation caused by World War I. Another group was to study all claims against the Dominican government after 1907 and to make recommendations for the settlement of those found legitimate. Similarly, military boards began to examine other problems, such as the Dominican prison system. In another scheme military officials undertook a poll of ayuntamientos all over the republic, asking them to submit lists of public works projects of both national and local importance. Dominicans, North Americans, and Puerto Ricans also participated in less formal discussions, analyzing various matters, examining proposed laws, and drafting projects.[99]

Slowly the military government created a policy and began to implement it. During the first half of 1917, it moved to improve education, to revive stalled public works projects and to plan new ones, to organize a public health service, to create the rudiments of the new constabulary (the Guardia Nacional Dominicana), to take a national census, to survey the nation's lands in order to improve the chaotic land title situation, and to better Dominican agriculture. Numerous other matters such as taxation, the disputed Dominican-Haitian border, the establishment of a national penitentiary, the improvement of communications, and reform of the judicial system would only "receive attention as rapidly as well digested programs can be thought out."[100]

These initial endeavors served to define most of the effort of the military government during the next seven years. Because the projects were complex, difficult to carry out, and costly, they often moved forward very slowly. Lack of progress and the incompetence of officials became a cause for complaint as early as September 1917, and some of the projects were still incomplete when the provisional Dominican government took over in 1922.[101]

The military government thus initiated the occupation of the Dominican Republic without having received a clear statement of future policy from Washington. And because it never received one, it was up to officials of the military government to create a policy, drawing on various sources to do so. Most of the decisions concerned concrete matters, such as what to do and how to do it. Certain broader matters, such as how long the occupation should continue, could not be decided in Santo Domingo. Some of these were never decided, despite various suggestions and some debate among U.S. officials.[102] Washington, clearly, had its attention focused elsewhere.

2
The Political Economy of the Military Government, I

One of Washington's primary goals in the several years of diplomacy which preceded the creation of the military government in November 1916 was the imposition of a number of reforms in the Dominican Republic. U.S. officials hoped that these changes, concerning the Dominican military, treasury, and public works programs, would bring financial and political stability and perhaps a measure of economic growth; if they did not, they would at least insure greater U.S. control. The establishment of the military government, however, temporarily obviated the need for greater control and opened the way for a different and far longer list of reforms, many of them based on the U.S. colonial experience which began in Cuba and Puerto Rico in 1898. Before long, projects would be under way in every ministry of the government which promised changes in nearly all areas of Dominican life.

It is important to remember, however, that because the military government had replaced the Dominican executive branch, the higher officials of the military government spent much of their time and energy on the routine tasks of running the national government. Despite their conscious desire to promote reforms and innovations, they had to continue ordinary administrative work, carry on extensive correspondence, supervise personnel, meet those who had business with the government, negotiate contracts, write budgets, review the actions of subordinates, and solve the many small problems which arose each day. The executive orders of the military government, which represent some of the more important concerns dealt with by military officials, are good indicators of the routine nature of most business: the largest number treat amendments to budgets, insignificant changes in laws, awards of pensions, ratifications of municipal actions, routine fiscal affairs, personnel appointments, proclamations of holidays, and various other matters equally commonplace.

The more significant actions of the military government were relatively few. Of these the major reform and development measures involved education, public health and sanitation, public works, and the creation of a more efficient and less political constabulary. These four were important because each package of reforms represented a consciously planned major commitment of the military government's human and material resources. And occupation officials put forward these programs, except for the constabulary, as examples of their best work whenever called upon to render an account to their critics or to their superiors in Washington.

In fact, much of what is generally known about these occupation programs has come from the military government's favorable self-appraisals, most notably *Santo Domingo: Its Past and Its Present Condition*, which became the basis for most of the sparse secondary literature on the subject. Virtually all such accounts repeat the same list of accomplishments which military officials set down to defend themselves against critics in 1920. Even the historian Melvin M. Knight, who indicted the occupation in many other areas, wrote hardly a critical word in his treatment of these four programs.[1]

It is necessary to look beyond the rosy picture painted by the military government propaganda. Doing so makes possible for the first time an informed assessment of the success or failure of these programs and, in part, of the occupation itself. It also opens the way to understanding more fully what military officials intended to accomplish, how they went about their work, what frustrations they faced, and how their work meshed with existing Dominican conditions.

It should not be in the least surprising that these programs were not what they were made to appear by military authorities. In fact, each of the four programs represents an originally ambitious plan much changed by varying degrees of compromise, inefficiency, incompetence, delay, insolvency, international political and economic conditions, resistance, and a variety of other factors.

In the final analysis, it is important to measure the success or failure of these four major programs in order to begin to evaluate the effectiveness of the military government itself. But what standards should be applied? Several criteria seem reasonable. (1) To what degree did the project as it was implemented measure up to the project as it was defined by its planners? In short, were military officials capable of doing what they had hoped? (2) How successful was each reform in meeting the needs of the Dominican people? Did the educational reform, for instance, provide a decent education to most young Dominicans, and did it solve the basic problems which had prevented that in the past? (3) How successfully did the reform survive withdrawal? Did it collapse, did it survive and perform as U.S. planners had intended, or was it substantially changed as the result of its existence in a completely Dominican milieu?

The Educational Program

The military government's work for the improvement of Dominican education began almost immediately, with the appointment of a commission of six prominent Dominicans. They were to investigate the existing state of education and make recommendations for its improvement and for the creation of "a system of education that will best serve the interests of the people of the Republic."[2]

There can be little doubt that the nation's educational system was poor when the military government took control. More than 90 percent of the nation's approximately 750,000 citizens were illiterate. Out of an estimated school age population of nearly 200,000, only 14,000 to 18,000 were enrolled in schools of any kind, and actual attendance was perhaps as low as 40 percent. Only Santo Domingo and Santiago had what might have been called school systems, while in most towns education was limited to a primary school with one or two teachers. In rural areas even primary education was usually lacking. Public education suffered from inadequate financial support, crude facilities, untrained personnel, and weak administration.[3] Parents were well advised, if they could afford it, to send their children to one of the state-subsidized private schools in the larger cities; in any case, these were often the only available facilities beyond the first two grades. As a result, education tended to be the prerogative of urbanites and the wealthy.

While this disastrous situation reflected the poverty of the country and the elitist attitudes of most Dominican leaders, it was not the result of total neglect. Beginning in the mid nineteenth century, various Dominicans such as Pedro F. Bonó, Padre F. X. Billini, and Salomé Ureña and the Puerto Rican Eugenio María de Hostos had worked to broaden and improve Dominican education. As a result, by 1900 education was at least theoretically free, obligatory, and available to both sexes, with more than five thousand students enrolled in primary, secondary, normal, and commercial schools. But none of these efforts had succeeded in bringing education to the Dominican masses.[4]

The military government's commission on education completed its work in late 1917. Soon officials published a completely
revised code of education, comprised of six separate laws, which
governed all levels of education, including special and vocational
schools and even the Catholic seminary. These laws, like earlier Dominican school legislation, called for compulsory education between the ages of seven and fourteen and for instruction to be free
and in Spanish, the latter a notable departure from U.S. colonial policy in Puerto Rico and the Philippines. They mandated a primary
curriculum which appeared reasonably well suited to the Dominican urban and rural masses, except for the absence of any study of
agriculture; the classical secondary curriculum, however, was of
limited relevance to those who were not going on to a university and
failed to answer the nation's need for well-educated nonprofessionals
such as technicians. The entire system, from primary schools to the
universities, was highly centralized, controlled by the Consejo Nacional de Educación, which was appointed by the central government.[5]

The foremost goal of the military government's reformed educational system was reasonable: to broaden and strengthen elementary
education. A basic education for the masses, officials believed, was
necessary both for economic growth and for the creation of a stable
and democratic government in the future. Based on this belief, the
military government and the U.S.-educated Dominican superintendent general of education, Julio Ortega Frier, worked to raise enrollments, to increase the numbers of schools and teachers, and to improve the quality of teaching. By 1920 officials boasted that nearly
half the school age population, almost 100,000 children, was enrolled, with a daily attendance rate of almost 85 percent. The most
remarkable increase occurred in the rural areas—in 1916 there were
perhaps 30 functioning rural schools with tiny enrollments; by 1920
there were 647 with 50,000 students.[6]

The greatest problem facing the expanding school system was
the lack of trained teachers. While lowering the requirements for
graduation from secondary and normal schools in 1918 probably
eased the problem temporarily,[7] the military government's basic solution was to raise teachers' salaries, which had been so low that
even normal school graduates had generally chosen to work in other
fields. The salary range of $8 to $60 per month before the occupation
rose to $15 to $150 by 1920, with rural elementary teachers and urban secondary teachers at opposite ends of the scale. These increases
allowed the school authorities, at least until 1920, to keep teachers'
wages competitive with those in other fields, which had risen steadily in response to war-induced inflation.[8]

Officials also used several other means to solve the teacher shortage. They increased the size of both schools and classes and, in rural areas, employed a double shift, with different students attending in the mornings and afternoons. These steps increased the number of students per teacher, as well as the cost efficiency of the schools; while education budgets rose dramatically, the annual cost per pupil dropped from $24 to $12.[9] Each of these measures was an innovative but partial remedy to a difficult problem which had plagued the Dominican school system for years.

The military government intended to improve the quality and content of education. Officials sought to upgrade teacher training and methods of instruction according to what was then in vogue in the United States. The government instituted summer schools for some teachers, worked to standardize the curriculum and textbooks, and introduced the latest subject matter, such as vocational and specialized elective courses, into the regular academic program. There is no evidence, however, that military officials tried to "Americanize" course content in other ways.

Expansion of the public school system also created an immediate need for school buildings. Not only did most rural areas lack them entirely, but education authorities found that in many towns existing schools were located in small, often inadequate rented buildings with rudimentary furnishings. To solve the problem in rural districts, officials encouraged the formation of parents' associations to erect schools "constructed of cheap material and very plain in every way." By 1920 these groups had provided 150 such buildings; after construction the associations continued to assist their local schools and teachers. In towns the authorities at first rented suitable quarters, well-constructed houses and larger buildings. Then in 1920 the military government began to encourage municipal governments to build new, permanent schoolhouses by providing loans for construction and standardized architectural plans for schools of one to six rooms. Education officials also began furnishing at least the urban schools with "good American desks, blackboards, [and] chairs" and equipped the nation's two public high schools with laboratories and libraries.[10]

The military government's treatment of secondary schools and universities was more controversial than its work at the elementary level. Given limited resources, the emphasis on providing a rudimentary education for the masses meant a corresponding deemphasis at higher levels. When the occupation began, officials found public secondary and normal schools operating in each of the twelve provinces. These, in the view of the marine officer in charge of public education in 1917, Rufus Lane, were entirely inadequate, "a drain on the public treasury, without rendering a corresponding service." For this reason the military government decided to withdraw most of its support from all but the Santo Domingo and Santiago facilities, which were greatly enlarged, "reorganized and equipped on a modern basis." Apparently five of the other ten also survived, limping along with limited aid as semiofficial facilities. Thus, by the military government's own admission, secondary education was improved by concentrating resources, but to the detriment of all except the nation's two largest cities.[11]

On the university level, the military government also followed a policy of retrenchment. Although the University of Santo Domingo was ancient, with roots in the early sixteenth century, it had often suffered from the misfortunes which had beset the Dominican people. Since the late nineteenth century, at least, the university had survived as a professional institute, without a faculty of arts and letters. In 1914, however, a general educational reform had remedied this defect. In 1915 the Dominican Congress authorized a second university, in Santiago; it opened in January 1916, with four professional faculties and two schools.[12]

Officials of the military government thought little of these institutions. Military Governor Knapp, himself a graduate of Yale University, privately referred to them as "two so-called universities, neither of high rank." In October 1917 he approved the closing of the Santiago facility and the elimination of the University of Santo Domingo's one nonprofessional faculty, letters, thus reducing its status once again to that of a professional institute. In subsequent years military officials slightly enlarged this small institution, boosting its enrollment from 110 to 169 by late 1920, and made a few improvements, raising professors' salaries and adding laboratory and clinical work to the education of medical students.[13] This deemphasis of university (and secondary) education made some sense, considering the basic problem of limited resources, but it had an unfortunate effect: it assured that the professionals, managers, and technicians whom the society so badly needed would not be available in sufficient numbers for several more generations.

After just three years, the military government had a highly creditable overall record in education. It had created a significant number of new schools, especially in rural areas, and had involved a much larger number of Dominican children than ever before in the educational process. At its high point in 1920, the public school system included 647 rural schools, 194 urban primary schools, a variety of secondary, vocational, and correctional institutions, and the university.[14] Moreover, the new system appeared generally well organized and supervised. But there were flaws in such a hastily created structure, and events would prove that it was built on shaky financial ground as well.

The flaws were easy to detect. By its own admission the government could not provide enough classrooms and classroom equipment, neither for those 100,000 students already enrolled nor for the other 100,000 still entirely outside the system. Statistics suggest that in 1920 less than one-quarter of the rural schools were located in even rudimentary buildings and that as many as two-thirds of all schools lacked such basic equipment as desks and blackboards.[15] A greater problem, one suspects, is that very little learning was accomplished in many schools. Large numbers of teachers, particularly in rural areas, had no more than an inferior grade school education themselves. The military government lacked the funds, facilities, and expertise to overcome these problems, especially that of teacher training.

As early as 1918, in a prosperous period, Military Governor Knapp was apologizing for the fact that the government's budget limitations would prevent needed expansion of the educational system. With the onset of a depression in late 1920, the situation quickly went from difficult to disastrous. Funds for new school buildings and equipment dried up, teachers suffered pay cuts—first of 20 percent and then of 50 percent—and eventually deficits threatened the system's very existence.[16]

In May 1921, the military government found itself forced by lack of funds to close the public schools, a move which inspired considerable Dominican protest. In spite of this protest, the schools were open only intermittently for the next three years.[17] Still worse, as the economic crisis continued authorities permanently closed nearly half the rural schools, as well as the correctional schools and other special facilities. In yet another economy move, the authorities put the urban primary schools on a double shift. "In this way," observed a marine officer, "more than 30,000 children have been left without schools and the remainder are receiving less training than before."[18]

The lack of funds and the intermittent closings soon reduced the public school program to a sorry state. In March 1922 a school inspector in the commune of Los Llanos, northeast of the capital city, filed a report which revealed this clearly. Of the twelve public schools in his district, only seven were operating. Of the other five, one had recently closed for unrevealed reasons, two were not operating because no teachers had ever been appointed, and two others had closed when their teachers resigned.[19]

The schools' economic crisis was, in part, of the military government's own making. Before 1921, war-induced prosperity had facilitated the expansion of the school system and had caused the military government to make some changes in the Dominicans' time-honored method of school financing. The changes, in more difficult times, proved inadequate. Up to 1919 the schools had depended on a patent tax on local businesses, a revenue source which was relatively immune to the uncontrollable fluctuations of the republic's internationally oriented economy. In forty years, depending on this system, there had been no school closings for financial causes. In 1919, despite warnings, the military government abolished the patent tax, making the school system dependent on the government's general revenues.[20] When these began a serious decline in late 1920, the school system was almost immediately in severe fiscal trouble.

In 1922, with the school system already crippled by the economic crisis, military officials instituted a new financial policy which did further damage. To relieve pressure on the declining general revenues, officials decreed that henceforth schools would receive the proceeds of a property tax which, it so happened, was then the object of a successful nationalist tax boycott. Thus the military government held up Dominican schoolchildren as hostages to the tax refusers. Sustained by nationalist fervor and the self-interest of wealthier Dominicans, whose children were in private schools and thus unaffected, the boycott continued and the quantity and quality of public education steadily declined. The schools were often closed, experienced teachers left the profession, and the support staff of inspectors and other officials was decimated.[21]

In early 1924, officials of the Dominican provisional government attempted to remedy the financial problem by again designating a patent tax to support education. Although this measure did not immediately undo previous damage, it did enable the new constitutional government which took office later that year to reopen the schools on a regular basis. However, enrollment was less than half what it had been in 1920.

The Dominican government established a mediocre record in the field of education after the occupation ended. A 1929 report noted the continuing construction of new buildings but also the fact that teachers' salaries were too low and that "the teaching staff is not sufficient in number to attend adequately to the necessities of public instruction in all parts of the Republic." In 1930 there was a total of 526 public schools serving 50,000 students, about the same enrollment as in 1918. Not until 1935 did enrollment surpass the 1920 figure, but by that time it comprised only one-third of school age children. The poor condition of Dominican public education continues today, especially in rural areas, a fact that can be confirmed by any inquiring visitor.[22]

An evaluation of the military government's program would have to applaud the dedicated effort to expand and improve public education. In the short run, officials created many new schools, improved existing facilities, and exposed a large number of Dominican children to at least the rudiments of education. But in the long run the military government was hardly more successful than its Dominican predecessors, its accomplishment limited by many of the same difficulties that had hindered previous educators. The military government's program could not solve the fundamental problem of producing large numbers of well-educated teachers in a basically peasant society, although intelligent planning somewhat alleviated the problem by boosting teacher productivity. Neither could military officials solve the underlying financial problem which threatened Dominican schools; in fact, they aggravated it by ignoring past Dominican experience. Military officials also failed to change the thinking of the Dominican elite on the matter of supporting public education. Without solutions to these problems, the military government's considerable effort was condemned to have a less than significant impact on future Dominican education.

Public Health and Sanitation

Another of the principal efforts of the military government involved the field of public health and sanitation, often lauded as one of the outstanding achievements of the occupation. A closer examination, however, reveals a less clear picture, a mixture of substantial effort and limited success.

Military officials found the republic's public health system and sanitary conditions sorely deficient in 1916. Sanitary and public health legislation, dating from 1912, existed, but such basic problems as shortages of money and trained personnel as well as poor administration had resulted in a program which was generally unimplemented and unenforced. Consequently, wrote a military official in a typical description, the "cities and towns were dirty, elementary sanitation was neglected, and the few hospitals in the country were in a sadly neglected state and totally inadequate. There was no real attempt at disease control."[23]

Less than a month after the establishment of the military government, officials demonstrated their concern about these conditions by naming a U.S. Navy surgeon, P. E. Garrison, as chief sanitary officer. His job was to oversee all health and sanitation activities in the republic, working both with marine authorities and with the existing Dominican health boards and officials. Work with the latter, however, proved frustrating. As Garrison's position was merely advisory, his efforts were often met with apathy and sometimes with passive resistance. Even when he received enthusiastic cooperation, the same problems which had crippled preintervention Dominican work continued to block significant progress. Much of what was achieved at first was owed to the efforts of local marine commanders to "obtain general cleanliness" in the occupied cities and towns. These officials encouraged both municipalities and individuals to clean up refuse, to abandon polluted wells, to install proper latrines, to clean and improve municipal facilities such as markets and abattoirs, and to put into practice various other elementary health and sanitation measures.[24]

While encouraging efforts under this arrangement, the chief sanitary officer had begun to study the republic's sanitation and health care situation and to formulate ideas for its improvement. His thinking on the matter, plus his day-to-day experience, served to convince him that "the existing laws and regulations for Public-Health organization and work in Santo Domingo are so incomplete and in many cases so ambiguous and contradictory that it is considered impracticable to conduct an efficient service under their provisions." With this in mind, Garrison drew up a comprehensive plan for reform and expansion. Since its implementation involved a large expenditure of money for a purpose not clearly within the mandate of the military government, officials referred the matter to Washington. There it remained for months, apparently ignored. Left temporarily to work with the existing system, Garrison's office began to issue a variety of laws and regulations. Some of these treated specific and pressing problems, such as the establishment of a more effective quarantine system, control of narcotic drugs, and regulation of prostitution by establishing zones of tolerance.[25] Others dealt with the legal structure which governed work in public health and sanitation.

Most of the latter legislation modified existing laws, particularly the 1912 sanitation code and the 1906 statute governing the Juro Médico, the board which licensed and regulated medical practice in the republic. The thrust of this legislation, the most important of which was Executive Order No. 196 of August 1918, was clear: it changed the decentralized Dominican health and sanitation system, with power at the local level, into a centralized bureaucracy controlled completely from Santo Domingo by the chief sanitary officer.[26]

Not until late 1919, owing to various administrative difficulties in both Washington and Santo Domingo, was the military government able to issue Executive Order No. 338, the Ley de Sanidad (Health Law), a unified code governing all aspects of health and sanitation.[27] The importance of this law, which superseded all previous legislation on the subject, lay in the ambitious scope of its intended accomplishment—to create at one stroke a system of health and sanitation for the entire republic.

The Ley de Sanidad reflected both the health and sanitation needs of the republic and the preoccupations of military officials. As of 1 January 1920, it established an intricate nationwide system under the centralized authority of a new cabinet-level office, the Ministry of Sanitation and Beneficence. In the health field the law specifically regulated the practice of medicine, pharmacy, and related professions, established standards for hospitals and other medical institutions, and created a national laboratory. It instituted measures to prevent and control communicable diseases, such as compulsory smallpox vaccination, a ban on prostitution, a quarantine service, and an improved system for gathering disease statistics. In the sanitation field the law established regulations for garbage removal, disposal of human wastes, and maintenance of sanitary conditions on all property, public and private. It instituted controls over the preparation and sale of food and drugs, as well as over water supplies. It also established codes for all public and private construction in regard to plumbing, sewage, and ventilation. Finally, the legislation created a system of enforcement.

The Ley de Sanidad, as well as the military government's other legislation in this area, had as its goals bringing order, efficiency, and science to health care and sanitation in the republic. The imposition of such criteria, it was believed, would result in more and better personnel and institutions and in an increase in the number of Dominicans who would benefit from modern health care and sanitation. The question, however, remains: to what degree were the laws effective in achieving these goals?

Certainly one of the two most serious problems facing the Dominican health care system was the grave shortage of doctors and other health professionals. In 1917 there were 95 doctors and licentiates of medicine in the entire country, approximately 1 for every 8,500 persons. Maldistribution, caused by doctors preferring to live in urban areas, aggravated the problem. The doctor-patient ratio varied from 1 to 2,500 in one province to 1 to 30,000 in another; within provinces, some 233,000 persons, almost a third of the population, lived in communes where there were no health care personnel whatever. Among doctors there were virtually no specialists, particularly in such needed fields as epidemiology. Because the national university's medical school was almost without equipment, instruction was, "for the greater part, theoretical." Few doctors, except for the 10 percent who had studied abroad, had practical experience in laboratory work, dissection, or surgery.[28]

How did the military government's health program address this problem? While the occupation legislation concerning the Juro Médico and the National Laboratory may have slightly improved the quality of medical personnel, it did nothing to produce more doctors, pharmacists, or even medical and sanitary technicians. In a sense, by creating more positions in the field, the military government's program created a greater, or at least more visible, shortage. Military officials' solution to this problem was to import critically needed medical and sanitary personnel from the United States, some of whom had served previously in other U.S. colonies, and from Puerto Rico. This remedy was of no use to the Dominicans after withdrawal; it also had the disadvantage of creating an employment pattern in which foreigners tended to hold the professional, supervisory, and technical positions while Dominicans were relegated to the bottom posts. Only in the area of professional nursing did the authorities promote a long-term solution, founding the republic's first nursing schools in La Vega and Santo Domingo in 1921. But these programs, with North American instructors and tiny enrollments, did not produce their first graduates, four in number, until mid 1923.[29]

What might the military government have done to remedy this lack of sufficient personnel? Can it be blamed for its failure to solve this fundamental problem? Probably, given the limited range of solutions which were available or acceptable to the military government, there was no immediate remedy. The difficulty of the problem, however, must not obscure the fact that, lacking any long-term solution, the military government's public health and sanitation program would most likely suffer a severe decline after withdrawal.

The second great obstacle facing Dominican health care and sanitation was a shortage of money. The military government inherited an inadequate system of finance; in 1916, both the national and the municipal governments combined had appropriated only $30,000, while private lotteries generated perhaps twice that amount for various philanthropic institutions such as hospitals and orphanages. By 1920 the military government and local governments provided $657,000 to the Ministry of Sanitation and Beneficence.

Approximately half of this increase resulted from the additional tax revenues generated by the extraordinary prosperity of the 1917 to 1920 period.[30] Military authorities could take credit for the rest. Executive Order No. 247 of 1918 and the Ley de Sanidad of 1920 required that municipal governments dedicate from 10 to 15 percent of their income, which was growing at the time, to public health and sanitation. In 1920 these local appropriations totaled $248,000. In addition, with Executive Order No. 420 in March 1920, the military government created a national lottery which within six months had added $125,000, earmarked for health and beneficence purposes, to the national coffers.[31]

These improvements in the financing of public health and sanitation were, it turned out, inadequate when a depression arrived in late 1920, just as the use of foreigners was, in the long run, an inadequate solution to the personnel shortage. The failure to solve these two fundamental problems was not surprising. Long-term solutions lay only in the eventual economic and social development of the country and/or in a move away from the republic's dependent and elite-dominated political economy. The military government was willing but unable to do the first and uninterested in doing the second.

Health and sanitation officials were somewhat more successful in dealing with health care institutions. While the military government saw the opening of only two new public (or charity) hospitals and a much needed leprosarium during its tenure, it considerably improved the five other hospitals which came under its jurisdiction in 1920 as the result of the Ley de Loterías. The law abolished a number of small private lotteries which had supported, but often inadequately, these institutions, forcing them to accept national regulation in exchange for funding. The additional revenues provided repairs to their buildings, new equipment, and, most important, expansions which increased the total number of charity hospital beds from about 100 to 450.[32]

The effort to improve the charity hospitals raises the important question of who benefited from the military government's health and sanitation policies. Poor urban dwellers benefited from the hospitals, since the middle and upper sectors patronized the well-equipped private clinics owned by physicians. The affected population in this case was typical on the one hand but not on the other. Most public health and sanitation programs were not particularly directed at the poor. The two most ambitious public health efforts, a campaign against infectious diseases and the endeavor to improve municipal sanitation, were meant to benefit the population in general, though their impact probably varied by class. On the other hand, the urban focus was entirely typical. The large majority of health and sanitation projects were either designed for or implemented only in urban areas.[33]

This is not to say that the military government was wholly insensitive to the health needs of poor and rural Dominicans. In 1918, for instance, certain government officials advocated improving the quality of health care in the republic by raising licensing standards for doctors, pharmacists, and other practitioners. This plan was rebutted and defeated by others who argued that the standards, considering the circumstances, were already high enough: "It is believed that the supply of technically qualified doctors and pharmacists is not sufficient to meet the necessities of the country; furthermore that the poor people, a very large percentage of the population, are not able to pay for the services of highly trained men." On the contrary, the military government sometimes lowered standards since "many practitioners, without scientific attainments, are capable of rendering valuable services to the people in need thereof."[34]

The absence of medical care in rural areas and in small towns troubled health authorities from the beginning. In 1917, for example, the chief sanitary officer proposed a plan to station a doctor with each of the small Guardia units scattered throughout the country, supporting him with government funds to fill a triple role as a military doctor, the local sanitary officer of the public health program, and the town physician. Though the plan proved impossible since the few Dominican doctors wanted nothing to do with the Guardia or the rural areas, U.S. military personnel serving with the Guardia received authorization to engage in private practice, which often included charity work among the poor.[35] A later effort to improve rural health services, mandated by the Ley de Sanidad of 1920, envisioned the extension and improvement of the traditional *salas de socorro*, small public dispensaries operated in some towns for poorer patients, as well as the expansion of the role of the "municipal doctors of the poor" associated with some of them. But administrative difficulties, caused by resentment over national encroachment on these local institutions, and then a shortage of funds crippled this effort.[36]

Another feature of the Ley de Sanidad intended to help poor and rural people was the ending of the monopoly of pharmacists over the sale of some kinds of medicine. By permitting merchants to sell patent and proprietary drugs and certain other common, nontoxic preparations, the law encouraged both price competition and the flow of these items into the countryside, where there were no pharmacies, for the first time. Moreover, the legislation presumably helped give rise to the Dominican penchant for self-diagnosis and self-medication and added one more technique to the repertoire of folk medicine-religion. The latter was exactly contrary to the intent of the law, one article of which sought to ban the use of "witchcraft, . . . obiaism [obeah], hoodooism, or other superstitious or deceitful methods" to cure physical or mental ailments. Though violations of this provision were punished by up to a year in jail, there is no evidence that it had any effect on the practice of popular medicine.[37]

The general public and doctors, pharmacists, bakers, plumbers, and others whose ways of living and working were affected by the new and sometimes complex health and sanitation regulations protested, resisted, stalled, evaded, and ignored the new law for months. For example, the work of the Division of Vital Statistics and Transmissible Diseases, a critical aspect of disease control, was "not . . . much appreciated by the general public" and undermined by "lack of cooperation by the physicians." Similarly, when the inspectors of the Division of Sanitary Engineering tried to enforce rules concerning waste disposal, plumbing, and ventilation in new construction, they encountered "considerable opposition to this work among contractors and property owners who do not appreciate the necessity and importance of same and do not take kindly to the simplest regulation."[38]

Part of the reason for this resistance to the new law was its content, but part was the manner in which it was enforced by inadequately trained and sometimes officious or even abusive inspectors. A Dominican otherwise favorably disposed to the military government's sanitary legislation noted that in the process of applying the law "numerous abuses and violent acts were committed, homes were violated, and individual rights were ignored."[39] One of the worst examples of this kind of behavior, in this case approved by higher officials and showing a gross insensitivity to the poor, occurred in Santo Domingo. There it became the practice of sanitation officials to tear down substandard dwellings whose owners could not or would not pay to improve them. "Quite a number" of small houses were destroyed as "unsanitary and a menace to public health," their owners and/or residents left uncompensated and homeless.[40]

Another reason for resistance to the Ley de Sanidad was opposition to the increased powers of the national government. Reactions of this kind involved not only individual Dominicans but ayuntamientos and local charity boards, whose members resented national interference in and regulation of matters which were traditionally local. Similarly, the imposition of national control over charity hospitals in 1920 provoked strenuous opposition from some quarters, especially from members of the elite who had previously controlled and received credit for these charitable works. The most famous case in this regard involved the military government's long struggle with the Junta de Caridad Padre Billini in Santo Domingo City.[41]

No doubt some of these complaints were only the natural concomitant of putting into effect such a broad program as the Ley de Sanidad. It was, after all, an alien system, based on esoteric scientific principles unknown to more than 90 percent of the population, which required changes in the way people lived their daily lives. Perhaps it was just a matter of education and time before people would understand and accept the requirements of the new law and it would begin to function effectively. That was the view of the navy medical officer who headed the Ministry of Sanitation and Beneficence when he wrote in early 1921 that "at least two years more are necessary before a really fairly efficient sanitary organization from the modern viewpoint can be developed."[42] Fate, however, deprived the military government of the time it needed.

By early 1921 a serious depression beset the republic, drastically changing the conditions under which the Ministry of Sanitation and Beneficence did its work. As national revenues declined, so did the department's budget; the national government's support fell from $253,115 in 1920 to $62,976 in 1921, and municipal contributions as well as income from the lottery also declined significantly. As a result, "only the absolutely essential work" of the ministry continued. "All other work has been greatly reduced or temporarily abandoned." On the local level, reported the military governor, "practically all municipal sanitation work has shown a serious and visible set back."[43]

After 1921 conditions remained adverse and eventually became worse. The only substantial work of the ministry consisted of combating epidemics of smallpox and typhoid and of finishing, with funds allotted to public works, several building projects which were under way. Otherwise circumstances limited official action to making generally minor improvements or attempting to enforce laws already on the books.[44]

In 1923, the first full year of the Dominican provisional government, the national budget of the Ministry of Sanitation and Beneficence was down to $35,820. The lottery was also much diminished, providing about $75,000 a year. Municipal funds were so low that many local health and sanitation officials "received no pay for months" and their morale was broken. Though health and sanitation standards had not fallen to preoccupation levels, according to U.S. military officials, they were declining rapidly. A primary cause of this was obviously the lack of money, but occupation officials also blamed the minister of health and sanitation, M. M. Sanabia, for an alleged lack of energy in his work. For his part, Sanabia came to believe that his task was fiscally impossible and resigned.[45] Clearly, the public health and sanitation program was in disarray.

There is every indication that by the time of the U.S. withdrawal in September 1924 there was little to show for the ambitious effort which occupation officials had begun in 1917. There remained a few more trained health and sanitation personnel, several new hospitals and asylums, and a number of refurbished institutions. Perhaps the most important survival was the new health and sanitation legislation and bureaucracy, although without adequate funding this was little more effective than the 1912 structure which occupation officials had abolished.

The surviving structure, in the view of the Dominican historian Luis Mejía, was important: "The intervention established public health and sanitation in the republic." It gave organization and impetus to a continuing interest in providing public health care facilities, he wrote, and in eradicating the infectious diseases, such as malaria and yaws, which continued to afflict the Dominican people.[46]

Yet, in terms of both the dimension of the problem and the broad scope of the military government's program, considerably less had resulted than might have been expected. Why? Basically, after much procrastination, the military government had tried to do too much at once. Its grand scheme was unsuited to Dominican reality, severely overtaxing the limited supply of money and personnel and thus assuring that no single problem received the concentrated attention and resources which the almost completely undeveloped public health and sanitation situation demanded. The personnel shortage also made necessary the use of numerous foreigners in both medical and administrative positions. This, as well as the fact that the program was established by fiat and that some of its provisions were unfamiliar, contrary to the interests of various groups and opposed to certain traditional Dominican values, generated resistance. This not only delayed the program's implementation but also weakened it, lessening its chance to survive withdrawal in a meaningful way. Finally, when all these factors were combined with a grave economic crisis, severe decline was all but inevitable.

The Public Works Program

The public works program was one of the military government's more successful endeavors. In just a few years it brought the Dominican Republic a greatly extended and improved road network, an upgraded telecommunication system, the rehabilitation of the all-important docks and custom houses, and the construction or restoration of various public buildings.

The public works program, like most of the major efforts of the military government, was a response to a long-perceived need and was built upon previous Dominican efforts. Since the administration of President Ulises Heureaux in the 1880s and 1890s, Dominican governments had directed attention to public works, especially to improvement of the country's miserable and undeveloped transportation system. Heureaux commissioned a government railroad from Moca via Santiago to Puerto Plata, which moved the import-export trade of the agriculturally rich Cibao, and he began work on several roads, including the north-south route connecting Santiago and Santo Domingo.

President Ramón Cáceres (1906–1911) began the nation's first comprehensive public works program under the supervision of a U.S.-imposed chief engineer. Cáceres' administration authorized construction of the British-owned "Scotch Railroad" from Moca to the port of Sánchez and was responsible for building the nation's first modern highways.[47] After his assassination in 1911, highway construction and other public works projects continued slowly but steadily until mid 1916, when the United States cut off all funds to the Dominican government. The total accomplishment up to that date was not impressive, a fact attested to by nearly all foreign visitors to the republic.[48]

Early in 1917, officials of the military government began to study the need for public works. They consulted with engineers, prominent Dominicans, local governments, and the Bureau of Insular Affairs in Washington about the United States' previous experiences in Puerto Rico and the Philippines. At the same time officials unsuccessfully pressured Washington to dismiss the director of public works, a North American engineer whom the State Department had forced on the republic some years before. "The Dominicans have some grounds for complaining against being forced to pay enormous salaries to incompetent American officials," reported Minister Russell in regard to the case.[49]

Military officials spent very little on public works during 1917, pending completion of their survey of the republic's needs. The few projects authorized were continuations of obviously important but incomplete Dominican efforts. Among these were several roads connecting important towns in the Cibao, various bridges including the one over the Ozama River at Santo Domingo, and harbor improvements in Puerto Plata and Santo Domingo. Another early project was the rehabilitation of the government-owned Dominican Central Railroad, which had become dilapidated and insolvent under the supervision of an incompetent U.S. appointee.[50]

By January 1918, the military government had developed a comprehensive scheme for public works which very much resembled previous Dominican plans. Officials projected spending more than $2 million on a variety of projects, including the completion of the highway from Santo Domingo to Santiago and then on to Monte Cristi, the development of secondary paved roads eastward and westward from the capital and connecting major towns in the Cibao, the building of various highway bridges, the improvement of port facilities, especially in San Pedro de Macorís, the surveying of the republic's topography and resources, and the construction of a new national penitentiary and a modern leprosarium.[51] With the State Department's approval, this became the basis of the public works program for the life of the military government.

Added to the original proposals over time were further extensions of the highway system, more port improvements, construction of new government buildings, and the improvement of the postal, telegraph, and telephone systems. Modernization of the latter included nationalizing the small private phone companies which had grown up in the various cities and stringing new lines, among them a short one which connected the Dominican and Haitian phone networks.[52]

The public works program began late, hardly before the middle of 1918; it then progressed very slowly and was much more costly than the officials of the military government had anticipated. In part this resulted from the inexperience of most military officials with such matters and the shortage of trained experts, North American or Dominican. Adding to this basic difficulty were others over which the military government had no control. Most important was the war in Europe. Steel, which was imported from the United States, was in short supply because of the production of military equipment. There was also a wartime shortage of shipping, making it extremely difficult to find transport for goods to Santo Domingo. Thus highway bridges lay uncompleted long after the piers were poured and the road had passed beyond. At the same time, wartime inflation caused prices for road construction equipment and for basic imported building materials such as steel and cement to skyrocket. For instance, the price of a barrel of cement delivered in Santo Domingo had risen from $.35 in 1914 to $2.40 in 1918.[53]

Other problems causing delays included the difficulties of finding contractors who would work at reasonable rates, of assembling enough qualified engineers, and even, some claimed, of obtaining sufficient numbers of laborers. A lengthy process of advertising, taking bids, and negotiating contracts eventually produced a small mixed group of Dominican and North American contractors and a force of engineers and draftsmen heavily dominated by North Americans and Puerto Ricans. Because not enough contractors could be found to work at reasonable rates, the military government took to managing many projects itself, which saved money but wasted much time and effort. The laborers were Dominican at first, as Military Governor Knapp refused to permit the import of foreign labor for road work. Military Governor Snowden later reversed this position, allowing large numbers of Haitians to join construction crews.[54]

Thus the start-up time in public works was lengthy. As a result, in December 1919 virtually none of the planned major roads or the larger public works projects was more than 50 percent complete, and a number were yet to be started. By autumn 1920, however, with most of the basic difficulties overcome and a large work force assembled, it appeared possible to complete the basic public works program, especially the highways, by mid 1921. This was not to be the case. The postwar economic boom collapsed in late 1920, prostrating the Dominican economy and sharply reducing government revenues. Forced to cut expenses, military officials suspended work on virtually all public works projects by January 1921, discharging 90 percent of the carefully assembled teams of engineers and most laborers, a total of some five thousand men.[55]

Work did not resume until July 1921, and then only on a limited basis, after the military government obtained an emergency loan of $2.5 million, a large part of which was intended for public works. But by late in the same year the military government was again in desperate economic straits and remained so until it obtained another loan for $6.7 million in March 1922. The expense of borrowing and the fact that, even with loans, funds were still scarce led to corner-cutting. After early 1921, for instance, narrow wooden bridges replaced many previously planned concrete structures. And authorities abandoned some projects altogether.[56]

By October 1922, when the military government handed over administrative control to a Dominican provisional government, it had completed a considerable number of smaller public works projects. These included secondary roads, school buildings, customhouses, wharves, bridges, the penitentiary, the leprosarium, and a host of minor construction and rehabilitation projects in transportation and communication. But, of the major highways, only the north-south route was more or less complete, leaving the eastern and western routes for the provisional government's continued attention. Persistent financial difficulties, however, prevented much progress. When the new constitutional government took office in July 1924, the eastern highway, named the Carretera Mella, was open only to El Seibo, and the western highway, the Carretera Sánchez, was complete only to Azua.[57]

To what extent was the public works program of the military government successful, both in an immediate sense and in terms of its legacy? What were its unintended results? And did it improve upon what the Dominicans would have done for themselves had there been no occupation?

Without question the military government accomplished an impressive task. Whatever the shortcomings of the work, military officials appear to have developed a coherent plan, administered it more or less successfully, and left behind many considerable improvements, especially the new highway system. And, because subsequent Dominican governments agreed that this work was important, they maintained and extended it. The Vásquez administration from 1924 to 1930 almost immediately undertook a comprehensive program of completing the major highways, of replacing the temporary wooden bridges with concrete and steel, and of building new roads. It also invested in irrigation projects and, for Santo Domingo, in a long-needed sewer system and aqueduct, which the military government had regarded as necessary but too costly. By 1929 the highway system had doubled in length and, noted a visiting U.S. commission, the roads were "well located and well maintained." At the same time, however, Sumner Welles noted the existence of "deplorable conditions" in the administration of public works.[58]

U.S. officials as well as Dominicans often voiced the hope that the transportation and communication network created by the public works program would promote Dominican economic growth, especially by stimulating agricultural production and marketing. They also believed that it would unite the country politically, eliminating regionalism by creating a closer community of political interests and by making it possible for a central government to exert effective military control over all parts of the nation. In fact, the U.S. withdrawal in 1924 was predicated in part on the belief that the new roads gave "security that order would be maintained by the new government."[59]

It seems likely that the improved roads and communications did stimulate at least limited economic growth. In particular the new highways began to reduce transportation costs, traditionally so high that they prevented the development of agriculture or the exploitation of natural resources such as timber in large areas of the republic. The new highways also changed some traditional economic patterns. Santo Domingo, for example, had never played a role in the export of cacao, which was produced in the north and the east. But, within one year of the opening of the north-south highway, seven million pounds of cacao a year were passing through the city's port. At the same time, the highways reduced the profits of the republic's two railroads and eventually caused the elimination of the Santiago–Puerto Plata route.[60]

It is also abundantly clear that the military government's public works program changed the country politically, though perhaps not in the way U.S. officials had envisioned. The relatively stable administration of Horacio Vásquez (1924–1930) gave the first indication that now a central government could successfully control the entire republic. But it remained for Rafael Trujillo to demonstrate clearly that the United States had left behind the basis, in the form of modernized communications and a modernized military, not only for unity and stability but for the most repressive regime the Dominicans had ever known.

Could the Dominicans have made the same progress in public works without suffering the occupation or the disastrous political scenario which followed? They had been well aware of the need for public works long before the intervention began; in fact, most of the military government's projects were based upon previous Dominican plans. If occupation officials accomplished the program faster than previous Dominican administrations, it can be argued that this was because of the extraordinary revenues which flowed into the Dominican treasury during World War I, not to mention the administrative and engineering skills which were available gratis to the military government. When military officials lost this financial advantage, their program floundered completely. It was salvaged, but only with large loans which the military administration obtained more easily and more cheaply than Dominican governments might have. Thus the military government was able to spend $2.2 million per year for public works, whereas previous Dominican governments had to manage on a mere $350,000 per year.[61]

There is, besides, convincing evidence that the Dominicans might have managed the public works program as well as did the military government. The program under the occupation had administrative problems which considerably diminished its effect. Although the military government was not always at fault, having inherited the poorly run U.S.-supervised public works department, some critics directly blamed the occupation authorities. "There is no doubt," wrote Sumner Welles in 1922, "but that in the years 1917, 1918, and 1919, hundreds of thousands of dollars of Dominican money were thrown away in the construction of public works. That, of course, was a very prosperous time, and the Military Government embarked on a program of extravagance and inefficient management in the public works, . . . which never would have been permitted in the United States."[62]

In summary, the public works program of the military government was a success, although the endeavor was hampered by serious problems which slowed the work, led to waste, and resulted in a less impressive achievement than was otherwise possible. But more important than the physical achievement was the fact that the Dominicans adopted the public works program as their own. Their interest in preserving and expanding the program enabled it to survive and flourish after the occupation ended.

The National Constabulary

One of the cure-alls which the United States proposed for the Caribbean and Central American states in the early twentieth century was the depolitization of the military. This process was to occur as the result of disbanding the existing armed forces and forming new constabularies, efficiently trained and officered, at least for a time, by North Americans.

The United States had demanded such a force for the Dominican Republic since 1915, and its creation became an early goal of the military government. Lacking guidance from Washington, Military Governor Knapp assembled a committee of North Americans in Santo Domingo to draw up a detailed plan for a constabulary. In

April 1917, the military government issued Executive Order No. 47, which appropriated $500,000 "for the purpose of organizing, equipping, and maintaining a national Dominican police force." The new force, called the Guardia Nacional Dominicana, would replace the old army, navy, Guardia Republicana, and frontier guard and would be staffed by U.S. officers "for the purpose of training the Guardia and of bringing it to a high state of efficiency."[63]

The plan for the Guardia Nacional represented the compromise outcome of a dispute within Knapp's committee over whether to establish an army or a police force. Marine General Pendleton had favored the former, Knapp the latter. In the military governor's view, the republic had no need for an army and could not afford to support one. There was no external threat to the nation and, should one materialize, the Dominicans could rely on U.S. "moral and physical" support. Moreover, he reasoned, a disciplined police force scattered over the republic in small units would not be susceptible to control by a potential dictator, nor could it topple the government.[64] The committee, however, only half deferred to Knapp's less than airtight argument, with the result that the new Guardia was crippled from the first by an unclear mandate. "It was never large enough to discharge the military functions incumbent on the national army and was too military to devote itself, except spasmodically, to its police duties," wrote Colonel Rufus Lane later.[65]

The duties of the new Guardia were many. It was to enforce civil laws, to act as a judicial police, to guard the frontier and the coast, to patrol the highways, and, as a supplement to marine efforts in the east, to combat insurgents. But formation of the 1,200-man Guardia proceeded slowly, as Washington dawdled over the military government's proposals and the Guardia's marine officers were burdened with other pressing obligations.[66] For months the organization limped along under an acting commandant, ordered to supervise the new force "in addition to his other duties." Not surprisingly, problems were common. There were so few supplies, for example, that for a time members of the new Guardia wore the uniforms of the disbanded Guardia Republicana and were forced to use antiquated equipment and even captured weapons.[67]

Attracting suitable personnel into the Guardia turned out to be difficult. By late 1918 the new force had a full complement of men but, complained a marine officer, "the recruiting was carried on . . . apparently more with a desire for numbers than for quality." Except for the exmembers of the disbanded Guardia Republicana, who formed the nucleus of the Guardia Nacional, few of the recruits had any military skills, it being chiefly poor country dwellers who were enticed by the promise of fifteen dollars per month and free room, board, clothing, and medical care. "Only a very small percentage of the men can read and write," commented an officer, "as most natives who are so fortunate as to acquire some education find more remunerative positions in civil life." [68]

The exmembers of the Guardia Republicana presented a different sort of problem. They were infamous for their lack of discipline and for their habit of preying on civilians, freely taking food and whatever else attracted them. Training would have helped alleviate this problem, but there was little or none. The Guardia's founders were aware of the need for training and had even begun a course for the first recruits, but the abrupt withdrawal of marines for service in Europe caused the military government to end instruction and rush the newcomers into service to combat unrest in several areas of the republic. Although these troops performed "as well as could be expected," they caused problems wherever they operated. As a result, the Guardia had an abnormally high rate of courts-martial. [69]

The recruitment of officers was even more difficult than that of enlisted men. The military government claimed that few Dominicans with the necessary education and status were interested in beginning a military career as a second lieutenant. Presumably such a person had better prospects outside the military, may have feared the stigma of working with the occupation forces, and had little desire to join an organization which, by virtue of its identification with the old Guardia Republicana, began its existence with a miserable reputation. The military government compounded the problem by making a feeble to nonexistent recruitment effort and by reserving all ranks above lieutenant for North Americans, thus assuring officer cadets that there was little chance for promotion.

So few Dominicans came forward that after a short while the military government began giving temporary commissions as first lieutenants and captains to marine enlisted men. This aggravated recruitment difficulties, for it meant that a Dominican second lieutenant would be commanded by North American officers who were in reality sergeants, corporals, and even privates. Few Dominicans were so unambitious or humble as to accept these conditions. Those who did generally came from the lower middle social stratum, men whose inferior social positions and general lack of opportunity caused them to accept this chance to gain status and a decent income. One of these was Rafael Trujillo, who joined the Guardia in 1919. [70]

Among the Dominican lieutenants there was a high rate of

failure. "The Dominican officers are not a success," wrote an un-sympathetic marine commandant of the Guardia. As they were not "from among the higher type of Dominicans, they have not the education, training, stability or character, honesty and natural aptitude or instinct requisite for good officers." A principal cause of their difficulty, noted a more reasonable officer, was that they received no training except what they picked up on the job.[71]

Adequate on-the-job training was also rather limited, for in virtually all cases the officers with whom these Dominicans worked were the temporarily commissioned marine enlisted men. These marines were not accustomed to command, nor were they trained for it. Of the Guardia's marine field officers in mid 1919, not one had served previously as an officer, nor was there "one who had experience in that peculiar line of police work necessary for the success of the Guardia."[72] Yet these officers faced a job calling for the utmost training, skill, and sensitivity. They had the task both of policing Dominican civilians and of managing their own ill-trained troops in a language which few of them could speak with facility, forcing some to command through interpreters. The job of these temporary officers proved so difficult that sixteen of the thirty-four marine noncoms serving with the Guardia had quit by mid 1919.[73]

Training would have helped these substitute officers, as it would have helped their Dominican counterparts. But there was no training. The military authorities recognized the need, but Washington refused to authorize more officers than were absolutely necessary for the basic staffing of the Guardia. As a result, officers were required to spend nearly all their time on duty with their companies in the field.[74]

Another handicap involved the Guardia's frequent changes in leadership. The organization's first commander was Colonel Buenaventura Cabral, the former chief officer of the Guardia Republicana, who was enticed to resign in December 1917 by the offer of the civil governorship of Azua. Thereafter, of the six marines who commanded the Guardia between 1917 and 1921, only one remained for more than seven months.[75] There could be little consistent direction or work for improvement.

The inadequate leadership, discipline, and training of the Guardia led to major problems. Various military government reports detail crimes committed by Guardia members, such as robbery, extortion, rape, murder, assault, and numerous violations of the Guardia's internal regulations. A North American visitor—who found them to have "a cocky, half-insolent air"—learned from a priest in El Seibo that the Guardia "included some of the worst rascals, thieves, and assassins in the country . . . , and these often egged the naive Americans [their marine officers] on to vent their own private hates."[76]

Marine officers were undoubtedly more thorough in investigating and trying Dominican Guardia members who had committed crimes than they were with their fellow citizens, even to the point of using them as scapegoats at times to cover up for guilty marines. But prosecutions did not end Guardia abuses, a fact indicated by the issuance of a new set of disciplinary regulations in mid 1920. The harsh rules, wrote Military Governor Snowden, were specifically designed to end the Guardia's poor discipline and its members' abuse, even torture, of civilians. Nevertheless, having left the fundamental internal problems of the Guardia untended, the military government continued to receive complaints "against the lawlessness of the Guardia."[77]

The behavior of the Guardia may have been despicable, but it was easy enough to explain. Guardia members were usually disadvantaged and uneducated, many had served in unruly and brutal military organizations before, and they were poorly commanded and virtually untrained. In addition, they were expected to police their own people, often in ways which seemed unnecessary and oppressive to ordinary citizens—the military government's efforts to regulate gambling, cockfighting, and prostitution stand as good examples. Because of their enforcement of these laws, their often belligerent demeanor and arbitrary methods, and their alliances with the occupying forces, members of the Guardia were often harassed. "Our men have been taunted and aggravated on all sides," wrote a marine-Guardia officer in 1919.[78]

In 1919, as the State Department began a reexamination of its Dominican policy, the dreadful state of the Guardia came to light. It was in no way prepared to take over from the marines should a U.S. civilian government or a withdrawal be instituted, and it could hardly fulfill its function of aiding marine efforts. The only solution to its problems, concluded Minister Russell and his State Department colleagues, was a complete reorganization, preferably, they added, under "white officers and not native Dominicans."[79] Little or nothing, however, changed.

"Not until January, 1922, did the Military Government see its way clear to fully organize the Guardia," wrote the military governor in 1924. This organization or, properly, reorganization finally occurred because in mid 1921 the United States announced a plan for U.S. withdrawal and reestablishment of a Dominican civilian government. Though the plan was postponed and later replaced by another, it had become clear that time was running out for the military government to attend to the Guardia. To accomplish this task, Washington sent Brigadier General Harry Lee to head the marine brigade in Santo Domingo in August 1921. What Lee found upon his arrival appalled him: "Officers and men were without training . . . their value as a military force was nil."[80]

General Lee's mandate with the Guardia was clear: it was to be reorganized, enlarged, trained, and its officer corps Dominicanized. As an additional requirement, noted Military Governor Samuel S. Robison, he had "been given unofficial instructions to 'lighten' the Guardia a little," presumably to accommodate Dominican elite prejudice against the organization.[81] General Lee set to work immediately. First he created the Publicity and Recruiting Bureau to attract new personnel. Then he established a new military school at Haina (a few miles to the west of the city of Santo Domingo, on the site of what was supposed to have become the national agricultural college) and enrolled the thirty Dominican officers of the Guardia. Although "this first course in military training which had ever been given native officers" had some problems, such as severe equipment shortages and a blatantly racist marine chief instructor who did not speak Spanish, it at least began a long-needed process. Twenty-one of the thirty Dominicans survived the course and were reattached to their units in late December 1921.[82]

Lee's second act was to restructure the institutional basis of the Guardia. Executive Orders Nos. 800 and 817 superseded the original 1917 legislation, creating a new organization of 1,200 enlisted men and 88 officers. Although the Guardia had recently been renamed the Policía Nacional Dominicana, the new force was now further than ever from Knapp's original concept of a national police, since it used the marines' more military organizational structure and procedures.[83] At the same time, General Lee and Military Governor Robison drew up a plan for the future. They envisioned a Guardia expanded to a total of 3,000 men, with a lengthy training program supervised by 246 marines. The latter were to remain for some unspecified time after "withdrawal," serving not only as instructors but as protection against possible revolutions.[84]

In mid 1922, however, the State Department agreed to a proposal for withdrawal which called for rapid training of the Guardia, prompt elimination of U.S. forces from command functions, and full withdrawal of U.S. troops. Robison and Lee were appalled by the plan, which gave them a few months to accomplish what they had planned to do in years and which, they believed, would result in a force inadequate to do its job. But their vehement objections brought no significant changes.[85]

In October 1922 a Dominican provisional government took office, gaining control of the Guardia except for the marines' two training centers, the one at Haina and a second at Santiago, which had opened early in the year. At these centers, troops of enlisted men passed through on a regular rotational basis, each receiving an eight-week crash course. And thirty out of sixty members of a second class of officer candidates graduated and became second lieutenants. By February 1923, after eighteen months of effort, military authorities had nearly doubled the number of Dominican officers and had provided at least basic training to the enlisted men.[86]

From March 1923 until July 1924, four hundred to five hundred men a month received advanced training in the centers. Although this schooling was surely improving the Guardia, there were occasional indications that the system of recruitment and training was functioning less than perfectly. In early 1923, for example, the director of the Guardia's southern district protested that "the majority of recruits who recently reported to this Division from the [Policía Nacional Dominicana] Training Center in Santiago are not only illiterate but were formerly discharged from the Service as undesirables."[87]

Soon after Horacio Vásquez took office as constitutional president on 12 July 1924, the marines ended their training of the Guardia.[88] Though the new force of about 1,300 officers and men was only slightly above the complement of the preintervention Dominican military, all observers agreed that it was better equipped, trained, and disciplined than ever before. Not incidentally, it was also more expensive, consuming between 21 and 26 percent of the national budget in the early 1920s and putting a considerable strain on the republic's always inadequate revenues.[89] Its leader was once again Colonel Buenaventura Cabral, whom the marines had retired in 1917.

The ultimate success of the military government in creating the new Guardia should not obscure the fact that, for six of the eight years of the occupation, U.S. authorities had failed completely to create an effective Dominican armed force. The lack of training and of a realistic program to recruit Dominican officers, combined with other negative circumstances, had produced a ragtag military organization with few capabilities. Thus the Guardia played a marginal role in the occupation, supplementing marine efforts in what officials believed were the least critical tasks. Only in the eleventh hour, compelled by the immediate prospect of a complete U.S. withdrawal, did military officials accomplish what they set out to do in 1917.

Given, however, the eventual creation of an effective force, one must ask the question: effective for what purpose? Was it the apolitical military envisioned by the United States in 1916, maintaining constitutional government and stability? The answer is clearly no. Even before the close of the intervention, there was some evidence of politicization within the new organization.[90] Within a year after the withdrawal, in mid 1925, Minister Russell charged that "politics is fast destroying the efficiency of the Dominican National Police"; as evidence, he pointed to several "purely political" personnel decisions, including the forcing out of Colonel Cabral and the promotion of two pro-Vásquez officers, Colonel Simón Díaz and Lieutenant Colonel Rafael Trujillo.[91] By 1926, according to the plausible charges of Federico Velásquez, the Guardia was deeply involved in the political process. Its new leader, Rafael Trujillo, had organized an intelligence service, at this point on behalf of President Vásquez; using marine intelligence techniques, his agents spied on meetings and other political events and submitted regular reports.[92]

By 1930, as the commander of the Dominican armed forces in a time of political unrest, General Rafael Trujillo had placed himself in a position to take power. He used the Guardia to help destroy the government of Horacio Vásquez and then as a base for taking control of the republic under his own rule. Trujillo maintained his corrupt and dictatorial rule for thirty-one years, with the Guardia an important factor in his survival.[93]

That the Guardia was able to control the republic so effectively was not entirely because of its improved organization, training, and equipment. Other aspects of occupation policy also contributed to its dominance. First, the military government had eliminated all the potential counterforces to the Guardia. Before the occupation the army, the Guardia Republicana, the navy, and the frontier guard were each under separate command; the Guardia's architects eliminated these in favor of a single force under one commander, leaving no institutional opposition should the Guardia be used in a tyrannical way. Second, the military government took energetic measures to disarm the Dominican population, leaving almost no one except Guardia members with firearms, thus eliminating an important resource for possible popular opposition. Third, the military government markedly improved the republic's telecommunications and roads. For the first time it was possible for the commander of the Dominican armed forces to communicate almost instantly with any major town in the republic and, more important, to move troops from one area of the republic to another in a matter of hours. Certainly each of these measures was justified in its own right, but the effect in regard to the Guardia was to create a force which was beyond challenge.

There is no better example than the Guardia Nacional Dominicana to illustrate the inability of the United States to impose reforms by fiat. The officials of the military government merely established an institution based on a U.S. model; they could not impose the values which lay at the core of that model. Traditional Dominican political culture rather than the poorly conceived (and, for six years, poorly executed) hopes of the occupiers shaped the Guardia.

Conclusion

Important common characteristics unite the efforts of the military government. These are worth noting because they put into relief certain shared patterns of planning and policy implementation which were significant in determining the nature of these programs and, ultimately, their success or failure.

To begin with, the programs of the military government had certain common antecedents and influences. One, of course, was Dominican. Not only were most of the reform efforts continuations and renovations of existing preintervention programs, but Dominicans had at least limited influence on the new programs. For instance, one source of the idea to create a national lottery, a possibility envisioned since the time of President Cáceres (1906–1911), was a regional congress of municipal governments, the Convención de Ayuntamientos del Cibao, which petitioned the military government to implement this proposal in 1919.[94] Similarly, the first effort to regulate prostitution, by creating a red-light district in the Barahona–Monte Cristi area of Santo Domingo City, was merely a municipal ordinance endorsed by the military government in an executive order.[95]

The second major influence on the programs of the military government was U.S. experience, both domestic and colonial. For example, the proposed 1920 law of vital statistics was based in part on "the model law of the United States Bureau of the Census." More important was the U.S. colonial experience. From it the military government borrowed not only various programs, such as that for public works, but also personnel.[96]

On the whole the occupation's reform programs tended to be more successful than earlier Dominican efforts (or, in the case of public works, earlier U.S. efforts). The reason was that the military government possessed a series of significant advantages. First among these was an extraordinary amount of available revenue, owing both to the unusual prosperity of the time and to the fact that the United States covered large expenditures formerly paid by the Dominican government, most notably the cost of executive administration. Another advantage was the military government's ability to issue and enforce new laws with less deference to Dominican sensibilities than was possible for a Dominican civilian government. Luis Mejía remarked on this when he noted in reference to sanitary legislation that "in a small arena like ours, where everyone is someone's relative, friend, or acquaintance, only a foreign power, without any of these ties, was able to complete this task."[97]

A further advantage was the fact that the military government had at its disposal a large number of well-trained personnel to carry out its tasks. Marine civil engineers administered public works, navy doctors and medics controlled and staffed public health and sanitation efforts, and experienced marines trained the Guardia Nacional. Moreover, with Washington in control, other U.S. groups volunteered aid. In public health, for instance, a party of doctors from the Harvard School of Tropical Medicine spent a summer on yaws eradication, the Rockefeller Institute financed a team to work on hookworm, and the American Red Cross staffed and equipped several hospitals.[98]

One unfortunate shared characteristic of a number of the military government's programs, including those noted here, was their creation without adequate reference to certain Dominican realities, particularly shortages of money and personnel. This meant that the military government had severe difficulties, even in times of prosperity, in staffing and paying for programs already mandated by law. And, when prosperity suddenly ended in late 1920, the military government soon found itself on the brink of financial disaster, with its projects crumbling. The programs in education and public health and sanitation became hollow shells of what they had been; the public works and Guardia projects survived only because authorities borrowed $2.5 million in 1921 and $6.7 million in 1922 to provide the funds needed to complete them.

The personnel problem was more complex. It was part of the military government's general failure, except in education, to involve Dominicans in these programs in significant ways. Neither in planning, except in the acceptance of occasional suggestions on an informal basis, nor in staffing, except in the use of Dominicans in lower-level positions, did the military government usually involve Dominicans in its reforms. Recruitment efforts, if any, were weak, in part reflecting a bias against Dominicans by many U.S. officials.

But the personnel problem also reflected a very real shortage of Dominicans possessing the skills necessary for higher-level positions. Aggravating this was the fact that the elite, those few Dominicans who had these skills, often refused to participate in these programs for reasons of pay, status consciousness, or nationalism. In any case, the lack of Dominican involvement led to the employment of foreigners in the majority of higher-level positions. This, plus the general lack of any effort to educate the Dominican people about what the military government was trying to accomplish, led to some resistance, especially in the area of public health and sanitation. It also contributed to the problems these programs experienced after withdrawal, since they were often left in the hands of Dominicans without sufficient training or experience who, by virtue of their unfamiliarity, did not share the vision which underlay their creation.

The exception to this pattern was education. This was partially because of the availability and willingness of Dominicans to serve and partially because of a more positive attitude toward Dominicans by the marine minister of education, Rufus Lane. From planning through implementation, Dominicans were involved from top to bottom. And Lane even sought support for the school system from private citizens at the local level through the formation of parents' societies, which were directly involved in such activities as school construction, local program planning, and aid to teachers. Such a grass-roots effort to involve and educate the public might have done wonders to encourage support for public health and sanitation, which instead encountered widespread resistance.[99]

The education program also escaped another problem which affected the other military government efforts: failure to provide effective administrative leadership. Among the principal ways in which this shortcoming became evident were the long delays, of two and three years, in getting programs planned, approved, and started, a matter which turned out to be of great import because of the depression of 1921. The blame for this tardiness probably lies as much with Washington as with the military government, but the slow and inefficient manner in which the military government completed projects after they had been approved suggests that the level of administrative competence was low.

Another shared characteristic of the major reforms was the tendency to centralize authority in Santo Domingo. This occurred in all four programs, even in the Guardia Nacional, which authorities had first intended to decentralize. Why? Because it was easier administratively to dictate and manage matters through the central government than to work through provincial or local authorities. Other factors influencing the trend toward centralization were historical and experiential—the Dominican government had long dominated provincial authorities, permitting limited autonomy only on the local level, and the military officials' own experience was with an authoritarian and very centralized command structure.

In the final analysis, how successful were the military government's education, health care and sanitation, public works, and constabulary programs? All fell short of their planners' expectations, although the public works and Guardia efforts eventually came closer than the others. The failure in this respect was owed heavily to the unrealistic goals of the military government, made with slight consideration of the limitations which the republic's economic and social conditions placed on efforts at development or reform.

But were the programs successful by other standards? Did they, for instance, make a substantial contribution to meeting the basic needs of the Dominican people? Considered in the short run, the answer for education and public health and sanitation would have to be positive—these improved for several hundred thousand Dominicans by 1920. And though the programs had substantial flaws, such as the failure of public health to deal adequately with the problems of rural areas, they had undoubtedly made a great advance over previous Dominican efforts. A large part of this progress was undone after 1920, however, when depression and then withdrawal stripped these programs of vital sources of money and personnel, leaving them considerably less successful in the end.

Concerning public works and the constabulary, the situation was the opposite. At first neither program was successful. But, with the addition of millions of dollars in extra funding in 1921 and 1922, both these projects were near to completion by withdrawal in 1924; the public works program provided the country's first adequate transportation and communication, and the Guardia was an efficient armed force. In these terms they were successful.

Finally, did these programs survive withdrawal? In regard to education and public health, the basic structure of these efforts remained but continuing problems severely limited both the quantity and the quality of their future work, assuring that they had relatively little impact on Dominican life for years to come. The situation was quite different in regard to public works and the constabulary. These two endeavors were at the peak of their development at the time of withdrawal. Though the departure of U.S. personnel surely had some deleterious consequences thereafter, a keen Dominican interest in both these programs kept them funded and running relatively effectively. Thus, in the sense that they survived withdrawal, they were successful. In the case of the Guardia, however, one must look beyond its survival as a healthy institution. Its planners had intended it to become an apolitical force, more a police than an army. But it is well known that in the Dominican milieu the Guardia lived up to neither expectation, becoming a totally political army.

3

The Political Economy of
the Military Government, II

During the six years of its active control of the administration of the
Dominican Republic, the military government was involved in a
wide range of significant activities quite apart from the much publicized endeavors in public health, public works, and education.
While the largest number of these concerned government finance
and the economy, others dealt with political, judicial, and social affairs. These efforts involved a variety of important matters, among
them the organization of the Dominican treasury and tax system,
agriculture, trade policy, development, the nature of the relationship
with the United States, the penal and judicial systems, and even
such social questions as the role of women. The large majority of
these measures bolstered the basic patterns of Dominican life, as
usually they were meant to. Military officials wanted to reform and
refurbish rather than to promote wholesale change.

The Impact of World War I

Agriculture and trade were the twin motors of the Dominican economy. Dominating both were the three major exports of sugar, cacao,
and tobacco. Of secondary importance were other exports, including
coffee, bananas, hides and skins, beeswax and honey, forest products,
and cotton. Also of lesser economic importance were the garden
crops which peasants produced for local consumption.[1] Aside from
agriculture, the republic's only other production came from the tiny
industrial sector, which made a limited array of consumer goods. Rather than manufacturing most of the industrial goods they needed,
Dominicans tended to import them. Manufactures, principally iron
and steel products and textiles, as well as common foodstuffs not
grown in the republic made up a large portion of the total imports.[2]

Ultimately, all sectors of the Dominican economy were dependent on the country's agricultural exports—without successful crops and good prices on the international commodity market, little cash flowed into the Dominican economy. Thus not only were factors and exporters dependent on the export trade, but so in the last analysis were importers, professionals, small business owners, artisans, and laborers. Even the government's economic health depended on the success of agricultural sales abroad.[3] The United States had long dominated the Dominican import trade, competing particularly with Great Britain and Germany. World War I had greatly reduced competition from these latter nations; by 1916 purchases from the United States amounted to 90.4 percent of the dollar value of imports.[4]

The structure of the Dominican economy remained basically unchanged during the period of the occupation, maintaining the trend toward modernization based on plantation agriculture, which had begun in the late nineteenth century. Leaders of the military government—although some of them harbored doubts about the benefit to Dominicans of continuing this pattern—did little to change it. Instead, most of the efforts of occupation officials were devoted to improving the economy as they had found it and to solving the immediate problems brought about by two severe crises, World War I and the postwar depression.

The numerous effects of World War I on the Dominican economy created difficulties for the military government. First, the republic's exporters were increasingly cut off from their traditional European markets, a fact especially important to growers of tobacco and coffee. Second, as the war escalated and the United States became involved, shipping became increasingly scarce. The Dominican economy, so dependent on import and export, soon suffered. Dominican crops which Washington officials judged nonessential to the U.S. war effort, such as cacao, became impossible to market, and essential imports became scarce. Third, Germans had long occupied important positions in Dominican economic life, especially as factors and exporters of the tobacco and cacao crops. The U.S. Trading with the Enemy Act of 1917 therefore made it impossible for U.S. citizens to deal with many of the republic's growers and traders. Fourth, external economic factors, as well as the scarcity of imports, resulted in sharp inflation.

How were officials to solve these problems? The loss of European markets—there was virtually no transatlantic trade in "nonessential" goods after 1916—offered only one solution. Exporters could divert their European shipments to the United States. But even this remedy met with a variety of problems. Some Dominican products, especially tobacco, were of a lower grade, difficult to sell in the United States. Worse yet, there was an increasingly severe shortage of shipping even to U.S. ports, especially after 1917 when the Clyde Line, the republic's main U.S. connection, cut its Dominican service from sixteen vessels to five. Aggravating this difficulty was the new War Trade Board in Washington, which controlled all shipping to and from the United States by a licensing system, granting licenses to products needed by the United States and denying licenses to other cargoes. As a result, sugar, of which there was a world shortage, passed freely, while other Dominican crops, especially tobacco and cacao, were denied passage. This differential treatment promised poverty for some regions and, wrote Military Governor Knapp, was doubly unjust to Dominicans. "Cacao, tobacco, coffee, honey, hides, etc., are commodities affecting Dominicans more than sugar. Sugar is produced by foreign capital; and to a large extent imported labor is employed. Other commodities are generally the result of the efforts of the Dominicans themselves, both in production and handling."[5]

Washington's regulations and the decline in Caribbean shipping caused other problems as well. Not least was the fact that a substantial interference with trade would cause a precipitous drop in customs revenues, the military government's main source of income. Second, Dominican consumers were threatened. Not only did the conversion of U.S. industries to war production and the general shortage of shipping reduce the flow of basic Dominican imports, but the War Trade Board also acted to restrict food shipments to Latin America, using the license system to reserve the lion's share for the United States and its European allies. By the end of 1917, Dominicans had begun to suffer serious shortages of certain basic consumer items, especially flour. Similarly, the war cut off the flow of raw materials to some of the country's few manufacturers.[6]

Military officials tried to devise their own solutions to these problems whenever possible. But the obvious fact that U.S. policies were the cause of many of the difficulties led to a flurry of petitions to Washington. Pleading for special treatment for the Dominican Republic, military officials argued that the Dominican people were suffering a hardship, that the military government was losing needed revenues, and that the United States was missing an opportunity to take over permanently the former Dominican trade with Germany.[7]

In response to these arguments, the military government obtained permission from the Department of the Navy to use naval vessels to transport the republic's stranded crops to the United States. It also extracted a series of concessions from the War Trade Board, including licenses for all Dominican cargoes moved in navy ships, freer passage to the republic of foodstuffs and other restricted materials (such as phosphorus and steel), and a more lenient interpretation of the Trading with the Enemy Act in regard to Dominican import-export firms. This last concession meant that the board still refused licenses to do business with German-owned trading houses but granted them for dealings with firms of other nationalities in spite of their allegedly pro-German (that is, neutral) sympathies.[8] The continued embargo on German firms, which made it nearly impossible for them to conduct business, not only ended German competition but created an opportunity for U.S. business interests to buy up blacklisted firms at favorable prices.[9]

The loosening of Washington's rules meant a partial return to normal conditions. To further the process, military officials took additional action in Santo Domingo. When flour remained unavailable for export to the Dominican Republic, the military government purchased 8.5 million pounds on its own account between May 1918 and January 1919. And, when Santo Domingo City's sole ice plant was without fuel to power the refrigeration process, military authorities provided the necessary coal from navy supplies.[10]

To the average Dominican, inflation was one of the worst aspects of the World War I period. Prices of foodstuffs, as well as a wide variety of other basic items, rose dramatically, influenced by worldwide inflation and by soaring shipping rates. One military government study showed the prices of thirteen basic imported foodstuffs to have advanced an average of 40 percent during the last six months of 1917; another showed the prices of such imported luxuries as dairy products and olive oil up 80 to 100 percent. Although outside factors caused much of the inflation, even the prices of many domestic foods rose. A December 1917 report noted that twelve out of thirty-two peasant-grown fruits and vegetables had advanced 100 percent or more in price during the previous year.[11]

Adding to the problem of inflation was what the military government saw as profiteering by merchants. Having discovered markups of from 40 to 100 percent over cost by some retailers of staple foodstuffs, military officials issued a press release in December 1917 threatening retaliation against "acts of extortion" by retailers, who "unrightfully are enriching themselves at the expense of their countrymen and are making the cost of living still harder to bear for all classes, but especially the poor one." Price increases, warned authorities, should not exceed the increases stated on invoices. A week later, the threat having gone unheeded, military officials seized all the flour to be found in San Pedro de Macorís and sold it for 10 percent above cost.[12]

In January 1918, military authorities formalized their campaign against local price inflation by creating the Office of Food Controller, which had the power to regulate food exports and imports, to fix food prices, to control food distribution, and to seize and distribute food as "the public welfare demands." Food Control Orders Nos. 1 through 5 placed fifteen basic imported foods on the controlled list and decreed that the profit on these items could not exceed 10 percent for the wholesaler and 10 percent for the retailer (3 and 6.8 percent on flour). The reason for price controls, explained the naval officer in charge of the program, was that "the economic conditions of the Dominican Republic, as well as of the whole world, are such that only nominal profits can be realized on the necessities of life."[13]

Although price controls lapsed after the war ended in late 1918, continuing inflation caused occupation officials to contemplate the resumption of "price control and price fixing." Instead they established food control stores at Santo Domingo and San Pedro de Macorís in 1919 and planned another for Santiago. By selling basic goods at low prices, officials claimed, these outlets kept down "the retail price of goods handled by local merchants and made it practicable for the poor people to secure such necessities of life as were handled by these stores at prices somewhat more within their means." It was to stock these shops with reasonably priced sugar that the food controller issued the famous Order No. 10, commandeering eight million pounds from the sugar estates, most of which had to be sold later at an immense loss. In early 1920, the government tried another price control tactic when it issued an executive order banning the export of meat, poultry, and eggs, justifying this law on the grounds that the supply was insufficient to meet Dominican consumer demand. Officials also wrote a rent control law, limiting annual rentals to 12 percent of a property's value, but for undisclosed reasons never issued it. At the end of 1920, with prices generally in decline and the food control stores losing money, the shops closed their doors, belatedly ending the military government's struggle against the pernicious effects of World War I.[14]

There was, it should be added, a positive side to the impact of World War I on the economy—namely, the increasingly high prices which Dominican commodities obtained on the world market. Although transportation and other problems somewhat limited the benefits during the war itself, aggregate trade grew each year. When the war ended, removing the obstacles to normal Dominican economic life, prices and production continued to climb. The result was the phenomenally prosperous year of 1920, during which the economy hit a peak it would not again equal until the 1940s.

Fiscal Reform under the Military Government

"The aim of the military government has been to organize the financial administration of the country on an honest and efficient basis, [and] to establish an equable system of taxation," wrote Military Governor Samuel Robison in late 1921 in regard to the fiscal reforms of the occupation.[15] The tasks were, in Washington's view, a fundamental part of the military government's mandate, for U.S. officials believed that the Dominican government's perennial problem of insolvency and its political instability were causally related. Curing one problem, officials hoped, would eliminate both.

Since 1905 the U.S.-directed Dominican Customs Receivership had controlled Dominican customs revenues; in June 1916, the receivership had arbitrarily seized control of internal revenues as well. It remained for the military government to assert its control over the management and disbursement of these revenues, a process which it began in December 1916 with Executive Order No. 9. The new law circumvented the customary auditing arrangement within the Ministry of Treasury and Commerce, putting aside the old Cámara de Cuentas and setting up a new Departamento Examinador de Cuentas, staffed with North American officials, "for the purpose of auditing all the revenue, disbursement, and property accounts of the Dominican government."[16]

As the audit proceeded, military officials began a gradual reorganization of the Ministry of Treasury and Commerce. Essentially following the instructions which Washington had given the ill-fated U.S. financial adviser in 1915, a coterie of U.S. officials worked to rationalize the ministry's bureaucratic structure, to modernize accounting practices, to revise budget practices, and, most important, to improve the systems of audit and accountability. In November 1920 Executive Order No. 563, the Ley de Hacienda, finalized the changes they had made.[17]

Another major task involved the settlement of all outstanding financial claims against the republic. In July 1917 military officials created the Dominican Claims Commission, a five-member Dominican–North American board, which examined 9,036 claims totaling almost $17 million, the largest amounts asked by Spanish,

Italian, and French creditors. In the end, after more than three years of work, the commission awarded slightly over $4 million on 6,287 claims.[18] Although the commission had a North American–Puerto Rican majority, it seemed to play no favorites, rejecting spurious U.S. claims along with others (despite pressure from U.S. senators in several cases) and using its special judicial powers to sentence some Dominicans, including the civil governor of the province of Barahona, to prison for making fraudulent claims.[19]

In order to settle the approved claims, the military government borrowed the money, issuing just over $4 million in Dominican twenty-year, 5 percent bonds. While those awarded less than $50 received their payment in cash, others received bonds, which had to be held for twenty years or sold to a New York bank at a loss of 8 to 12.5 percent. These options were not popular among Dominican claimants, many of whom needed the money immediately and could ill afford the discount.[20]

Simultaneous with the effort to improve the internal workings of the Ministry of Treasury and Commerce, occupation officials began an effort to increase the government's income by improving the collection of internal revenues. This effort, predicated on mere enforcement of existing tax laws, paid immediate dividends, almost doubling internal revenues between 1916 and 1917. By 1919 additional collection refinements, the financial turnaround of the government-owned railroad, and general prosperity had caused receipts to triple without adding significant new taxes.[21]

The military government also sought to modernize the old tax structure and to develop new sources of revenue. To accomplish this, in late 1917 military officials brought in a taxation expert from the United States, Professor Fred R. Fairchild of Yale University. By spring 1918 they had received Fairchild's comprehensive study. His report documented the obvious facts that customs receipts comprised the greatest share of the national revenues and that the remainder consisted of excise taxes, neither of which were dependable sources of income. Fairchild's work on local revenues was equally important, as it revealed an incredibly complex and often unfortunate system of taxation which had previously escaped analysis. Few municipalities kept adequate records, he found, and most of the revenues flowed from excise taxes and local tariffs, the latter levied not only on imports from elsewhere in the republic and abroad but sometimes on a locality's own exports as well.

Fairchild's report concluded: "The fundamental weakness of the Dominican revenues, national and local, is the almost complete reliance on indirect taxation. The system is unjust in that a heavy burden is placed on the necessities of the poor, whereas the property and income of the well-to-do go practically scot free. The system is furthermore a heavy drag upon trade and industry." His study soon resulted in legislation. The Ley de Rentas Internas (Internal Revenue) of 1918 essentially combined a series of old taxes into a simplified new tax, with the result that collections almost doubled. A similar modification of the Ley de Patentes, a municipal tax used to support education, more than tripled revenues.[22]

More significant was the new property tax of 1919. Prepared with Fairchild's help, it was the first attempt at direct taxation in the republic's history. Officials intended this tax not only to provide a major new source of revenue but to shift some of the tax burden onto the shoulders of those best able to pay.[23] Opposition to the tax, beginning in 1921, severely crippled and eventually destroyed it. However, its initial success inspired treasury officials to attempt another direct tax, an income tax. The new tax, which imposed a rate of from 2 to 15 percent on incomes above $2,000, was ready in late 1920. But officials failed to publish it, possibly because of the economic decline which began at that time.[24]

The national lottery which the military government introduced in 1920 was of far greater eventual benefit to the national treasury than the attempt at direct taxation. While politically retrograde, it proved an effective means of persuading people to part with their money to support necessary state services. In 1924 the lottery generated $662,000, one of the largest sources of national income outside of customs.[25]

How successful were the fiscal reforms of the military government, and what impact did they have subsequently? The reforms of the internal organization of the Ministry of Treasury and Commerce yielded mixed results. They rationalized an antiquated system, increasing its efficiency, but they in no way hindered future graft and corruption, the prevention of which had been another alleged U.S. goal. Reforms of the tax system proved on the whole more successful and important. Both the rewriting of old tax laws and the improvement of collection practices resulted in greatly increased internal revenues.[26]

The military government's stress on internal revenues, for the obvious reason that customs revenues could not be easily increased, proved valuable to postoccupation Dominican administrations. Before 1916 Dominican governments usually drew about 90 percent of their income from customs; in 1925 the Vásquez government obtained only 40 percent from this source, 60 percent internally.[27] This not only increased the total revenues of the Dominican government but considerably reduced the degree of U.S. economic control through the receivership.

The major failure in the area of taxation was the property tax. This first attempt at direct taxation in the republic was a highly laudable effort to tap a major but unused source of tax revenue and to begin to shift the tax burden, to modify the elite's historic unwillingness to contribute a fair share to the support of essential state services. But the property tax's effectiveness was destroyed by the elite's narrowly defined self-interest, the economic hard times of the 1920s, and the selection of the tax as a nationalist issue. Nonpayment, it soon became clear, was an effective way of crippling the military government. However, the lottery, a kind of indirect and voluntary tax, did succeed and became a major source of revenue for future Dominican governments.

In balance, the fiscal system which the military government left behind was greatly improved, but it was still inadequate to meet the needs of the republic, especially in less prosperous times. Even with the neglect of such basic areas as education and public health after 1920, the military government, the provisional government, and the new constitutional government usually operated in the red.[28]

Ending Protectionism: The Antinational Tariff of 1920

In 1919 the military government embarked on a complete revision of the Dominican tariff. Carrying out this project was the Dominican Tariff Commission, a five-man committee dominated by North American and Puerto Rican representatives. The commission began with general instructions to revise the tariff of 1910, to eliminate inconsistencies, and "in general, to recommend an appreciable reduction in the rates of duty on imported articles which are not produced in quantity in this country and which are ordinarily classed as necessities in contrast to articles of luxury." The tariff's purpose, according to military authorities, was to promote freer trade, adequate revenue, economic development, and, with lower prices, the welfare of the consumer.[29]

By late 1919 the commission had completed its work. The new tariff, which took effect as of 1 January 1920, lowered rates an average of 38 percent and placed nearly 250 items on the free list. Among the items allowed free entry were vehicles and other transportation equipment, agricultural machinery and tools, industrial machinery, building materials, and, "in general, articles necessary for the development of the republic." Other items receiving significant reductions were foodstuffs, metal manufactures, oil and chemical products, and pharmaceuticals.[30]

The result of the tariff change was a fairly substantial loss of revenue to the republic, though the exact amount is difficult to calculate, and a much more favorable trading situation for the western industrial nations, especially the nearby United States. That the flood of manufactured goods invited by the new tariff would help develop the republic seems highly unlikely. On the contrary, the rush of new imports even threatened the nation's few existing industries, especially the producers of tanned leather, shoes, and matches. Likewise food imports, though they may have benefited consumers, threatened local food producers, even coffee growers, who found themselves menaced by the entry of the cheaper Brazilian product.

The tariff soon brought protests and calls for increased protection, but occupation authorities failed to respond.[31] When a Dominican government took power in mid 1924, it moved to reestablish a protective tariff barrier for both industry and agriculture. But since, according to the terms of the 1907 and 1924 treaties, it could not change the tariff without the permission of the U.S. government, it accomplished the same purpose with an internal tax.[32]

The reestablishment of protection reflected not only the Dominican desire to shelter home industries and agriculture but also a reaction to a virtual double cross by the United States. One reason for Dominican support of the 1920 tariff was that Washington had led the Dominicans to expect that generous treatment of U.S. exports would be rewarded with a reciprocal trade agreement.[33] But, when it was time for the U.S. response, all that issued from Washington was a miserable letter from the State Department which "noted with satisfaction" the new Dominican tariff and "sincerely regretted" the impossibility of responding in kind. Reciprocity faced insurmountable obstacles in Washington from well-entrenched Cuban and U.S. colonial interests, whose products competed with those of the Dominicans. Neither the military government's aggressive advocacy of this quid pro quo in Washington, the continuing agitation for reciprocity in Santo Domingo, nor the later calls for a treaty by such figures as Sumner Welles could change this.[34]

From today's perspective, the failure of the republic to obtain reciprocity from the United States was a blessing—in closing off the U.S. market to Dominican sugar, Washington slowed the further rapid advance of sugar monoculture and forced Dominicans to attend to other aspects of their resource base. If the military government had obtained the treaty, one observer has remarked, the entire nation "would have found itself covered with cane."[35]

While the failure to obtain reciprocity may have somewhat frustrated the expansion of sugar, the tariff of 1920 prevented the growth of nearly everything else. The tariff, with its emphasis on an open market, increased the flow of both manufactures and food products from the United States and, by default, confirmed the Dominican role as a supplier of a few plantation crops to the industrialized North Atlantic powers. While this arrangement also served the needs of the Dominican planter and merchant elite, it was decidedly contrary to the long-term interests of the Dominican people.

The Economic Crisis of 1921 to 1924

In late 1920 a sudden economic collapse ended the extraordinary prosperity of the immediate postwar period. The depression lasted with severity into early 1923, and recovery was a slow and irregular process. Its effects were devastating in both the private and the public sectors, sorely testing the military government's administrative and economic skills as well as its new fiscal arrangements.

The depression, like most of the economic forces which affected the republic, began outside the country. One of the early signs of its arrival was the collapse of commodity prices for Dominican products in New York. The price of cacao, for example, had fallen to its lowest point in thirteen years by December 1920, and in a few months the price of sugar had cascaded from an olympian twenty-two cents per pound to less than two cents.[36] The effect within the republic was almost immediate. With many planters unable to sell their crops and to pay their debts, a host of economic difficulties spread through the economy, drying up credit, producing unemployment, substantially reducing retail sales, and causing government revenues to dwindle.

The response of occupation officials, who little suspected the profundity or the length of the crisis at its beginning, was to provide short-term relief to affected agricultural and business interests. Working intensely with chambers of commerce and the representatives of affected industries, the government began by buying up and storing the Dominican tobacco crop, investing almost a million dollars to save growers from having to sell at a loss. At the same time officials considered a similar valorization scheme for cacao but rejected it because the future prospects for cacao seemed worse than those for tobacco. This could hardly have been true. By the time the military government's agents had sold the last of the tobacco in mid 1923, they had incurred a loss of $689,000.[37] A surprising reversal of the general policy of aiding planters was the action occupation authorities took in early 1921 in regard to the sugar companies, forcing them to take a loss of $1.25 million on the eight million pounds of sugar which military officials had requisitioned earlier for the food control stores.[38]

Merchant importers, like planters, were also in difficult straits, having heavily overordered at high prices in 1919 and early 1920. By late 1920 they found themselves with huge inventories, particularly of cotton goods, which they were unable to sell, preventing them from paying their creditors. To make matters worse, the Dominican import houses claimed that "merchants in adjoining islands" were buying fresh stocks in New York, where prices had fallen, and were preparing to import them to Santo Domingo, where they would sell them at below the Dominicans' 1919 and 1920 costs. To save themselves, local merchants asked for a six-month embargo on the import of cotton. This the military government obligingly provided, but only after forcing the reluctant merchants to reduce prices.[39]

In a similar scheme, a delegation of merchants, bankers, and foreign rice dealers persuaded the military government, through the Office of Food Controller, to embargo imports of rice for some months. Though the military government also set a maximum price on rice to prevent profiteering, the obvious effect of its action was to save the profits of a few rich and influential persons at the expense of Dominican consumers. The representatives of labor and others protested loudly but to no avail.[40]

Another action taken at the request of the merchants was the issuance of a new bankruptcy law in 1921. This legislation, modeled on a Philippine law of 1909, contained several provisions favorable to the nation's beleaguered merchants, including one which enabled them to suspend payments to creditors temporarily without being forced to liquidate their businesses. At the same time, and again at the merchants' behest, the military government began a study of the entire Dominican commercial code, of which the old bankruptcy law had formed a part. No other important legislation seems to have come from this, however, although the 1921 bankruptcy law turned out to have such flaws that it was replaced after just six months.[41]

Unfortunately for ordinary Dominicans, the military government aided them much less than it did elite merchants and planters. Military officials spoke of the need to expand public works and other government projects in order to provide additional employment for the masses of unemployed, but, after a few months of trying this approach, they began to follow a new policy of retrenchment within the government which had exactly the opposite effect. In late 1920, with both internal and customs revenues in rapid decline, occupation officials slashed the projected 1921 budget by 50 percent, forcing each ministry to propose a program of reductions. Thousands of persons, both administrators and workers, lost their jobs. Programs were reduced in every case. Some, like public works and education, were suspended. And others, like the forestry service and the agricultural college, were ended permanently. Those employees fortunate enough to keep their jobs found their salaries, when paid at all, cut back 50 to 60 percent between early 1921 and April 1922. And, shortly after the restoration of full salaries, the government decreed a longer workday for its employees, first extending the traditional five-hour workday to six and one-half hours and, after protests, reducing it to the six hours which it remains today.[42]

The scenario of drastic budget cuts, mass firings, and salary reductions, which destroyed much of what the military government had worked for four years to build, was not, it should be noted, what officials had wanted. They had, in fact, originally planned to float a loan of $10 million which, they believed, would have allowed for the maintenance of both essential services and the new programs, as well as for some expansion of public employment and aid to key economic sectors. Officials were so confident of obtaining this loan, having arranged it earlier in 1920 with the State Department in order to accelerate the public works program, that at the beginning of the economic downturn they freely spent all their reserves to create new jobs and aid tobacco farmers. Much to the surprise of the military government, however, the State Department reversed its position on the loan when it decided late in 1920 to effect a withdrawal as soon as possible. This, with the worsening economic situation, left the occupation government in dire straits, with no options but to retrenchment or bankruptcy.[43]

The effect of budget cutting was not immediate. The military government's financial situation grew so desperate by early 1921 that Washington had no alternative but to authorize the issuance of up to $1.2 million in short-term certificates of indebtedness. Rapid use of $800,000 allowed the immediate survival of the government but left much of its work at a standstill. Military officials continued to plead for a larger loan, asking for $5 million. Finally, in June 1921, the State Department authorized a four-year loan of $2.5 million.[44]

The relief provided by the June loan was only temporary. The continuing decline of the republic's economy and of the military government's finances, the short term and high monthly payments of the new loan, and a successful boycott of the property tax combined to create a critical situation by late December 1921. Monthly revenues by then totaled about $200,000, enough to service out-standing loans but only half of the government's expenditures. With salaries unpaid since October and bills of almost half a million dollars in arrears, military officials found that bankers would not even accept the remaining $400,000 of authorized certificates of indebtedness unless a new and larger loan was assured. With the situation clearly impossible, in March 1922 Washington finally approved a loan of $10 million, of which $6.7 million would be emitted immediately. Of this total, $4.5 million would be obligated to retire the 1921 loan and certificates of indebtedness, to meet internal debts such as salaries, and to liquidate the tobacco purchase debt. That left, after bankers' charges of more than $635,000, about $1.6 million, mainly for completion of the north-south highway and the building up of the Guardia Nacional.[45]

The loans which the military government was forced to seek in 1921 and 1922 were an embarrassment. They called into question the ability of the United States to manage Dominican affairs and made clear an obvious double standard, for Washington would have soundly condemned any Dominican administration which had found itself in a similar predicament. Furthermore, these loans raised ethical questions, for they were made by a U.S. military government with U.S. bankers on behalf of an occupied nation. The appearance if not the substance of impropriety was there, and various critics, both North American and Dominican, have since made charges of collusion and indecently high interest rates.[46] The collusion, if it existed, was among the bankers themselves or between the bankers and the State Department. More likely, there was no collusion and the loans' unfavorable conditions merely reflected the bankers' normal practice of fleecing those who, including poorer nations, have few credit alternatives. The evidence concerning the military government shows that officials worked hard to avoid unfavorable rates of interest and, in general, dealt with bankers warily. In fact, in 1921 the military government instituted the first-ever audit of the 1907 $20 million loan, finding that the Guaranty Trust Company of New York had for years made illegal charges and engaged in other doubtful practices. These had cost the Dominican treasury $228,000, which the bank was forced to return in 1923.[47]

The March 1922 loan stabilized the finances of the military government, though still on a net deficit basis. With the additional help of a new sales tax created in February, the military government limped along until the establishment of a Dominican provisional government in October.[48] Though general economic conditions remained dismal for the rest of 1922, the resurgence of commodity prices in early 1923 to a level which again permitted profits marked the beginning of a slow revival. But this gradual improvement did not result in immediate fiscal recovery. The provisional government operated at a loss through 1923 and 1924, forcing Washington to approve a loan of $2.5 million in 1924 to bring the new constitutional government into office on a sound basis. "This money was deemed necessary," wrote José C. Ariza, the new Dominican minister in Washington, "to continue public works . . . and to meet urgent needs of the Government."[49]

The 1921 to 1924 period had made clear an important economic and political reality. The Dominican Republic was a poor and underdeveloped country, dependent and extremely vulnerable to world economic forces. When these forces operated to the detriment of the republic, it was all but impossible for the government, or the rest of society, to function properly. The military government, despite its various reforms and many advantages, could manage no better than most Dominican governments in similar circumstances.

The Military Government and the Process of Development

The military government undertook a number of measures meant to further the economic development of the republic. By far the most important of these were the major public sector investments in roads, harbors, port facilities, and communications. In the private sector military officials also developed a variety of projects, primarily in agriculture and secondarily in forestry and mining, reflecting the belief of Military Governor Knapp that "the future material prosperity of Santo Domingo will be, I believe, principally dependent upon agriculture."[50]

The heart of the military government's program in agriculture was an extension service. Beginning with one instructor in June 1917, the service had thirty-five agents scattered over the country by late 1920. These instructors farmed small demonstration plots, worked with individual farmers to solve specific problems, tried to persuade farmers to adopt modern methods, formed local agricultural committees (of which there were 1,644 by 1920), and worked in a variety of other ways—developing agricultural fairs, for example—to promote the improvement of agriculture. The agents also acted as distributors for the rural services. One of these imported simple agricultural implements, such as plows, seed drills, and cultivators, and sold them to farmers at cost. Another distributed free vegetable seeds in order to promote vegetable growing for home consumption and local markets. A third imported cattle, hogs, goats, and poultry for demonstration and breeding purposes.

The second major element of the agricultural program established experimental stations. The main center at Haina, just west of Santo Domingo City, eventually consisted of a variety of modern farm installations run by foreign specialists in agricultural science. It was at this location that the North American director of agriculture and his staff engaged in research and promotional activities. They worked to develop healthier and more productive seeds for traditional Dominican crops, to introduce useful plants, and to eradicate common infectious diseases of Dominican plants and animals. There were also substations in experimental agriculture at Monte Cristi and Constanza, with two others planned for Santiago and El Seibo. The station at Monte Cristi specialized in research in cotton growing, a basic cash crop of the area; that at Constanza, in a temperate zone in the mountains, experimented with such crops as wheat and northern fruits. In other actions, agriculture officials issued various publications and planned a college to train young Dominicans in scientific agriculture.[51]

The military government's agricultural program, according to Military Governor Knapp, was designed "to show the Dominican people how to raise larger, better, and more varied crops, the proceeds of which will accrue to Dominicans themselves and not go in large measure to foreign corporations." Thus few resources went to sugar interests, while aid to such Dominican-controlled commercial crops as cacao and tobacco was common. To help the latter, for instance, the agricultural service employed experts in both tobacco and cacao and promoted various laws to improve the quality of these crops so that they would bring a better price on the international market.

Critics charged that the military government's agricultural program did little for the vast majority of Dominican farmers. In fact, U.S. officials were aware of this problem, and they designed such services as demonstration plots, traveling agricultural instructors, free seed distribution, and instructional movies partly with the peasant farmers in mind. But persuading peasants to abandon such traditional techniques as slash and burn in favor of more modern methods met with little success. Though this failure resulted in part from flaws in the military government's approach, there can be little doubt that the peasants' resistance to change was extraordinarily great. It was to the credit of the military government's director of agriculture, Holger Johansen, that he learned enough about peasant farming to understand its time-tested principles and to accept that, given the conditions (such as lack of capital) under which the peasants operated, their methods were often best.[52]

Much of the agricultural program had its origins in the United States, the home base of the director of agriculture and most of his technical staff. But there was also a Dominican foundation. About 1900 the Congress established the positions of inspectors of agriculture, and in 1902 the Vásquez government began working for the standardization and improvement of export crops. By 1909 the Cáceres administration had created a separate Ministry of Agriculture and Immigration. It also appropriated $30,000 to hire a foreign agricultural expert and to create two agricultural experiment stations. But insufficient funds, administrative disorganization, and the fact that the inspectors of agriculture, enlarging upon their function of inspecting rural labor, had become more police than agricultural officials meant that none of these efforts had much improved agriculture.[53]

Was the military government's program more successful than previous Dominican efforts? It seems likely, given a larger and better-trained staff and more ample funding, that the occupation program did promote some agricultural improvement, especially among more educated farmers. But Ministry of Agriculture reports indicate that little had been accomplished with peasants. Moreover, the program had serious shortcomings, particularly its failure to provide some form of agricultural credit. Lacking funds to provide loans themselves, officials were leaning in the direction of rural cooperatives to meet credit needs. But the depression of late 1920, which reduced the ministry's funding by more than 30 percent, prevented any action in this area and ended many other projects, including the extension service.[54]

Because the military government's 1922 loan specifically provided some funds for agricultural work, officials were able to reinitiate several projects. But the interruption and diminution of funding, followed by the resignation of the discouraged director of agriculture, seriously crippled the ministry's efforts until 1924. Beginning in that year, the new Vásquez government took a strong interest in agricultural development. It retained the main experiment station, which was moved to Moca in 1925, and finally created the long-planned college, staffed by foreign agricultural experts. It continued some of the military government's programs, such as the improvement of Dominican livestock, and created new ones of its own, apparently experiencing some success with irrigation and agricultural diversification.[55]

Occupation efforts to promote development in the private sector outside of agriculture were limited. The government lacked financial resources, and military officials rejected a primary method of bringing in foreign investment, the concession. Furthermore, like most of the Dominican elite, officials had a limited view of what was possible or proper to develop. Thus their few nonagricultural endeavors were concentrated in a field traditionally seen as appropriate to Latin America, the development of raw materials for export, namely, forest products and minerals. Other obviously neglected areas of the economy such as manufacturing and commercial fishing remained without attention.

The military government's work in forestry consisted of making a preliminary assessment of the republic's timber resources and then writing a law to protect them and govern their use. To carry out the original assessment, military officials invited two North American experts, one from the Smithsonian Institution and one from the Department of Forestry at the University of Puerto Rico at Mayagüez. Both saw great potential riches in the republic's vast expanses of nearly virgin forest, and both recommended the immediate passage of a law to prevent the random destruction of the forest, especially by peasants burning off the land for new fields and pastures.

Officials issued two executive orders on this matter in 1919 and 1920. One, the Ley Forestal, governed the use of Dominican forests and created a forestry service under the Ministry of Agriculture and Immigration. The other, the Ley de Reserva Forestal, established government protection over broad forested areas extending from western Azua to Samaná. Since funds for adequate personnel and enforcement were lacking, these laws were probably not very effective even before 1921, when depression-related budget cuts eliminated the entire forestry service. In any case, all this activity had little effect on the republic's timber exports, which remained quite small until after the occupation. Neither did it affect the forests controlled by several U.S. corporations, whose vast holdings were said to exceed the total acreage controlled by the sugar interests; they continued to let the timber stand unused, pending the development of better transportation.[56]

Mining legislation was no more successful. The military government appropriated funds for a geological survey of the republic's mineral resources in 1918. Then it moved to reform the 1910 law which governed mining concessions. The object was to better protect Dominican interests, particularly to see that, when concessions were obtained, they were used for mining rather than for speculative purposes, as frequently occurred under the old legislation. In reviewing outstanding concessions, some belonging to U.S. citizens but the majority to Dominicans, military authorities canceled more than half of them. While this represented an improvement, it did not cause any significant mining to begin.[57]

The discarded Ley de Minas of 1910 reflected the Dominican elite's view that development would occur only when foreigners with capital and expertise were attracted to the republic by laws favorable to their interests. Such was also the thinking behind the 1911 Ley sobre Franquicias Agrarias (Agrarian Concessions), which authorized a generous set of concessions to agricultural entrepreneurs. However, the military government, unlike the elite, did not stand to profit by these laws and took a less favorable view of them, seeing such legislation as detrimental to Dominican interests. While the military government would allow "foreign enterprises authorized and conducted strictly according to Dominican law," explained C. C. Baughman, a naval officer serving as a cabinet official, it "would not permit them to have concessions of a character that allowed them to exploit the country." With this policy in mind, occupation authorities rewrote the mining law and, in 1919, abolished the Ley sobre Franquicias Agrarias.[58]

Seeing their role as "trustee for the Dominican government in defense of the interests of the people," military officials avoided awarding major concessions and took a dim view of those who sought them. "The Military Government here," wrote Military Governor Knapp in 1917, "is very much pestered by would be concessionaires, almost invariably Americans, who seem to feel that the existence of Military Government by the United States in Santo Domingo is for the benefit of Americans who are coming down here to exploit Santo Domingo for the good of the aforesaid Americans."[59] Not surprisingly, the anticoncession policy was unpopular in some quarters. A lawyer for several U.S. corporations complained that potential investors were "given little encouragement by the military authorities" and that "the Dominican government showed greater interest in attracting foreign capital" and had been "more considerate of Americans and other foreigners."[60]

In 1919 and 1920 the military government clearly displayed its coolness to two groups of investors, one with ties to the United Fruit Company, who wanted the military government to grant subsidies and a bond guarantee for construction of a railroad from Santo Domingo through Santiago to Manzanillo Bay in the northwest. After the military government had repeatedly rebuffed the self-serving proposals of both groups, one of them tried to apply pressure through a U.S. senator and the secretary of the navy. But military officials stood their ground, arguing that the railroad would barely serve the needs of the Dominican people but "would favor certain [U.S.] interests who hold large tracts of forest land in the country back of Manzanillo Bay." Either group was welcome to build the railroad, wrote Military Governor Snowden, but neither would receive subsidies, bond guarantees, or other favors. That ended the matter.[61]

In another revealing case, occupation officials repelled the effort of Behn Brothers of Puerto Rico (which later became International Telephone and Telegraph) to take over the Dominican telephone system. They did so in spite of the fact that the company had nearly completed arrangements for a franchise with the preintervention Dominican government. Instead the military government nationalized the existing Dominican private companies, which were small and inefficient, setting up a government telephone service which it proceeded to modernize and expand.[62]

The military government's virtual ban on concessions to foreigners, combined with the Dominican elite's traditional preference for speculative and nonproductive investments such as land and other real estate, meant that there were few large investments in the private sector during the 1916 to 1924 period. Virtually the only major investments were expansions of existing or previously planned sugar estates, motivated mostly by the extraordinary demand for sugar from 1914 to late 1920. Offsetting the limited activity in the private sector, however, was the military government's heavy spending in the public sector for infrastructure. Though the immediate economic benefits of this investment flowed mainly to agriculture and trade, there remained the possibility that it would serve as a basis for future development in other areas.

Other Occupation Programs

Of the many other actions of the military government, a few stand out as especially significant, either for what they attempted or, less often, for what they accomplished.

Military officials implemented a number of reforms meant to improve the administrative effectiveness of the Dominican government. One of the more important of these was the attempt to establish a civil service, then a popular panacea in U.S. reformist circles. In 1920 Executive Order No. 452 established the national Civil Service Commission, modeled on the Puerto Rican system.[63] One of the cardinal purposes of the reform was to eliminate partisan political considerations from the hiring and firing of government employees. Ironically, this basic principle was first violated by the military government itself when, in mid 1921, it systematically fired every government employee who had signed a nationalist protest against the Harding Plan of withdrawal. With this inauspicious beginning, it is not surprising that the provisional Dominican government felt free to suspend the civil service law "temporarily" in 1923 and that the new constitutional government ignored the law almost completely.[64]

The census of 1920 was a more successful undertaking. It was the republic's first thorough national census, a considerable improvement over the various local censuses and informal national efforts of the past. The census not only yielded a count of the republic's 895,000 citizens but provided data for other purposes, such as computations regarding health and the economy. The primary flaw in the military government's effort was that it conducted the census with a temporary organization, having earlier closed down the statistics bureau set up under the Cáceres administration. This, presumably, was one of the reasons why the Dominican government made no new national census until the 1930s.[65]

Military officials also made a number of significant reforms of the Dominican judicial system. Often suggested by Dominican advisers, these reforms bettered the administration and delivery of justice by modifying and improving the judicial structure, penal procedure, court facilities, archives, and judicial salaries. At the same time, authorities began scrutinizing the conduct of judges and lawyers more closely and suspended several lawyers from practice for lengthy periods. They also issued an executive order which required lawyers to work *pro bono* for indigent defendants.[66]

Prison reform was less successful. The Dominican prison system in 1916 was primitive in the extreme, with overcrowded, unsanitary, and inhumane conditions. The military government at first hoped to institute a broad reform based on that in the Philippines, but instead it slowly implemented a piecemeal program. It worked to clean up older prisons, tried to improve the prisoners' diet, sanitation, and general health, opened two correctional schools for young male offenders, and built a 500-man national penitentiary in order to create a more spacious and healthier environment for long-term prisoners. Other aspects of this reform outlawed the use of stocks, leg irons, and other ancient and inhumane devices and called for the training of prisoners in useful trades.[67] However, as late as mid 1920 overcrowding, poor diet, and unsanitary conditions in Santo Domingo's Ozama Prison continued to cause outbreaks of beriberi and other diseases among the prisoners. The state of the Santiago prison also remained terrible—"the worst I have ever seen in my life," commented a marine officer familiar with Dominican jails—and there was no money to improve it. Thereafter, the arrival of the depression in late 1920 considerably worsened matters, even causing the permanent closing of the correctional schools.[68] There is no evidence that any improvement of prison conditions survived withdrawal.

Occupation officials decreed some social legislation, much of it treating women and children. Executive Order No. 375 hoped to encourage marriage and decrease the rate of illegitimate births by replacing the "complex and expensive" regulations of the old marriage law with simplified legislation. The old law, explained military officials, "militated against the interest of woman by making it impracticable for her to obtain the sanction and protection of matrimony for the sexual unions into which the social conditions force her." A related law, Executive Order No. 168, required fathers to support their children, regardless of the question of legitimacy. And military officials at least contemplated the complete abrogation of article 340 of the Dominican civil code, which prohibited the investigation of paternity, denouncing this provision as "an iniquity, . . . the protection and refuge of seducers and corrupters."[69]

"Women should have equal rights with men under the law," opined Military Governor Snowden on an occasion when he observed the law operating prejudicially against a woman. Although the military government demonstrated a somewhat ambivalent legal position on women, alternating between protection and equality, the actions of higher military officials generally accommodated, in both legislation and practice, the movement for women's rights which was developing in western culture at that time. For example, Executive Order No. 201 established that women had the right to practice law. Similarly, Executive Order No. 338, the Ley de Sanidad, specified that "women are eligible for the practice of medicine, dentistry, pharmacy, or any of the medical professions or trades . . . under the same conditions as men." Military officials also opened government clerical jobs to Dominican women, a radical innovation at the time. In 1922 the military government sent a Dominican woman, Ana T. Paradas, to a Pan American conference in Baltimore which treated the political and economic status of women and related issues.[70]

The military government's accommodation of Dominican women caused a male backlash. Some blamed the occupation for corrupting Dominican women, both because individual North Americans, including officers' wives, set "bad" examples and because the military government offered women opportunities which had not been available before. "The Yankees are threatening the traditional modesty of Dominican women," warned publicist Horacio Blanco Fombona in a speech. Specific complaints (which reflected a certain class orientation) included such matters as women beginning to drive cars, becoming typists "and neglecting the kitchen," going to market "as though they were servants," wearing dresses with hems cut too high and necklines too low, and dancing in public cafés and restaurants.[71]

Conclusion

In late 1920 the creative work of the military government came to a virtual halt. There were two reasons. First, the State Department was about to issue the plan of withdrawal which became known as the Wilson Plan. With this in mind, it ordered occupation authorities not "to effect any alterations of the law of the Dominican Republic other than are immediately necessary for the best interests of that country," a provision which it interpreted narrowly.[72] Second, the severe depression which began in late 1920 made it impossible to pay for many projects already under way, much less for new ones. Lost as a result were a variety of well-advanced proposals for innovative legislation, including an income tax law, a law reestablishing a bureau of statistics, and a law creating a system of workers' compensation, which would have been the first attempt at social insurance in the history of the republic.[73]

Nonetheless, the military administration had compiled an extensive record of governmental action and reform in just four years. And, despite the fact that officials had modified the republic's economy, political life, judicial system, and social organization, they nevertheless generally supported and strengthened the basic patterns of Dominican society. This was especially true in the economic field, where military government actions and programs tended to revitalize and support an economy geared to the interests of plantation agriculturalists and merchants. This in turn insured that basic social and political patterns would continue in the near future, as the post-occupation Vásquez administration demonstrated. Ironically, it was the new Guardia Nacional, meant to insure the status quo, which would break the traditional mold of Dominican life after 1930.

A number of factors explain the supportive role played by the military government. First, the occupation programs were reformist. Their authors wanted to eliminate inefficiencies and inequities, but they had no thought of radically changing the Dominican economy or society. Second, members of the Dominican elite served an important advisory role in formulating the military government's programs. Therefore, many projects reflected, or at least did not harm, elite interests. Third, inertia carried the Dominican economy and society along a certain path. Most occupation programs, even if they were contrary to this direction, did not operate on a large enough scale to deflect the republic from its original course.

4

The Military Government, the Sugar Industry, and the Land Question

The rapid growth of the sugar industry in the late nineteenth and early twentieth centuries was the most important economic development in Dominican history. A crop of minor importance in 1870, sugar had become the nation's premier export by the time the military government took control in 1916. In the process of gaining this predominance, sugar had changed the republic, not only the areas where it was grown but also the nation as a whole. Where cane flourished, corporations reduced poor but independent landowners to occasionally employed day laborers, transformed self-respecting rural householders into crowded renters in slumlike settlements, created a monoculture which destroyed the country's ability to produce its own foodstuffs and raw materials for industrial processes, and in most cases transferred the land, and the profits which it earned, into foreign hands. Moreover, as the new crop came to dominate the republic's agricultural export economy, Dominicans became ever more dependent on the vagaries of the international commodity market. The expansion of the sugar industry also strengthened the economic ties to the United States, which further enabled Washington to manipulate Dominican internal political affairs.

The importance of sugar in Dominican life thus lent a special significance to the military government's actions in this area. And it happened, because one of the sugar growers' greatest concerns was land tenure, that sugar became the focus of a major legislative endeavor of the military government. Thus, better than any other, this effort elucidates the occupiers' thinking on several important policy issues, particularly their responsibility to the Dominican people and their relationship to foreign capitalists, especially to the North Americans.

A Historical Sketch of the Sugar Industry

Planters had grown sugar on the Dominican portion of the island of Hispaniola since the sixteenth century, but until the last quarter of the nineteenth century agriculturalists had cultivated only small quantities, which they processed in small and primitive factories called trapiches. Two events were to change Dominican sugar production. First was the Spanish reoccupation of the republic from 1861 to 1865, which brought civil war but also Spanish and Italian immigrants interested in the development of commerce and agriculture. Second, and more important, was the Ten Years War in Cuba, from 1868 to 1878, which sent Cuban sugar planters to the Dominican Republic in search of new sugar lands and security. The Cubans brought with them capital and an advanced sugar technology, including the steam engine for power and transport and modern refining techniques. Cane planting and processing increased accordingly, and by the 1870s extensive modern sugar cultivation had begun.[1]

Most of the sugar expansion took place on the southeastern coastal plain of the republic, an area which even in its undeveloped state reminded a North American traveler of "the vast sugar plains of Cuba." Other, less spectacular increases in sugar cultivation took place in the southwest on the Barahona peninsula and around the town of Azua, in the north near the town of Puerto Plata, and in the south on the outskirts of Santo Domingo City.[2]

Expansion continued into the twentieth century. At the time of the harvest of 1920–21, the republic had twenty mills in operation, producing some 1,818,968 tons of cane and, from that, 199,708 tons of sugar. Most of the sugar was in a partially refined form known as muscovado, which was shipped to the United States, Canada, or England. Dominicans themselves used not more than 5 percent of their production, consuming it as table sugar or using it for the manufacture of alcohol.[3]

Sugar rapidly became the most important component of the Dominican economy. In the banner year of 1920, the $45 million earned by sugar exports represented a figure 423 percent greater than that of the republic's three other largest exports combined. In 1926 sugar production accounted for 88.5 percent of Dominican export tonnage and approximately 60 percent of export value. The sugar companies claimed that the Dominican government received about 65 percent of its $7.4 million total income in 1926 from sugar-related taxes, paid either by the sugar estates themselves ($1 million) or by company laborers, other employees, *colonos*, merchants, and others "directly dependent on the sugar industry" ($3.8 million).[4]

The world commodity market was of critical importance to sugar producers. A high price meant large profits, a low one spelled disaster. During the first four years of the occupation, the sugar market pushed steadily upward in response to the shortages caused by World War I. The growers in the Dominican Republic, as elsewhere, responded to the stimulus of higher prices by putting more and more land into production. The world sugar market spiraled to an all-time high in 1920 but then, as a result of overproduction, crashed. This sharp decline, plus an unfavorable U.S. tariff, reduced the value of Dominican sugar exports by more than two-thirds in one year.[5] Sugar exports from 1916 to 1922 were as follows.[6]

Year	Tons	Value
1916	122,642	$12,028,497
1917	131,499	13,386,463
1918	120,032	11,191,399
1919	162,322	20,697,761
1920	158,803	45,305,620
1921	183,611	14,338,354
1922	171,542	9,192,173

The impact of this loss on the Dominican economy was tremendous, precipitating a major financial crisis for the military government.

The occasional economic crises which beset the sugar industry as well as the cutthroat competition tended to drive small operators out of business, leaving the field to the larger, more heavily capitalized estates. Increasingly, North American companies dominated the surviving elite. By 1925, just twenty-one major estates remained, occupying at least 438,000 acres; by 1926 these occupied an estimated 520,000 acres. Of the twenty-one, twelve U.S.-owned companies controlled more than 81 percent of the total acreage.[7]

The conversion of more than half a million acres of land to the cultivation of sugar inevitably caused a number of important changes in the small republic, particularly in the east. Major economic problems resulted, including the transfer of the domestic economy into foreign hands, the increasing dependence on the international commodity market, and a decreasing ability to produce an adequate domestic food supply because of the destruction of diversified agriculture. And another, equally important change occurred, a social one: the transformation of the mass of the people in the affected regions from independent, small-holding agriculturalists into a rural proletariat, laborers totally dependent on the sugar companies for employment and, often, for their shelter and food as well. The human price of this loss of independence was high, as several nineteenth-century critics, including Pedro F. Bonó and Eugenio María de Hostos, noted when they saw the process first at work in the 1880s.[8]

Bonó and de Hostos were, however, among the very few who at any stage protested the increasing development of sugar cultivation. Those most adversely affected, the peasants, were inarticulate and politically weak. Among the more powerful educated elite, few questioned the wisdom of what they saw as economic progress. Furthermore, such development promised to enrich the elite, who were the chief Dominican beneficiaries of the expanding economy, servicing its needs as professionals or provisioning it by importing and selling consumer and capital goods. They also stood to profit from land speculation, and some became involved directly in sugar production.

After Bonó and de Hostos, the few Dominicans who challenged sugar's growing importance generally concerned themselves with the increasing preponderance of North Americans in the sugar industry rather than with the inherent social and economic drawbacks of a plantation economy. A small group of radical nationalists, among them Américo Lugo, warned that, in a small nation like the Dominican Republic, "the loss of private property implies the loss of sovereignty." Another writer, Persio C. Franco, stated: "If with the lands of the entire republic occurs what has occurred with those of San Pedro de Macorís, La Romana, and Barahona, the Dominican Republic will be a myth."[9]

There is little doubt that the increasing U.S. economic presence did harm Dominican sovereignty. But both sectors of the sugar industry, Dominican and foreign, were responsible for a more direct and visible cost: the destruction of the peasants' way of life. As cane fields replaced their homes and *conucos,* the farmers either had to leave the area, probably migrating to a town or into adjacent hillier country, or they had to accept jobs with the sugar companies which had taken over their lands. Of those displaced persons who stayed, only a few were able to obtain year-round employment in the mills. The fate of most was to work as cane cutters, a physically demanding but low-paid job which lasted only three to six months a year. The better positions in management or even in the mills (for example, that of a panboiler or chemist) went to foreigners, who were paid on a much higher scale.[10]

The conditions which the average sugar worker faced were appalling. When men or women could obtain work, they received a basic wage of fifty to sixty cents for an eleven- to twelve-hour day. In some circumstances the base might fall to thirty cents; for piecework under exceptional conditions, it might rise as high as eighty or ninety cents.[11] These wages were insufficient for survival, claimed the first Dominican labor leaders in 1919. They advocated a minimum wage of at least a dollar per day, an amount which only a few skilled employees, such as mechanics, could then expect. In addition, two conditions aggravated the inadequacy of the pay: seasonal layoffs and the practice of paying the workers at least partly in *vales*, scrip redeemable only in the company stores.[12]

Only the company store and company-owned housing enabled the peasant-turned-laborer and his family to survive the six months or more of unemployment which followed the harvest each year. At the company store, credit for the overpriced goods made up the difference between income and the price of the family's meager necessities. The workers' debts assured the sugar estate of cane cutters for the next season. A marine officer who had watched the operation of these small stores advised that they be shut down, noting cynically: "As for their bodegas, . . . their stock is chiefly rum, the doctrine of most centrals being that the laborer will not work if he has money in his pocket and that rum in the bodegas will help deprive the laborer of his money."[13]

The company-owned houses, grouped in small settlements called *bateys*, provided squalid shelter for employees and their families. Of cheap construction and soon decrepit, the small houses lacked the amenities of electricity, running water, and plumbing, although these services were available to the houses of administrators and to the mill itself. The *bateys* were overcrowded in general, but this was especially true of the *barracones* or barracks, into which the single workers squeezed. Conditions were unsanitary, and medical services, both doctors and pharmacies, were generally lacking. Reports indicated that some 70 percent of Haitian migrants suffered from yaws and that other diseases such as dysentery, leprosy, malaria, and elephantiasis were rampant. Even the privileged indoor workers of the mill were likely to encounter unsanitary and dangerous conditions, and none of the workers was covered by any form of social insurance.[14]

A 1926 report by a U.S. consul in Santo Domingo provides rare documentation concerning the sugar workers. Their living conditions, the consul wrote, were "primitive in the extreme," often worse for Haitians and other imported laborers than for Dominicans. "Most of these laborers exist solely on a diet of yams, bananas (plátanos), and other fruits, the average expenditure for food being estimated at from 15 to 20 cents per day." A pound of meat, for a special occasion, might cost half a day's wages. "A cheap shirt and a pair of drill trousers suffice for the men and are worn until useless. For women a cheap cotton dress answers the clothing problem," while "the children for a considerable number of years are devoid of clothing of any kind." When new clothes were needed, the lowest quality, marketed expressly "for common laborers," was still expensive, with shirts priced at $.60 to $2.50, trousers at $2.50, and shoes at $2.25 to $4.50. But, the consul added, "in most cases common laborers do not buy shoes. They use a special kind of slipper [sandal] prepared by Dominican shoemakers which sell at retail from 50 to 70¢ per pair."[15]

The pressure of living and working in the environment of the sugar estates led to frequent violence within the *bateys*. This, plus protests about the generally deplorable conditions, led military authorities to study the situation in 1920. But neither the military regime nor the two subsequent Dominican administrations made any improvements.[16]

A variety of factors, including control of the land and political influence, enabled the sugar corporations to maintain these terrible conditions among workers. Another factor was the companies' habitual practice of importing much of the labor needed during the harvest, which both prevented workers from organizing and depressed wages. By far the largest number, perhaps as many as 100,000 legal and illegal migrants, came from Haiti annually. Much smaller numbers, 3,500 to 6,500 a year from 1916 to 1921, arrived from neighboring non-Spanish Caribbean islands. Under contract to the sugar companies, the migrants worked for the season and then returned to their homes, except when they obtained permits to stay or remained illegally.[17]

The sugar companies argued that they needed these contract workers because there were not enough Dominicans to complete the harvest each year. Both the Dominican and the U.S. military governments accepted this rationale. In fact, evidence exists that the republic had high levels of unemployment and underemployment and thus much available labor. It seems likely that the sugar companies found it cheaper to import foreigners than to raise wages to a level which would attract more Dominicans. Such was the argument of the fledgling labor unions of the republic, which saw the policy of importing thousands of braceros as a threat to their wages, working conditions, and employment itself.[18] But these small groups of workers had insufficient power to cause the military government to change its policy.

Migratory workers had problems above and beyond those of Dominican workers. In 1922, Haitians charged that their nationals were paid lower wages than Dominicans for the same work and that labor contractors deliberately misinformed them concerning the

The cabinet of President Francisco Henríquez y Carvajal in 1916. From left to right, sitting: Emilio Prud'homme (Justice and Public Instruction), Federico Henríquez y Carvajal (Interior and Police), Francisco Henríquez y Carvajal, and José María Cabral y Báez (Foreign Relations). Standing: Miguel Máscaro (War and Navy), Francisco Peynado (Treasury and Commerce), and Eladio Sánchez (Immigration and Agriculture). Eliseo Espaillat (Development and Communications) is not pictured.

Followers of Vicentico. The guerrilla leader is probably the figure dressed in white, second from the right.

Guerrilla leader Martín Peguero, in the white hat, with another guerrilla, Juan Francisco Guerrero, photographed in September 1920 following a clandestine interview with a Dominican admirer.

Guerrilla leader Ramón Natera and Máxima de la Cruz in 1921.

A guerrilla, his arms held aloft by two comrades, slain in combat with the marines in 1921.

Guerrilla leader Tolete posing for his picture in 1926.

Curious Dominicans surround a marine plane at Laguna de Campiña, outside of El Seibo, in 1920.

The eastern district commander in 1919 and 1920, Colonel J. C. Brecken-ridge (third from the left), with fellow marines and a Dominican onlooker, Luis F. Morel.

A group of marines out on a patrol. Their Dominican guide is on the far right.

One side of an identification cedula, used in the east during the guerrilla war, which contains the picture and fingerprints of a peasant farmer from near El Seibo. The reverse side of the cedula, signed by three Dominican civil officials, including Pedro A. Pérez, the governor of El Seibo Province in 1918.

Fabio Fiallo, the modernist poet, in prison garb in 1920. After Fiallo's jailing for violation of censorship regulations, this photo was circulated widely for propaganda purposes.

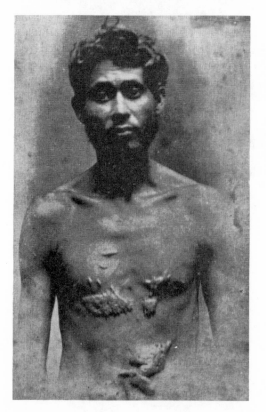

A 1920 propaganda photo of the tortured peasant Cayo Báez, showing the scars on his chest. When the editor of the magazine *Las Letras*, Horacio Blanco Fombona, published this photo, the military government closed his press and deported him.

Demonstrators against the continuing occupation fill Santo Domingo's principal plaza during the Semana Patriótica of 1920.

A marine takes notes during a market. The style of the colonial house in the background is typical of elite homes and businesses in the early twentieth century.

A marine and Dominicans gather around a phonograph outside a typical rural thatched hut.

A prison work gang toils under marine supervision.

Marine instructors drill recruits of the Guardia Nacional.

Motorized marines pose at the Ozama River gate of Santo Domingo's colonial wall.

Marines and Dominican onlookers line the dock at Santo Domingo during the arrival of General Harry Lee in 1921.

The Dominican backers of the Hughes-Peynado Plan. From left to right: Horacio Vásquez, U.S. Minister William Russell, Sumner Welles, an unidentified U.S. functionary, Federico Velásquez, Elías Brache, and (probably) Francisco Peynado.

wage scale to persuade them to migrate. Migrant working conditions on some estates in the early 1920s were so bad that the British colonial government eventually opened an office on the island of Saint Kitts to keep track of British contract laborers and to boycott estates which had records of abusing workers. Critics singled out the estates of the Vicini family, particularly La Angelina, for censure because of unusually poor housing and working conditions, especially the practice of refusing to return injured and uninsured workers to their home islands.[19]

Though the cane workers represented an obvious target for unionization, the republic's infant unions avoided them for some time, except on the issue of braceros, which affected all Dominican workers. This avoidance is understandable when one considers that Dominican unions were organized around crafts, that they were small and poor, and that the cane workers were exceedingly difficult to organize. In 1919, however, the Dominican labor movement began showing interest in the plight of the sugar workers. And by early 1920 workers had organized a union on one of the largest sugar estates, Consuelo, and soon were on strike against the recalcitrant management.[20]

If the life of a sugar company laborer was so bleak, why would peasants part with their land and their old way of life? Some had no choice, since they did not own the land on which they lived and worked. Residing on the underutilized estates of larger landowners, when the land was sold and converted to sugar they had to leave or work for the sugar corporations. The majority of peasants owned land, however, and were persuaded or forced to sell by the sugar companies. A company representative would begin by offering a good price for the land. In some instances, that was sufficient. The prospect of ready cash, perhaps made more tempting by the dizzying effect of rum provided by the potential buyer, helped encourage sales. If this sort of cajolery failed, land buyers could move toward trickery, threats, and violence.[21]

Violence by the sugar companies, as much as it may have existed, is not often recorded. On one occasion in 1918, however, a marine colonel reported a battle between peasants and the workers of one Johan Leevy, affiliated with the Consuelo estate, as merely a "normal fight between Leevy's men and the natives they are attempting to oust." It would appear that the colonel had seen such affairs before. By such actions, the officer noted, "Leevy was rapidly increasing his great land holdings. . . . He lays claim to immense tracts north of Consuelo." A few years later, investigators of conditions in the sugar industry noted allegations that sugar companies commonly took and held land "more by force than by legal process."[22]

There was, however, an alternative to buying and selling or to the use of violence. Sugar corporations could seize the land by legal means. Peasants often lacked a legal title to their land or held an insufficient title. Even if a valid deed existed, the chaotic land title system dating from colonial times often resulted in a lack of corroborating evidence for the title or in spurious duplicate titles. The laws which Dominican congresses had passed to clear up the situation tended to favor the sugar corporations and other entrepreneurs, if for no other reason than the ability of the companies to hire the best lawyers and to pay for extensive litigation.[23] Peasants faced with sacrificing their land to pay a lawyer, the courts, and other expenses, such as surveyors' fees, were probably well advised to sell immediately.

The sugar companies sometimes obtained titles to whole villages. In 1921 the Central Romana estate burned to the ground two such hamlets, El Caimoní and Higüeral, which stood in the path of its expanding fields. One hundred and fifty families were left homeless, the company having made no provisions for them.[24]

Another method of obtaining land was to persuade peasants to become independent *colonos* for the sugar company, raising sugarcane under contract for the estate. This was a risky undertaking for the peasants, who had to borrow money from the company in order to sow the cane and to live during the months before it matured. Their land served as collateral, and as long as crops were good, peasants could repay their loans and earn a small to moderate profit. But if a year of drought occurred, or if peasant landowners were unable to work because of sickness, or if for any other reason the crop was small or failed, they would be caught in an endless cycle of debt, until they eventually produced a crop owed entirely to the sugar company or lost their land.[25]

Another class of *colonos* existed who were in a significantly better position than peasant *colonos*. They were essentially entrepreneur-administrators, many of them European-born, who worked their own land or land rented to them by a sugar company. How well they fared depended on how much land they possessed. They had their own capital or could borrow it at reasonable rates, and they hired laborers to do the actual work. For example, Ramón Morales, a merchant from La Romana, was a prosperous *colono* who negotiated various contracts with the U.S.-owned Central Romana sugar corporation. One contract specified that for a period of five years Morales "agreed to cut, haul and deliver sugar cane on about 700 acres of land" belonging to the estate. He received $1.50 per ton of delivered cane and should have grossed between $20,000 and $25,000.[26]

Sugar Politics

What was the attitude of the military government toward the large sugar companies? What role did military officials play in aiding the expansion of sugar cultivation? The available evidence is ambiguous. On the one hand, the policy statements of the officers highest in the military administration often displayed a marked animosity toward the sugar industry. On the other, the military government's actions in many cases strongly favored the sugar producers.

A similar ambivalence marked the attitude of sugar company managers. They encouraged the original intervention and, after the military government was in operation, they often applied to it for favors. But in the end, according to a knowledgeable contemporary observer, the corporations felt that the military authorities had "treated them badly" and that a Dominican government would have been more responsive to their wishes.[27] In particular, they resented the wary attitude of military officials toward foreign concessions and the failure of the marines to end the lengthy guerrilla war in the east, which was decidedly unfavorable to their interests.

The stated policy of military officials, taken separately from their actions, is quite clear. Military Governor Knapp wrote in August 1917 to the secretary of the navy concerning the need in the Dominican Republic for developmental capital, admonishing that it be used carefully so as not "to bring about a practical economic slavery of the Dominican people." And he noted the use of capital by the sugar corporations in particular: "I am far from convinced that the large business corporations that are in Santo Domingo engaged in agricultural affairs are of very great value to the Dominican people. They do give employment to a certain number but the large sugar estates import labor to a great extent to carry on their work. I would greatly prefer to see the Dominican people, and especially the poorer classes, brought to the point where they can work a small plot of land on their own account and leaving the fruits of their labors in Santo Domingo, than to see great companies come here into Santo Domingo and exploit the country, taking out of it immense sums in the form of their profits." Referring to sugar company officials and their lawyers, Knapp wrote a year later: "My impression . . . is that they thought [the military government's] principal duty was to further the interests of Americans here in their schemes, some of which need the closest supervision as they have not been conceived as far as we can judge with much consideration of the interest of the Dominican people."[28]

Military Governor Thomas Snowden also stressed his independence from the sugar companies on various occasions, although he was much less clear than Knapp on the economics of sugar capitalism, a fact which further confused his actions. In 1920, in reply to labor union criticism, he wrote: "It is believed to be true that at present the sugar industry is not dealing fairly with either laborers or consumers. The nation has a paramount proprietorship in the land and it is not equitable for foreigners to exploit the land for their own interest and to also exploit the nation."[29]

What could be more definite than the stated positions of these two men, whose word was virtual law in the republic between 1916 and mid 1921? Yet why were so many of the significant actions of the military government favorable to the sugar corporations when their interests were involved?

Momentarily leaving aside the difficult question of why, let us establish here the fact that the period of the military government was a fruitful one for the sugar interests. On many smaller questions, including the flow of braceros to the sugar estates, legislation concerning the working conditions of laborers, and the right of workers to unionize and strike, military officials favored the corporations, either by instituting positive measures or by failing to take action. On many larger issues, especially that of laws affecting the ability of the sugar companies to swallow up large portions of the country's arable land, the military government completely capitulated to foreign interests, ignoring those of the Dominican people. Yet there were a few exceptions. The military government's program of land taxation was a major setback for the sugar companies. And in 1921 military officials forced the sugar interests to take a $1.25 million loss, caused by the crash of the market in late 1920, on sugar which the same authorities had earlier commandeered from the growers at a bargain price.[30]

Why, then, did the contradiction exist between the military government's statements and most of its actions? The answer is paradoxical: military officials *were* acting in accord with *what they saw* as the interests of the Dominican people. Occupation planners, for example, decided that the land title situation was in need of reform and set out to create a program which would clear up the difficulties, believing that they were doing so in the interests of the Dominicans. That their program was favorable to the sugar corporations was not accidental, but it was nevertheless secondary in the minds of military officials. Similarly, the military government created the land tax in answer to what they saw as a need of the Dominican people, implementing the tax over the vehement protests of the sugar companies.

An important consideration, then, is *how* the military officials determined what was best for the Dominican people and, secondarily, *whom* they identified as the Dominican people. Unfortunately, a number of factors combined to hinder officials from perceiving the situation correctly (in terms of their stated goals) and thus prevented the transformation of their altruistic statements into beneficial policies.

What were these factors? On the practical level, there was a natural inclination for military officials to attempt to transfer programs and institutions which had been successful at home to their new environment, without recognizing that the essential differences between the two societies would ultimately make the transfer impossible. Philosophically, the higher officials of the military government were consciously or unconsciously believers in nineteenth-century liberal economics and capitalism, the principles of which, when translated into laws and policies, often favored only a few. Thus, military officials might oppose the sugar corporations on certain questions yet create policies which favored them. Military Governor Snowden, for example, believed that wages and working conditions in the sugar industry were unfair to the workers yet acted to prevent their correction by invoking laissez-faire principles against union activity: individuals, he contended, had the right to negotiate with their employers as equals but not to persuade others to engage in a strike.[31] Snowden was caught in the past. By the early twentieth century, capitalism itself had advanced beyond the conceptions of the nineteenth century, using concentrations of wealth and power to obviate the old liberal system and to victimize those who continued to believe in it.

Liberal, capitalist conceptions invoked the necessity of putting the resources of the Dominican Republic to work. With that in mind, the military government passed laws, such as that on land registration, which ultimately benefited wealthy and powerful individuals and corporations. Aggravating this and other predispositions of the military rulers was the fact that they lacked the training to solve many of the complex social and economic problems which confronted them. They little understood the negative implications of some of the projects created by their advisers and other interested parties.

Their inexperience also left them vulnerable to a variety of strong influences. Two of the most important of these were the precedents of past Dominican policy and the opinions of the elite, that "better class of Dominicans" with whom higher military officials had most of their dealings. Both past policy and elite opinion were favorable to increased foreign investment.[32] A third strong influence on military policymakers was that of the State Department and the Customs Receivership. Both of these agencies were particularly sensitive to the needs of U.S. business, much more so, it appears, than the Navy Department. The higher officials of the receivership, in particular, were sometimes intimately connected with large corporations operating in the republic. Fourth, landholding companies themselves were anxious to offer advice, particularly in favor of new land title legislation.[33]

Thus a combination of naïve predispositions, of inexperience, and of strong influences from interested outside sources led to the creation of policies which were in many cases contrary to the occupiers' original intentions. In no other area was the contradiction between policy intentions and policy implementation so great as in land legislation. And in no other area did an economic policy have such a baneful effect on the future lives of ordinary Dominicans. New laws of the military government greatly improved the sugar companies' ability to procure land for their expanding domains and thus assured that the dominance of a one-crop economy, already possessed of a firm foothold in 1916, would be unshakable after 1924. That a Dominican government would have wanted or would have been able to do differently is doubtful, considering the performance of Dominican administrations before and after the occupation. But that is not the issue, for the United States had usurped Dominican sovereignty.

Land Registration before 1916

The land title system of the Dominican Republic was an antiquated and confused remnant of the three-century colonial experience. Before 1916 several Dominican governments had addressed the issue, but their efforts generally failed to resolve the basic problem. Nevertheless the new laws, written in the interests of modernization, generally enhanced the position of the corporations over the traditional landholders.

Land titles originating in the colonial period were often troublesome, in part because they referred to trees, rivers, rocks, and other landmarks which had long ago disappeared or moved. Furthermore, old titles were often incomplete or imperfect, owing especially to the numerous transfers recorded on them. Some were lost. And the very manner in which titles were granted or passed on led to confusion, even when they were in perfect order. This was particularly so of the most common type of colonial titles, known variously as *pesos comuneros, pesos de posesión,* and *acciones.* The *pesos comuneros* originated from royal land grants, often circular plots. When land passed from one generation to the next, the descendants received shares, or *pesos,* of the whole title. The actual land, meanwhile, generally remained undivided for various economic and social reasons.[34]

Titles to property were therefore held collectively. Each share specified that its owner had a right to some percentage of the total circular property but did not specify which part of the circle belonged to whom. Theoretically, in order to divide the land for use, the titleholders would all have to meet and agree upon the division. In practice, however, an extralegal arrangement prevailed when land was divided. Time-honored usage determined the division, so that a particular family might occupy the same portion of the communal land year after year.

The system of *pesos comuneros* worked well enough as long as the use of the land was limited and as long as the system operated among the local inhabitants of an area, among a community of families who passed the land on to descendants or who sold or traded it to one another within the community. But problems arose with outsiders, especially those with business in mind. Entrepreneurs were unwilling to buy land and make improvements without knowing what specific part of a larger landholding they could legally call their own. Therefore, Dominicans who favored the economic modernization of the republic or who were involved in the expanding sugar sector of the economy increasingly saw the old system of land titles as an obsolete obstacle to economic expansion.[35]

In April 1911, mindful of "persons with capital available for investment in agriculture," legislators passed a law entitled the Ley sobre División de Terrenos Comuneros, which sought "the surveying, marking of boundaries, and division of the *terrenos comuneros.*" The law attempted to facilitate the division of communal land and to establish clear titles by allowing any coproprietor of such land to demand that it be surveyed and permanently divided by a court, each coproprietor receiving title to a specific piece of property.[36] It was the first law which attempted to regularize the procedure for dividing communal lands.

The impulse which led to the writing of the law on communal lands also brought into existence the Ley sobre Franquicias Agrarias

of June 1911. Although this law, which concerned government concessions to agricultural entrepreneurs, did not attempt to deal with
the land title situation, it also smoothed the way for foreign investors. The legislation conferred on modern agricultural enterprises a
long list of privileges which fostered their expansion.[37]

In May 1912 the Dominican Congress passed a more comprehensive land title law, the Ley sobre Inscripción de la Propiedad Territorial. The new law called for the registration of *all* rural land titles
within one year, preparatory to a cadastral survey of the republic. It
was a further attempt to regularize landholding and, in particular, to
stop the great proliferation of false land titles. As land values soared,
the fabrication of titles became a big business, especially for the
communal lands of the east where sugar cultivation was spreading.
And forgery was simple; so many records had been lost or destroyed
over the years that verification of documents was often impossible.[38]

The case of the Barahona Company, located in the southwestern
region of the republic, illustrates how entrepreneurs could use the
laws passed during 1911 and 1912 to their advantage. Organized in
1916, this New York–based corporation quickly created the second-
largest sugar estate in the country, claiming ownership of 49,400
acres by 1925. The estate's meteoric expansion was facilitated by
two factors: the purchase of a massive number of *pesos comuneros*
and the acquisition of extensive water rights, a necessity in the
largely arid Barahona region.[39]

By 1917 the company's titles to communal lands totaled 10 percent of the registered land in Barahona Province. Although it was of
"public notoriety" that many of these titles were false, having been
purchased from two men later indicted for forgery of titles, the company had hired the best lawyers in the country and continued to take
what it wanted. According to a 1918 to 1919 protest against the company's actions by small farmers, these outsiders were "taking advantage of the ignorance and poverty of the coowners and inhabitants of
the Neyba Valley who, for lack of unity and financial resources, cannot hire a good lawyer to defend their legal rights."[40]

Water rights presented a second problem. The Barahona Company had several times asked the military government, under the
Ley sobre Franquicias Agrarias, for the right to use a large portion of
the water of the Yaque del Sur River. To grant even half of the company's latest request, claimed the protesters, would ruin the many
small communities located along the river's banks, as water was already in short supply. More than ten thousand inhabitants of the region would have no choice but to become tenants of the estate.

The military government, prompted to investigate by the pro-

tests, promised to rebuff the company's extravagant claims for water, as it had done once before in 1917. But the investigation also
found that the company's actions were legal, if sometimes brusque,
under laws instituted by Dominican congresses and that the conflict
basically arose from the miserable land title situation. In that regard
the military government's hands were tied, claimed the investigators, noting that the laws gave "people with money an advantage
over those who had little or none." Significantly, the area's elite advised military officials to ignore the pleas of these small agriculturalists, believing that the Barahona Company's multimillion-
dollar investment would much improve the economy of the region.[41]

Land grabbing, it should be added, was not the exclusive prerogative of large corporations. A Mr. Descombes, apparently a foreigner residing in Sabana de la Mar in Samaná Province, is a case in
point. Using the 1911 Ley de Terrenos Comuneros, he attempted
with some success to force sixteen men and their families from their
land and homes, despite the fact that they were "hard-laboring men
. . . who have been working for years . . . on these lands."[42]

Thus the laws which the Dominican Congress passed in 1911
and 1912, insofar as the legislators intended them to correct the difficulties associated with the terrenos comuneros and land titles in
general, failed to achieve their goal. When ordinary citizens became
entangled in these laws, they were often victimized, either by unfair
execution of the laws or by their inability to hire lawyers and to
participate equally in the legal system. But more often the laws remained unimplemented. With the country embroiled in civil war
much of the time between 1911 and 1916, Dominican officials neglected many administrative tasks. Besides, peasant landowners
were little inclined to comply with the legal abstractions spun by
legislators in Santo Domingo. Had the peasants, for instance, known
about the 1912 registration law, which is problematical, they probably would not have rushed to register their titles—for they believed,
as a Dominican writer has noted, that "each time officials asked
them to bring their titles to a public office, it was for the purpose of
despoiling them of the documents." The response to the law of 1912
was so limited, in fact, that in late 1915 the Dominican Congress
contemplated passage of an entirely new statute to deal with the title situation. Despite reported support for the legislation by "the
best element both native and foreign," the only measure to emerge
was a prorogation of the original law, which extended the period for
inscription of titles to the end of 1916.[43] There the matter rested
when the military government took over.

The Land Legislation of the Military Government

U.S. officials had often expressed an interest in the matter of Dominican land titles. As early as 1911, U.S. Minister William Russell wrote the State Department to describe the problems associated with the title situation, and in 1914 Minister James Sullivan reported that "I have frequently discussed the question of introducing a proper system of land titles with members of the Dominican government, and have found them favorable to such a change." When Russell returned to the Santo Domingo legation in 1915, one of his instructions directed him to press for a cadastral survey, which would both clarify the title situation and pave the way for possible future taxation. And in November 1915 President Woodrow Wilson himself wrote to Dominican President Juan Jiménez, strongly suggesting that the Dominicans resolve the confusion concerning land titles in an "expeditious manner."[44]

The reason for the interest of U.S. officials is not difficult to ascertain. In the words of a former member of the diplomatic corps, the State Department believed that "the uncertainty about titles . . . was an obstacle to the country's economic development and especially to the expansion of the plantations of the large American sugar companies." Representatives and owners of the sugar estates agreed.[45]

In line with the military government's typically cautious approach to reform in the early days of the occupation, Executive Order No. 27, the first concerning land matters, simply extended the long-expired original period of inscription for the registration law of 1912. Extending the deadline did nothing, of course, to solve the problems which previous extensions had failed to solve. In September 1917, Minister Russell wrote to the State Department urging prompt new action on land surveys and registration, claiming that "it is not exaggeration to state that there are at present falsely manufactured titles to more land than is comprised in the area of the republic, and titles continue to be manufactured."[46] But military officials continued to move carefully and slowly, seeking the knowledge and services of experts in the fields of land tenure and taxation and deferring action until they had more information.

In the spring of 1918, the military government's tax expert, Fred R. Fairchild of Yale University, decided that "reform of the land system," especially "bringing order out of the chaos of land titles," was a necessary prerequisite to obtaining another of the occupiers' primary goals, that of financial reform, since the latter involved instituting taxation on land.[47] But the matters which these reforms would treat were so complex that it was 1920 before legislation appeared. In the meantime, authorities continued to postpone the final deadline for registration of land titles under the 1912 law until December 1919, when Executive Order No. 363 ordered a halt to all partitions begun or contemplated. The government's action caused considerable unrest, for it contained provisions blatantly favorable to the sugar companies and it ended or significantly curtailed the work of numerous persons, especially surveyors and notaries.[48]

Finally, on 11 July 1920, after a year and a half of labor on the legislation, the military government published the Ley de Registro de Tierras as Executive Order No. 511. The new law was a comprehensive attempt to reform all past laws on the subject of rural lands and titles, superseding both the 1911 Ley de Terrenos Comuneros and the 1912 Ley sobre Inscripción. The twin goals of the Ley de Registro were "to register without delay all lands located within the territory of the Dominican Republic" and to bring about "the demarcation, survey, and partition of the *terrenos comuneros.*"[49] To facilitate these matters, the law provided for a cadastral survey of the republic, a new system of land registration, and a new court, the Tribunal de Tierras, which would adjudicate cases involving land and administer the other aspects of the law.

The law required that all landowners register their titles with the Tribunal de Tierras, which would refuse to register any title which was not clear. Cases in which there was any question about ownership or boundaries went before the tribunal. The Tribunal de Tierras was also responsible for administering the cadastral survey, choosing which areas to survey first according to the "public interest." A new office of the national government, the Dirección General de Mensuras Catastrales, would carry out the actual surveys.[50]

How had the military government determined its new policy, and what was the effect? In 1917 the marine head of the Ministry of Justice and Public Instruction, Colonel Rufus H. Lane, began to study the land title situation, assisted by Francisco J. Peynado, the noted Dominican jurist and statesman, whose frequent legal services to the sugar companies left him well informed on these matters. Then in April 1919, with the groundwork completed, Military Governor Snowden appointed a board to prepare a concrete proposal. Although the matter under consideration was of vital importance to Dominicans, U.S. citizens comprised the entire six-member committee.[51]

Within several months the board had before it two concrete proposals regarding the *terrenos comuneros,* one by Francisco Peynado and the other by the receivership official, J. H. Edwards. Edwards

was hardly a disinterested party. Shortly after the committee had decided its course, he resigned to become president of a corporation
owning half a million acres of Dominican land. His proposal had the
backing of the entire committee save Colonel Lane, who found
Peynado's work "infinitely superior." His views ignored, Lane resigned from the board in disgust.[52]

Among those most interested in the proceedings were large
landholding companies. The legal representative of a number of the
largest sugar corporations, Frank H. Vedder, followed the board's de-
liberations carefully. Vedder vehemently objected to Peynado's proposal, even attacking Peynado personally, particularly because of a
provision to staff the new land court with members of the existing
Dominican judiciary. Instead Vedder wanted a new court, appointed
by the military government, whose members, like Vedder himself,
would be U.S. citizens. "To my mind," he noted, "it would be impossible to obtain Dominicans of the necessary conditions and qualifications for such a court, except possibly in a minority."[53] Obviously,
Vedder believed that his clients' fortunes would be more secure under his proposal. And his point of view prevailed. The military governor appointed two U.S. citizens and one Dominican to the new tribunal. The U.S. appointees had previously served with the colonial
administrations in the Philippines and Panama.[54]

The new system of land registration was that proposed by
J. H. Edwards. It was, in the words of Francisco Peynado, "for the
most part a literal copy of 'The Land Registration Act' of the Philippines," based on the Torrens system of land registration developed in
Australia. Peynado, after reviewing the new law, thought the system
good enough to introduce to the republic but noted that some of its
features were incongruent with other aspects of the Dominican legal
system and that the new law in some ways favored U.S. lawyers,
court officials, judges, and surveyors over their Dominican counterparts. Other specific articles of the law also worried him, especially
a provision which gave title to landholders after ten years' possession. All in all, he concluded, one had "to ponder the losses which
the landowners of this country, especially the poor campesinos,
could suffer under this system."[55]

Subsequent events confirmed Peynado's judgment. Basically,
the law was a suitable remedy for what had been a chaotic and, given
an expanding population and heavier land use, an increasingly untenable situation. But for many Dominicans the price of the solution
was a high one, since sugar companies and other land-extensive operations used the new law to assist them in adding thousands upon
thousands of acres to their properties. The new law did not always

protect the real owners and users of the land, noted the jurist Manuel Ruiz Tejada: "The displacements which occurred in the east—to the great discontent and damage of the injured—came about precisely after the passage of the Ley de Registro de Tierras and were a necessary consequence—albeit sad—of the need to execute the judgments of the Tribunal de Tierras."[56]

The difficulties of the law were not so much with its specific provisions as with the ways in which it functioned in the Dominican social milieu of 1920. The large sugar companies and other corporations and individuals, using a tiny part of their comparatively vast resources, could hire the best lawyers and engage in extensive litigation to use the new law to their fullest advantage, as they had used previous laws and as they would have used any law based on liberal, capitalist conceptions. Peasant landowners could hardly afford the cost of defending their own legal interests, and the military government provided no remedy for them.

If the 1920 law seriously failed some of the Dominican people, in a broad sense it did accomplish what its writers intended. Two leading authorities on Dominican land laws, jurists Alcibiades Albuquerque and Manuel Ruiz Tejada, agree that the law was a positive step toward solving a most difficult problem. In at least one respect, however, the implementation of the law failed to fulfill its writers' expectations. The law had established a program for universal cadastral surveys, which were essential to solve the land registration problem. But by 1922, owing to the financial difficulties of the military government, these surveys had ended except on lands belonging to wealthy agricultural interests. The sugar corporations, which wanted the surveying continued, paid $7,450 a month to keep the military administration's Office of Surveyors functioning and provided manual laborers to assist surveying teams on their lands. In districts where no private corporations were willing to foot the bills, the surveying stopped indefinitely.[57]

Thus economic circumstances considerably blunted the effect of the law's provisions for a cadastral survey. In 1923, the new Dominican provisional government compounded the difficulty when it amended the 1920 law, making voluntary, in most cases, the formerly compulsory nature of the survey process. As a result, the settlement of the land title situation dragged on for years—a tenth of the country remained unsurveyed in 1966.[58]

Critics of the Ley de Registro were often nationalists who saw their country's interests threatened. And some opposition arose purely because the law was imposed by a foreign power. But the nationalists also spoke for the otherwise voiceless peasant landowners, as Félix E. Mejía did when he argued that the new law "in some of its provisions made possible the veritable plundering of small-holders of *terrenos comuneros.*" Worse still, Mejía saw the law as part of a possible plan to enable the occupiers to pillage the republic, "to squeeze its natural riches as from a sponge, leaving only the remains to the Dominicans." Mejía and others also worried that this law and related ones might be another chapter in the long history of moves toward annexation.[59]

Some groups had more personal reasons for protest. Prominent among them were the republic's surveyors. The new statute, they complained through their national association, enlisted them as government employees while they carried out surveys for the Ley de Registro. This provision, as well as other "ridiculous and onerous conditions," would cause them to lose status.[60] One suspects also that they feared loss of more than status, for the chaotic world of land dealings had previously afforded many opportunities, legal and illegal, for personal enrichment. Surveying, noted one commentator, was "one of the most lucrative professions."[61]

The surveyors eventually threatened not to cooperate with the new law until some changes were made. Military Governor Snowden, never noted for his reasoned responses to opposition, wrathfully denounced them, threatening to call in foreign surveyors if there was "any strike or boycott." The surveyors quickly dropped their demands for everything except more money. This too officials refused to grant, probably because the surveyors' conditions of employment were already quite favorable, including a seven-hour workday and salaries up to $250 per month.[62]

The Land Tax

The second major element of the military government's land policy was the imposition of a land tax. The impost was important as a major new revenue source, as the republic's first attempt at direct taxation, and as a policy in sharp conflict with the economic interests of large landowners, including U.S.-owned sugar and timber corporations.

The military government's land tax represented ideas drawn from a variety of sources. Important among them were several Dominicans, including Francisco Peynado, as well as Fred Fairchild, whose 1918 study guided nearly all efforts at tax reform during the occupation. Relying heavily on Fairchild's ideas, military officials worked nearly a year before publishing the Ley de Impuesto sobre la

Propiedad on 10 April 1919. The preamble of the law stated its writers' purposes, which were to provide municipalities with a new source of revenue to replace taxes which the military government was gradually abolishing and to reduce the taxes paid by the poor by placing "the burden of taxes upon those best able to bear them and upon those who reap the greatest benefits from the national wealth."[63]

The new tax, an annual one, was first due on 31 July 1919. The rate ranged from .5 percent on the value of land not exceeding 2,000 tareas (6.435 tareas = 1 acre) to 2 percent on land exceeding 10,000 tareas, while the rate on permanent improvements was .25 percent. Communal lands fell under special provisions which the law's writers hoped would force their survey and division. Property owners assessed their taxes, subject to review by the government; violators of the law incurred fines or, in extreme cases, seizure of their land. The obvious intent of a tax based solely on size was to force landowners to make their land productive or to sell it to someone who would. Military officials claimed privately that, if one took the income of a property into account as well as its size and value, the effective rate of taxation could vary from 20 percent for 10,000 unused tareas to 4 percent for 10,000 tareas of sugarcane.[64]

"The imposition of the land tax is a most radical measure," reported U.S. Minister Russell, "and no former Dominican party in control would have dared to undertake it." Although large landowners would complain, he noted, "the Dominicans at large, that is the poorer classes, will not suffer . . . , and if the measure can be carried through without much general opposition it will be a most important reform over existing conditions."[65]

The owners of the large sugar estates were among the first to protest the new law. Representatives of the sugar companies and other landholding corporations, the largest number of which were North American, banded together in the Sugar Association of Santo Domingo. They presented a petition to the military governor even before the first taxes were due, protesting the graded taxation, "double taxation," and the alleged unequal and discriminatory taxation on communal lands. The military government stood its ground, however, and refused to modify the law until it had been tried. The refusal prompted the Sugar Association and its spokesman, lawyer Frank Vedder, to send a protest to the Navy Department in Washington.[66]

The Sugar Association, however, found the military government fully supported in Washington. Secretary of the Navy Josephus Daniels informed Military Governor Snowden that he was pleased with the land tax, that the military government could "be sure that the American-owned sugar estates will not be successful . . . in the matter of evading taxation," and that he had already elicited support for his views in the State Department.[67]

By late 1919 the military government could report that the only resistance to the tax, by "certain wealthy foreign sugar companies," had ended and that all was "proceeding without friction."[68] Then, having stood their ground, military officials retreated from their position and in September 1920 issued Executive Order No. 545, which reduced the tax and discarded the graduated rate based on size. The effect for large holdings was to lower the rate of taxation from 2 percent to .5 percent. The move might be construed as a sell-out to the sugar interests, except that the revised legislation doubled taxes on improvements, of which the sugar companies had millions of dollars' worth. What brought the change about is not clear, but at least some disinterested outsiders, such as Fairchild, had counseled that a reduction would be a positive step. The sugar companies, having failed to obtain relief on other grievances, continued thereafter to seek changes in the law. In 1923 they approached the new Dominican provisional government, hoping to obtain a 50 percent reduction in their taxes and changes of other aspects of the law which they had previously found unfavorable.[69] The sugar interests were unsuccessful.

In the end, several forces would combine to destroy the land tax, but the sugar corporations would not figure prominently among them. Rather, the agents were depression and nationalism. When the depression began in late 1920, propertied citizens turned almost immediately to the still new tax as a way to alleviate their problems, suggesting its further reduction or suspension. When the military government refused, Dominican nationalists, who saw the tax as the illegitimate offspring of an illegal government, took it up as a symbol around which to rally opposition to the occupation. Landowners needed little encouragement to avoid payment of their taxes, enabling the nationalist movement to build an effective protest.[70]

The tax boycott, combined with other economic problems, soon had the military government in desperate financial straits. After pursuing the time-consuming and immensely unpopular path of seizing and auctioning off the lands of some tax resisters, military officials tried a new tack—which was to force Dominicans to pay the tax by making the school system totally dependent on it. Even this spiteful measure failed, however, and the property tax remained a casualty of the nationalist opposition. Ironically, the sugar companies and other foreign corporations kept paying and thus bore by far the greatest burden of the tax.[71]

The boycott had fatally crippled the land tax, however. After 1921 the new system lost its effectiveness, and it outlived the occupation by only a few years.[72] Nevertheless, the land tax is a good example of a case in which the military government pursued a policy independent of the powerful U.S.-based corporations which operated in the republic, doing so in the interests of the Dominican people. Military officials deserve credit for their effort, albeit futile, to use the land tax to implement a progressive social and political philosophy.

Other Policies Affecting Land

The military government promulgated other laws which affected land and land use, although none of them was as important as the 1919 Ley de Impuesto sobre la Propiedad or the 1920 Ley de Registro de Tierras. They are significant, however, since they represent an effort to create a comprehensive policy on land use.

Public lands were the object of various legislative efforts. At first the military government focused on retrieving state lands and other property which had been usurped or otherwise obtained illegally. An investigation yielded several instances in which socially prominent families or groups had usurped state lands, which the military authorities then confiscated for the government. The most famous case involved not only land but a public building which for many years had been used by an elite Masonic lodge.[73]

In several other laws, the military government anticipated the creation of a comprehensive land policy. In May 1919, military officials suspended the 1905 Ley sobre Concesión de Terrenos del Estado (Law Concerning the Granting of State Lands) until "another more adequate law can be prepared and promulgated" and repealed the 1911 Ley sobre Franquicias Agrarias, one of the laws which had encouraged the takeover of Dominican lands by foreign corporations. The immense importance of the latter was considerably reduced because it provided that rights acquired before May 1919 would not be impaired. But the comprehensive land policy, for unknown reasons, never materialized. Only the July 1919 Ley sobre Conservación y Distribución de Aguas en Regiones Aridas (Law Concerning the Conservation and Distribution of Waters in Arid Regions), which established that such waters were public property subject to government control and laid down rules to assure their fair distribution, and the December 1919 Ley Forestal, which created a forestry service, indicated the direction in which military planners were heading.[74]

The military government's legislative program concerning land and land use is significant because of its close relationship with the future economic and social history of the Dominican Republic. But it is also important as a key to understanding the program of the occupation in general. Its complex and contradictory nature is typical of that of the entire intervention, for it represents the outcome of the efforts of a government which was willing but unprepared to accomplish the job which it faced. It reveals clearly the mixture of naïve good intentions, of conflicting needs and interests, and of manipulation from powerful outside sources. And it shows the difficulty that an interventionist foreign power will always have in trying to produce changes, however useful or necessary, in another society.

5

Guerrilla War in the East: Origins

From 1917 to 1922, the peasants of the eastern region of the Dominican Republic successfully waged a guerrilla war against the forces of the U.S. military government. This conflict stands, along with the campaign against Augusto César Sandino in Nicaragua in the later 1920s, as the major military involvement of the United States in Latin America in the twentieth century. And it deserves a place in the series of guerrilla wars which the United States has fought, from the Philippines to Vietnam. Yet the record of the Dominican conflict has largely been buried or lost.[1]

The guerrilla struggle was significant. For five and a half years the marines failed to control most of the eastern half of the republic. Ranged against them at various times were eight to twelve guerrilla leaders who could enlist up to six hundred regular fighters and who could count on the support of numerous part-time guerrillas, as well as on the aid and sympathy of the general population. The guerrillas, using their environment and experience to advantage, fought a marine force which possessed superior equipment and training. The fighting led to a stalemate, and in 1922 the guerrillas agreed to a negotiated conditional surrender. It was a capitulation at least partially predicated on the then impending withdrawal of U.S. forces from the republic.

This chapter, based primarily on the records of the U.S. military government, explores two basic questions. Who were the guerrillas? And what motivated them to fight? The answers have come especially from the examination of two factors: first, the nature of eastern Dominican society, particularly the traditional political system and the new economic influences at work in the region, which undermined long-established patterns of life; second, the marines' conduct of the antiguerrilla war and their treatment of Dominicans.[2]

The Roots of the Guerrilla War

When the military government sent marines into the east in early 1917, they encountered a still thriving vestige of nineteenth-century politics, the caudillo system. This irregular type of rule, which bestowed power and authority upon men who could combine military skills, economic resources, personal strength, charisma, friendship, family ties, and the ability to manipulate followers, had deep roots in Dominican history. During the nineteenth century, while the republic's political institutions were developing, Dominicans were often at war, fighting the Spanish, French, Haitians, or each other. The result was a society heavily influenced by caudillos, who soon came to dominate the nation's political life. Despite later reform efforts, the caudillo system persisted into the twentieth century, with a few regional caudillos such as the northwesterner Desiderio Arias assuming great national political importance at the time of the intervention.[3]

The east had not boasted a regional leader of Arias' stature since the days of President Pedro Santana in the mid nineteenth century, but caudillo politics nevertheless continued to play a prominent part in eastern life in 1916. In fact, the east offered a particularly secure environment for this tradition because meager improvements in transportation and communication had hardly challenged the historic isolation and near independence of most of the region. A kind of dual government existed. Alongside of the highly centralized de jure structure of provinces, communes, and sections, with a civil governor and other officials appointed by the national government, there was a de facto power structure dominated by popular local leaders, the caudillos.

A relationship existed between the two structures, because national political factions bid for and depended on the support of local and regional leaders. Once a faction gained control of the central government of Santo Domingo, it could exercise its power in the east only when the area's popular leaders, under specified conditions, agreed to cooperate with its officials. As a consequence, national administrations actively sought the allegiance of local and regional caudillos, often with simple cash payoffs, government concessions or franchises, or appointments to public positions, such as the military command of a province or the garrison of a town or simply a minor position with the rural police.[4] If a government could not obtain the support of an important regional figure, it had to concede him virtual autonomy in his own territory. Alternatively, it had to back a rival caudillo with arms and money in an attempt to defeat him.

The central government could not rely on its own military forces to support its authority against the caudillos. The Dominican army was small and so poorly trained, commanded, equipped, and paid that it provided little threat to anyone except the law-abiding and defenseless members of the lower class who fell afoul of its petty extortions and graft. In any case, the caudillos often controlled the army. As Sumner Welles noted, "the military branch of the Dominican Government was inevitably the means through which, by corruption or promise of corruption, revolutions were engineered." Not being able to count on this "meager Dominican soldiery," Military Governor Harry Lee later wrote, the central government had shown a "chronic attitude of passivity and tolerance" toward the caudillos.[5]

Local military chieftains, employed with the government or not, might rebel at any time. In mid 1915, for example, a fairly serious uprising occurred in the east as part of the general restiveness against the administration of President Juan Jiménez. Though some casualties had resulted, the national government allegedly pacified the rebels and their followers by promising road construction contracts and appointments to the rural police, as well as by providing safe-conducts to Puerto Rico for the leaders. Authorities continued their policy of accommodation when, a few months later, they brought another eastern caudillo to the capital and "in order to quiet him . . . assigned to him a salary of $150 a month for doing nothing."[6]

The east's population accommodated itself to the caudillo system. Although the influence of these traditional leaders was ultimately felt in every sector of society because of their military strength, it fell most heavily on rural areas and very small towns. In that milieu no cohesive class or caste barriers frustrated the acceptance of the caudillo, who was most often a poor countryman by birth and upbringing. The tradition-oriented inhabitants admired, feared, and respected him as an authority, and from among these country dwellers he recruited his followers. The only potential countervailing force in the countryside was that based on wealth. But the interests of the few leading landowning families and the sugar corporations were no more able to control the caudillos than was the central government. Instead, they manipulated the caudillo system to protect their own interests, paying one of the stronger local leaders to guard their crops and property.[7]

In most of the east's large towns, all closely related to the extensive rural areas which surrounded them, the personal influence of the caudillos was quite strong, at least among the poorer citizens. Even the elite of such towns as El Seibo, Hato Mayor, and Higüey, composed of landowners, a few professionals, and the more prosperous merchants, were forced by political realities to deal with the caudillos, although the elite set themselves apart socially and in other ways. Their financial interests were somewhat adversely affected by the caudillo system, for the warfare with which it was often associated caused economic declines, reduced business and professional incomes, and provided justification for forced levies against elite wealth and property. Elite political interests were also in conflict with the system. Inasmuch as the members of the upper stratum furnished personnel for the higher offices of the de jure governmental structure, they were tied to the national political system rather than to the regionalism of the caudillos. But their political survival was ultimately related to the goodwill of the traditional rural leaders.[8]

Only in the city of San Pedro de Macorís, the third-largest in the republic by 1916, did these traditional rural leaders have minimal influence. The city's obvious sources of independent strength lay in its size, approximately twelve thousand people, in its wealth, and in the international ties which resulted from its being headquarters for the republic's sugar production and export. Perhaps even more important was the process of urbanization, which weakened ties with the rural area surrounding the city (except for the neighboring sugar estates) and resulted in a separate social structure in which the rural chieftains had no place and thus no power. San Pedro de Macorís' leading citizens, though they might ally themselves with the caudillos for political ends, could bargain from a somewhat more equal position than other citizens of the east.

Thus, local and regional caudillos effectively held power and maintained or broke the peace in most of the eastern region. When the military government confronted this situation in late 1916, it both failed to understand it and completely misjudged its strength. Military officials had learned during 1916 that some people in Macorís, as well as the sugar companies, strongly opposed the dispatch of marines to the east. But the military authorities decided to ignore this opposition after they discovered that "the sugar estates were practically paying blackmail to bad characters to keep them from looting and burning, a part of the understanding being apparently that they themselves would keep other bad characters off."[9]

Military officials saw this situation as anarchic and criminal and were determined to put an end to it. But, when they sent in troops to enforce the authority of the central government, the local and regional leaders, whose prestige and power derived from the threatened system, went to war. As they had done many times before, the caudillos determined to force the central government to deal with them.[10]

In the caudillo system, then, lie the roots of the guerrilla war which desolated the east for over five years. But an important question remains. If the caudillo system existed in other parts of the republic, as it did, why should guerrilla war develop only in the east? The answer seems to be that, in other areas of the country, various factors thwarted or redirected the energies which might have sustained revolt.[11]

First, the east, more than other isolated areas of the country, had wealth and population in conjunction with a favorable topography. Thus, food, money, and other supplies were readily available to the insurgents. And the sizable though by no means dense population of the east provided the guerrillas with recruits, shelter, and, most important, an extensive system of intelligence.

More important, the east's rapidly changing social and economic structure distinguished it from other regions. The expansion of the sugar latifundios had had a severe impact on a significant portion of the eastern population. Independent peasants whose families had lived in the region for generations, farming *conucos* (garden-size plots), suddenly found themselves pushed from the land, forced to leave the area or to become part of the seasonally employed rural proletariat.

The condition of the uprooted Dominican peasantry corresponds closely to that which Eric Hobsbawm has found most favorable to social banditry. Upsurges of this phenomenon, he writes, often "reflect the disruption of an entire society, the rise of new classes and social structures, the resistance of entire communities or peoples against the destruction of its way of life." The aptness of Hobsbawm's analysis in a Latin American context has also been noted by Louis Pérez, whose research on social banditry in early twentieth-century Cuba reveals a situation nearly identical to that of the eastern Dominican Republic.[12]

The east's caudillo leaders could count on a substantial number of displaced and bitter peasants and many others who, similarly threatened, sympathized with them. And this bitterness was easily directed toward North Americans, whose corporations were among the chief beneficiaries of the land acquisitions. A perceptive marine officer noted in 1917 that "the principal thing the provincial peasants have been taught about the foreigner is that he is trying to deprive the peasant of his land and . . . to impose new and undesirable forms of living. So it is easy for the bandit [as the marines preferred to call the guerrillas] to convince the peasant that the bandits' (assuming the character of revolutionists against [a] foreign government) and the peasants' interests are the same and that the peasant should help."[13]

Many of the men who fought with the caudillo-led bands were from the sugar *bateys,* the company-owned villages in which the workers lived. As James McLean, a marine officer who for a time commanded the Guardia Nacional in the east, noted unsympathetically in 1919, the guerrilla ranks included "a number of voluntary recruits from the riff-raff among the unemployed who were hanging around the sugar estates." Fighting alongside the guerrillas at least provided a livelihood for the landless and unemployed worker, if not for his family, and it was a convenient way to even a score with oppressors who were protected by the law. After the negotiated surrender of guerrillas in 1922, military officials found a significant percentage to be men who had recently lost their land. Realizing the relationship of landlessness and unemployment to the guerrilla war, the military government implored the sugar companies to increase "steady employment" during 1922 and to open up more land for *conucos,* so that the sugar work force could maintain itself during the months after the harvest. "Any lack of employment," stated the military governor, "will have the most disastrous results in the increase in banditry."[14]

Marine documents indicate that the insurgents generally fought close to home. The greatest number came from the sugar-growing heartland of the east, an expanse centering on Hato Mayor and El Seibo and running south to the coast. Others came from adjacent areas—from the north coast near Sabana de la Mar, from the east in the vicinity of Higüey, and from the west around Monte Plata and Bayaguana. Most of the peasant partisans, both leaders and followers, were Dominicans. Despite the presence in the eastern cane fields and the company-owned *bateys* of many imported laborers from Haiti and the British Caribbean, only a few Haitians and virtually no British West Indians were present in the guerrilla ranks.[15]

Guerrilla Political Motivations

Two of the most important questions about the guerrilla war concern the political nature of the movement. Were the insurgents politically conscious? If so, at what level? Many bits of evidence indicate that all the guerrillas had at least inchoate political motives: they resented the changes in their lives which resulted from the loss of their land to the large corporations; they resented being unemployed and poor; and they resented the fear and insecurity brought into their daily existence by the aggressive and arbitrary acts of the occupying marines. Some guerrillas, moreover, were conscious that these issues were important to their struggle. They would, for instance, recruit followers by informing peasant smallholders that the North American corporations were planning to take over their land.[16] Going one step further, various guerrilla leaders and groups openly identified themselves as political revolutionaries and claimed regional or national goals. They also conducted themselves, on some occasions, as an irregular government, exacting taxes, enforcing popular law, and dispensing justice.

This is not to say, however, that purely political considerations motivated all guerrillas. As in most movements of this kind, both leaders and followers were sometimes moved by personal rather than political factors. Intergroup rivalries at times led guerrilla bands to fight one another; such rivalries were survivals of the caudillos' preintervention competition for personal power and influence. Vicente Evangelista, for example, allegedly imprisoned a rival guerrilla leader and turned him in to the marines in 1917.[17] In addition, small groups of actual bandits took advantage of the social turmoil brought on by the guerrilla war, and even the organized guerrillas sometimes committed criminal acts against fellow Dominicans.

Nevertheless, evidence surfaced regularly during the entire course of the war which revealed the political consciousness of the insurgents. In 1918, for instance, a group of marines was scouting near Las Pajas, guided by a local official, the second alcalde of the section. An unidentified group of insurgents surrounded the marines and a battle began. At one point, the alcalde called out, taunting the guerrillas for being *gavilleros*, the Dominican word for rural bandit. Back came numerous cries to the effect that "we are not *gavilleros*; we are revolutionists!"[18]

During and after 1919, one of the most prominent groups operating in San Pedro de Macorís and eastern Santo Domingo provinces was that led by Eustacio "Bullito" Reyes. These guerrillas called their troop La Revolución, and when seizing money, arms, or other supplies from their victims they identified themselves as such.[19] And in 1920, on the eastern edge of the zone of hostilities, between La Romana and Higüey, an unidentified guerrilla unit accosted a mail carrier and sent him and his mail unmolested back to Higüey with a letter carefully explaining that the guerrillas were revolutionaries, not killers. A marine report noted that this and similar incidents indicated that the "bandits" were "trying to pose as revolutionists" in order to "gain assistance and recruit for their bands."[20]

By far the most important partisan leader was "General" Ramón Natera, who campaigned with large groups between 1918 and 1922. In 1921, Natera devised an obviously nationalistic operation which forced the military government to recognize the political motivations of the guerrillas. In the fall of that year, Natera and his men abducted the British manager of the La Angelina sugar estate. They released him unharmed after two days, when he agreed to Natera's demand that he and the other estate managers make known to the U.S. government the political and patriotic goal of the guerrillas— that the United States should terminate its occupation of the Dominican Republic.[21]

Corroborating the guerrillas' direct statements is evidence which shows that they saw themselves as a kind of government. In January 1922, for example, marines discovered the burial site of four men. The epitaph on a board above the grave read: "Emilio Gil, Miguel de León, Reimundo Ramos, Juan Moraldo: shot for having robbed the store Margarita, December 22, 1921, Ramón Natera"; and in three places the board had the inscription "General Ramón Natera," imprinted with the rubber stamp which Natera used in his correspondence. The marine report on this incident noted "that Ramón Natera purports to be a ruler in the section of the woods north of La Campiña and that he undertakes to punish raids made upon the cane field bodegas when the raids are not made under his direction and control." This system of justice applied equally within insurgent ranks. During a raid on a sugar estate bodega in early 1921, the guerrillas executed one of their troop on the spot for a violation of discipline.[22] Departure from the guerrillas' code of ethics compromised their all-important relationship with other Dominicans.

Evidence indicates that the guerrillas regarded their seizures of money and property as a kind of taxation, as material requisitioned for a political movement. They "look upon themselves as heroes, and the food and clothing which they steal as prerogatives of their position," wrote an incredulous marine lieutenant. In a similar vein, a marine officer reported in late 1920 that a wealthy farmer living near Higüey had been "fined" one hundred dollars by the guerrillas.[23]

Occasionally, marine reports suggest that the guerrillas had some connection with the national political structure and with the bourgeois party system. But no national politician was ever directly implicated in the guerrilla activity, despite numerous investigations by the military government.[24]

Other Guerrilla Motivations

There can be little doubt that personal factors provided at least as much motivation for many guerrillas as did patriotic or politico-economic considerations. And by far the most important of these personal factors was that of hatred and fear of the marines and the marine-controlled Guardia Nacional Dominicana. The marines, as they fought to exert U.S. control over the eastern Dominican Republic, frightened, insulted, abused, oppressed, injured, and even killed hundreds of Dominicans, combatants and noncombatants alike, who lived and worked in the area of hostilities. No more effective agent existed for the guerrilla cause.

These abuses ranged from major atrocities to minor, if infuriating, rudeness. If cases such as that of a marine captain who allegedly machine-gunned to death as "bandits" some thirty peasants working in a cane field were exceptional, other incidents such as that involving a group of armed marines who invaded a party at a social club in El Seibo and drank up the champagne were so common that many probably went unrecorded.[25] Also common and often recorded, but only occasionally punished, were serious crimes such as the well-documented case of Altagracia de la Rosa. As this teenage peasant prepared dinner one evening in December 1920, four armed marines entered her house in Ramón Santana, raped her, and then held her and her mother prisoner for ten days. No charges were brought against the marines involved.[26]

A variety of factors underlay the friction between the marines and the inhabitants in the east. To begin with, the Dominican peasants feared the marines because they were outsiders. In peasant eyes, the invaders had an unfamiliar physical appearance, they dressed queerly, they spoke an unintelligible language, and they practiced unfamiliar customs. Besides, the marines were armed and many of them were brusque, discourteous by Dominican standards, and not a few were abusive.[27]

The marines arrived in the Dominican Republic completely unprepared for the experience. Most enlisted men had little education; neither officers nor enlisted men knew anything about Dominican culture; and few could speak Spanish.[28] Affected by the jingoistic nationalism prevalent in the early twentieth-century United States, many North Americans possessed a patronizing attitude of superiority, the belief that they had taken up what Military Governor Thomas Snowden referred to as "the white man's burden; the duty of the big brother."[29] Such attitudes flourished in the impoverished, exploited, and underdeveloped Dominican Republic.

More important than ignorance or chauvinistic nationalism was the deeply ingrained antiblack racism of most marine officers and men. North American racism found a fertile soil in the Dominican Republic, "a country whose people," Military Governor Harry Knapp noted, "are almost all touched with the tarbrush." The marines' prejudice caused them to look down upon Dominicans generally, but the problem became even worse among the peasants of the east, poor and darker-skinned than many other citizens of the republic. Furthermore, the marines were accustomed to patterns of white superiority and black subservience in both the northern and the southern United States, a fact which in the Dominican Republic led to marine abuse and Dominican bitterness.[30]

Race was a potential irritant in any encounter between Dominicans and marines. Several North Americans living in Santo Domingo reported that marines commonly referred to Dominicans as "spigs" and "niggers," a habit also noted by visitors. When a writer accused marine officers and men of using the terms "spig" and "spik," Military Governor Knapp came to their defense, questioned whether officers would do so, and denied that the enlisted men's use of this "slang" caused bad feelings among Dominicans.[31]

A typical incident occurred on the streets of San Pedro de Macorís. An offended black artisan reported, probably in cleaned-up language, that when he and a marine corporal accidentally brushed each other in passing on the sidewalk, the corporal whirled around and yelled, "Look here, you damned negro! Don't you know that no damned negroes are supposed to let their body touch the body of any marines?! And that they are always to give them way in the street!" The marine then assaulted the man. The victim, an English-speaking immigrant, fully understood and reported the encounter. The provost marshal of San Pedro de Macorís essentially refused to investigate the matter, and it was dropped.[32]

In another instance of abuse, one which involved the killing of several men, all testimony against the marine defendant was discounted by the marine officer in charge of the investigation because of "the unreliability of the Dominican as a witness under oath . . . and . . . the hopelessness of finding any Dominican who can differentiate between what he has seen and he has heard." The charges in the case, the investigator argued, coming from "an individual of different race . . . who has no conception of honor as we understand it," would best be dropped. Because of "the wide gulf separating the white from the negro race," because of the basic "difference in psychology," the officer added, the Dominican "race has a totally different conception of right and wrong from that held by the white race." Finally, the marine officer in charge of handling the case suggested prosecuting the complainant, in order to maintain "the prestige of the white race."[33]

The conduct of the guerrilla war itself greatly frustrated the marines, at times leading to abuse of Dominicans. The North Americans were not prepared to fight a guerrilla war. They found themselves in often futile pursuit of an elusive enemy, repeatedly fell into ambushes and other tactical situations of the guerrillas' choosing, and were unable to establish permanent control over any area. Even when they began to understand the guerrillas' style of warfare, the marines still suffered a severe handicap: they were strangers in an environment in which the guerrillas had lived all their lives. And, unlike the marines, the guerrillas blended into that environment perfectly, making it difficult for the North Americans to distinguish guerrillas from *pacíficos* (as the noncombatants were called).[34]

Gradually the pressures of war made the guerrillas and the *pacíficos* less and less distinguishable. As the war dragged on, women and sometimes whole families joined the insurgent bands, living with the men in semipermanent camps. Among the *pacíficos*, the increased tempo of war produced a growing number of refugees, particularly peasants fleeing the aggressive marine patrols which scoured the eastern countryside. While some peasants fled to nearby towns, others responded by secreting themselves and their families, moving deeper into the east's backcountry. During 1918, marines began to discover peasant homes, sometimes even small villages, hidden in the forest amid food-producing *conucos*. The dwellers usually fled at the marines' approach, but evidence left behind, such as a child's primer, told clearly who they were. The marines showed a strong tendency to identify any house found in the forest as a "bandit house," any *conuco* as a "bandit *conuco*," and any families as "bandit families."[35] And they commonly burned these homes and their contents. Although the marine command attempted to stop this practice on the grounds that such homes would serve as gathering places where patrols might easily locate insurgents in the future, the burning persisted.[36]

When the marines arrived at one of the rural hideaways in time to witness the flight of the inhabitants, they fired at them, even though most were unarmed. "People who are not bandits do not flee at the approach of marines," noted one officer.[37] In a typical incident in 1918, a marine detachment located two peasant homes north of Hato Mayor, at the foot of the Manchado Hills. "There were two bandit houses," wrote Sergeant Morris Stout, Jr., "and I would say, four men, four women and some children occupied same." When the families fled the approaching intruders by climbing a steep hill next to the houses, the marines "formed a skirmish line and opened fire, but all got away except one woman and child and one horse and saddle." This particular incident brought an admonition from marine headquarters in Santo Domingo to "exercise extreme caution in firing on fleeing parties which contain women and children." But a 1919 communication, not five months later, revealed that a marine raid had severely wounded three of the four children of one "bandit."[38]

More "bandits" resulted from such marine actions. Olivorio Carela, a follower of the guerrilla leader Bullito Reyes, testified that he joined the guerrillas when "American forces had fired at his house and he had run away to take refuge." Another guerrilla, Ramón Batía, said in an interview that, after a marine captain had threatened his life, he believed that "his only remaining option was to flee into the hills." There he joined the guerrilla leader Vicente Evangelista and later formed his own group.[39]

As the war progressed, the marines began to discover that in fact no clear line divided the guerrillas from the *pacíficos*. Many guerrillas fought seasonally or, more commonly, operated year-round on a part-time basis. A peasant tilling a field might be behind a rifle thirty minutes later, ambushing a marine patrol. Moreover, a large number of rural inhabitants belonged to an informal fifth column of guerrilla sympathizers. As the marines began to grasp the situation, they came to treat everyone as the enemy.

It was simply not safe to be in areas where the marines were actively pursuing guerrillas. Numerous incidents occurred in which people who could not or would not reveal information concerning the guerrillas were beaten, tortured, and killed or, if they were more fortunate, imprisoned. A peasant might also be the object of gratuitous violence by the marines, such as rape or the destruction of a home or other property. Ever present was the danger of being attacked as a suspected guerrilla.[40] One might also be robbed by individuals or groups who used the guerrilla war as a cover for criminal behavior. As a result of all these circumstances, the whole central area of the east became, in the words of a marine commander, "a scene of desolation and long abandoned homes . . . a sad and pitiful spectacle."[41]

The *pacíficos* were not the only victims of marine abuse. The guerrillas themselves sometimes suffered brutal treatment, torture, and even death while captives of the marines. In one 1918 incident, a marine lieutenant murdered eleven jailed followers of Ramón Natera. He explained that he became angry after having heard that a friend of his, a marine captain, had been killed in an encounter with guerrillas.[42] One of the more common methods of eliminating guerrilla prisoners was to shoot and kill them while they "attempted to escape." In 1919, after two and a half years of such incidents, marine authorities in Santo Domingo cautioned marines in the field to secure prisoners more carefully, since "there is always suspicion produced by reports of this character that the prisoner was given an opportunity to escape so that he might be killed." Nevertheless, such reports continued.[43]

In time, nearly the entire population of some eastern areas was involved in the war. The marines faced not only full-time guerrillas in the countryside but those who had stayed behind in towns and villages. These rural centers became hotbeds of guerrilla activity, serving as centers for intelligence, for the gathering of money and supplies, and for recruitment. Many of the "so called bandits or gavilleros have relatives in all the outlying towns and it is understood that they are frequently visited by the gavilleros," noted one marine report. "Certain towns such as Jagual, Los Llanos and to a certain extent, Hato Mayor, are notorious headquarters of bandits," commented another.[44]

Large numbers of guerrillas also came from the sugar estates to the south. In periods of guerrilla inactivity, a marine lieutenant surmised, many of them "can be found in the southern district near the [sugar workers' villages] and living in the houses of the sugar cane workers. Some of them may even be working the sugar mills." In any case, he continued, "it is a certainty that they are being supplied with rum, clothes and all sorts of supplies by their friends around the mills."[45]

A Dominican who watched the events in the east unfold described the effects of the marine presence quite clearly: "The gavillerismo [rural unrest] increased with the occupation, or was created by it, . . . because of the increasing danger and difficulty of living in those districts. . . . When someone . . . was killed, his brothers joined the gavilleros, to get revenge on the marines . . . Some joined the ranks inspired by patriotism, but most of them joined the ranks inspired by hate, fear, or revenge."[46]

Efforts to Eliminate Marine Abuse

Higher officials of the military government soon became aware of the developing pattern of marine abuse in the east and took some corrective action. There were orders banning certain practices, as well as admonitions and prosecutions of marines whose conduct was obviously questionable. But the remedies were frequently weak and ineffective, either because of lack of enforcement or because of the difficulty of controlling the hour-to-hour conduct of units in the field. Also, the marines' court system was often a mockery. Furthermore, many officials devised rationalizations which enabled them to ignore much of the evidence which steadily accumulated during the occupation.

Military officials did make efforts to get Dominicans to come forward with their charges, but few chose to do so.[47] Many who had experienced or witnessed the marines' system of justice, based on provost courts, believed that to bring charges was useless and possibly dangerous, since those who did so were sometimes jailed, fined, harassed, or physically harmed. Otto Schoenrich, a North American writer of moderate opinions who was well acquainted with the Dominican Republic and the occupation, wrote that "the provost courts have gained the reputation of being unjust, oppressive and cruel, and seem to delight in excessive sentences. These provost courts, with their arbitrary and overbearing methods, their refusal to permit accused persons to be defended by counsel, and their foreign judges, foreign language and foreign procedure, are galling to the Dominicans, who regard them with aversion and terror."[48]

Military records indicate that the marine investigating officers and courts of justice deserved their poor reputation. Investigating officials in general showed themselves unsympathetic to the views of Dominican complainants, often accepting the word of North Americans over that of a Dominican as a matter of course. Like the officers in charge of preliminary investigations, the military tribunals were notoriously biased in favor of marine defendants. Prosecutions of offending marines were often halfhearted, and sentences—if any— were light, especially when the defendant was an officer. One Dominican observer commented: "When an American officer has committed a crime, the effort of his superiors is to hide it, to prove the innocence of the criminal, believing that to admit the truth would tarnish the honor of the American forces."[49] On the other hand, the court system was often prejudiced and occasionally vindictive against Dominican plaintiffs. And Dominican defendants could expect the worst. Clearly, the marines viewed the court system as a weapon to be used against the guerrillas and their supporters.

The 1920 case of Pelegrín Castillo typified the misuse of the judicial system. This man, a lawyer, accused Marine Captain Charles R. Buckalew of killing four guerrilla prisoners in cold blood and of other atrocities, such as crushing the testicles of a prisoner with a stone.

Although evidence pointed unequivocally to the captain's guilt, a preliminary court of inquiry, headed by Marine Lieutenant Colonel C. B. Taylor, found the evidence unreliable and suggested that Buckalew "deserves praise and not censure." Furthermore, the court recommended that Castillo be stripped of his right to practice law.[50] He was then tried by a military court for making false accusations. Much later, such massive evidence accumulated against Buckalew that he was made to stand trial before a military court. Despite the defendant's confession, which essentially corroborated Castillo's earlier charges, the court acquitted Buckalew on technical grounds.[51]

Other cases indicate that the courts' refusal to give credit to the allegations of Pelegrín Castillo was not unusual, although the negative bias would have been still greater had he been a peasant farmer or a laborer.[52] One marine investigator commented that the process of investigating peasants' complaints was not even worth his trouble, as he would never recommend bringing charges against a marine because "the evidence given by the average Dominican in the country is worthless."[53]

Not only was the testimony given by Dominicans discounted by the courts, but clear evidence exists of the intimidation of witnesses. Such intimidation prevented some cases from ever reaching the courts and prevented others from being tried fairly. One instance of the former involved a man who volunteered to turn in some firearms. A marine, assisted by members of the Guardia whom he commanded, apparently believed that the man had knowledge of the whereabouts of additional arms and so began to torture him, beating his testicles with sticks and burning his feet. His daughters were taken naked from their house and forced to watch, and then all of them were imprisoned. Complaints concerning the incident subsequently produced an investigation, but it reached no conclusion because witnesses were afraid to talk.[54]

During one of the investigations into the misconduct of Captain Buckalew, all the prosecution's witnesses suddenly "voluntarily recanted and acknowledged that they falsely testified," thus making it "impossible to establish the truth of the accusations made against Charles R. Buckalew."[55] It is reasonable to conclude, in light of Buckalew's later confession of guilt, that the witnesses recanted their truthful testimony under duress.

Some of the sentences of the military courts were so blatantly unfair that higher military officials protested. Occasionally this caused a retrial or the reopening of an investigation. In one case involving the killing of prisoners, Military Governor Harry Knapp called the acquittal of the obviously guilty marine defendants a "shocking occurrence, utterly reprehensible." On another occasion, Secretary of the Navy Josephus Daniels wrote that he viewed with "distinct regret and disapprobation" the "inadequate sentence" given to a marine private for a serious offense.[56] In 1922, Marine Lieutenant Colonel Henry C. Davis was dismayed to discover that, of a number of Dominicans sentenced to five years' imprisonment at hard labor for alleged guerrilla connections, "none of these men were legally tried but were 'railroaded' into jail." Tried by a provost court in San Pedro de Macorís, the prisoners had not been allowed to present witnesses on their behalf, nor did any prosecution witnesses appear against them, a procedure approved by Rear Admiral Thomas Snowden, the military governor at the time. Lieutenant Colonel Davis believed that "other cases of this kind" existed and asked for a special investigation.[57]

Dominicans ordinarily received harsher treatment in the military courts than did marines. Though there are not many precisely comparable cases recorded, a revealing exception occurred in early 1922. A group of four armed marines disguised as peasant insurgents was flushed out of the brush by a marine patrol. An investigation proved that the marines had set out on a "robbing expedition in the Consuelo [sugar estate] settlements," one of several in which they had participated. For this crime, they each received a sentence of thirty days' imprisonment on bread and water.[58] Dominicans tried for similar but less devious acts received sentences of from five years to life.

The failure of the system of military justice to deal fairly with Dominicans caused them to distrust and fear it and eliminated legal recourse for those mistreated by the marines. Another obstacle to any effective crackdown on marine misconduct lay in the tendency of military officials to ignore, suppress, or make excuses for those incidents which did come to their attention.

Among the explanations which the authorities of the military government gave for the misconduct of troops in the field was that the problem originated with Dominicans of the Guardia Nacional fighting under marine command rather than with the marines themselves. Since Guardia members lacked adequate training, argued Military Governor Knapp, their breaches of discipline were a natural "reversion to the intolerable conditions which existed in the late preintervention Dominican Army and Guardia Republicana."[59]

The Guardia *was*, no doubt, a source of problems. But the responsibility for abuse and atrocities lay as much with the marines. This fact became obvious in the case of Captain Charles Merkel, whose infamous deeds are still remembered in the east in the 1980s.

Marine authorities arrested Merkel in October 1918, only after the archbishop of Santo Domingo interceded on behalf of the terrified citizens. Charged with numerous incidents of torture and murder, Merkel conveniently committed suicide while in marine custody. The military government then dropped its investigation and brushed off his numerous atrocities as singular and isolated incidents, attributable to his Germanic ancestry rather than to marine attitudes, the problems of fighting a guerrilla war, or the occupation itself. Captain Merkel, wrote Military Governor Snowden, was "a German who used the well-known German methods on the native population."[60]

The use of the German issue in the Merkel case was not unique. From 1917 to 1919, marine officers, especially those in intelligence, tried diligently to prove that the Germans were responsible for the peasant uprising in the east, providing money, arms, and other supplies. So receptive were marines to this thesis that some high-ranking field officers saw guerrilla attacks as coordinated with German offensives in Europe.[61]

In the years following Merkel's death, as it became clear that other marines had been involved in similar atrocities, officials created a new rationalization. Many officers in the east, they explained, were actually corporals and sergeants who, without further training, had been hurriedly promoted to captain because of the World War I officer shortage. "It is hardly equitable," argued Military Governor Knapp, "to expect young and inexperienced officers, some of whom have just been appointed from the ranks, to be thoroughly familiar with all the regulations and rules of warfare governing their conduct."[62]

Charges made by C. M. Ledger, the British chargé d'affaires in San Pedro de Macorís in late 1921, indicate clearly that both the abuses and the failure to deal adequately with them continued throughout the war. Ledger sought an investigation into events surrounding the killing in cold blood of a British citizen, a black worker from Saint Kitts, by marines. The chargé, who saw this incident as part of a "reign of terror," mentioned several *bateys* from which the inhabitants had fled after incidents during which marines had beaten men and raped women. Though the marines were theoretically protecting the *bateys* from guerrilla raids, the chargé noted, their conduct was worse than that of the guerrillas, who were "not in the habit of killing their victims nor of interfering with their women folk." He asked for a thorough investigation. Military officials at first ignored the charges, but repeated demands finally resulted in at least limited action. Indications pointed strongly to a particular marine officer and his unit, but the investigator seemed unable to produce sufficient concrete evidence for anything more than a minor charge against one enlisted marine. Eventually the entire matter was quietly shelved and the criminals remained free.[63]

The occupation forces compiled a lengthy record of wrongdoing, even if, as appears likely, not all cases were included. The most blatant offenses occasionally resulted in investigations, trials, and convictions. But, in a sense, these judicial processes were irrelevant: the abuses had already occurred, the peasants had learned to hate the marines, and the guerrilla cause had gained adherents.

Only in late 1921, during a U.S. Senate investigation of the military occupations of the Dominican Republic and Haiti, did many of the details concerning marine misbehavior come to light.[64] By then the damage had long since been done. The only beneficiaries were those who could somehow obtain a sense of vindication from the far-off, after-the-fact hearings, which in themselves did not declare anyone innocent or guilty or pass any sentence.

Conclusion

In early 1917, representatives of the military government had disembarked in the east to carry out what appeared to be a relatively simple task: the pacification of a few local troublemakers and the establishment of the authority of the central government. But, when the marine leaders attempted to implement their orders by riding roughshod over the traditional autonomy of the east, they created an armed uprising. Thereafter, the tension and resentment associated with the region's rapidly expanding sugar industry and the resulting social and economic dislocations, as well as the anger which the marines' own mishandling of the conflict generated, stimulated and prolonged the uprising.

There can be no doubt that the marines' opponents were something other than the "bandits" born of military government propaganda and accepted by subsequent writers—they were peasant guerrillas fighting for principles and a way of life. Although the precise nature and degree of their motivation remain open to definition, it is certain that in many cases both the guerrillas and their leaders were conscious of political issues.

6

Guerrilla War in the East:
The First Years

The dispatch of marines to the eastern region of the Dominican Republic in 1917 provoked immediate armed opposition. The plains
around San Pedro de Macorís and the hills to the north soon rang
with the opening shots of a guerrilla war which would continue,
with periods of greater and lesser intensity, for more than five years.
The initial phase of the conflict corresponded roughly to the first six
months of 1917. This was followed by a period so tranquil as to convince the military government of the east's virtual pacification. But
the events of 1918 dashed these hopes of peace. Despite all marine
efforts, the level of violence again escalated. And as the war continued it gradually became part of eastern life, bogging down the marines in a seemingly unending conflict. By early 1919 military officials judged the situation so out of control that they tripled the
number of marines in the eastern provinces.

The Campaign of 1917

The marines encountered opposition almost from the moment they
landed at San Pedro de Macorís. The first marines sent to that city,
seventy-two enlisted men and four officers, were dispatched from
the Santo Domingo garrison to reconnoiter and to assert U.S. control
over the area. They landed at Macorís on 10 January 1917, amid
assurances by the provincial governor and other officials of the
friendly intentions of the Dominicans of the city. The tranquillity of
the disembarkation was marred, however, by the patriotic gesture of
one young man, seventeen-year-old Gregorio Urbano Gilbert, who
rushed onto the dock and fired a revolver at a group of marine
officers, killing one and wounding another. The military government rushed reinforcements of about 250 men to Macorís.[1]

In the view of the military government, one of the places of primary importance in the San Pedro de Macorís area was the large U.S.-owned sugar estate, Consuelo, which lay to the north of the city. Unrest had been reported at Consuelo even before the disembarkation had been completed. Salustiano "Chachá" Goicoechea, a caudillo who had often participated in political uprisings, had taken to the bush with one hundred to two hundred armed followers upon hearing of the marines' arrival. Almost immediately a detachment of marines under Colonel Hiram Bearss set off to subdue Chachá, now labeled a bandit. The opposing forces fought briefly in what was to be the first battle of an irregular war which was to last for over five more years.[2]

For the next several days Chachá led the marines on a chase, finally eluding them completely to the north near the town of Hato Mayor. At that point, having lost his quarry, Bearss scattered men to the various places where it was rumored that Chachá might go and offered a reward of three hundred dollars for the rebel leader, dead or alive.[3]

Except for Chachá and his followers, the situation in the east seemed under control after five days. San Pedro de Macorís, capital of the province and the largest city in the region, remained quiet, and its officials and police appeared anxious to cooperate with the occupation forces. But disturbing information came from the countryside, allegedly infested with "bands of robbers" who were killing other Dominicans and robbing and otherwise threatening the property of sugar estates in the vicinity. The estates' managers appealed for protection. Although another forty men had recently joined the previous reinforcements of the Macorís garrison, the marine command recommended a troop increase for the region as well as payment of salary arrears to the Guardia Republicana, a fragment of the preintervention Dominican military, whose members were expected to be useful allies once they received their back pay. Another recommendation proposed that sugar mill managers and some foreign residents keep guns for self-protection.[4] Further troop increases came very slowly, however, owing to the demands of the war in Europe.

The military government encountered increasing opposition as it attempted to consolidate its authority in the east. Although Chachá and two of his followers surrendered for unexplained reasons after less than a month of occasional fighting, two new leaders became the focus of marine attention: Vicente Evangelista, known as Vicentico, and Pedro Celestino del Rosario, called Tolete.[5] Military officials soon learned that Vicentico, like Chachá, was one of the region's popular caudillo leaders who had often participated in revolutions against the Dominican government before the intervention. There were also reports of a third but minor leader, Ramón Natera, who with a small band sometimes cooperated with Vicentico.[6]

By late January, after several engagements with the guerrillas, marine officers confidently reported Vicentico routed and his band broken up. In response military authorities ordered the Dominican forces of politician and general Fidel Ferrer, who had helped pursue Chachá and Vicentico, disarmed and disbanded. But weeks later, in response to a number of "alarming reports," another punitive marine expedition went out to eliminate the supposed remnants of the group. After six unsuccessful days of searching, the expedition suffered a surprise attack by Vicentico and some forty men at El Cerrito. The marines, with three men wounded, again claimed heavy Dominican casualties, including Vicentico.[7]

During late March and April, the countryside was relatively quiet, although military reconnaissance indicated that the "Evangelista forces are determined and will fight" and that the El Cerrito attack had been made "with full knowledge of the numbers they were to engage." Vicentico, however, apparently decided to avoid further confrontations and broke his band into small groups, perhaps because of the arrival of marine reinforcements in the town of El Seibo, the provincial capital on the northern edge of the Macorís sugar region. Furthermore, with the arrival of the peak employment season in the sugar industry, many of his men may have drifted away to jobs on the sugar estates.[8]

The marines, unable to locate the guerrillas, had to content themselves with such militarily unproductive acts as burning houses known to belong to Vicentico's family in the area of Magarín, La Candelaria, and San Francisco, just west of El Seibo. They spent most of their time scouting and tracking down vague rumors of "insurgents," as the marine command still occasionally labeled the guerrillas. Seeking information in the small villages of the east proved frustrating. Even in towns like El Gato, a known rendezvous for Vicentico and his followers, the inhabitants claimed to have no knowledge of them whatsoever.[9]

This spirit of noncooperation was provoked in part by the conduct of some of the marine forces. Lieutenant Thad T. Taylor's entry into El Seibo in February 1917, according to later testimony, was marked by abusive and arbitrary behavior. He and others broke into homes to search for arms, threatened citizens who failed to produce weapons, imprisoned local officials, and generally treated all citizens "as if they were animals." Under certain officers, unsupervised marine patrols in the countryside were similarly abusive to both peaceful peasants and suspected guerrillas; some Dominicans lost their lives by virtue of the *ley fuga*, the shooting of prisoners who "attempted to escape."[10]

The refusal of most easterners to cooperate with the marines was to remain a basic pattern throughout the insurgency. In June 1917, a marine commander observed that "while people are terrified by Vicentico, they hate us so that they will not give us information of any value." While Dominicans in the city of San Pedro de Macorís seemed willing to help the marines, an attitude that the marine officer attributed to the fact that the people there owed their livelihoods to U.S. interests, outside the city, in Macorís Province and in most of El Seibo Province, conditions were very different.[11]

The marines soon discovered that even the officials of many towns favored Vicentico or Tolete over the military government. In cases where such sympathies became obvious, the wholesale replacement of town officials followed. Even the ayuntamiento of El Seibo, one of the largest eastern towns with a population of about two thousand, suffered a purge when a marine officer reported that the administrative council was an "inefficient body, half hearted in carrying out the laws, afraid to move against a bandit like Vicentico, and more than half unfriendly to the American forces, underhandedly." Nor was El Seibo unique, he added. The failure of rural authorities throughout the area to move against insurgent activity made clear the need for a complete "reorganization of the political affairs of Seibo province." Not surprisingly, there is little evidence to show that the marines' replacement of officials was effective. If the new appointees seriously supported the military government, they endangered their lives and property.[12]

In May 1917, Vicentico and his forces struck in a way that was sure to arouse Yankee wrath: they captured and executed two U.S. citizens who had ignored Vicentico's warnings to leave the area. The men were surveyors for the Central Romana sugar estate, the U.S.-owned concern which was appropriating large tracts of land north of the town of La Romana, about twenty miles east of San Pedro de Macorís.[13]

Conflicting testimony obscures the reason for Vicentico's action, but it was widely believed that he had killed the surveyors simply because they were North Americans. The legal representative of the Central Romana estate wrote to the State Department demanding protection for the firm's employees, noting the manager's claim that Vicentico had threatened to "kill all Americans who fell into his hands." A subsequent claim concerned reports which alleged that Vicentico had ignored the surveyors' pleas that they were not with the U.S. military forces, telling them: "You are Americans, and that is all sufficient." [14]

By midsummer the marines discovered that Vicentico claimed to be leading a revolution against the military government, a position which brought him "some help and sympathy from the citizens." Moreover, the "bandit" offensive was taking on an increasingly military appearance. Vicentico and Tolete, a marine report indicated, both wore khaki uniforms, as did some of their followers, and Tolete's group wore distinguishing marks on their uniforms or hats. Some persons suggested increasing the pressure on Vicentico by offering a large reward for his capture, but Military Governor Knapp rejected the idea, saying that such a reward might "make the bandit a hero in the eyes of the people of Seibo Province." [15]

Marine officers worked hard to combat the insurrection but were unable to make significant gains. Various descriptions of the campaign during the first half of 1917 reveal their frustration. In late May, two lieutenants and their thirty men reported searching the country around Hato Mayor for four days. On the fourth day, checking out a tip from a local official, they were passing along a wooded trail when suddenly "rifle fire was opened on us from the bush at close range." As the marines began to return the fire, the guerrillas melted back into the undergrowth. Afterward, "numerous scouting parties were unable to pick up any information of this band." Not only had the marine unit been caught in a trap, probably baited by the village official, but they were unable to follow up the contact. Another visit to the area a week later failed to turn up anything after three days of searching; in addition, it rained, and "exceedingly bad roads were encountered on the return trip, many delays being caused thereby." The marines, after two weeks' hard work, were back where they had begun: "The latest rumor of Vicentico Evangelista is that he was in Magarín with 60 armed men." [16]

The marine battalion commander, Henry C. Davis, in detailing the activities of officers operating under him, related several episodes which revealed the marines' unpreparedness for guerrilla war. One lieutenant reported that he had Vicentico surrounded, having caught the guerrilla leader with his back to a range of low mountains to the north; the marine officer, having measured his opponents' mobility in terms of that of a regular army, was surprised when Vicentico withdrew over the sierra toward Sabana Grande. On another occasion, a lieutenant made contact with Tolete and pursued him. But the heavily equipped marines had to stop when their pack animals gave out. In yet another incident, Davis himself received word of the location of the camp of a lieutenant of Tolete called Ballido (perhaps Bullito Reyes). The guide to this camp, through "fear or ignorance," led the marines on a three-hour hike to cover a distance which should have taken three-quarters of an hour. "Needless to say," Davis wrote, "Ballido had been informed." Because guides are afraid, he continued, they "invariably take the longest instead of the shortest route to a point."[17] More likely, the guide's circuitous route was designed to allow time for another person to reach the guerrillas and warn them of the marines' approach.

The marines were not trained to fight guerrillas, nor were they properly equipped to fight in the tropics. Although they had a surfeit of such supplies as blankets, they completely lacked, for instance, mosquito nets. As a result the commander of one of the marines' key units in El Seibo reported in the summer of 1917 that he feared an outbreak of dengue fever among his troops would become an epidemic. For this reason, he curtailed operations until he could procure the nets necessary to protect his men.[18]

Until mid 1917, marine forces in the east were insufficient to do much more than protect a few base camps, although the number of troops gradually rose during 1918 to about three hundred. One cause of the military government's manpower difficulties was Washington's withdrawal of some marines for the new campaign in France. To replace them, a "considerable number of the newly organized Guardia . . . were rushed into the field," in fact "before they were fit for service," and the Central Romana sugar estate was authorized to organize and arm a private police force.[19] Members of the Guardia, because they were untrained and poorly equipped, were poor soldiers. One U.S. commander recommended that in combat the Guardia should be placed between the marines and the enemy to prevent the Guardia's flight and to safeguard U.S. personnel. "They are a menace to our troops if in the rear, as they fire in all directions, mostly in the air, and accompany their firing with loud shouts, even throwing their rifles in the air."[20]

After 10 June 1917, the leader of the antiguerrilla campaign was Lieutenant Colonel George C. Thorpe, the new commander of the Third Provisional Regiment. Thorpe's unit was charged with military control of the entire eastern region. In his initial reconnaissance, he found the countryside unsettled. Some of the land of the large sugar producers was going untended, and even the peasant smallholders had stopped bringing farm produce into the larger towns. Thorpe blamed this situation on fear of Vicentico and Tolete, although the farmers' inactivity was probably more correctly attributable to the presence of the marines, who were roaming the area and were beginning to believe, with some justification, that all peasants were their enemies.[21]

Thorpe, attempting to maximize his limited manpower, tried to extend the marines' physical presence over a larger area by splitting his forces into smaller, more mobile units of about twenty, each with an officer or at least a seasoned sergeant in command. Small detachments were out for days at a time from unit locations at La Romana, El Gato, Higüeral, Guaymate, Higüey, and El Seibo, living off the land and scouring the countryside for information on the guerrilla bands. Several of these places were *bateys*, located on the Consuelo, Porvenir, and San Isidro estates. After Vicentico's slaying of the Central Romana surveyors, the North American–owned sugar companies were increasingly eager for protection.[22]

Thorpe also worked to introduce other changes which would aid the marines' military effort. He cautioned his troops to be courteous to all Dominicans, as this was crucial to the "pacification" effort, and to practice constant reconnaissance, memorizing trails in their areas in order to compensate for the tremendous disadvantage caused by the unfamiliar terrain. Thorpe tried to maximize his meager transportation and communication resources, but he had little with which to work. Roads were nonexistent in the rough, forested terrain favored by the guerrillas; even in the immediate vicinity of the sugar estates, roads were little more than paths for bull carts. Thus it was often better to utilize the few private railroads which traversed the cane fields. As for communication, the only available equipment was a telephone line between La Romana and Guaymate and two marine radios, one only partially serviceable.[23]

Thorpe's innovations, however, were ultimately insufficient and led to unforeseen problems. In particular, some of the small, unsupervised field units began to terrorize the eastern population as they searched the countryside for information, arms, and guerrillas. Meanwhile, the guerrillas continued to be elusive: the marines were generally unable to make contact with their bands. Even the dispatch of small detachments into the forest in the hope of drawing the guerrillas' fire by their very weakness usually failed to produce results. The guerrillas attacked at times and places of their own choosing, in the most favorable circumstances only, and generally they broke contact at will. They owed their advantages to their high mobility, their knowledge of the terrain, and their excellent intelligence network, sustained by peasants and townspeople alike. In a word, Thorpe admitted after less than a month in command, the situation looked hopeless.[24]

The Surrender of the Guerrilla Forces

Almost as Thorpe made his pessimistic appraisal, the situation changed. The marines made contact with Vicente Evangelista through two Syrian-Dominicans, Antonio Draiby, a sugar *colono* who had organized eighteen of his workers into a paramilitary force to search out the guerrilla leader, and Agapito José, a merchant whose small store near the hamlet of San Francisco was close to Vicentico's center of operations. The two, acting in the belief that the rebels' surrender would bring them a reward of ten thousand dollars, conveyed Vicentico's proposal of a conditional surrender to military authorities.[25] But Military Governor Harry Knapp dashed hopes for a negotiated settlement by curtly rejecting the offer. He refused to deal with a "hunted criminal" and demanded an unconditional surrender. Ignoring the fact that the marines could seldom locate the guerrillas, Knapp ordered Thorpe to pursue Evangelista relentlessly and capture or kill him.[26]

The conditions of surrender asked by Evangelista, as reported by Knapp, seem at first glance to obscure his motives for fighting; he requested amnesty, a commission in the Guardia Nacional, and the right to bring some of his followers into the Guardia with him.[27] But Vicentico was following a time-honored political formula of the regional caudillos by offering his support to the central government in exchange for certain considerations.

Military Governor Knapp's rebuff did not end negotiations with the hunted guerrilla leader. The two intermediaries, Draiby and José, kept the lines of communication open. Working with a marine sergeant, William West, who posed as a battalion commander, they opened a series of talks with the "negro bandit and murderer." One of the negotiations took West into Vicentico's camp, which he found occupied by about 245 men and very well guarded. Visitors had to pass through a series of eleven sentry posts, and the entire camp was surrounded by a "network of trails by which the whole force could escape in case any outpost were attacked."[28]

After several delicate bargaining sessions, which were eventually joined by Commander Thorpe, Vicentico agreed to surrender. On 4 July 1917, the guerrilla leader and about 200 of his men presented themselves in El Seibo. All but 40 men, who kept revolvers, gave up their weapons, and the marines allowed 142 to return to their homes the following day. The next morning, Vicentico, his brother-in-law, and his father were sent to San Pedro de Macorís with Sergeant West and a marine guard, while Thorpe and the Forty-fourth Company took the remaining men, numbering about 60, to La Romana and then by ship to Santo Domingo. This group, according to later testimony, had been told that military officials had selected them "as important men 'to be employed in the Guardia Nacional.'" In the meantime, guerrilla leader Tolete, now calling himself a general, had also surrendered. Thorpe claimed that Tolete's capitulation resulted from a feud with Vicentico, who had threatened to kill the rival leader; other sources suggest that Tolete had received promises of a high political office in return for his cooperation.[29]

Vicentico's reason for surrendering is not entirely clear. It is obvious that he and his followers were not beaten militarily. Possibly the insurgent leader believed that it was useless to try to defeat the marines, whose vastly superior weapons and organization had a devastating effect on the guerrillas when battles were waged in the open or under other conditions in which the guerrillas did not have a decided advantage. In any case, there are strong indications that Sergeant West and Draiby made false promises to Vicentico. Although their conversations were only sketchily recorded, several sources, including a journalist who obtained his information from the marines in El Seibo about 1920, say that the guerrilla chieftain received assurances similar to his original demands, including an officer's post in the Guardia.[30] In any case, undoubtedly Vicentico and his followers would not have capitulated had they not been led to expect fair and moderate treatment.

The surrender of Vicentico and Tolete stripped the resistance of its leadership. The marines, it appeared, had finally obtained control of the east. Peace might have followed despite the continuing tensions generated in the region by serious social and economic changes and despite the fact that the military government had created many enemies during its 1917 campaign. But essential to this peace was reasonable treatment of Vicentico and his followers, combined with a policy of mollifying the alienated inhabitants of the east. This was not to be the case.

On 6 July 1917, marines shot and killed Vicentico while he was "attempting to escape." The victim, at the time of his death, was a shackled prisoner under a marine guard charged with moving him from San Pedro de Macorís to Santo Domingo for trial. The nearly universal belief was that the marines had deliberately murdered

Vicentico. Higher officials of the military government suspected the same, but the military's subsequent investigation took the testimony of Vicentico's guard at face value and set aside the case. "Even the marines themselves," noted an observer several years later, "do not often boast of the killing of Vicentico."[31]

After the insurgent leader's death, the military courts began a process of railroading many of his followers to the gallows, all promises of positions in the Guardia having been forgotten. Forty-six were tried, and twenty-six were found guilty and sentenced to be hanged. Rules of evidence and fine points of law were ignored. Notwithstanding the fact that these men had voluntarily surrendered and, at least, might have expected moderate treatment, the courts, with the approval of high officials of the military government, were bent on avenging the deaths of two U.S. citizens and on making an example of the Dominican defendants. Though it was hard to obtain solid evidence, admitted Brigade Commander Joseph H. Pendleton, "every member of the band richly deserves death for his crimes." Military Governor Knapp endorsed Pendleton's views.[32]

The severity of the sentences meant an automatic review by the judge advocate general and the secretary of the navy. As a result, the military government carried out no executions. Most of the men received reduced sentences of ten to fifteen years; twenty-one of the twenty-six so sentenced were not released until the last days of the U.S. control in July 1924.[33]

Certainly the murder of Vicentico and the harsh trials of his followers worsened the position of the military government in the east by creating further bitterness and distrust, especially among the released men who had been comrades-in-arms, neighbors, and often relatives of those sentenced to prison. The military government gave the Dominican peasants a personal reason to fight by its vindictive handling of the Vicentico group. "There is at least a grain of truth in the . . . assertion that the killing of Vicentico made all Seibo turn gavilleros," wrote a visiting North American journalist afterward. "The province wants revenge for what it considers the treacherous betrayal of one of its popular heroes."[34] The military government also insured that, for a long time to come, few guerrillas would negotiate with or surrender to the military authorities. Future recruits to the guerrilla movement would know that once they had begun to participate openly there could be no turning back, no matter how adverse the conditions, for the penalties were too great. And, as regarded the twenty or thirty men still thought to be active after Vicentico's surrender, they had little alternative but to continue their armed struggle. The military government, in effect, managed to keep alive a decimated and demoralized guerrilla movement by backing it into a corner.[35]

At a glance, however, conditions appeared much better in mid 1917. Of the three most active eastern caudillo leaders, Vicentico was dead, Tolete had surrendered and was in prison, and Chachá had surrendered and was tried, sentenced, and released on a suspended sentence. Of four other leaders of uprisings before the intervention, Juan Calcano and Emiliano Rojas were in prision, Julio Bonetti had died, and General Ramón Batista had been killed in the 1916 shoot-out with marines in Villa Duarte.[36]

Enthusiastic reports concerning the new situation in the east flowed across the desk of the military governor. The marine brigade commander claimed, on the basis of reports by both marine and civilian personnel, that "peace and quiet are now the order of the day in the Provinces of Seibo and Macorís . . . for the first time in many years." One of Vicentico's pursuers, Sergeant William West, now an acting captain in charge of a Guardia unit, made an inspection trip through large areas of El Seibo and Macorís provinces and concluded that the insurgency was dead. He found each place he visited, including the area from which Vicentico's family came, "quiet and free from lawlessness and bandits, and the natives well contented." And because of this atmosphere of peace, large quantities of farm produce were flowing to market in a normal fashion.[37]

On the basis of these and other optimistic appraisals, the military governor reported to the secretary of the navy that the insurgency in the east was ended: "While it may be too early yet to state with confidence that the whole country is so pacified and that there is no prospect of any uprising or banditry . . . I shall be very greatly surprised and disappointed if disorder of any magnitude whatever should break out in the future."[38]

The Resurgence of Guerrilla War

Only occasionally during the fall of 1917 and the spring of 1918 did reports of minor guerrilla activity suggest that the war might not be over. Sightings of insurgents came especially from the northern part of the east, the area between Hato Mayor and El Seibo north to the coast of Samaná Bay. The marines and marine-commanded Guardia units methodically checked each rumor but seldom connected with their quarry. A typical report in May 1918 described investigations of "bandits" at Las Cañitas and near Hato Mayor. Both leads produced nothing. Instead of pursuing guerrillas, the detachment spent

time in Sabana de la Mar supervising a town cleanup of latrines, pig-
pens, backyards, vacant lots, the markets, and the abattoir and meeting with the ayuntamiento to discuss ways of increasing town revenues. Routine military drills helped keep the troops occupied.[39]

The most visible leader in early 1918 was Ramón Natera, who
had remained in the field after the surrender of Vicentico and Tolete.
The marines made many attempts to kill or capture him which were
utterly unsuccessful, as were efforts to persuade him to surrender.
Eventually, marine officers decided to employ trickery, but even
these efforts failed because they depended on easily identified marine or even Guardia personnel. Finally, however, irregular troops
under the leadership of Delfín Trinidad, a minor caudillo, took to
the field, ostensibly to raise a revolution against the military government. When, after these revolutionaries had fought several staged
battles against the marines, Natera joined them for the purpose of
taking the town of Hato Mayor, he and his men were captured. But
the next day Natera escaped during an attack on his marine guard—
probably organized by other guerrilla leaders still at large, including
Ramón Batía, Llilo Ferrer, and José Cuba.[40]

In this operation and others during 1917 and 1918, Dominicans
were an important part of marine actions against the guerrillas. Besides serving as officers and troops in the Guardia, they worked as
advisers, as in the case of former caudillo leader Juan Calcano, who
helped plan the operation against Natera. They served as *prácticos*
or guides for marine and Guardia units and they gathered intelligence, as did Bullito Batía, brother of Ramón, before he joined the
guerrillas. After mid 1918, however, U.S. military officials carefully
eliminated Dominicans from positions of authority, thereby limiting
the latter's effectiveness. Irregular units disappeared completely, and
the Guardia fought only under U.S. officers. Not until late 1921
would the marine command again place independent Dominican
units in the field, at which time they would once more prove their
superiority to the marines in fighting a guerrilla war.

Although military officials admitted to "some bandit activity"
in the east during the late spring of 1918, they regarded it as unimportant. Reports of the military governor during the first six months
of the year emphasized that "quiet and good order have continued to
prevail," and they minimized events that apparently contradicted
this view. The killing of a marine sergeant serving as a captain with
the Guardia, for example, "appeared to be an act of assassination,
pure and simple, committed from ambush by one of the lawless element; and does not appear in any way to have been anything more
than a case of sporadic violence." By June 1918, officials judged

northwestern El Seibo and southern Samaná provinces so quiet that they no longer stationed marines there on a permanent basis.[41]

Perhaps more significant than the occasional guerrilla actions were the increasingly frequent accusations of misbehavior made against marines and members of the Guardia. The misbehavior was real, this being the period of the worst atrocities of Marine Captains Charles Merkel and Thad Taylor, known locally to Dominicans as El Tigre and El Tifus (Tiger and Typhus), and of other abuses as well. But a confidential investigation, which merely resulted in the suspension of one Guardia officer and the transfer of Taylor to Santo Domingo, generally brushed the criticism aside as inconsequential and unjustified.[42] This augured ill for the future.

The general appearance of tranquillity in the east began to break down during the summer of 1918. The quickening of guerrilla activity at this time of year was to become an annual occurrence, directly related to the end of the sugar harvest and the beginning of the season of unemployment. By July, Lieutenant Colonel Thorpe was speaking of the "present uprising." Intelligence reports indicated that large numbers of guerrillas had begun to congregate in the center of the eastern region, with some groups moving southward over the mountains and others, often unemployed sugar workers, coming up from the south.[43]

In August guerrilla leaders Ramón Natera, Ramón Batía, Tomás Mota, and Juan Pablo met, with 150 of their men, near the village of Vicentillo. Outside of the central region, on the eastern coast near Higüey, marines battled an estimated 40 to 50 guerrillas. Their leader, Marcial Guerrero, and 3 of his men were killed. Several weeks earlier, the same group had invaded the center of the town of Higüey at dawn, waving a Dominican flag and shouting nationalist slogans. They left after taking the guns of the municipal police.[44]

The marines estimated guerrilla strength during the month of September 1918 at six hundred men, who were in "open insurrection." Now added to the previously noted leaders were Martín Peguero, Nicolás Pimentel, and Carlos Chavaría (Echavarría?). The insurgents' tactics and organization had improved greatly. Leadership was better defined than at any time previously, and firearms and other supplies were seemingly more plentiful. Several ambushes, using decoys, were expertly executed during August and September.[45]

Private Alvin B. Kemp, who was stationed near the town of Dos Ríos in 1917 and 1918, provided a rare account of the antiguerrilla campaign through the eyes of an ordinary soldier when he wrote home to the editors of the *Literary Digest*. His unit, in the midst of "swamps, rivers, mosquitos, and wilderness," had few facilities of any kind and limited equipment. "Our bunks," he noted, "are made of poles and covered over with what is known as 'Jagwa' [yagua], or common palm-tree leaves . . . and the houses we occupy are covered by these leaves also." Their food, most of which was canned, was brought in monthly along with mail and other supplies by oxcarts or packtrains of mules. "As for our manner of operating," wrote Private Kemp:

> We go out in a detachment of from twenty to thirty men in command of a captain, a lieutenant or, on occasion, a sergeant. We carry our blanket roll and ammunition and a corporal carries on his shoulder a Lewis machine gun, and this gun is passed from one to another as one tires, which isn't long, for we sometimes hike as far as thirty miles a day across the mountains and open swamps with this tropical sun. . . . Sometimes we go out for as long as ten days. On these occasions we take two or three pack-mules for rations and packs. We search hidden trails out—there are no roads—and search the mountains for bandit camps and stray natives who look suspicious. . . . We have two mounted outfits operating with us, but they don't seem to be as successful as the infantry, from the fact that they make too much noise approaching. These natives are very sharp-witted and can easily step aside ten paces into the brush and laugh as we go by.[46]

An incident at the hamlet of Dos Ríos during September 1918 is illustrative of the marines' difficulties in fighting the guerrillas. Shortly after a detachment of eleven men arrived there, they sensed a tense atmosphere and noticed people conversing guardedly. After the marines left the town, guerrillas ambushed them as they were crossing a river. Finding themselves in an impossible tactical position, the marines took cover, held their fire, and waited for the concealed guerrillas to close in. When the marines finally opened fire, their only targets were puffs of smoke and movements of underbrush. When the guerrillas called off their attack, the battle ended, despite marine efforts at pursuit. In his report, the marine officer nevertheless insisted that his men had inflicted more damage than they had received; though he had seen no actual guerrilla casualties, he estimated twenty enemy dead and more wounded. But another description of the attack, by a sugar estate manager, suggested that the marines, although suffering no casualties, lost their horses and provisions and failed to kill any of the guerrillas.[47]

Exaggeration and optimism were common features of marine reports. In August 1918, for example, an officer claimed positively that his men had killed guerrilla leader Bullito Batía and four of his followers, one a woman.[48] But Batía, very much alive, continued to fight the marines until May 1922.

As the Dos Ríos encounter suggests, the guerrillas were extremely flexible. Another incident a few days later underscored the point. A detachment of marines was traveling between Las Pajas and Dos Ríos when a woman invited them to cook at her house. Her husband arrived but departed soon afterward to "look for cattle." A short time later the house was surrounded by guerrillas, perhaps eighty of them, and a fierce twenty-minute fight ensued. The marines sustained two wounded but believed that they had inflicted a much larger number of casualties on the guerrillas.[49]

Wounded marines presented a serious problem. Almost the only medical services in the east were those furnished by the marines themselves. They located permanent medical installations at San Pedro de Macorís, El Seibo, and La Romana, supplementing these by small, semipermanent posts created "from time to time as the military situation requires." But the number of wounded overtaxed the facilities, reported the regimental surgeon in 1918; besides, services were so limited that seriously wounded men had to be carried by boat to the field hospital in Santo Domingo City in order to receive adequate care. The regional hospitals were better suited to treating the illnesses which continually plagued marines. In 1918 the commonest diseases among troops in the east were malaria, which accounted for 24.9 percent of all illness; venereal disease, 16.1 percent; and dengue fever, 14.7 percent. Malaria was the most serious in another respect: it caused 31.7 percent of all sick days.[50]

Marine Response to the Renewed Insurgency

By late August 1918, the growing insurgency had become a serious concern to U.S. officials. "I have the honor to report," wrote Minister Russell to his superiors in Washington, "that banditry in the eastern part of the Republic, in the Province of Seybo, has assumed more serious proportions than at any time since the military occupation began." He documented his statement by mentioning several ambushes recently suffered by marine units and an attack on the Santa Fe estate near San Pedro de Macorís. The guerrillas, he noted, were well supplied with arms and ammunition.[51]

The sugar companies were also alarmed. The manager of the

Consuelo estate sent a message to his company's parent corporation in New York, which promptly relayed it to Washington, complaining that numerous recent attacks on Consuelo *colonias* and bodegas had netted the raiders several thousand dollars. Some three hundred marines, the Consuelo manager fretted, were finding it impossible even to locate the perpetrators. Conditions were so unsettled that no one would work; even the notoriously hardened *colonos* had left the fields.[52]

Marine leaders were unable to understand the reason for the upsurge in guerrilla activity. Pressed to supply an explanation to authorities in Washington, they passed over marine and Guardia brutality and other possibly relevant factors and pointed the finger at "pro-German propaganda." The insurgents' "German assistants and backers have not been asleep and have been using every effort to reinforce and keep alive this lively insurrection," wrote Lieutenant Colonel Thorpe.[53]

In order to combat the renewed resistance in 1918, Commander Thorpe made various changes and improvements in marine tactics, equipment, and communication which reflected an improved understanding of the guerrilla war. The marines continued to operate in small units, but, rather than making long patrols, each covered a limited area very thoroughly. Commanders were instructed to search every house and to collect information on each of the inhabitants, using cameras when available to "fix identity." Marine officers were also instructed to determine who favored the military government, so that they could serve as reliable rural officials, as members of the marines' secret service, or merely as trustworthy sources of military intelligence. Radios came into increasing use, greatly improving marine communication and coordination. By September 1918, a radio network existed between San Pedro de Macorís, El Seibo, Hato Mayor, and Las Pajas, replacing the old system, which depended mainly on infrequent messengers escorted by guards. Marine officers also began to recognize and guard against common guerrilla tactics. Troops were warned to "suspect all natives that accost you on the trail and seem to want to talk, challenge anyone coming out of the bush," and arrest and imprison any Dominican "whose conduct is questionable."[54]

Along with these small changes, the marine command in the east made one major innovation, adopting a new tactic called concentration. The concentrations or *reconcentraciones*, as the Dominicans knew them, involved rounding up all the people in a district and herding them into a few large centers while the "bandits," or those who failed to report to the centers, were hunted down. The

purpose was simply to separate the "good" folks from the "bad" folks
and to cut off the guerrillas from their sources of supply and information. Ironically, the new tactic recalled that of the Spanish General Valeriano Wyler, whose concentration camps in Cuba a few
years before had prompted loud condemnation from the government
and people of the United States.

In mid August of 1918, Lieutenant Colonel Thorpe issued Campaign Order No. 1, which commanded all inhabitants of a large area
of the eastern region to go to concentration camps located in various
larger rural centers. Within seven zones of operation, each zone commander was to contact the head officials and their aides of each village in order to "advise all good people to get in from the country
before 6 P.M., Saturday, 24 August, 1918, bringing in all food they
will require for a month, including cattle, poultry, etc." In the meantime, each zone commander was to scout his area thoroughly and
prepare to begin intensive operations at 8:00 P.M. on 24 August. Following the deadline, marines would imprison armed Dominicans
found in the countryside; they would shoot any persons who attempted to flee. And they would arrest those without weapons,
sending them to a military field camp for interrogation.⁵⁵ Instructions called for concentrations at La Romana, El Seibo, Los Llanos,
and the *bateys* Monte Coco and San Felipe. Attendance at the camps
was, at least technically, voluntary. Perhaps closer to the truth was
the announcement by one alcalde that "those who failed to go would
be considered enemies of the government," although military authorities vigorously denied the statement.⁵⁶

Few appraisals of the concentrations and the accompanying military campaign were positive. Only the plan's originator, Lieutenant
Colonel Thorpe, saw it as a success. He believed that the guerrillas
had been driven to such an unfavorable position that they had been
forced to break up their larger groups and that many were willing to
surrender but feared that they would be killed. He even asked for
permission to arrange for the surrender of guerrillas under the protection of an amnesty. Santo Domingo officials approved but so
hedged the amnesty with restrictions that they destroyed whatever
chance of success the program may have had.⁵⁷

Thorpe's report on life in the concentration camps was as favorable as his assessment of the military situation. Although the in-
ternment of large numbers of men, women, and children in small
Dominican towns posed difficult problems concerning accommoda-
tions and food, Thorpe found "the concentrated people . . . very
comfortable—few have ever been so comfortable in their lives—and
all were happy." Besides, two of the camps boasted doctors who

treated "the horribly diseased people who had arrived from the country innocent of any previous medical attention."[58]

The management of the sugar estates, on whose lands three of the camps were located, provided a decidedly opposite view of the concentrations. A New York law firm representing the Consuelo, Porvenir, San Isidro, and other companies wrote the major general commandant of the marine corps and quoted the reports of various managers to show that the originally promising concentrations had much worsened the military situation. The insurgents seemed to operate more boldly than before, coming and going almost freely from the sugar company areas and taking advantage of the desertion of the countryside to raid unprotected company stores. Between 24 August and 11 September 1918, with the concentrations still in progress, guerrillas had made five attacks on Consuelo bodegas alone, each of which resulted in losses of several hundred dollars or more.

Although Thorpe had contended that the work of the sugar plantations benefited from the captive labor supply, the Consuelo estate reported that the concentrations had entirely disrupted the season's schedule. Although there was only a limited amount of fieldwork available, even that was not completed. Workers refused to leave the *bateys* except during the day and even then returned in the early afternoon. Most of those concentrated had no means of support, and the sugar companies did not consider "charity work" their obligation. One report on 1,589 people at the Monte Coco *batey* on the Consuelo estate said that, although some did odd jobs, "most of them are deprived of any definite means of sustenance." Of other groups, an estate manager commented that "we are doing the best we can to take care of them, but have no work for them and they will soon be hungry. Some are already taking their chances and going out to the country to bring in food. They say they might as well get killed as die of hunger." In another *batey*, a company official considered sending his charges to San Pedro de Macorís, where the government might support them. In fact many families went on their own initiative to Macorís, where according to the governor of the province they wandered the streets, living "without resources and in sanitary conditions which could facilitate the spread of any disease."[59]

A Dominican supporter of the military government saw the concentrations as a personal disaster: ". . . when the reconcentration was stablished [sic] by the Militar [sic] Government, my state [sic] became the property of the bandits and they stole the cattle by lots of considerable number of heads." Another Dominican observer of events in the east, Julio Peynado, whose family had close ties with the sugar industry, believed that the concentrations actually "increased the 'gavillerismo.'"[60]

The concentrations illustrated the marines' inability to understand their enemy. It was impossible to separate the insurgents from the *pacíficos* because no clear line divided them. Though the concentrations might have isolated active insurgents from their bases of supply, intelligence, and fresh manpower, the benefit was lost when the concentrations lasted for only a limited time and covered a restricted territory. Nor did the strategy solve the basic problem of forcing the guerrillas to confront the marines—the guerrillas either remained quiet or went off to relieve unprotected areas of arms, ammunition, other supplies, and money. Finally, the guerrillas might join the concentrations with everyone else. There, as part of a marine plan to fix identification during the concentrations, they would receive a cedula of identification with which to prove their status as reliable citizens in the future. As identification ultimately depended on officials of the local community, there was little chance the insurgents would be given away.[61]

Since the concentrations were very inconvenient for the Dominicans, frightened them, and further impoverished them by making them gather idly for a month and eat up their provisions of food and livestock, it seems likely that considerable resentment against the military government was the chief result. Though some may have appreciated the medical attention they received, the detrimental aspects of the concentrations were the only ones which the majority of the people experienced.

One of the most significant results of the concentrations was that they exacerbated the already difficult relationship between the sugar companies and the military government. Where the large estates had once maintained peace by paying off and cooperating with caudillo leaders, under the military government they found their property under frequent attack and their work disrupted. With the marines apparently unable to prevent these problems, managers of sugar properties felt compelled to complain frequently. During the concentrations, their protests mounted to a crescendo. Worse, the managers more and more often took their problems directly to Washington rather than to Santo Domingo, a practice which occupation officials greatly resented. The military government in turn viewed the sugar companies with a jaundiced eye. Officials charged that sugar managers often complained about nothing, that they were totally self-interested and failed to cooperate with the military government, and even that they caused some of their own problems by abusing Dominicans.[62]

After the fall of 1918, no love was lost between the military government and the sugar companies, especially the Consuelo estate. This poor relationship hindered the marines' antiguerrilla effort, for the managers of the sugar estates, heading informal intelligence networks formed by thousands of employees, were the most knowledgeable English-speaking residents of the republic on eastern affairs. But, even if they were still inclined to advise the military government, the military government was scarcely willing to listen. Ironically, the two parties most interested in the pacification of the east had become antagonists, both trying to discredit one another in Washington and neither cooperating in Santo Domingo.

The expanding guerrilla movement, the evident failure of the concentrations, and the marines' inability to enforce even a policy of containment or of "pushing bandits back from settled points" made increasingly obvious the need for more marines. Though Military Governor Knapp resisted this for some time, continued depredations by the guerrillas and the heavy pressure exerted in Washington by the sugar companies eventually forced the military governor to act. In November 1918, he requested that "the Brigade be temporarily increased by five hundred men." As this number represented an increase of 266 percent over the previous record-high troop strength in the east, lengthy explanations and apologies accompanied the request.[63]

The request for additional troops was one of Rear Admiral Knapp's last acts as military governor. On 18 November 1918, he departed from Santo Domingo, soon to join the U.S. delegation to the Versailles Conference. Brigadier General B. H. Fuller, commander of the marine brigade, became acting military governor; on 25 February 1919, he was replaced by a new military governor, Rear Admiral Thomas Snowden.[64]

Changing the Guard, 1919

Early in 1919 the eastern command still awaited additional troops. Faced with continuing unrest and lacking a positive response from Washington, the military government renewed its manpower request, meanwhile increasing strength in the east by other means. Because Barahona and Azua, in the west, had been totally quiet for a year, all marine units there were moved to El Seibo, leaving the marine-officered Guardia behind to keep order. Other troops were pulled out of the Santiago command in the north and sent to Hato Mayor.[65]

Finally, in February, U.S. Marine Corps headquarters announced its decision to send a larger unit to patrol the east. On 26 February 1919, the 1,091 men of the Fifteenth Regiment, newly arrived from the United States, replaced the 300 men of the Third Provisional Regiment, which had operated in the east since 10 January 1917. In a final report, officers of the departing unit noted that in two years of operations it had made over one hundred contacts with the insurgents, suffered battle losses of only six killed and eighteen wounded, and had inflicted much heavier losses on the guerrillas.[66]

Just before the departure of the Third Regiment, its new commanding officer, Colonel Carl Gamborg-Andresen, had toured the east and prepared a confidential report on operations against the guerrillas. He began by breaking down the category of those who are "conducting . . . armed insurrection against the government" into "professional highwaymen" and "common criminals." He identified the leaders of the "professionals" at that time as Ramón Natera, Martín Peguero, Ramón Batía, José Cultico, and Félix Laureano, known as Chiquito, and noted that the center of their strength and scene of many of their operations was the hilly area north of the sugar estates and east of Hato Mayor.

The commander acknowledged that fighting this irregular war was extremely frustrating. The guerrillas seemed to know every marine move, despite elaborate and tiring efforts to deceive them with feints and night or secret movements, while the marines' information was almost always outdated or inaccurate. Most people refused to confide in the marines, the officer surmised, because they feared the guerrillas or sympathized with them. Moreover, the nature of the countryside made operations both dangerous and unproductive. Flank protection was impossible and concealment was easy, so ambushes were common. The guerrillas fought when they wanted to fight. Various marine measures, such as the use of field radios and the increased employment of Dominican members of the Guardia with each marine unit, had improved the bleak situation only slightly.[67]

The wholesale replacement of the seasoned marines in the east by newly arrived personnel crippled the military government's pacification effort. Years of accumulated field experience were lost. The new officers and their men had to learn by costly trial and error what it was like to fight an irregular war, as continual reports of marine debacles during 1919 attest.

The Fifteenth Regiment moved slowly while acclimating itself to this new environment. It continued the tactics of the Third Regiment, using small units for patrolling and tracking down leads, while working to improve intelligence and communication. The new unit's first large-scale operation was also modeled on the actions of its predecessor.

In April 1919, the new district commander, Colonel J. C. Breckinridge, organized another concentration. That he did so suggests that communication between the departing and the arriving commanders was something less than candid, since many agreed that the concentration of August and September 1918 had been a failure. The operation lasted only forty-eight hours and affected but two sections of the province of San Pedro de Macorís, Las Cañadas and Juana Lorenza in the commune of Los Llanos, both allegedly inhabited by large numbers of "bandits or bandit sympathizers."[68]

Some six hundred Dominican peasants trailed into the concentration site by 20 April 1919. While marines combed the countryside, those gathered at Los Llanos listened to a military band, which played almost continuously for two days, and heard speeches by Breckinridge and the civil governor of San Pedro de Macorís explaining the positive aims of the military government.[69]

Military reports on the concentration varied. One commander noted that "no able bodied natives were reported being encountered in the entire district" around Los Llanos, Dos Ríos, and El Salto, while others encountered numerous "friendly natives," many of whom professed to have no knowledge of the concentration. In any case, there were no contacts with identifiable guerrillas. Despite rumors that various guerrilla units were about to surrender, no important groups ever did.[70] One possible source of such rumors was the peasants' considerable excitement and fear around Yerbabuena, Las Claras, and Sabana Grande on 22 April, when planes dropped bombs in the suspected locations of guerrilla units.[71]

Perhaps because the idea of the concentrations was not his own, District Commander Breckinridge was more willing than his predecessor to appraise the strategy critically. He concluded that "as a military measure the concentration was productive of no good results. The good males came in and the bad ones remained out, but were not found."[72]

Besides local resentment, there seemed to be no immediate adverse reactions to the concentrations. But the growing protest of Dominican nationalists after 1919 and increasing awareness of the occupation in the United States and elsewhere eventually led to criticism in the press. On several occasions in 1920 and 1921, Military Governor Snowden and his staff had to defend the concentrations to the secretary of the navy, who was smarting under attacks on this policy by newspapers in Latin America, the United States, and Europe. Snowden defended the policy as a military necessity and claimed that its use was limited to short periods under the most humane conditions.[73]

Breckinridge, who appears from his correspondence to have been an intelligent, relatively enlightened commander, did not comprehend the reasons for the insurgency. Having rejected in his own mind the original thesis that large numbers of the peasants were actually bandits, he naïvely surmised that their readiness to follow guerrilla leaders was the result of not understanding the goals of the occupation. He hoped to correct this misunderstanding when he explained to those assembled for the concentration that the military government sought "peace and tranquility to the end that there may be prosperity and happiness in Santo Domingo." After the concentration ended, Breckinridge continued his policy by going on a speaking tour throughout El Seibo with Civil Governor Antonio Ramírez.[74]

Junior officers were no better informed than their superiors. One marine lieutenant decided to make a frontal assault on his own ignorance: "I made several inquiries as to the reason for the existence of so much banditry, and learned that in addition to the fugitives from justice, and those who found banditry an easy way to make a living, there was a class of bandits who gave as an excuse patriotic motives. These bandits boast that they have driven the Spanish and the Haitians from the Republic and will soon drive the Americans out." Confronted by one element of the truth, the incredulous lieutenant dismissed it, remarking that the information "was obtained from native sources, and can only be considered in that light."[75] The lieutenant's evaluation of his information points up another factor favorable to the guerrillas. The marines were armed, aggressive outsiders; intimidated Dominicans often told them what they wanted to hear or, in other situations, deliberately deceived them. Only occasionally did the marines learn the truth. As a result, they built up great distrust for Dominicans and believed less and less of what they heard, even when it was true. And the guerrillas did all they could to exploit this situation by purposely spreading rumors and false information.

7

Guerrilla War in the East:
Stalemate and Resolution

By May 1919, during the third year of the guerrilla war, the military government had amassed 1,480 men in El Seibo and San Pedro de Macorís provinces. Stationed at twenty different points were 81 officers, 40 hospital corpsmen, and 1,359 enlisted men. The largest numbers were at the city of San Pedro de Macorís (270), Consuelo (222, including 127 in an aviation squadron), Hato Mayor (198), El Seibo (196), Las Pajas (112), Dos Ríos (76), Guaymate (64), La Romana (63), Higüey (56), and San Rafael del Yuma (40). Most of the remaining men were at posts concentrated in a small area north of the sugar company properties around El Seibo and Hato Mayor.[1]

In June the military government, in recognition of the fact that the eastern region constituted a special problem, designated it as a separate military district, with headquarters in San Pedro de Macorís. The new district, like the two already in existence, would report to the brigade commander in Santo Domingo,[2] but the eastern commanders would have somewhat more freedom to make on-the-spot decisions than previously.

A Stalemated War

With these changes, the guerrilla war took on the form in which it would continue, substantially unaltered, into 1921. The east became the barracks, and an occasional battleground, for an army of occupation. The marines, their documents show, were stalemated and increasingly demoralized. The spirit of innovation represented by the ill-fated concentrations disappeared. The marines now settled into a routine existence, patrolling the countryside by day and retreating to towns and outposts at night. Pursuit of the guerrillas became *pro forma*. The basic policy was one of containment, which at least kept up the appearance of military government control in the sugar-producing areas to the south. Marine-guerrilla confrontations generally occurred in the more remote wooded and hilly areas to the north and east, although there was some geographic ebb and flow to the war, according to the fluctuating intensity of the guerrilla effort.

Because of its limited success in combating the guerrillas, the military government played down this aspect of the occupation. If complaints brought the issue to the surface, as occurred in the spring of 1919, military authorities became defensive. Military Governor Thomas Snowden, replying to criticism by Minister William Russell, wrote that any "intimation . . . that the banditry situation in Santo Domingo is not well in hand is absolutely untrue. The so-called bandits in the Dominican Republic are located in the Provinces of Seibo and San Pedro de Macorís which have always contained unruly elements. These are not really bandits, but bands composed of a few real outlaws, refugees from justice and such simple countrymen as they can impress. They are without organization, move about in small parties, [and] have no political aims whatever." To Minister Russell's suggestion that a civilian government might provoke less opposition than the military government, Snowden replied that "stealing by work-avoiding criminals will exist under any form of government." Most of the people, he argued, "are absolutely happy and content in an assured peace." Not all marines were as blind to the situation as the military governor. A second lieutenant reported from San Pedro de Macorís that "labor conditions are very bad in this section of the country, and might be the basis for bandit trouble. The people receive very low wages, averaging less than a dollar per day, while they are only able to work three or four days a week." The lieutenant's words fell on deaf ears.[3]

A quarterly report for the spring of 1919 on the military situation in the east spoke of engagements "from time to time" with guerrilla units which were usually small but which sometimes included up to 200 men. Except for a flurry of activity near Bayaguana, northeast of the city of Santo Domingo, most insurgent actions were in the central area of the east. Marine officials estimated guerrilla casualties for the period to be "about 150."[4]

The words "from time to time" euphemistically described perhaps twenty-five battles during the quarter, many of which were no credit to the marines. Typical is a report by an inexperienced second lieutenant of the Fifteenth Regiment. He and his small detachment spotted three men who "appeared to be a little nervous and immediately aroused my suspicions." As he and his men advanced, he noted another ten men ahead. The marines quickened their pursuit, only to find themselves suddenly caught in cross fire between one hundred guerrillas on either side of them.[5]

Even from such disastrous encounters the marines often emerged with surprisingly few casualties, owing to the guerrillas' often inadequate firearms and allegedly inaccurate marksmanship. Generally, the insurgents seemed to suffer more dead and wounded. But, cautioned a military official, "as bandits take great care in removing their dead, the number of bandits actually killed is difficult to ascertain."[6]

The body count was an important measure of success in a war which offered no clear territorial gains, but the marines' claims of dead and wounded were, at best, honest estimates. Typical was a report which read: "The [ammo] pouch was cut by a bullet and blood stains were found nearby. Also a shattered belt buckle was found and from that, I believe, two or three bandits were wounded or killed."[7]

The fact that wounded men took advantage of the terrain to hide themselves also frustrated the body count. One marine, Major T. E. Watson, unsuccessfully searched for dead and wounded in the thick grass of a potrero. Having been robbed of the fruits of his victory, he adopted a unique solution: "I endeavored three times to set this potrera [sic] on fire but was unsuccessful."[8] Higher authorities apparently failed to protest his action, which would have burned to death the seriously wounded.

During 1919 and 1920, the marines' inability to locate the guerrillas remained their most fundamental problem. Their basic strategy of searching continually with small detachments had produced very limited results. To increase their effectiveness, they used a network of spies which operated in the east as well as in other areas of the country. Sometimes exguerrillas were so employed, in exchange for amnesty. They also served as *prácticos*, men openly working with the marines as informants and guides.[9] At times they identified known guerrillas and often led the marines through the maze of trails which crisscrossed the east. One *práctico*, an exguerrilla, led the marines to a group of secluded houses near Cibahuete where some of the followers of Ramón Natera and Cecilio Aponte slept on Sunday nights. An attack on the place killed a number of men as they ran unarmed out of a house—the women were "allowed to surrender."[10]

Marines periodically raided the houses of known insurgents and their families, as well as rural camps, rendezvous, and supply areas. Some actions resulted in the death of women and children. Dozens of reports detail unsuccessful searches for guerrillas, often in response to rumors that proved false or led the marines to guerrilla camps after the inhabitants had departed. Sometimes promising leads were lost because poor roads made movement slow or impossible. In July 1919, one officer admitted that he had to abandon an attempt to reach a guerrilla band in the Bayaguana-Pulgarín area because of such difficulties. Another noted the failure of an operation when his trucks became mired on a muddy road for two days.[11]

When contact was established, it was usually on the guerrillas' terms. But even open confrontations often ended less than successfully for the marines because of the guerrillas' ability to retreat. Reports repeat each other time after time: "It was plain to see that this fight was developing into another foot race"; "we pursued the bandits, but could find no trace of them"; "discovered no trace of enemy." Such escapes were not accidental. Guerrillas planned their camps and their tactics with routes of withdrawal as a prime consideration.[12]

The two opponents' advantages remained approximately the same throughout the war. The marines' superior training, organization, and arms (especially machine guns) made short work of the guerrillas in open confrontations. But the guerrillas' mobility, knowledge of the terrain, and intelligence network enabled them to avoid most such battles and to plan engagements which gave them the advantage. Thus, despite the guerrillas' inferior arsenal as well as their limited formal training, they were formidable opponents.

The marines had difficulty enough when, as was often the case, they themselves were the focus of insurgent operations. But when the guerrillas deliberately avoided them and turned their attention to other endeavors, such as those necessary to provide themselves with money and supplies, the marines were at a complete loss. Guerrilla units made continual raids on small stores and municipal treasuries and collected forced contributions from wealthy citizens and from the sugar companies. The marines could not prevent this sort of activity because they did not know where it would occur next.

The insurgents controlled the countryside, except near the marines' relatively few permanent garrisons. While this fact did not determine the loyalty of most easterners, whose social and economic ties led them to sympathize with the guerrillas, it usually prevented those few who might have been willing to cooperate with the marines from doing so. Whenever the marines were away, civilians were at the mercy of the guerrillas.

One Yankee sympathizer described his suffering to the military government in hopes of obtaining monetary compensation. Antonio Sarmiento, a Dominican, apparently befriended U.S. officers soon after they landed in San Pedro de Macorís. When Chachá and his followers took some cattle from his land in the province of El Seibo, Sarmiento offered his services to the provost marshal of San Pedro de Macorís. He first aided the marines in a practical way when he learned that a group of guerrillas was waiting in ambush near El Cerrito for an expected marine column. He notified marine officers and they sent out reinforcements, who attacked the guerrillas and killed ten of them. "The Gavilleros," reported Sarmiento, "knew what I did, and began to hate me and rob me more than before." When he persisted in associating with the marines, he began to receive anonymous letters threatening his life and the destruction of his property. So Sarmiento stopped visiting his estates. Finally, when guerrillas menaced his mayordomo, he left and the lands remained entirely unattended. The experience left Sarmiento "a ruined man."[13]

There can be little doubt that Sarmiento's experience was the common lot of those who turned their backs on the insurgents. Since the marines could not protect most people in the countryside, those who wanted to remain there or who owned property and wanted it unharmed had to cooperate with the guerrillas. Vulnerability was a particular problem of the sugar *colonos*. In June 1919 guerrillas killed a *colono* of the Quisqueya estate, T. W. Pockels, and attempted to kill another, Antonio Draiby, who often cooperated with the marines. "As a result of this," wrote the estate manager, "all of our men are abandoning all their property and moving into the Central. We have no place to house any more."[14]

Towns were also vulnerable. The absence of the marines meant that the guerrillas—and the petty criminals who used the turmoil of the times to their own benefit—could make free use of municipal treasuries or the cash and goods of local merchants. Frequent complaints brought marine and Guardia forces in and out of a number of small towns. After a Guardia unit relocated from El Valle in the commune of Sabana de la Mar, the community was raided three time by "bandits" and the town leaders asked for the reestablishment of a military unit there. When the town of Ramón Santana, in southern El Seibo, suffered a series of robberies soon after the departure of a marine detachment, town officials requested the unit to return. Military authorities instead instructed the officials to form a local police force. They did so, and in addition a marine patrol visited the town once a week.[15]

It is possible that actual bandits, as opposed to organized guerrillas, were the cause of some of these complaints. Since many insurgents came from and visited such small towns as Ramón Santana and depended heavily upon the cooperation of ordinary Dominicans, they were not likely to commit acts which would alienate the inhabitants of these rural centers. But it is equally possible that guerrillas *were* responsible for the robberies and that the local elite, as distinct from the rest of the population, asked for the return of the marines or Guardia. The self-interest of merchants and other wealthier citizens may eventually have estranged them from the proguerrilla sentiments of their neighbors.[16]

Such a cleavage between the inhabitants of some towns is suggested by a report of an attack on the town of Diego by "General" Ramón Natera and his followers. Marine investigators noted not only the robbery of a local bodega and the death of four Dominicans (without specifying who they were) but also the fact that the group picked up twenty new followers. Another foray, against a bodega at Dos Ríos, a known center of insurgent activity, added ten men to the guerrilla contingent. Clearly the guerrillas found more support than opposition.[17]

From 1918 until the end of the guerrilla war, Ramón Natera was by far the most important guerrilla leader. His living arrangements in 1919 revealed his status. Natera lived not with his followers in their large camp but in a nearby location "guarded by a few of his special, trusted men." Even other members of his group were ignorant of precisely where he stayed, and if outsiders wished to visit him, he met them in places other than his personal camp. Natera and his men usually traveled by foot, moving by day or by night, in groups of up to fifty men; they lived off cattle and produce which they gathered. They were always well informed of marine actions, since *pacíficos* in the area reported to Natera's men.[18]

Other leaders besides Natera were very active. A new group, called La Revolución, appeared during 1919, led by Eustacio "Bullito" Reyes. It operated in San Pedro de Macorís and eastern Santo Domingo provinces and, like other groups, its members spent much of their time in the forested hills, pursued by the marines and occasionally fighting them. In 1920 Pedro Celestino del Rosario, called Tolete, a guerrilla who had surrendered in 1917, escaped from prison while serving a sentence of twenty years' hard labor; soon he had gathered a group of up to fifty well-armed followers.[19]

Marines met the renewed insurgency with a new weapon. During 1919 they began to use airplanes against the guerrillas, for both bombing and strafing. In April, during the concentration in the Los Llanos commune, bombs were dropped on suspected areas of guerrilla strength, apparently as much to intimidate the populace with a show of power as to harm the guerrillas. Typically, guerrillas made their own use of the new tactic, spreading the rumor that marine aircraft would fire on women and children seen outside their houses.[20] In July, a pilot flying over a savanna between Hato Mayor and Mata de Palma spotted a large group of men. When they began shooting pistols at his plane, he dove straight at them, firing; he and his copilot apparently killed six.[21]

More commonly, military officials used planes for mapping, conveying messages and personnel, and scouting for guerrillas in the wide areas uncrossed by roads. In one incident, a pilot located a large guerrilla encampment and, with his plane, led a marine detachment there. On the peaceful side, the republic's first airmail service carried letters between the east and Santo Domingo. These activities were all the work of a 130-man marine aviation squadron, established in February 1919 at an airfield on the Consuelo estate and later moved to San Isidro, which today remains the main base of the Dominican air force.[22]

Marking Time

During 1920, the military government's policy of containment (or, more properly, exclusion) seemed to be operating more effectively than ever before. In January 1920, Military Governor Snowden reported to a Massachusetts-based importer of coffee, cocoa, and spices that, unlike conditions in 1919, "it is now quite safe to travel in and around La Romana and San Pedro de Macorís, D.R." The situation, however, left a large part of the interior of the east in guerrilla hands. Snowden noted the need for more effective marine action in El Seibo in early 1920, saying, hopefully, that the guerrillas "are now broken up into small bands and require running down." To carry out this mission, the military government once again lobbied for more troops, first requesting 2,500 and then 2,950. Washington officials balked at the second request but eventually provided the 2,500.[23] Reinforcing the marines were members of an expanded Guardia Nacional Dominicana, local police, and private forces of the sugar companies, called *guardas campestres* or rural guards.

A military official described the *guardas campestres* as "special police officers for the landed estates whose appointments are ratified by the Governor; . . . their authority is restricted to the estate by which they are appointed." They became more effective in 1920, when Military Governor Snowden authorized weapons for them. The idea of the *guardas campestres* was not new. The concept dated from a 1907 Dominican law, and Central Romana had had such an armed force since 1917. In 1920, as the other estates increased their security, military officials ordered the large force at Central Romana reduced to fifty men, who were compelled to give up their military titles and uniforms and otherwise show clearly that they were not members of the marines or the Guardia Nacional.[24] The military government did not want the transgressions of these private armies blamed on the regular forces.

Perhaps more important than the peace-keeping efforts of the *guardas campestres* was the fact that the sugar companies, or at least their *colonos*, went back to the old system of paying protection money to the guerrilla leaders (if indeed they had ever abandoned the practice). This reversion to old ways apparently took place after the fiasco of 1917 and 1918, when at least some of the sugar companies had cooperated with the military government against the guerrillas. But when estate managers found that the marines could not give them adequate protection against the guerrillas, who robbed company bodegas, carried off payrolls, and burned cane fields with virtual impunity, some apparently chose a reasonable alternative—to pay the guerrilla leaders. And evidence suggests that the military government tacitly agreed to the new spirit of accommodation.[25]

There is no doubt that the guerrillas could still strike within the marines' defensive perimeter. In December 1920, for instance, a group of twenty-two guerrillas under Tolete took money, shoes, and other merchandise from the Quisqueya sugar estate between San Pedro de Macorís and Los Llanos. In addition, Tolete "demanded an additional sum of money from the administration."[26]

The marines claimed that they protected the sugar estates by keeping the insurgents away from the sugar areas. But the fact that many guerrillas lived in sugar estate *bateys* and even worked for the sugar companies contradicted their argument. "Every sugar estate has amongst its own employees emissaries of the bandits, who are working peacefully by day and in connection with bandits at night," commented one official.[27]

As an indication of conditions outside of the marines' well-armed enclave in the east, the usually optimistic Military Governor Snowden advised a U.S. citizen who was interested in farming in Higüey not to go there. "The conditions around Higüey and Seibo are normal," he claimed, "but some petty thieving is taking place." In the same month, September 1920, a marine officer reported five active "leaders" in the Higüey area alone, and this was on the periphery of the usual area of guerrilla operations. These five commanded from fifteen to seventy-five men each, depending on circumstances.[28]

The east, both within and beyond the marines' area of defense, showed the strain of war. The region's central area had been virtually abandoned, except for the towns. A visitor passing through the district north of the town of El Seibo in 1920 spoke of seeing a "cacao conuco, or tiny plantation, overgrown with brush and weeds and with the scarred ruins of a hut in one corner of it. More of them lined the way for mile after mile, all abandoned for the past three years."[29] Within the towns, municipal facilities were unclean and poorly administered. The jail at Higüey was a "pigpen," wrote one marine officer. Similarly, the streets of La Romana were "filthy" and the town itself was a "hotbed of vice and corruption, and the source of numerous complaints." Mail service was very inefficient, especially between La Romana and El Seibo, and a telephone line which had connected the two towns was almost entirely down, with some people using the wire for fences. Public works, especially the roads, showed virtually no progress. Even some schools were closed because of fear of violence in areas of marine operations.[30]

The development of roads was of great importance to the military government. Military Governor Snowden remarked in 1919 that "the building of roads through the heart of the country facilitates the opening up of new farms and at the same time facilitates military operations against the bandits. . . . It is not believed that banditry can survive the opening up of the country." Marine Colonel J. C. Breckinridge, for several years the eastern commander, agreed. "The continued extending of roads and opening up of business have done more to pacify the country than any amount of military force could have done," he argued.[31]

Roads also offered the possibility of ending political regionalism. "A highway," stated one high-ranking officer, "would bring the people more in contact with the Capital, thus giving the Central Government an opportunity to control political conditions. Previous to the United States Military Control every province resembled a feudal state controlled by a Military leader, who from time to time levied tribute on the merchants, sugar estate managers, and Central Government." Such leaders, he noted, "are now known as bandits." The author of this illuminating remark was a new military governor, Rear Admiral Samuel S. Robison, who replaced Rear Admiral Thomas Snowden in June 1921.[32]

A Growing Insurgency, 1921

The marines' military position in the east deteriorated during 1921. A financial crisis which hit the military government late in 1920 had caused a halving of the Guardia's manpower nationally, from one thousand to five hundred, and marine morale seemed on the ebb. Even the policy of containment was sinking from sight, as the marine commanders' lax pattern of patrolling the countryside only by day gave the guerrillas free run of the small towns and of the entire countryside at night. And, besides serious problems in the guerrilla heartland, there were renewed reports of guerrillas to the north of the mountains, in the vicinity of Sabana de la Mar.[33]

Conditions had so deteriorated by March 1921 that the transfer of prisoners from El Seibo to San Pedro de Macorís was impossible without a large armed escort. Similarly, by April the post office in the east had stopped accepting registered mail known to contain money, owing to losses to the guerrillas. Several banking houses, including the International Banking Corporation, the fiscal agent of the military government, and the merchants of El Seibo asked the marines to provide an armed guard for one or two money shipments per month.[34]

The director of internal revenue reported that guerrillas had held up a number of his agents and relieved them of their money and clothes near Higüey and in the province of San Pedro de Macorís, especially near Los Llanos. But guerrilla policy, he noted, seemed to be to kill only those who carried firearms. Meanwhile, a marine officer in Los Llanos, responsible for protecting the agents, reported that he had scarcely seen the guerrillas. The results of his inquiries to residents of the area were not helpful—some said that they had seen no guerrillas for months, while others volunteered that the insurgents came into town often to buy supplies and to visit relatives.[35]

Sometimes sugar companies suffered as well. In one of a number of reports in early 1921, the civil governor of San Pedro de Macorís claimed that guerrillas were increasing in numbers and audacity. Counted at "over one hundred and fifty, well armed with carbines and revolvers," they had been seen all over his province and just recently had made five raids on four separate sugar estates, in which amounts of money up to four hundred dollars were lost. A lawyer for the La Angelina estate reported other raids on *bateys* in which clothing, other merchandise, and money were taken from company stores and officials. Worse than the material losses, however, was the fact that, since the attacks brought "further demoralization of the laborers . . . the amount of cane ground has only been about one-fourth of what would have been done had there been no raids."[36]

Besides the problem of the war itself, the military government had to acknowledge that its relationship with the so-called pacific inhabitants of the eastern region was far from healthy. When, in February 1921, a military official ordered the transfer of all court records at El Seibo to San Pedro de Macorís, he found that "it is impossible to obtain a carpenter in Seibo who will construct packing boxes for the archives, and that it is further impossible to hire any method of transportation in Seibo for the actual transfer of the archives." Since he also feared that "an effort might be made while the archives are in route from Seibo to Macorís to either capture or destroy them," the military government had to use marines to crate, move, and guard the archives.[37] The incident showed an aversion not only to the officials of the military government but also to the law, which had come to represent oppression to ordinary Dominicans. The marines used military courts as an instrument of war, and the sugar corporations used the civil courts to deprive peasants of their land.

A Crisis: Devising New Responses

In September 1921, an event occurred which shook the military government out of its desultory prosecution of the guerrilla war and out of its self-imposed delusion that all guerrillas were apolitical bandits. "General" Ramón Natera stole onto the grounds of the La Angelina sugar estate during the night of 27–28 September and abducted the manager, Thomas J. Steele, a British citizen, after he failed to respond to Natera's demand for five thousand dollars.[38] Steele went free, unharmed, after two days' imprisonment on the condition that he call a meeting of all the estate managers and that they together, under threat of death from Natera, explain to U.S. officials in Washington the patriotic goal of the guerrillas—that the United States end its occupation of their country. The managers of the six principal U.S.-owned estates were anxious to comply. On 4 October, the managers informed Natera by letter that they would send his message to their New York offices, which would then forward it to Washington.[39]

The kidnapping of Steele caused an uproar both in Washington and in Santo Domingo. The immediate military reaction was to put the entire Fifteenth Regiment, as well as some special troops from Santo Domingo, into the field to pursue Natera, under the leadership of a new eastern district commander, Lieutenant Colonel William C. Harllee.[40]

Harllee, under considerable pressure to eliminate the guerrillas, moved to revamp marine strategy. He created a system of "standing patrols" to supplement the roving units which had dominated marine tactics since 1918. The new patrols, "in concealment during the hours of daylight," located themselves "at strategic points to cover all roads and trails, thereby denying their use to the bandits." They particularly guarded the area around Jagual, El Naranjo de China, and Ramón Santana, the suspected location of Natera's headquarters. Military authorities also sent small marine detachments to as many villages as possible, where they operated during the night, checking all activity and gathering information. Each unit was to include a Spanish-speaking marine. These individuals were so scarce that the Santo Domingo command had to pool Spanish speakers from all over the country and send them to the east.[41]

Perhaps the most important change in late 1921 was the development of the cordoning-off technique. In a series of intensive operations which lasted until March 1922, the marines and the Guardia cordoned off large areas, sweeping through and picking up all "suspicious" characters and forcing them to undergo a process of identification which, if positive, resulted in their imprisonment. According to a marine spokesman, the new tactic was meant to counter a common guerrilla mode of operation, in which the enemy made a raid, fled into the woods, dispersed, and hid. When the marines ended their search, the fugitives left the bush "appearing like any other citizen" and went about their normal jobs, safe because peaceable citizens feared to report them. So the marines decided to move into guerrilla-dominated areas and identify these part-time insurgents.[42] Military authorities thought the identification possible because they had developed a large group of informers, including a number of exguerrillas, and a new screening process which protected the identity of those who gave information against their neighbors. Some idea of the scale of the marines' use of spies and informers is provided by the size of the yearly budget allotment to the intelligence service. It received about twenty-five thousand dollars for its activities all over the republic, an amount which officials claimed in early 1922 was too small, owing to the increased effort in the east. The total is large in light of the fact that monthly payments to active operators averaged around twenty dollars, seldom reaching fifty dollars.[43]

The new technique appeared successful at first. Within a few days the marines arrested nearly fifty alleged "bandits or bandit accomplices," who were soon to be "tried and punished for the unlawful acts for which they are individually or collectively responsible." A marine report detailed several of these operations: "An assembly of people within the region bounded by Chicharrones, Las Callas, Mata de Palma, El Salto, Las Pajas, and Monte Coco was conducted and the people were assembled at Chicharrones and one hundred and five men who were identified as bandits were tried and convicted." A few days later the marines surrounded the area just to the south, bounded by El Salto, Las Pajas, Quisqueya, Los Llanos, and Las Cañadas. Five hundred and sixty-eight people were collected, and one hundred and one were "identified as having engaged in or associated with bandit activities."[44]

The drumhead trials of those caught in these dragnets were open to considerable abuse, as was the process of collecting and identifying the suspects. In fact, the Los Llanos operation produced allegations which portrayed the two-day marine takeover of the town as a psychological if not physical reign of terror. Los Llanos' male citizens were brusquely rounded up, threatened, and penned up overnight in tiny quarters while interrogations and house searches proceeded; the next day they were tied together and forced to march some miles to a neighboring town to undergo the identification process. Afterward provost courts, often using the flimsiest of hearsay evidence, convicted a large number of citizens and sentenced them to heavy fines or to prison at hard labor. "We imagined, Sir," the town's leaders protested to Military Governor Robison, "that we were in Teutonic concentration camps, over there in old Europe, in the days of the great War."[45]

The military government was forced to conduct a serious inquiry because of the citizens' protest, which was picked up and endorsed by the now active nationalist movement in Santo Domingo, and because it was under scrutiny by a U.S. Senate committee which was investigating the occupation. Changes in the marines' method of operations soon resulted. Citizens will "not be collected, tied, and marched to distant points," Eastern District Commander Harllee ordered. "Civil and municipal officials will not be interfered with or prevented from performing their duty, nor will any persons of known good standing be held for identification." If any identification party wants to see large groups of citizens, he continued, it will go to the people rather than moving them. Believing that these changes would make an obviously unpleasant procedure somewhat more acceptable to those who experienced it, Lieutenant Colonel Harllee continued to conduct these roundups. It was, he argued, more effective than the old "system of aimless patrolling."[46]

Despite Harllee's changes, it is likely that the identification process alienated many more than it captured, as would any program, no matter how scrupulous its administration, which removed a significant number of a community's members and sent them off to jail. In November 1921, a delegation of officials from the sugar estates told the military governor that "consternation reigned among the natives in that vicinity to such an extent that they believe that the present operations were on the whole having a bad rather than a good effect, due to the belief of the people that they were being persecuted."[47]

Fear that their community would soon be cordoned off may have led the citizens of the Los Cocos section of Dos Ríos, in the heart of guerrilla country, to send a delegation of forty-three men to Commander Harllee to volunteer their services to the military government.[48] Though Harllee accepted this most unusual demonstration at face value, it is possible that its participants merely hoped to avoid later accusations of banditry.

Even while the cordoning-off operations continued, officials began to doubt their efficacy. After a month's use of the new tactic, Military Governor Robison noted that the marines had arrested and convicted a "fairly large number of unimportant people" but that the guerrillas themselves proved "very elusive." He could consider only one captive, Ramón Natera's wife, as "fairly important." The participation of Guardia members was valuable, he noted, but their decreased number limited their possible effectiveness. Hopefully, Robison added, the opening of the cane-cutting season after October would diminish both unemployment and "banditry." The military governor's hopes soon fell. Military intelligence reported that unemployment continued high during November and that as a result guerrilla recruiting had been quite successful. In fact, most groups seemed to "have more men than they can arm."[49]

In spite of, or perhaps because of, the cordoning-off operations, which represented a break with the previous marine accommodation of the guerrilla movement, there was an increase in the insurgency and in the number of guerrillas in late 1921. Marine officials identified ten distinct major groups in El Seibo and Macorís provinces, as well as numerous small bands of "unemployed laborers" who committed petty crimes while "styling themselves 'bandits.'" The most famous leaders were still Ramón Natera and Tolete, while other men followed Martín Peguero, Cabo Gil, José Fabal, Ramón Batía, Julio Núñez, Andrés Polanco, and El Capitán, whose real name was unknown.[50]

Worse than the increase in activity in late 1921 was the fact that guerrilla operations were again spreading beyond the core area in El Seibo and Macorís. The men of Martín Peguero and his son often operated in eastern Santo Domingo Province. They were frequently near Bayaguana and had four times struck the town of Guerra, little more than fifteen miles from the city of Santo Domingo, to take weapons from civil officials. Even further afield, the leaders Perún de la Cruz, José Parades, and his son, Luis Parades, were operating in Pacificador Province and reportedly had struck as far northwest as the provinces of Espaillat and Puerto Plata.[51]

This continuing warfare was very hard on the economy and the people of the east, particularly on the peasants of the guerrilla core area. But even the best-protected persons, the foreign personnel of the sugar companies, felt insecure after the seizure of Steele at La Angelina. One North American employee of the International Banking Corporation came to San Pedro de Macorís early in October to look after his firm's interest in the Quisqueya sugar estate. Because of the presence of marines stationed there, he judged it safe enough to bring his wife, while taking the precaution of securing a permit to carry arms. But shortly afterward rumors indicated that the guerrillas had made demands on Quisqueya's owner, Juan Castro, who left the estate for the safety of Santo Domingo. Hearing these reports, the representative lost no time returning to San Pedro de Macorís; shortly thereafter he left for the United States, motivated by "fear only."[52]

Rumors also abounded in military circles. In October, military intelligence reported the smuggling of arms into the country from Puerto Rico and warned of a guerrilla campaign to seize the weapons of the *guardas campestres* and the mayordomos of the sugar companies. A more sober estimate of the situation in November 1921 discounted smuggling; most guerrilla weapons had been in the country before the occupation. Some of these were in good condition, but the insurgents were seriously short of ammunition.[53]

In late 1921, Eastern District Commander Harllee determined to eliminate the places of refuge in which guerrilla units had hidden and rested in the past. He pursued his plan in January 1922 by marching into the center of a territory bounded by Hato Mayor, El Seibo, Guaymate, and Los Chicharrones. Harllee believed that a primary camp of guerrilla leader Natera was located in the middle of this district, somewhere just southwest of the junction of the Anamá and Soco rivers, a central point from which trails radiated outward to the whole district. By searching the territory on foot and with aerial patrols, he hoped to locate the spot and establish a regimental field base nearby, thus eliminating the sanctuary. To the same end he worked to improve all the roads in the region, so that main roads would be open to motor vehicles year round and secondary ones to bull carts. Where there were no roads, such as in the Jagual Woods, Harllee used provost prisoners to cut 140 miles of wide trails which so crisscrossed the area that no point was more than half a mile from a trail. He also mapped isolated areas for the first time.[54]

Harllee's campaign made guerrilla life somewhat more difficult in late 1921 and early 1922. A follower of Ramón Natera, a *guarda campestre* who had joined the guerrillas after a raid by Natera on the Santa Fe sugar estate in mid September 1921, detailed this period to his marine captors. At first he had lived at a place called Caño Famiel, south of Ramón Santana, until a marine probe in that area caused a relocation eastward to the Jagual woods. During a month and a half in the Jagual woods, a succession of camps had been established near La Noria and El Regajo, each of which usually held about fifty men. Then, when the marines began operating in the Jagual area, Natera moved his men north to the Arroyo Lucas section, "east of the Soco River and between La Campiña and Seibo."[55] Each of these moves, all within a very small area of the south central region, was a successful effort to avoid direct clashes with the marines.

Some guerrillas, unlike Natera, decided to leave the scene of active marine operations altogether. Reports of contacts from outside the insurgents' heartland began to come in during the fall of 1921 and multiplied in early 1922, with many occurrences in eastern Santo Domingo and western San Pedro de Macorís provinces. The appearance in the area of Guerra and Bayaguana of men who were thought to be outsiders fleeing from the operations in El Seibo caused the civil governor of Santo Domingo Province to ask for Guardia detachments in those towns and in Monte Plata, Yamasá, and La Caleta. There were also incidents at Los Llanos and at La Mula *batey*, where a guerrilla group robbed a bodega of $160 and merchandise. To the north, in the commune of Sabana de la Mar, four towns reported robberies of money and merchandise from bodegas and even from a few families, which was very rare. On the eastern edge of the insurgents' core area, guerrillas were active in Magdalena, near Higüey, and in Chavón Abajo, northeast of La Romana.[56]

1922: An Honorable Surrender

During the first months of 1922, military leaders continued to employ the cordoning-off technique and to use small patrols for careful probing of the countryside. In early January, for instance, an intensive campaign by the marines and the Guardia resulted in four contacts, one with a hundred guerrillas in a camp of thirty-two dwellings. Although most of the insurgents escaped, the marines captured a hundred hammocks, eighty blankets, clothing, and firearms. The civilian who led the marines to this camp, Antonio Draiby, was the same person who had arranged the negotiations with Vicente Evangelista in 1917. Thereafter, in late January, contacts diminished, with only two inconsequential clashes for the rest of the month.[57]

Despite doubts about the effectiveness of the cordoning-off operations, Commander Harllee ordered several in early January 1922. In one case, the entire Fifteenth Regiment encircled the town of El Cercado, just north of Hato Mayor, and its surrounding area. As the troops moved inward, tightening the ring, they collected "all suspicious characters" and took them to Hato Mayor for identification. Informers pointed out 54 people as being connected with the "bandits," and they were immediately tried and sentenced by a provost court. A few days later the encirclement of the woods north of Jagual, an area correctly thought to serve as headquarters for Ramón Natera, netted 530 "suspicious characters." Marines and their assistants identified and sentenced 98 persons as somehow being associated with the guerrillas.[58]

Yet, when the cordoning-off operations were over, the military government's highest-ranking marine officer assessed them as failures. The roundups had led to the identification and conviction of some individuals associated with the guerrilla movement, but they "did not, however, cause the cessation of banditry, nor result in the capture of bandit leaders, and in fact the various bandit groups were unusually active during the latter part of February and the first part of March."[59]

Meanwhile, the east continued to present a miserable spectacle. District Commander Harllee described the core area, between Hato Mayor and El Seibo and running to the south, as deserted. "By nature," he observed, "this [is] a beautiful and fertile section, fairly well supplied with water and which ought to be a region of many prosperous and happy homes. . . . The roads in that area have been entirely neglected. Large trees across them bespeak the fact that bull carts have not traveled over the roads."[60]

In the spring of 1922, military officials decided to change their course because, in the words of two marine chroniclers, "the Marines were no nearer to stamping out banditry than they had been three years before." They abandoned the cordoning-off operations and put to use two other ideas. One was amnesty, a proposal which had been revived several times since 1917 but which had always been unsuccessful because of the harsh terms offered to those who surrendered. The second was the creation of civilian, pro–military government guerrilla units to search out and destroy the enemy which had for so long successfully eluded the marines. To carry out this operation, the military governor appointed a new commander for the eastern military district, Colonel Charles H. Lyman, previously in command at Santiago.[61]

Both policies evolved in 1922 only after the discovery of new information concerning the guerrilla movement, several months of study, and trial runs. The more liberal policy of amnesty, for instance, developed with the slow realization and admission by a few highly placed military officials that the "bandits" had political grievances—that they were, in effect, revolutionaries. Certainly Ramón Natera's seizure of Steele at La Angelina was one cause of the complete reversal of what had been the military government's official position ever since 1917. Another was information which military authorities obtained from the civil governor of Santo Domingo Province, Juan Francisco Sánchez. In mid October 1921, following raids on the town of Guerra by Martín Peguero, Governor Sánchez asked military authorities in Santo Domingo for permission to use a traditional Dominican strategy, that of trading amnesty for surrender, as "these men were formerly workers of good standing in those communes [Guerra and Bayaguana]."[62]

The commanding general of the marine brigade, Harry Lee, mulled over the idea. Intelligence, he said, ascribed only one killing to Peguero's group (committed in conjunction with Tolete), and the evidence was weak. So Lee concurred with Governor Sánchez, adding that "amnesty is usually granted to revolutionists and insurrectionists and . . . it is evident that Peguero and his band consider themselves to be revolutionists." Besides the laying down of arms, Lee suggested the following terms: the group should disband; members should pursue peaceful occupations; the military government should receive members' names, addresses, and physical descriptions; and the amnesty should not include killings.[63]

The military government apparently forgot about Peguero at this point but soon employed another version of the policy in the northern district. Colonel Lyman, at that time still the commander of the Fourth Regiment in Santiago, sent word to the two groups of Perún de la Cruz and José Parades that, if they surrendered, the provost court would try them for military offenses and then release them on one-year suspended sentences conditional on good behavior. The amnesty would not, however, guard them from civil punishment if it were due. Within a week Luis Parades turned himself in, and shortly afterward so did his father, José, and some of their followers. They were tried and given suspended sentences, as were their followers, and it was hoped in early December that Perún de la Cruz would soon follow their example.[64] This act of moderation on the part of the military government, based upon a more intelligent analysis of the insurgency, represented a great advance toward a more realistic policy.

The second proposal for combating the guerrillas was originally the idea of a Dominican, Carlos V. de León, who had formerly worked as chief clerk in the Ministry of Interior and Police and as director of the Labor Bureau. He argued that Dominican civilian irregulars, rather than marines or Guardia members, should be used to combat the "gavilleros." In the first years of the insurgency, he had presented his plan to Brigade Commander Joseph Pendleton and then to Pendleton's successor, B. H. Fuller, he said. But, because it conflicted with the ideas of the officers in charge of the antiguerrilla campaigns and depended on Dominicans for its execution, the plan was not accepted. "Nevertheless, five years of failure should suffice to prove that regular troops, not accustomed to the country, its language, habits, trails, hiding places and system of gorilla [sic] warfare, are not the ones . . . that can easily wipe out gangs of criminals well versed in said affairs and with the most exact knowledge of every inch of the country," de León wrote in October 1921.[65]

Although the military authorities hesitated to place confidence in de León's judgment because he had been discharged from his post in the military government for "malfeasance in office," his idea was soon presented again along with that of amnesty. In November 1921, E. I. Kilbourne, Enrique Jiménez, Eugenio Despaigne, and (Juan or Nicolás?) Santoni, representatives of sugar estates in the east, called on Military Governor Robison to report the negative results of the cordoning-off operations and to ask for their discontinuation. As an alternative, they proposed that "a committee of prominent Dominicans be requested to cooperate with the military authorities in selecting other natives to go into the field with the Guardia to apprehend bandits or that Governor Ramírez, of the Province of Seybo, be given authority to select his own assistants and work directly with the Policía Nacional [the Guardia] in the woods while the Marine bodies continue as now to protect the sugar estates." In addition, "they thought that a Proclamation of Amnesty for such bandits as believed themselves to be fighting for their country would have a good effect and that there would be no difficulty in naming a few such leaders, but that no offers be made to criminal leaders such as Natera and Tolete." As for the latter men, every effort should be made to capture them, a task best accomplished by Dominicans because of their greater knowledge of local affairs and geography.

The commanding general, Harry Lee, when asked to comment on the proposal, noted positively that the estate managers had both property and crops at stake and that they "understand the psychology of the inhabitants." He suggested that the group continue to develop these ideas and, as a vehicle, he arranged a conference between the managers and the civil governors of the provinces of El Seibo, San Pedro de Macorís, and Santo Domingo.[66]

At a mid November meeting, the conferees drew up specific plans for both the paramilitary groups and the amnesty, proposing a trial run of the new strategy in the province of San Pedro de Macorís. The civil governor, Juan Félix Peguero, would recruit forty reliable civilians to add to ten small units of the Guardia Nacional. Each group would have ten men—four unarmed civilians and six members of the Guardia armed with rifles. The marines would maintain their regular positions while the Guardia-civilian groups combed the countryside, limiting marine support to raids on known guerrilla camps at Caño Famiel and La Noria and to other special occasions when the units needed assistance. A simultaneous offer of amnesty would, hopefully, deplete guerrilla ranks of all those not charged with capital crimes. The military governor approved a ten-day test of the program, adding that he thought the civilians should be armed and that he did not want the total cost to go above six hundred dollars.[67] Evidence of the trial run, if it took place, has been lost, but in any case military authorities continued to develop the twin proposals.

Meanwhile, information continued to reach the military authorities which gave them a clearer picture of the eastern situation and added weight to the argument for amnesty. There were further indications that the guerrillas were politically motivated and that many of the insurgents were, in normal times, hardworking and law-abiding citizens who had been provoked into opposition by the military government. Such was the thesis of the Congreso Nacionalista del Seibo in a public statement made to the military government in November 1921. No amount of marine warfare, its members wrote, would eliminate the problem of violence in the east. On the contrary, they argued, the coming of the marines had caused the insurgency, which "had its origin in the suppression and conquest of the year 1916." Though they accepted the military government's designation of the insurgents as bandits, they argued that those involved were good people who had been driven into a life of banditry by fear of military rule, by the disrespectful, arbitrary, and harsh marines, or in angry reaction to the occupation itself.

The statement of the congress, which was sent to Military Governor Robison and others, was one of the first instances in which members of the Dominican elite gave recognition to the war in the east. Most of the signers were young men from influential families in the eastern region, and all were members of the Junta Nacionalista Dominicana, an antioccupation political group which supported the deposed president, Francisco Henríquez y Carvajal. One of the central purposes of their document was to capitalize on the ill feelings caused by marine activity in the east, most recently the cordoning-off operations, in order to call for reestablishment of a civilian national government.[68]

Another insight into the insurgent movement resulted from the surrender of guerrilla Juan José José. José had fought for three months with Ramón Natera and then turned himself in to Governor Peguero of San Pedro de Macorís, a friend of his family. The governor vouched for José, saying that he came "from a good family at Seibo" and describing his responsible past as a policeman in San Pedro de Macorís and as a *guarda campestre* at La Campiña for the Santa Fe sugar estate.

In deference to José's influential friend, Eastern Commander Harllee gave the exguerrilla his freedom in exchange for information about Natera and a promise of future cooperation with the marines. At the same time, Colonel Harllee conveyed the story of the entire incident to Military Governor Robison and Commanding General Lee and proposed making a general policy of amnesty: "I would like very much for all of Natera's group to quit the bandit business and those who do so and return to work and give us assistance in locating this Natera and the active members of his group will not be treated with severity."[69]

During the winter of 1921–22, the military government decided to proceed along the lines of the plans drawn up in November by creating new civilian units, called civil guards, to carry out an intensive antiguerrilla campaign. These aggressive patrols, stationed at Consuelo, Santa Fe, Las Pajas, Hato Mayor, and El Seibo, would each consist of fifteen "thoroughly reliable Dominicans" led by a marine officer and several marine noncommissioned officers. Aside from loyalty to the military government, the criteria for unit members were their knowledge of guerrilla tactics and familiarity with their respective areas of operations. As the marines judged all Dominicans to be poor marksmen, each recruit received a marine rifle course.[70] Officials also made plans for an amnesty. The military government promised specific, generous terms to all insurgents who surrendered, even to those previously excluded from such offers, like Ramón Natera and Tolete.[71]

The civil guards were ready in April 1922. Normally a guerrilla offensive would have occurred at this time of year. Unemployment surged as the busy season ended at the sugar estates; the mills of La Angelina, Porvenir, and Consuelo had closed. But the normal late spring resurgence of warfare never occurred. The civilian groups went into operation in April and proved extremely effective at reaching the insurgents.[72]

The twofold approach of amnesty and the use of the civil guards quickly produced the desired results. The first voluntary surrender of a guerrilla leader since 1917 came on 6 April 1922, when Andrés Polanco turned himself in at Bayaguana. He was followed six days later by the famous Tolete, who, with his followers and those of Martín Peguero, had just come under heavy attack by a marine unit after one of the civilian groups had located them. Although Tolete's group had successfully retreated from the battle and still had firearms "in excellent condition,"[73] Tolete had apparently seen the writing on the wall. For the first time, he faced an opponent acquainted with him, his tactics, and his territory, and this opponent was also well trained and equipped.

After Tolete, other guerrillas began to trickle in, especially the members of Martín Peguero's group. In the first days of May, negotiations were opened between District Commander Lyman and Ramón Natera. They arranged a cease-fire, whereby the military government suspended all operations in the east, and on 5 May 1922 Natera, together with another leader, Cabo Gil, surrendered to Colonel Lyman at Cañada del Agua, north of Consuelo. Lyman remained in Natera's camp as a hostage while Natera and Gil rode into Consuelo to meet with other marine officials. Following the discussion, Natera and Gil, still armed, returned to their camp, promising to bring in their followers within several days. Although Gil apparently had second thoughts and remained out for a short while, Natera led in his band on 8 May. On the same day, Ramón Batía surrendered at Hato Mayor, as did his brother, Bullito, on 9 May. Martín Peguero surrendered on 13 May at Vasca, leaving only Cabo Gil, who finally turned himself in on 22 May at El Seibo. The entire operation went smoothly, except for one incident in Higüey on 14 May, when a group of three marines and six local police attacked and killed a minor leader, Ferro (Lillo?) Peguero and five of his followers. Marine officials promptly initiated an investigation.[74]

Other than those who came in with Natera, very few followers presented themselves before 14 May. The last guerrilla surrendered on 31 May 1922, bringing the total to 140.[75] This was only the hard core of the guerrilla movement. There had been hundreds of others, some of whom had already been imprisoned and many of whom, only occasionally involved in the fighting, had returned home previously.

A Pax Americana

The military government paroled the guerrilla leaders as they surrendered. They returned for their trials on 14 to 16 June 1922. All except Tolete "were sentenced to be confined at hard labor for a period of fifteen years, but the punishment was remitted on the condition that each ex-bandit leader, during a period of eleven years and three months, conduct himself in such a manner as would warrant suspension of the sentence." Tolete, who had escaped from previous incarceration, received a sentence of twenty years' hard labor, suspended for fifteen years.[76] Similarly, each of the followers stood trial and then went free on parole. After the guerrillas' surrender, many men previously jailed on charges of banditry or aiding banditry requested pardons. Except in special cases, the military government granted these men their freedom. Even Gregorio Urbano Gilbert, the young patriot who killed an officer on the dock at San Pedro de Macorís in 1917, obtained release after Archbishop Nouel and the papal apostolic delegate presented a petition of clemency to the military governor.[77] The only guerrillas remaining in jail until the end of the occupation were the former followers of Vicentico and Tolete, who had all received long sentences in 1917 and who had no friends in high places.

Following the final guerrilla surrenders, Commanding General Harry Lee sent letters of commendation to each group of civil guards, thanking them for their cooperation with the military government. The contacts which they had made and the losses which they had caused the insurgents, he explained, "were largely, if not primarily responsible for the presentation and surrender of the bandit chiefs and their followers to the military authorities."[78] Military Governor Robison also thanked the sugar estate administrators, particularly E. I. Kilbourne of the Consuelo estate, who had been one of those chiefly responsible for the formation of the civil guards and for the negotiations with the guerrilla leaders in April and May.[79]

The military governor again contacted the sugar estates a short while later, concerning unemployment. Recalling the difficult task of ending the guerrilla war and praising the contributions of the sugar companies, Robison noted that the surrendered guerrillas were now in need of jobs. Although some exguerrillas had *conucos*, he explained, many did not. "It is considered that the good behavior of the latter will be assured by steady employment and your good efforts in this respect will be appreciated." As a second measure, he requested land for *conucos*, so that the sugar workers could feed themselves during the months of unemployment. Finally, Robison forbade the sugar estates to solicit government permits to import laborers until "all sources of labor in the vicinity of your Estate and in other parts of the republic be fully explored and exhausted." When he had sent out a similar request in March, he had received only vague promises to increase employment, along with various reasons why it was not practical to do so.[80]

The military governor also tried to create more work in other areas of the economy. He canvassed local public authorities in Santo Domingo and other towns and sought to increase the number of jobs offered by the military government itself, particularly on the eastern highway. Somehow, the military governor insisted, he had to create fuller employment in order to "guard against a condition of unemployment and resulting lack of good order."[81]

Although armed opposition to the military government ended in May 1922, Robison's concern about employment shows that military officials were more cautious than in the past about the possibility of a resurgence of guerrilla activity. The military governor further revealed official apprehensions in June, when he began to promote the establishment of civil armed guards on a permanent basis for each of the sugar estates. He was also adamant with Sumner Welles, the special commissioner sent by the State Department to negotiate a treaty of withdrawal with the Dominicans, that a marine outpost remain at Los Chicharrones while the occupation continued. This post was located in the heart of the guerrilla area and, the marines believed, served as a quieting influence. It was also a good place from which to keep watch over the guerrilla leaders, who, Robison noted, were "men of considerable force of character."[82]

In September 1922, in accordance with the plans to end the occupation signed in July, the marines concentrated their forces at just two locations in the east, Los Chicharrones and San Pedro de Macorís. The permanent garrisons at Hato Mayor, El Seibo, Higüey, Los Llanos, and Guerra departed and left the task of policing the region to the Guardia and local authorities. A skeleton force remained at the two points of concentration until April 1924.[83]

In fact, the apprehensions of military officials were not realized. Guerrilla leaders assented to the new situation and, in at least some cases, even cooperated with it. For example, Ramón Goico, the chief of the municipal district of Ramón Santana, reported in mid 1922 that Ramón Natera had visited some areas for him to make sure they were peaceful. Several reports of friction between exguerrillas, including Natera, and local authorities proved upon investigation to be the fault more of abusive officials, perhaps testing their authority, than of the exguerrillas.[84] In Natera's case, however, another, perhaps inevitable confrontation eventually occurred. In a dispute with a *guarda campestre* from the Porvenir estate, Natera was shot to death in November 1923.[85]

As for organized guerrilla activity, there was none after May 1922. Only a few reports of "banditry" broke the tranquillity of the east during the remainder of that year, these incidents being the work of small groups which were usually soon captured. Intelligence reports for all of 1923 reveal not one incident of outlawry of any kind.[86] By October 1922, life in the east had returned to normal. William E. Pulliam, the receiver general of Dominican customs and a past critic of the policy of the military government in the east, at last had words of praise. The roads from San Pedro de Macorís, he noted, were open to all nearby towns. The countrypeople could now market what they raised, and a considerable amount of fresh produce was coming into the city. Owners were reopening cacao plantations in the region which had been completely abandoned for several years. The situation in general was excellent.[87]

A Retrospective View

Why, after five and a half successful years of warfare, did the guerrillas opt to surrender in May 1922? What combination of factors caused them to agree to end the war? Viable military alternatives remained, such as a retreat from the populated central section of the east to more mountainous areas. Life would have been harder there, but it would also have been much easier to elude the marines.

It is likely, however, that the guerrilla leaders, acting to conserve their own strength or for patriotic reasons, thought that they had accomplished their ends by the spring of 1922, as it was obvious to most Dominicans by this time that the United States wanted very much to end the military occupation. The much publicized negotiations which led to U.S. withdrawal were under way, and a tentative agreement was reached by June 1922. The insurgent leaders could not have known that the traditional structure they fought to preserve would never function again.

What of the guerrilla leaders' inarticulate followers? What of the peasants fighting in protest against the usurpation of their small holdings? Certainly their frustrations were unrelieved. The military governor's plea to the sugar estates to increase employment during the postharvest *tiempo muerto*, and to provide *conucos* for those workers who had none, was an insufficient answer to their problems. But, deprived of their traditional leaders by the surrender, neither peasant farmers nor cane workers showed any desire to continue to fight.

Changing perspectives within the military government matched those on the side of the guerrillas. The arrival of new officials, especially Military Governor Samuel Robison and Brigade Commander Harry Lee, who were more open to reexamining the nature of the war than earlier military officials had been, was also important in ending the five-and-a-half-year struggle. Their willingness to listen to civilian experts from the eastern region brought Robison and Lee to accept the war as a revolutionary insurgency motivated by political and economic grievances. This understanding caused significant changes in marine strategy. The cordoning-off operations, though militarily ineffective, may have weakened the base of guerrilla support—the general population—by making it more dangerous for people to harbor insurgents or to provide other means of support. More effective was the use of civil guards. These groups, knowledgeable in guerrilla war and well acquainted with the terrain, were able to put considerable military pressure on the insurgents. And complementing the civil guards' work was the earlier decision of Commander William Harllee to get the marines off the main roads and into the woods, especially in the guerrilla heartland to the south of Hato Mayor and El Seibo.

All these factors, political and military, contributed to ending the insurgency. During the entire war the marines, in some 370 recorded contacts with insurgents, claimed to have suffered only 13 killed and 40 wounded. Guerrilla casualties, according to a fanciful marine estimate, were 950 killed and wounded.[88]

In part, the guerrilla war had been the last gasp of a declining political system. In their surrender, the guerrilla chiefs paid obeisance to a new way of political life. They may have hoped that the new order would last only until the marines departed. If so, they were wrong. No longer would the central government be forced to negotiate with the eastern caudillos to gain the region's allegiance. Never again would these traditional leaders successfully defy the central government or raise their followers in rebellion.

Certain changes insured the destruction of the old system. The military government had greatly improved transportation and communication and was continuing to do so. For the first time, however tenuously, the east was joined to the nation. And, even more important, the Guardia Nacional was slowly able to replace the marines. Soon it would hold an effective monopoly of power, directed from the nation's capital. In the future, easterners who wanted to affect the destiny of their region would have to go to Santo Domingo to do so.

About a year after the guerrillas' surrender, an incident occurred which graphically illustrates the basic shift in power. In May 1923, the *síndico* of Mata Palacio, a police official responsible to the central government, complained that Tolete had interrupted a meeting at which the *síndico* and the local inspector of public instruction were urging the citizens of the area to pay their taxes. Tolete declared loudly that he was in charge of the commune, arguing that the officials refused to recognize his authority because he would not allow them to collect taxes invented for their own benefit. When the peasants at the meeting continued to support the *síndico* and the inspector, Tolete began to call the officials thieves and cowards and the discussion nearly degenerated into a fistfight.[89] Though nothing more came of this argument than a complaint to higher authorities, the incident symbolizes the great change which had taken place in the east. No longer did the word of a popular leader represent a force greater than that of an official of the central government, even when the official was promoting something as unpopular as taxes.

8

The Nationalist Campaign for Withdrawal: 1917–1921

The United States withdrew its forces from the Dominican Republic in September 1924. The primary cause of the withdrawal was a campaign waged by Dominican nationalists and their allies against the occupation. Their eight-year political struggle served to make the military government's rule increasingly difficult, brought the competence of the U.S. overlords into question, caused the interventionist foreign policy of Woodrow Wilson to become an issue in the U.S. presidential campaign of 1920, and brought the United States severe embarrassment and difficulty in its international relations. Once these combined pressures had resulted in a withdrawal plan, a continuing nationalist effort forced its rapid implementation.

The Frustration of the Nationalist Campaign, 1916–1918

One of the first acts of what was to become the nationalist campaign was President Francisco Henríquez y Carvajal's visit to the United States in December 1916. Accompanied by his son and secretary, Max Henríquez Ureña, the Dominican president tried to obtain a change in U.S. policy. But it soon became clear that his arguments fell upon deaf ears. Instead, the Dominicans lodged an official protest, gave the press some interviews critical of the occupation, and left for Cuba.[1] Apparently suspecting that the occupation might last for some time, President Henríquez presented a confidential and unsigned memorandum to the State Department before he left Washington. The memorandum protested the continuing occupation, proposed the substitution of a U.S. civil regime for the military one, and suggested various concrete policies which the occupation government might follow to solve some long-standing Dominican problems.[2]

From the first, the ousted president and persons associated with him led the nationalist movement. Very soon after the proclamation of the military government, they laid down the principles which would guide the nationalist movement in its campaign against the occupation: (1) maintenance of constant protest in the United States, Latin America, and Europe; (2) preservation of Dominican unity, especially against signing or submitting to any pact which would legitimize the U.S. presence, such as had occurred in Haiti; (3) creation of a directorate to guide the resistance and of three traveling embassies, one each for the United States, Latin America, and Europe; and (4) establishment of a network of *juntas nacionalistas* in the Dominican Republic for the purpose of collecting contributions to support the directorate and the embassies.[3]

Cuba was to be the headquarters of the nationalist campaign, since the absence of civil liberties in the Dominican Republic prevented any open political action there. The island offered various advantages. Cuban nationalists, having troubles of their own with the United States, made the Dominicans welcome. Cuba had good communication with both the nearby Dominican Republic and the United States. Moreover, President Henríquez had established a home and a medical practice in Santiago de Cuba in the years before his election in 1916. Finally, the Dominican chargé d'affaires in Havana, Manuel M. Morillo, had, in concert with other Dominicans, already paved the way for the nationalists by organizing several acts of protest against the intervention.[4]

At first, events seemed to favor the nationalists. A number of Dominican diplomats, in Washington, Paris, Havana, and the Virgin Islands, brought international publicity to their country's plight by defying the new military government. At the late January conference of the American Institute of International Law in Cuba, attended by Latin American and U.S. jurists, the Dominican case received considerable attention. Delegates returning from the meeting, as well as other contacts, caused the Dominican case to be taken up by "prominent people and important journals" in the United States. Similarly, the Latin American press gave the Dominican case frequent coverage. This was facilitated by the work of Morillo in Havana, whom the heavily censored Asociación de la Prensa had named as its foreign representative, "with instructions to carry on a programme of publicity against the actions of the American government in Santo Domingo."[5]

The Dominicans put their case before the world successfully. But their success was limited and continued to be ever more limited by the focus of U.S. and world attention on World War I. By late winter 1917, with the United States preparing to enter the conflict, the nationalist leaders decided to suspend their infant campaign for the duration of the war.[6]

In the interim, the brothers Henríquez returned to their professions in Cuba, Francisco as a doctor in Santiago and Federico—who had been a presidential candidate in 1916—as a professor in Havana. Twice during 1918, Federico returned to the Dominican Republic to test the wind for the nationalist cause, and twice he was disappointed. Of likely supporters, he wrote, "the majority—some because of fear and others because of pessimism—avoided all commitment." Of those few who were willing to identify openly with the nationalists, despite censorship and the tight surveillance by the military government's intelligence services, many were younger Dominicans, a number of them former students of the brothers associated with the Academia Colombina.[7]

But Dominicans in 1918 were still divided over how to deal with the occupation, explained politico, lawyer, and sugar *colono* Enrique Jiménez in Santo Domingo. A few advocated rising up in arms, seeing this as the only alternative to permanent loss of independence. Another group despaired of the ability of Dominicans to run their nation successfully and thus accepted the occupation. Members of a third element, which included "a very large number of intellectuals," were engaged in a massive debate over the moral and legal questions of the occupation which had the effect of completely immobilizing them. The best policy, argued Jiménez, was to end this debate, to acknowledge the occupation as a temporary fact, and to work with it for necessary political and social reform.[8]

The Reawakening of Nationalism, 1918–1919

The end of World War I, some Dominicans believed, would bring about a change in U.S. policy in Santo Domingo. With this in mind, a group of eleven young men met in Cuba on 11 November 1918, the day of the European armistice, and took the first step toward revitalizing the Dominican nationalist movement. The eleven, three Dominicans and eight Cubans, formed the Sociedad de los Once. One of the first acts of this new group was to spawn another, the Comité pro–Santo Domingo, with branches in Havana and Santiago. The committee, packed with illustrious and wealthy Cubans, primarily provided financial support. But it also offered first-rate connections, among them direct links to at least three Cuban newspapers which could provide publicity, printing facilities, and access to international wire services.[9]

Within a short time, the group had raised twenty thousand Cuban pesos to send President Henríquez to the Versailles Conference in early 1919. There he would press for inclusion of the Dominican case in the docket of oppressed nationalities whose cause President Wilson claimed to champion in his famous Fourteen Points. Little resulted from the effort, however, as the United States succeeded in blocking consideration of U.S. hegemony in the Americas. Henríquez' activity was thus limited to lobbying among the diplomats present at Versailles. He received promises from several Latin American nations to raise the Dominican question with the United States after peace was made. With great difficulty he obtained an interview with J. H. Stabler, the chief of the Division of Latin American Affairs of the State Department, to whom he presented several memoranda on the Dominican situation. But Stabler refused to negotiate, reportedly telling Henríquez that "American matters would have to be dealt with in America." Although tempted to press his case further, the Dominican leader decided on a course of nonconfrontation and returned quietly from Europe.[10]

Shortly after the unproductive trip to Versailles, President Henríquez met for talks in New York with his brother, Federico, with his sons Pedro and Max Henríquez Ureña, and with writer and diplomat Tulio M. Cestero and the noted lawyer Francisco Peynado. The small group of nationalists had also invited the leaders of the three main political factions, plus Archbishop Adolfo Nouel, to join them, on the assumption that Washington would be prepared for serious negotiation after the Versailles Conference; but one by one they refused, citing the weakest of excuses. The purpose of the New York meeting was to plan a strategy and to strengthen the organization of the nationalist effort. The conferees laid plans for establishing other Comités pro–Santo Domingo as solidarity and fund-raising groups, first in New York and then in the capitals of Latin America. On the suggestion of Peynado, the group at first named itself the Junta Nacionalista del Exterior, but it was soon generally known as the Comisión Nacionalista Dominicana; it became the coordinator of nationalist lobbying and propaganda in the United States.[11] Notably absent from the group's plans was an effort to strengthen the *juntas nacionalistas* and the nationalist movement in the Dominican Republic.

After the New York meeting, the Comisión Nacionalista traveled to Washington to pursue negotiations with the U.S. government. To this end President Henríquez attempted to see President Wilson, but, for the third time since 1916, he was turned away. Official doors remained closed until the group approached other Latin American diplomats, particularly those of Uruguay, who interceded. There followed in September and October a series of conversations with State Department officials and representatives of the Bureau of Insular Affairs of the Department of War (what amounted to an office of colonial affairs).[12]

The very moderate argument advanced by President Henríquez and the nationalists in approaching the State Department was that the United States had no legitimate reason to continue the occupation. With World War I ended, hemispheric security was no longer a pressing issue. The Dominican Republic was again in a quiet and prosperous condition, and its people were anxious to regain control of their own affairs. President Henríquez suggested that Washington immediately begin a gradual process of turning the government in Santo Domingo back over to Dominicans. He envisioned "a process, which must not be lengthy, of reorganizing the country politically and administratively, in accordance with a plan for broad legal reforms, similar in many ways to those carried out in Cuba during the intervention of 1906 to 1909, that is, preparation of basic laws which would assure the people's liberty and give them control of the functions of government." As a first step, he argued, it was necessary to establish a climate conducive to full political discussion by abolishing censorship and the provost courts. Then the military governor should create an advisory council of representative Dominicans to advise him during this process.

Henríquez also stated his willingness to renounce his claim to the Dominican presidency to allay charges that he sought reestablishment of Dominican sovereignty in order to regain power personally.[13] He believed that circumstances compelled him to take this moderate position: "In view of the insuperable difficulties which the State Department raised against the claims of the Dominican people," he confided in a letter to a supporter, "I found myself obligated to seek the gradual reestablishment of my country's government."[14]

Several members of the Comisión Nacionalista remained in Washington until the fall of 1919, at which point lack of money as well as various personal and business obligations forced them to return to Santo Domingo and Cuba, leaving only Tulio Cestero behind to maintain communication with the State Department and the Latin American embassies. The diplomatic negotiations, it then seemed to the nationalists, had produced positive results. The State

Department, it appeared, was listening and reconsidering its policy. President Henríquez wrote of "confidential promises" concerning reforms made to him by State Department officials, and Cestero remarked hopefully that "our efforts are beginning to bear fruit."[15] However, their optimism, as events of the next year would prove, was ill founded.

With the war in Europe ended, the Dominicans also found North American intellectual and political circles more receptive to their ideas. They found themselves invited to a series of distinguished gatherings where they were able to present their case. And by late 1919 articles began to appear regularly in the *Nation*, in the *New York Times* and its journal, *Current History*, and in *Reforma Social*, a New York publication disseminated throughout Latin America. Sympathetic pieces also appeared in such diverse publications as the *Yale Review*, the *Washington Post*, the *New York Tribune*, the *Journal of International Relations*, and *Metropolitan Magazine*. As a result of this publicity some organizations began to support the Dominican cause, most important among them the American Federation of Labor and its president, Samuel Gompers, who directed a letter of protest to President Wilson on behalf of his organization.[16]

A number of the Dominicans' North American contacts were facilitated by Horace Knowles, a New York lawyer and exminister of the United States to the Dominican Republic and Bolivia. Knowles, who had a wide network of contacts in the Republican party and with the press, met President Henríquez through Francisco Peynado. When the exofficial showed a sympathetic interest in the Dominican cause, the nationalists retained him as their U.S. legal counsel. His services would prove valuable.[17]

The growing nationalist campaign in the United States had its parallel in Europe and Latin America. In Europe the most vigorous proponent of the Dominican cause was Enrique Deschamps, the former Dominican consul in Paris. His actions, especially in Spain, resulted in numerous newspaper articles and several petitions protesting the occupation which were directed to President Wilson. One of the petitions bore the signatures of representatives of all the parties in the Spanish parliament. The center of Latin American propaganda remained Havana, from which the nationalists kept a steady stream of information flowing to the rest of Latin America, especially to journalists, press associations, and sympathetic governments.[18]

One of the outstanding successes of the Latin American propaganda during this period involved the publication of a speech critical of the intervention by Cuba's noted jurist Emilio Roíg de Leuchen-ring. Made to the Sociedad Cubana de Derecho Internacional and sent from Havana by cable, the speech attracted widespread attention in Latin America and the United States. In Colombia its publication provided ammunition for a pro-Dominican campaign in the prominent daily *El Tiempo* and, eventually, for a condemnation of the intervention by the Colombian congress.[19]

These propaganda efforts soon began to receive Washington's attention. As the State Department's Sumner Welles noted, Secretary Robert Lansing was constantly aware of the "increasing apprehension among the Republics of Latin America" over the Dominican situation. "Protests both informal and formal, emanating from Latin American Governments, prominent publicists in South America, and from associations throughout the continent, were being addressed continually through the summer and autumn of 1919 to President Wilson, urging the termination of the occupation and the reestablishment of a Dominican government."[20] The result of Latin America's growing concern with the occupation was more than embarrassment—it increasingly interfered with U.S. diplomacy there.

The pressure on Washington translated into pressure on the military government. One of the sorest issues concerned the lack of basic liberties, particularly freedom of the press, under the military government. When, as a result of this criticism, the State Department began to demand precise information from military officials on their policies concerning freedom of the press and of assembly, it found that, the military government's protestations notwithstanding, these freedoms were severely curtailed.[21] Shortly thereafter, the State Department began to pressure the military government to abandon its policy of prior censorship.

The general repressiveness of the military government—censorship, severe limitations on political activities, and the force represented by armed marines, the provost courts, and the military government's network of spies—was a primary reason why the nationalist movement had remained weak and unorganized within the republic itself. Virtually the only breach in this tight ring of control was made by a series of newsletters written by President Henríquez. Sent in from abroad and circulated from hand to hand, they sought not only to inform but to break the apathy which prevailed among the Dominican people toward the occupation. Henríquez sometimes urged specific actions, such as the formation of patriotic juntas, and in nearly every case he sought contributions to support the nationalist campaign abroad. The military government complained of his "constant flood of circulars" and worried about his possible influence on the political situation.[22]

A second factor which detracted from the nationalists' effort at home was political divisiveness. Even while the Comisión Nacionalista had attempted to negotiate in Washington, the traditional infighting had continued in Santo Domingo between the political parties. This disturbed the nationalists, who felt that their credibility in Washington was undermined by the petty squabbles at home. More disturbing were the occasional direct attacks on their efforts by the traditional political parties, jealous of the nationalists' increasing political importance. In November 1919, for example, the party of Horacio Vásquez published a letter questioning the actions of Henríquez and Cestero and even suggesting that they were preparing to give away Samaná Bay in their negotiations. In another case, Dr. Henríquez' call for "a political and administrative organization identical to that which governs the island of Cuba" occasioned a malicious rumor that he approved of the Platt Amendment, which he emphatically denied.[23]

The nationalists' less than total support at home was reflected in the difficulty they had collecting funds for their efforts. Their campaign was costly, involving travel, publication, international communication, and sometimes the living expenses of those who had given up their regular professions to work for the nationalist cause. Much of their support before mid 1920 came from Cubans, often through the Comités pro–Santo Domingo. Contributions came occasionally from Santo Domingo, where a few individuals such as Francisco Peynado contributed disproportionately, but many others were affected by what one supporter called a "sleeping patriotism."[24] In November 1919, Alicia Gutiérrez de Cestero and a group of women in New York City founded the Comité de Damas pro–Santo Domingo to solicit funds in New York, the Dominican Republic, and Latin America, but their campaign was rather unsuccessful. Therefore, individual nationalists often found themselves having to borrow from friends, spending their savings, and even selling family property to survive.[25]

Toward the end of 1919, a change was afoot in the Dominican Republic which eventually resulted in a much strengthened nationalist movement. Several forces promoted this turn of events. Among them, to be sure, were the activities of Dr. Henríquez and the Comisión Nacionalista in Paris and Washington. Although Dominicans had at first viewed his work as ineffective and hopeless, this attitude had begun to change. The newsletters with which he peppered the republic found a large underground circulation, eventually stirring up hopes, rumors of plans to soften or end U.S. control, and, in Military Governor Snowden's view, "considerable agitation and unrest." Meanwhile, members of the Comisión Nacionalista in Washington, unaware of Snowden's exaggerated claims of their effectiveness, saw the lack of "visible support from the Dominican people" as a political embarrassment and moved to revitalize the *juntas nacionalistas* and the leadership of the nationalist movement there. In so doing, they helped create a base for the active movement which arose in 1920.[26]

Among the other causes of the change in Santo Domingo was the military government itself. Since 1916, the officials of the military government had encouraged the passive acceptance of the occupation by a majority of Dominicans with repeated public assurances that the United States had no intention of permanently destroying Dominican sovereignty. In July 1919, however, Military Governor Snowden, often the author of injudicious remarks, noted to a group of Dominicans at a school dedication his belief that the United States should continue to govern the Dominican Republic until its present generation of small children had reached maturity. Snowden's chance remarks caused an immediate wave of protest, including a condemnatory petition signed by thousands of Dominicans. The State Department eventually forced him to amend his remarks, to declare publicly that the United States had no intention of staying longer than was necessary to enact some basic reforms, though he continued to argue privately that the occupation should continue for ten to twenty years.[27]

The patriotism stirred up by Snowden's remark became plainly visible in September and October of 1919 with the visit of a Spanish poet, Francisco Villaespesa, to various Dominican cities. Readings of his poems of Hispanic solidarity ("Canto a la raza") and of support for the Dominican nation ("Canto a Santo Domingo") were greeted with thunderous applause; it was "the first display of popular patriotic passion" since 1916, wrote the noted intellectual and nationalist Américo Lugo. In Puerto Plata, a marine intelligence officer reported that Villaespesa's visit created "considerable unrest."[28]

In early November 1919, the U.S. State Department further stirred Dominican hopes for withdrawal by forcing Military Governor Snowden to appoint a *junta consultiva* or consulting commission of four influential Dominicans who were to study and propose various reforms which would eventually facilitate U.S. withdrawal. Although Snowden had opposed the commission's formation, he hoped that "this might appease the desire of the Dominicans for a voice in their country's affairs." The commission consisted of Archbishop Adolfo Nouel, Francisco Peynado, Federico Velásquez, and Jacinto R. de Castro, moderate to conservative public figures who had generally cooperated with the military government.[29]

The commission, although modeled on an earlier suggestion made by President Henríquez to the State Department, was a total surprise to him and his followers, who refused to join it. "The news could not have been more surprising, since nothing formal had been arranged with the State Department concerning this matter."[30] Nevertheless, the group began its work almost immediately. After an initial cordial meeting with Snowden, the group wrote three memoranda during November and December, the second and third mainly reiterating the points of the first. The commission's proposals were essentially the same moderate ones that President Henríquez had been making in various memoranda since 1916. They suggested a series of new or rewritten laws concerning elections, the organization of communal and provincial governments, control of the treasury, conscription, and the presidential succession, as well as two immediate reforms of military government policy: (1) abolition of prior censorship and its replacement by a set of precise guidelines to prevent journalistic abuse of the military government and (2) limitation of the provost courts' jurisdiction to military personnel.[31]

The majority of politically involved Dominicans at first welcomed the junta's formation. The *Listín Diario*, Santo Domingo's most influential paper, warmly welcomed the junta in an editorial, and even Military Governor Snowden found himself pleased with "the cordial reception which the measure is everywhere receiving." But the prospect of the junta upset a small and influential group of more radical nationalists, who believed that it represented a departure from the original nationalist policy of a united front against the military government. Washington, the radicals believed, would seduce the commission members into a compromise which would legitimize the occupation. The junta, Américo Lugo wrote later, resulted from President Henríquez' "false" and "dangerous" doctrine of "reestablishment of national sovereignty after reforms." The reforms themselves were often acceptable, argued Lugo; the evil was that the military government rather than Dominicans would implement them.[32]

The nationalists, it turned out, had little to fear from the *junta consultiva*. Although Military Governor Snowden appears to have been prepared to treat the junta's suggestions seriously, he refused to implement its preliminary proposals regarding censorship and the provost courts. He abolished prior censorship, but, in a nearly insulting rejection of the junta's request for a precise and narrow code to curb possible excesses of the press, he issued a very vague "Reglamento para la censura." Later codified as Executive Order No. 385, the new regulation laid down a wide range of injunctions, even prohibiting articles and speeches which "portrayed the present condition of Santo Domingo in a manifestly unjust way." Such provisions, the junta correctly feared, could be used for the wholesale repression of the rights of free speech and assembly. Snowden also declined to abolish the civilian jurisdiction of the provost courts because, as he confided to a friend, no Dominican court could be trusted to try offenses committed against the military government.[33]

Snowden's rebuff showed the commission's powerlessness and brought it under increasing verbal attack both in the press and on the street. Behind the scenes, President Henríquez and his followers rejected the junta as an "inadequate version of what we have asked for and continue to demand," lacking both authority and an unoppressive environment in which to operate. On 7 January 1920, the members submitted their joint resignation, saying that it would be necessary to remove the twin threats of censorship and provost courts before the process of reform could proceed. Until that time, the Dominican people would lack the all-important freedom to discuss the proposed reforms.[34]

Confrontation: The Semana Patriótica and the 1920 Censorship Cases

The awkward and contradictory U.S. policy put forward by the more liberal State Department and begrudgingly implemented by the Department of the Navy's conservative military government had effects in Santo Domingo which Washington little intended. The long-quiet nationalists found a cause to combat in the junta while moderates, basically willing to cooperate with the military government, were embarrassed and increasingly alienated by the refusal of Military Governor Snowden to meet them halfway. In sum, U.S. policy had the effect of mobilizing the nationalists and of increasing support for their position among previously uninvolved Dominicans. A polarization was beginning to take place which could only undermine support for the military government and damage its ability to rule.

One sign of this was the formation of a new nationalist organization in February 1920. The creation of some of the more radical nationalists, led by Fabio Fiallo and Américo Lugo, the Unión Nacional Dominicana was a reaction both to U.S. policy and to the threat of compromise represented by the *junta consultiva*. The union had two guiding principles: the immediate reestablishment of the republic as an absolutely sovereign state and a prohibition against any collaboration with the military government which might limit Dominican sovereignty after U.S. withdrawal. The new group was open to anyone, regardless of party affiliation, who accepted its principles. The members paid dues according to their ability, were organized on a provincial basis, and were to recruit new members, collect funds, and coordinate nationalist propaganda. From the larger organization came a Junta Central Directiva, which was to direct nationalist activities both inside and outside the country. Within a month the organization published the names of its officers and of nearly three thousand members, as well as a statement of adhesion by a large number of Dominican women. Subsequently, various groups, including the Congreso de la Prensa, voted their support.[35]

The Unión Nacional, with its leadership located within the country, quickly became the most important nationalist organization in the republic, and it remained so until mid 1922. Though it could hardly be said to have had a popular base, it at least began to mobilize a sizable part of the elite and the middle sectors. In this sense it was a tremendous boost to the efforts of President Henríquez and his associates. Yet the new organization was also a threat to them, for much of its leadership stood in opposition to Henríquez' moderate stance. By mid March, Military Governor Snowden reported hopefully that the union had "split up into two antagonistic parts, the radicals and the conservatives." But though there were differences, essentially centered on the more moderate members' willingness to negotiate with the U.S. government to regain sovereignty gradually, the group survived and flourished. At the same time, the articulate and persuasive radicals continued to exert a heavy influence on the union and its politics, which frequently forced Henríquez and his followers toward the radical point of view. The group early demonstrated its strength when, in April 1920, it opposed and stopped a movement, backed by moderates, to send the *junta consultiva* to Washington to end the stalemate over censorship.[36]

The creation of the Unión Nacional brought together in an effective and open organization the growing number of Dominicans who rejected or at least questioned the occupation. As though drawing strength from this display of numbers, Dominican individuals and groups began small but collectively significant actions to oppose the occupation. In March, for example, an article appeared in the Santo Domingo and Santiago press, calling for an immediate end to the occupation and vaguely threatening violence if it continued. The article, wrote a marine commander, created much comment, "all of it hostile to the U.S., and much of it of a very violent and excited character."[37]

In the east a noted lawyer and exsenator took an unprecedented action in bringing charges of brutality against a notorious marine. Although the marine went unpunished and the lawyer himself was brought before a court-martial on a retaliatory, trumped-up charge, a group of distinguished citizens openly challenged the right of the military to try the lawyer.[38]

In San Francisco de Macorís, the *junta nacionalista* asked all businesses to join in a brief strike upon hearing that a member of the U.S. House of Representatives, William E. Mason, had called for an investigation of the occupation. This action, part of what the U.S. chargé called the "considerable agitation" resulting from the news, brought its organizers a warning from the military governor.[39]

In Santo Domingo, representatives of the country's considerable Masonic movement held a five-day congress to consider ways of bringing the occupation to an end. Among other matters, they drafted a letter to fellow Masons in South, Central, and North America, a vivid statement protesting the occupation—particularly the brutal methods with which it had often been associated.[40]

The importance of these relatively insignificant acts of protest lies in what they represent collectively. By early 1920, for the first time since the beginning of the occupation, a group of Dominicans was openly challenging U.S. control of their nation. One result was to bring this issue to the forefront and to popularize and legitimize protest. Once this process began, a spirit critical of the occupation and conducive to active protest spread in ever widening circles. Another result was that the officials of the military government felt compelled to react to these challenges, often in repressive ways, and so were increasingly cast in the role of oppressors.

The first major act of protest against the intervention was the Semana Patriótica or Patriotic Week 12 to 19 May 1920. This was designed to raise both consciousness and money, the former to increase awareness of and resistance to the military government and the latter to help finance the work of President Henríquez and the nationalist missions abroad.

The two main cities of the republic, Santo Domingo and Santiago, were the chief centers of activity during the week, although nationalists in many towns and villages arranged local events. The week was marked by a barrage of publicity and rhetoric. Writers and public speakers vied with each other to boost patriotism and to question the authority and actions of the military government. One editor, Manuel Flores Cabrera, even changed the name of his newspaper from *Las Noticias* to *La Semana Patriótica*. And fund raising for the nationalists' work abroad went on continuously. Especially active in this work was a new organization, the Junta Patriótica de Damas. Approximately $115,000 was collected and sent to Dr. Henríquez to continue his antioccupation campaign.[41]

Although the military government tried to pass off the Semana Patriótica as a "patriotic colic," officials were seriously concerned and soon acted to demonstrate their control. "I gave them all the rope they wanted," wrote Military Governor Snowden in reference to the events of the week, "but have now hauled in the slack." Hauling in the slack involved imprisoning three participants in the Semana Patriótica and trying them before the hated provost courts. The military government arrested Luis Conrado del Castillo for a speech which he delivered in Santo Domingo's Parque Colón and two journalists, Rafael Emilio Sanabia and Oscar Delanoy, for articles which they had written or published.[42] The three were found guilty of having violated Executive Order No. 385, Military Governor Snowden's modified version of censorship, which forbade all criticism of the military government which incited or might "tend to create" public disquiet or disorder. They were given heavy sentences, such as Sanabia's imprisonment for two years at hard labor and $2,000 fine. Although these sentences were eventually reversed by the U.S. secretary of the navy, the immediate effect was to galvanize the nationalists and to promote an even greater confrontation between the military government and its growing number of critics.[43]

One of the reasons for the military government's draconian treatment of the nationalists was that the North American officials were frightened, having convinced themselves that the Semana Patriótica was the prelude to a revolution and that any concessions on the matter of free speech would be seen as "evidence of our weakness." Military Governor Snowden wrote anxiously to Washington, begging that the marine brigade be increased from 2,000 to 2,950; and the marine commanding general, Logan Feland, prepared a plan of battle. Furthermore, Snowden alleged, revolutionaries had departed for Cuba and Mexico with Semana Patriótica funds to buy arms, and a society of assassins had formed to eliminate U.S. officers. "My own life has been threatened," he wrote. Convinced by Snowden's hysteria, the Navy Department moved to increase the marine contingent to 2,500. Subsequent investigations in Santo Domingo, Cuba, and Mexico failed to turn up any evidence of arms purchases or the revolutionary movement, as in fact there had been none.[44]

Despite the harsh treatment of the three nationalists, or perhaps because of it, a host of others began to write pieces critical of the occupation which were viewed by military officials as violations of the law. Eventually the authorities jailed more than twenty publishers, journalists, poets, and other intellectuals, many of them connected with the republic's most important families. Two, moreover, were of international stature: Fabio Fiallo, a modernist poet renowned in all of Latin America, and Américo Lugo, an internationally known intellectual and statesman.

The Dominican nationalists were outraged at the military government's cavalier suspension of basic liberties and at the treatment of the republic's leading citizens as common criminals. But they also realized that they had an issue which would be invaluable for criticizing the occupation. Soon articles attacking the trials and the military government began to appear all over Latin America and in the United States.[45]

The arrests and trials were questionable on a number of grounds. In the first place, the supposed violations often appeared inconsequential to outside observers. Américo Lugo's offending article, for instance, had previously appeared in *El Tiempo* in Puerto Rico. Lugo's Puerto Rican publisher, Judge Willis Sweet, a friend of the military government and of Admiral Snowden, could see "nothing tending to incite the people to violence" and hardly even any "harsh criticism" in the article. Snowden admitted as much but argued that Lugo had to be judged in light of the fact that he sought "in collusion with others to keep up a propaganda to excite the ignorant or weak minded to some overt act of rebellion against the existing government of the country which could only result in the loss of life of innocent persons."[46]

If to most observers the offenses of the Dominican journalists seemed slight, the sentences of the military courts appeared harsh and excessive. The initial sentences for Fabio Fiallo and Manuel Flores Cabrera were for five years of imprisonment at hard labor and fines of the then immense sum of five thousand dollars.[47]

Further, the trials raised the question of jurisdiction. Some defendants, among them Américo Lugo, refused to recognize the military government's censorship legislation on the grounds that the occupation itself was a violation of international law. Lugo and others also questioned the right of the military government to try Dominican civilians in U.S. military courts and in some cases refused to defend themselves.[48]

When they did choose to do so, defendants and their lawyers found their efforts curtailed by the military government. Officials chose to view the judicial immunity of nationalist lawyers, judges, and other court officials—which enabled them to present the nationalist point of view freely in court—as "a cloak for the willful maligning of the Government" and threatened to prosecute them also.[49]

Finally, since the censorship trials were clearly travesties in a legal sense, on this basis they were eventually overturned by the Department of the Navy. In overthrowing the sentences of Luis C. del Castillo and Rafael Sanabia, for example, Washington authorities noted that the cases as tried were "prejudicial to the interests of the accused" and allowed practices "not entirely consistent with fair dealing and certainly not in accord with the theory or practice of the [Navy] Department."[50]

The 1920 censorship cases prompted the State Department to seek the abolition of the censorship laws, as well as the provost courts, with renewed vigor. But, despite the pressure from Washington and the immensely unfavorable publicity accruing to the military government as a result of the summer 1920 arrests, military officials maintained the laws and even continued to arrest journalists occasionally. In a particularly famous case, the military government arrested and deported Horacio Blanco Fombona, the Venezuelan-born editor of *Las Letras*, for having published a photograph of a peasant victim of marine torture, Cayo Báez. By December, however, it had become clear that Washington officials would not ordinarily permit enforcement of censorship and that those sentenced under the law would be released. At that point, with pressure growing because of the impending announcement of a withdrawal plan, the military government made a partial retreat. Snowden abolished the old law and issued in its place two new laws, Executive Orders Nos. 572 and 573, covering sedition and defamation.[51] Although these were almost as vague and open to abuse as the old law, they were in fact employed more cautiously. Censorship was seldom a serious issue thereafter. And the new approach to censorship had the secondary effect of removing some of the pressure against the provost courts, which remained unchanged but less frequently used until the end of the occupation.

The glaring injustice of the censorship cases created an environment in the republic which was receptive to the propaganda of the most radical nationalists and which was more openly hostile than before to the military government. Not surprisingly, the press organized itself and in the fall held an avowedly nationalistic Congreso de la Prensa, which representatives of thirty-five Dominican publications attended. One of the resolutions of the congress supported the nationalist campaign to end all connections, official or personal, between Dominicans and officials of the military government, labeling all citizens who persisted as traitors.[52] The campaign made it increasingly difficult to recruit Dominicans to work in or with the government, and "it practically ended social intercourse except in a few instances." The hostile situation, remarked Military Governor Snowden, "forced the clubs [the Unión and the Juventud] to stop sending invitations to myself and [members of] the government." Even on the street the forces of occupation found "an undercurrent of hostility among the people." Though this was true "especially in the larger towns," in the countryside people were also "afraid to express their friendship openly."[53]

The Continuing International Propaganda Campaign

Favorable resolution of the censorship cases resulted largely from the considerable propaganda campaign waged by the nationalists outside of the republic. The center of this effort was Havana, from which the president of the Cuban Asociación de la Prensa, Dr. Modesto Morales Díaz, alerted the press associations of other Latin American countries concerning the cases of Fabio Fiallo and others, stressing such alarming details as the fact that the provost court had the power to condemn Fiallo to death. Soon urgent and angry messages were pouring into the White House and the State Department from concerned Latin Americans, and writers in Latin America, the United States, and Europe were giving the matter worldwide publicity. "More than any single incident," one writer has observed, "the Fiallo case brought the Dominican cause before the world."[54]

The cause célèbre over Fiallo in the United States was but part of a continuing campaign of publicity, including public debate, pushed by the nationalists. Tulio M. Cestero had worked steadily in Washington and New York during late 1919 and early 1920 as the official representative of the Comisión Nacionalista. His return to Havana in April to his regular position as the editor of the *Heraldo de Cuba* turned out to be only temporary, as the Fiallo case brought him once again to Washington in early August 1920. During his sojourns in the United States, Cestero pushed the White House and the State Department to treat seriously with the nationalists concerning withdrawal; he propagandized the Congress, lobbied the Latin American diplomatic community, developed institutional support from U.S. labor unions, and carried on a constant effort to inform and mobilize both the Latin American and non-Hispanic communities in the United States, utilizing the press and other forums.[55]

Cestero's efforts in the diplomatic area were long unproductive. Despite the rays of hope which had illuminated the Dominican-U.S. discussions up to October 1919, the departure of President Henríquez for Cuba at that time seemed to end the State Department's willingness to talk. Cestero found his letters and calls scarcely acknowledged. Important steps, such as the formation of the *junta consultiva*, were made without consulting or even informing him in advance. Attempts to go around the State Department directly to the White House were completely fruitless. In early March 1920, Cestero wrote in near disbelief of "the barrier of presidential seclusion." Only later in the year, in the wake of the censorship crisis, did genuine discussion resume. Cestero, joined once again by President Henríquez, met regularly with U.S. officials in the fall of 1920. The talks began with protests against censorship and the arrests, then moved to broader questions of policy.[56]

Cestero's propaganda was more productive than his diplomacy. Ironically, his most successful effort in this area resulted from mounting frustration over his fruitless negotiations. In March he made a last effort to communicate through diplomatic channels, presenting to the State Department serious charges—physical abuse of civilians by the marines and capricious and harsh use of censorship—which he believed merited discussion. When once again he was rebuffed, he precipitated what became a major embarrassment to the U.S. government.[57]

On 3 April, Cestero sent every member of the U.S. Senate two letters severely critical of the occupation, one written by the archbishop of Santo Domingo, Adolfo Nouel, to U.S. Minister William Russell and the other his own, a near copy of the charges he had made to the State Department the week before. Nouel's letter raised the issue of various brutal acts reputed to have occurred in the east and questioned both the ability and the integrity of the military government. The charges were so serious as to produce an immediate uproar. While U.S. officials might dismiss Cestero as a chronic critic of the occupation, the prestigious Nouel had generally cooperated with the military government and had been a member of the *junta consultiva*. Explanations were immediately asked of an uninformed and embarrassed State Department, which promptly demanded a complete accounting from the military government.[58]

Cestero had stirred up a hornet's nest in Washington and, in the process, created a sensational news item that was carried in the international press. In Santo Domingo the news resulted in considerable excitement and the false hope of a quick withdrawal. Destroying this hope, wrote a prominent U.S. official there, was likely to "seriously and permanently affect the friendly feeling between Dominicans and Americans."[59]

Thanks to the efforts of Cestero, who was often aided by Horace Knowles, the press of the United States had begun to increase and broaden its coverage of the occupation in 1920. Led by the *Nation* and *Current History*, reporters covered not only the charges emanating from Nouel's and Cestero's letters but also the matters of mismanagement, racism, favoring of U.S. economic interests, and various abridgments of civil liberties and democratic practices. Even more important was the changing perspective of the coverage; whereas a majority of U.S. newspapers and periodicals from 1916 to 1919 had favored the occupation, a majority of the same publications had reversed their view by 1920.[60]

The Dominican publicity campaign generated public interest in the occupation as well as other forms of attention in the political and academic worlds. William E. Mason, a Republican representative from Illinois, took an interest in the occupation, thanks to his introduction to Tulio Cestero by Félix Córdova Dávila, the Puerto Rican delegate to the U.S. Congress. Mason, who had become convinced that the United States should withdraw from all its colonies, introduced a resolution on 7 April 1920 calling for an investigation into the Dominican occupation. But it never came to a vote. Some months later, when Indiana Republican Representative Oscar Bland introduced a similar resolution, the House again failed to act.[61]

The academic world also took up the topic of the United States' Dominican policy in a conference at Clark University in Massachusetts. The May 1920 event was widely reported, and its proceedings were published as a book. The general tenor of the conference, wrote a marine officer who participated, was "adversely critical, and the military government of Santo Domingo came in for a severe scoring."[62]

Most important was the support which the North American labor movement offered to the Dominican cause. The link to Samuel Gompers' American Federation of Labor and its infant offspring, the Pan American Federation of Labor, was made through José Eugenio Kunhardt, a Dominican who about 1916 had organized the Confederación Dominicana del Trabajo, the Dominican Federation of Labor. Kunhardt's sympathies became markedly pronationalist, which he demonstrated clearly in 1919 when he gave his organization a second name, the Hermandad Comunal Nacionalista or Nationalist Communal Brotherhood. Gompers recruited Kunhardt and his organization for the Pan American Federation of Labor and invited the Dominican leader to address its international conference in New York in late 1919. Kunhardt accepted and provided the delegates with a hearty condemnation both of labor conditions in the republic and of the military government. His speech resulted in a thorough investigation of both matters by two representatives of the AFL, Peter J. Brady and Anthony McAndrew. Their probe was facilitated by the nationalists through Tulio Cestero and, when completed, was the subject of several conferences with representatives of the Wilson administration.[63]

In fact, the nationalist-AFL connection provided Cestero with his only direct access to the Wilson administration until late 1920. When Gompers wrote to the president or cabinet officials concerning the occupation, investigations and explanations followed. Eventually Secretary of the Navy Daniels even proposed to Cestero that he explain the Dominican position to the Wilson administration through the good offices of Gompers.[64]

The work of the nationalists and their allies in the United States paid an unexpected dividend when the occupation almost accidentally became an issue in the presidential campaign of 1920. In August the former assistant secretary of the navy and Democratic vice-presidential candidate, Franklin Roosevelt, boastfully raised the matter of U.S. control in the Caribbean, and the Republican presidential candidate, Senator Warren G. Harding, took up the issue. As president, he declared in a direct reference to Roosevelt's claim to have written the 1918 Haitian constitution, "I will not empower an Assistant Secretary of the Navy to draft a constitution for helpless neighbors in the West Indies and to jam it down their throats at the point of bayonets borne by United States marines." Utilizing damning evidence from the *Nation* and other periodicals, Harding lambasted the Democrats' Caribbean policy and in effect committed his future administration to withdrawal from Santo Domingo.[65]

The nationalists were elated over the developments of the Harding campaign, even though they realized that such rhetoric might easily be forgotten after the election. In any case, the occupation as a campaign issue and the continuing fallout over the censorship cases resulted in extensive and often favorable publicity for their cause in the latter half of 1920.[66]

Both the military government and the State Department attempted to counteract the occupation's negative publicity. The military government used various public relations techniques, providing services and information to visiting journalists and itself publishing

Santo Domingo: Its Past and Its Present Condition, a book which lauded the achievements of the military government in such fields as education, public health, and highway construction. The State Department often recommended this work to correspondents inquiring about the Dominican Republic. In addition, the department prepared a five-page statement on U.S. accomplishments in Santo Domingo and sent it to all U.S. diplomatic officers in Latin America with instructions to "have it published in the leading periodicals in the country to which you are accredited, but in some form that will not make it seem to be merely official propaganda." Subsequently the piece appeared in the newspapers of at least six countries, each time as an unsigned article.[67]

Spurred on by successes in the United States and in possession of the $115,000 generated by the recent Semana Patriótica, the Comisión Nacionalista met in Cuba in August and in October to plan for the future. In short, its members decided to redouble their efforts in the United States and to begin a more active campaign of propaganda in Latin America. In the United States, lobbying in Washington would continue and a new office of propaganda, the Dominican Republic Information Bureau, would be opened in New York City. In Latin America, contacts with journalists, politicians, and diplomats would continue as before, and several members of the commission would carry out a long-postponed plan of travel through South America to campaign against the occupation. In Europe, Enrique Deschamps would continue his lobbying in Spain, France, and Belgium and before the League of Nations.[68]

Even before the more active campaign began, Latin Americans were showing a greatly increased concern with the Dominican occupation. The censorship cases generated hundreds of articles critical of U.S. policy beginning in the summer of 1920. In August and October, the Colombian congress passed resolutions pointedly celebrating the anniversary of the 1863 to 1865 Dominican rebellion against Spain and condemning interventionism. And in November, when the military government imprisoned and exiled Venezuelan editor Horacio Blanco Fombona for publishing a photograph of the tortured Cayo Báez, the Latin American press publicized the incident widely and caused the governments of Uruguay and Brazil to make official protests against the continuing occupation. At about the same time, according to Sumner Welles, "the press of Mexico, Colombia, Cuba, Argentina, Chile and Ecuador, as well as that of the Central American Republics, commenced a determined campaign against the policy undertaken by the United States in occupying the Dominican Republic."[69]

Thus the ground was well prepared for the nationalist mission which sailed for South America in December 1920. The Dominican delegation, which included Federico Henríquez, Max Henríquez Ureña, and, for part of the trip, Tulio Cestero, hoped to galvanize Latin American public opinion and to influence Latin American governments to intercede on their behalf with Washington. The first part of the nationalist excursion was timed to coincide with the visit to Rio de Janeiro, Montevideo, and Buenos Aires by U.S. Secretary of State Bainbridge Colby, who was on a fence-mending tour of Latin America. Everywhere, wrote Fabio Fiallo, Colby's footsteps were haunted by the "subtle shadow" of the Dominicans, whose very presence called into question his "declarations of good faith and continental brotherhood."[70]

The Dominicans' five-month tour, which included visits to the capitals of Brazil, Uruguay, Paraguay, Argentina, Chile, and Peru, was a resounding success. In each country except Brazil, they spoke to the president and other high officials, receiving pledges of solidarity. Personal contacts, numerous speaking engagements, and sympathetic coverage in the press generated voluminous pro-Dominican propaganda among the intellectual and social elite of Latin America. This pushed the matter of North American imperialism into the forefront of daily discussion, adding further tension to the United States' difficult relationship with Latin America and thus encouraging a reorientation of U.S. policy.[71]

The First Withdrawal Plan

On 23 December 1920, the United States offered the Dominican people a program of gradual withdrawal which came to be known as the Wilson Plan. A proclamation issued in Santo Domingo declared that the United States intended to "inaugurate the simple processes of withdrawal from the responsibilities assumed in connection with Dominican affairs." The process was to begin with the appointment of a new *junta consultiva*, which would revise certain Dominican laws and draw up a number of constitutional amendments preparatory to actual withdrawal.[72]

Though written hurriedly by Sumner Welles, the Wilson Plan represented a rethinking of the Dominican policy which had been going on for nearly two years, since early 1919. A number of influences determined the shape of the new policy, particularly the extensive talks with Dr. Henríquez and Tulio Cestero in 1919 and 1920 and a series of consultations within the State Department, with the officials of other agencies, and with a number of outside experts, mainly men with experience in other U.S. colonies. Common among the suggestions of those consulted, with the exception of the two Dominicans, was the need to formulate and state a definite policy, to assign overall authority to a single U.S. government agency, to convert the military government into a civil one (with a U.S. administration modeled on the second intervention in Cuba), and, in some cases, to withdraw (but in conjunction with the imposition of strong controls, such as in Cuba under the Platt Amendment or in Haiti).[73]

Compared to the conservative suggestions which preceded the Wilson Plan, the new proposal was the essence of enlightenment and a testimony to the persuasive skills of Henríquez and Cestero. In the fall of 1920, the two Dominicans had generally pushed for some version of President Henríquez' proposal for gradual reestablishment of Dominican sovereignty, beginning with the abolition of censorship and the provost courts, the creation of a Dominican advisory council to map out legal and other reforms, and then the gradual reconstitution of an independent government. In fact, the Wilson Plan bore some resemblance to points which the Dominicans had proposed, but Secretary of State Colby, on the advice of Sumner Welles, apparently chose to ignore Henríquez' counsel that certain provisions would be totally unacceptable to the Dominican people. State Department officials also failed to consult with the two representatives over the specific details of the proposal before its publication on 23 December.[74]

The Wilson Plan almost immediately stirred up an "epidemic of protest" in the Dominican Republic. It offered withdrawal, but some of its terms were positively objectionable, and others were so vaguely defined that many Dominicans correctly feared they would be no better than the terms refused by them between 1914 and 1916. "Today's proclamation," declared the headline of an extra edition of *Las Noticias*, "has laid out a formula which the Dominican people cannot accept without abdicating their sovereignty." The protest was led by the Unión Nacional Dominicana, which issued a statement condemning the proposed constitutional and legal changes, especially as they were to be written and ratified under the eye of the military government. Conscious of the constitution and puppet government which the United States had previously forced on Haiti, the nationalists would permit no change in their fundamental law. The Unión Nacional's views were strongly backed by the Congreso de la Prensa.[75]

The Unión Nacional, as in its campaign against the 1919 *junta consultiva*, condemned any form of cooperation with the occupiers on the grounds that it would lead to a compromise of Dominican sovereignty. Instead, its members proposed a formula of *evacuación pura y simple*, withdrawal with no strings attached. This was totally unacceptable to the U.S. government, and an impasse resulted.

The first requirement of the U.S. proposal was the setting up of the *junta consultiva*. But the political environment in Santo Domingo made it very difficult to find Dominicans who were willing to serve. Anyone who did, wrote Military Governor Snowden, was "denounced by the press as a traitor." Eventually seven accepted, including the four members of the 1919 junta. Although they imposed conditions on their acceptances, they were nevertheless subjected to considerable pressure to resign. This continuing controversy, as well as the change of administrations in Washington, apparently prevented the commission from accomplishing very much.[76]

What caused the Dominicans to reject the Wilson Plan so forcefully? One factor was their previously mentioned suspicion of the plan's vague terms, as well as outright disagreement with some of its specific proposals. Another was their perception of the situation in early 1921. The nationalists saw North Americans as divided on the question of the Caribbean interventions, and they believed that the situation in Washington was changing in their favor; so did their U.S. counsel, Horace Knowles, who according to Francisco Henríquez advised the nationalists "to reject forcefully the plan proposed by the State Department." Colby, Wilson's last secretary of state, was believed to be anxious enough to improve relations with Latin America to be vulnerable to continuing Dominican pressure.[77] Even should he refuse to compromise with Dominican demands, a new secretary of state under Harding would replace him. And Harding, some Dominicans mistakenly believed, would quickly grant them their sovereignty without compromising conditions.

Weakening the Dominicans' position was the obvious fact that they were also divided. While the radical nationalists stood in total opposition to the Wilson Plan, some moderates regarded it as a base which, if modified, could lead to a fair settlement. Still other Dominicans accepted the plan as it stood. Some took this position because they thought that Washington would refuse to grant more generous terms; others feared that simple withdrawal would lead to chaos and that the reforms necessary "to destroy political personalism and caudillo rule" would be forgotten. The pro–Wilson Plan group included some important persons, such as the head of a major political party, Federico Velásquez. Nevertheless, by early 1921 one faction was ascendant. That group—"which is radical and represents the great majority of citizens, who ask for restoration pure and simple"—had taken control of the nationalist movement.[78]

The divided opinion over the Wilson Plan was particularly troublesome to President Henríquez. His approach to this and other issues was fundamentally moderate, at least in part because he believed that the State Department would refuse to consider a radical line. Thus his first advice to his followers on the Wilson Plan, which appeared to be based on some of his earlier suggestions to the State Department, was to study the proposal with an open and positive attitude. Yet many of his followers in the Dominican Republic were heavily influenced by the radical Unión Nacional, which in this and other cases criticized Henríquez' position as the prelude to a sellout. The president's efforts to thread his way between Washington and the radicals was apparently unsuccessful, for he found his "middle position" misunderstood by both sides. Eventually, with the Unión Nacional's position clearly dominant, Henríquez had to shift his position to agree with the radical line. The probable result was to diminish his influence in all quarters. While he had been forced to abandon his remaining supporters, his radical critics still regarded him with suspicion, and Washington viewed him as an unreliable negotiator with insufficient influence at home.[79]

Moderate nationalists made an attempt in early 1921 to resolve the conflict within the nationalist movement and to end the impasse between Washington and the radicals. José Eugenio Kunhardt, the labor leader, and Rafael Estrella Ureña, a youthful political leader only later associated with the radicals, put forward a proposal to accept the Wilson Plan but to implement it under Dominicans rather than the military government. This strategy, which apparently represented the combined thinking of President Henríquez and the secretary of the Comisión Nacionalista, Rafael César Tolentino, was also rejected by the radicals, mainly because U.S. troops were to remain until the required reforms were completed.[80]

The Dominicans believed that the Wilson administration was especially vulnerable to pressure in the last months of its existence in early 1921. Horace Knowles bombarded State Department and other officials with letters asking for a policy change, and President Henríquez traveled from Cuba to Washington in late January in the hope of negotiating a withdrawal agreement. Events seemed to favor their campaign when, in February, the Senate Foreign Relations Committee reported favorably upon a resolution calling for an investigation of the Dominican and Haitian occupations. But neither this threat nor the pressure from continuing protests and a generally bad press in the United States and Latin America caused the State Department to alter its December proposal.[81]

The Harding Plan of 1921

The Dominicans eagerly awaited the March inauguration of Harding in expectation of a fundamental change in policy. The nationalist moderates gathered a negotiating team in Washington, including President Henríquez, Tulio Cestero, Rafael César Tolentino, Manuel M. Morillo, and Fabio and René Fiallo, as well as a group of U.S. advisers, Horace Knowles, William E. Pulliam, the former receiver general of Dominican customs, Ernest Gruening of the *Nation*, and Ira Bennett, editor of the *Washington Post*. From early March until June, the Dominicans met with various officials of the Harding government, including Secretary of State Charles Evans Hughes, Subsecretary Henry Fletcher, Secretary of the Interior Albert Fall, Chief of the Latin American Division Sumner Welles, and eventually President Harding himself. Their discussions centered on possible alternatives to the Wilson Plan.

Among the proposals of the Dominican negotiators was an interim multiparty junta of nationalists which before withdrawal would govern, call elections, and carry out specified reforms agreed upon by Dominican and U.S. representatives. The U.S. officials, though cordial and encouraging, long remained vague and noncommittal concerning their views. Finally, having concluded that the Wilson Plan was unworkable, Welles strangely proposed an even more objectionable settlement which specifically included recognition of the U.S. right to intervene to carry out the 1907 treaty, U.S. control of the Dominican treasury, a national guard commanded by U.S. officers, and Dominican approval of all acts of the military government before withdrawal. The Dominicans found this plan totally unacceptable.[82]

In the background to the negotiations was a steady stream of petitions, protests, and news commentary generated by the nationalists and their allies. To begin with, President Harding's inauguration brought a flood of congratulatory letters from Dominican individuals and groups asking for an immediate end to the occupation. As time passed without a withdrawal, more serious protests surfaced. Particularly important were discreet inquiries from the governments of Argentina and Brazil and several protests from the U.S. and Latin

American labor movements.[83] To show good faith, President Harding sent his secretary of the navy, Edwin Denby, on a tour of the Dominican Republic. His meetings there with influential and cordial Dominicans at polite receptions took place amid a barrage of nationalist newspaper articles, broadsides, and demonstrations.[84]

On 2 June the U.S. negotiators informed the Dominicans that the State Department had prepared a revised plan of withdrawal, based on the previous discussions, to be announced by a new military governor, Samuel S. Robison, on 14 June 1921. This withdrawal plan, which would soon become known as the Harding Plan, was a somewhat softened version of the earlier U.S. position. It called for ratification of all acts of the military government, for validation of a $2.5 million loan for public works and other immediate expenses, for possible extension of the receivership to internal revenues, for a U.S.-officered Guardia Nacional, and for elections under U.S. tutelage, followed by withdrawal within eight months. Significantly absent was the right to intervene. But the proposal as it stood was unacceptable to the Dominicans, and they continued talking to the State Department through Sumner Welles, both to clarify details of the plan and to gain further concessions.[85]

The basis of the Dominicans' objections was obvious, for the Harding Plan contained a number of features against which they had been struggling since before 1916. Nevertheless, the moderate nationalist negotiators believed, at least in early June 1921, that the plan represented a significant improvement in the U.S. position and that it was open to still further modification. The nationalists had obtained their "basic points" and with further discussions could overcome the objectionable features, wrote President Henríquez to several Dominicans.[86]

In Santo Domingo, however, the plan produced an immediate and considerable negative reaction, "a hot blast of protest," wrote Minister Russell. In the capital city a group of some three thousand persons organized by the press (most of which now supported the nationalist cause) demonstrated in front of the military governor's home; Robison appeared on the balcony and promised to make their sentiments known in Washington.[87] Editors and organizations condemned the new plan in newspapers and handbills, and large numbers of important political figures, including moderates, published letters disavowing Washington's proposal. From La Vega the pro-U.S. governor, Teófilo Cordero Bidó, wrote the military governor that "the majority of the people in the country are dissatisfied with the principal clauses of said proclamation" and that he agreed with the protesters that there were too many unnecessary controls. Reports of like sentiments also arrived from Santiago, Sánchez, Barahona, and elsewhere.[88]

Robison's proclamation caused the formation of several new nationalist groups. By far the most important was the Junta de Abstención Electoral, which was to remain influential into 1924. The main purpose of the new organization was to fight against the election proposed by the Harding Plan and to boycott it if it did occur. Two groups of younger nationalists, the Asociación de Jóvenes Dominicanos in Santiago and the Asociación de Jóvenes Independientes in Santo Domingo, also formed in opposition to the new U.S. proposal.[89]

The newly installed military governor and his staff were somewhat bewildered by the strength of the demonstration against the Harding Plan. A Dominican subsecretary of state for the Department of Interior and Police explained the reaction to his superiors as a result of failed expectations. The Dominicans, he noted, had viewed Robison's installation as military governor as the arrival of freedom's messenger, in accord with the pronouncements of Harding before his election. Thus the proclamation of 14 June, with its many qualifications, was a great disappointment. It was not surprising, continued the official, that as a result the nationalists, the influential Masonic fraternity, the church, and even the municipal officials of Santo Domingo had opposed the plan and its proposed elections.[90]

The protests in the Dominican Republic surprised not only the military governor but also higher officials in Washington and even the negotiators for the Comisión Nacionalista. Realization of the strength of the nationalist movement there, which at this moment was heavily influenced by Américo Lugo and the radical leaders of the Unión Nacional, forced President Henríquez to adopt a more confrontational attitude toward the United States. This was reflected in a memorandum which he presented to the State Department fully a month after the publication of the plan; in it he made repeated references to the "steadfast attitude assumed unanimously by the people" and declared his intention to adhere to the desires of his constituency. "The people absolutely refuse to cooperate in the execution of the plan proclaimed on 14 June," an indication, argued Henríquez, that Dominicans must be allowed to reorganize their government without interference from the United States.[91]

Even as protests continued, the military government went forward with plans for the withdrawal. Military Governor Robison announced the first step of the process of electing a new government, to begin in August. Occupation officials initiated studies on the state of the public works program, on government finances and the proposed bond issue, and on possible changes to the Dominican constitution. And Robison announced the formation of an advisory panel of eight prominent Dominicans, including representatives of the leading political factions. They met and formed several committees to draw up revisions of certain laws, based in part on suggestions made to the State Department by President Henríquez on 9 October 1919.[92]

Military Governor Robison also made several efforts to conciliate Dominican public opinion and to bring Dominican leaders over to the U.S. position. First he issued a statement of clarification on 6 July 1921 which slightly softened the original proclamation by further defining and limiting some of its vaguer terms. Then he held a series of meetings with influential Dominicans, including several with the leaders of the principal parties, who "showed some desire to cooperate" but appeared cautious of public opinion. Robison's persuasive efforts were nearly successful. Several moderate nationalists wrote secretly to President Henríquez, urging him to accept the Harding Plan. But in the end the Dominicans remained more or less united and continued to voice their now standard objections to U.S. control of the elections, of the Dominican military, of internal revenues, and of the process of making constitutional changes. The general pattern of Dominican counterproposals called for the United States to hold elections, evacuate, and then negotiate further details with the new sovereign government, a position clearly unacceptable to Washington.[93]

The glue which held the Dominicans together was the domestic propaganda effort of the radical nationalists, who at this point had the most vocal, visible, and organized movement and who could count on the support of a large part of the press. One of the chief objects of the radicals' attention continued to be President Henríquez, who, as an unquestioned nationalist and the defender of a moderate position, seemed to represent a greater threat to the radicals' *pura y simple* position than the more conservative Dominican leaders.[94]

Several months after the announcement of the Harding Plan, it was clear that a deadlock had developed. This forced the military government to delay the upcoming elections and to postpone withdrawal indefinitely. Meanwhile, in Washington, contacts between the Dominicans and the State Department continued only in the most desultory way. President Henríquez and Tulio Cestero found Sumner Welles and the State Department uninterested in negotiating the Harding Plan, unwilling to "modify a single point."[95]

Both sides had substantive reasons for not accepting each other's proposals. But in addition both parties saw possible advantages in stalling. The State Department, knowing of the Dominican differences, hoped to exploit them and to negotiate with the moderates; Washington believed that eventually the majority of Dominicans would be willing to compromise in order to regain their independence. To encourage this, Military Governor Robison maintained a great distance from the nationalists while continuing communications with the leaders of political parties in Santo Domingo, none of whom appeared deeply committed to nationalist principles.[96]

The nationalists, nevertheless, believed Washington to be under increasing pressure to compromise. The economic crisis which had begun in late 1920 posed ever more critical fiscal problems for the military government. And in August the U.S. Senate made its first moves toward an investigation of the occupations of Haiti and the Dominican Republic. The nationalists were convinced that the revelations from these hearings would cause the United States such great international and domestic embarrassment that the State Department would become far less concerned with the exact details of withdrawal. It was only necessary to wait and to preserve the unity of the Dominican leaders.[97]

Ironically, the policy against which the nationalists struggled in 1921 was a liberalization, the culmination of a long and acrimonious debate between the military government, represented by the Navy Department, and the State Department over who would establish policy for Santo Domingo and what that policy should be. In essence, the military government had advocated continuing the occupation and taking a hard line against the nationalists, while the State Department, sensitive to the effect of the occupation on its diplomacy in Latin America, wanted out. By May 1921 the State Department had clearly gained the upper hand, and it controlled U.S. policy in Santo Domingo until the end of the occupation. The representative of the military government who dealt with the State Department's Sumner Welles concerning policy matters recognized his powerlessness by early May, noting that "it was absolutely no use for me to talk further"; new ideas "made no dent in Mr. Welles' armor."[98]

9

The Nationalist Campaign,
the Hughes-Peynado Accord,
and Withdrawal: 1921–1924

The year 1921 ended as it had begun: there was no agreement between U.S. officials and Dominicans concerning a plan to end the occupation, and the two sides remained far apart. Although 1922 seemed to offer little hope of change, with the United States hardening its position, private diplomacy by Francisco Peynado broke the impasse in the spring. His agreement, which soon led to the reawakening of Dominican political life, also had the effect of dividing the weakly united nationalist factions. In the two following years, as Dominicans moved toward elections and the military government toward withdrawal, the nationalists found their influence growing steadily weaker.

The Pact of Puerto Plata and the U.S. Senate Committee

The last months of 1921 were a time of continuing stalemate and of jockeying for advantage. In Santo Domingo the Harding Plan remained on a back burner, while two other matters dominated the political scene. One was the Puerto Plata conference, a nationalist attempt to foster and safeguard unity among leading Dominican politicians vis-à-vis the United States. The second was the December visit to Santo Domingo of the U.S. Senate committee investigating the occupations of Haiti and the Dominican Republic. Both of these events turned out to be of great importance to the future course of the struggle over withdrawal, mainly because of their failure to meet nationalist expectations.

The nationalists saw their most important task in late 1921 as the maintenance of unity against the demands of the Harding Plan. With President Henríquez now closer to the radicals, the greatest threat to unity came from the leaders of the preintervention political parties, whose commitment to nationalist principles was weak and whose desires for power, as later events would confirm, might lead them to make undesirable compromises with Washington. Also important was the need to formulate a clear and workable Dominican counterpolicy which might lead to withdrawal, for the public as well as the political leaders appeared increasingly anxious for a settlement. With these matters in mind, delegates from President Henríquez' *juntas nacionalistas* went to a regional meeting in El Seibo in August and proposed a meeting of party leaders with Henríquez in order to reach a common agreement on questions relating to the restoration of Dominican sovereignty. Later the Horacista political party took up the idea and discussed it with other groups, and the Puerto Plata conference of December 1921 resulted.[1]

The pact of Puerto Plata of 7 December 1921 pledged the signing parties to honor nine articles, which comprised a plan of action for the Dominican people until withdrawal was finally accomplished. The nine articles dismissed most of the Harding Plan's principal points, pledged the signers to adopt various constitutional and administrative reforms, and assured the continued existence of the Comisión Nacionalista abroad. The pact also created the Comité Restauradora or Committee of Restoration, headed by President Henríquez, who was to represent the Dominican people until a new government was installed and to oversee the election of that government. Among those included in the Comité Restauradora were the leaders of the political parties supporting the declaration (the only refusal came from notedly pro-U.S. Federico Velásquez), national church and Masonic leaders, representatives of the various nationalist groups of both moderate and radical persuasions, and delegates from the Asociación de la Prensa, from the Colegio de Abogados, from the Confederación Dominicana del Trabajo, and from other "groups of a public character."[2]

Military Governor Robison noted after the conference that it "practically rejects the entire proclamation" of 14 June and that it made unacceptable counterproposals as well. This surprised Robison, for Horacio Vásquez had previously told him that he agreed with all the U.S. proposals except the military mission. Making matters more ambiguous was the fact that since the conference, in private talks with Robison, some of the signers had told him that their adherence to the pact did not signify their agreement with all its points. Nevertheless, the military governor made a bleak assessment: "The present situation with regard to effecting the disoccupation is at a standstill."[3]

On 9 December 1921, while the Puerto Plata conference was

still in session, the U.S. Senate Committee on the Occupation of Haiti and Santo Domingo began its hearings in Santo Domingo. The committee, which arrived in the capital city from Port-au-Prince, had been in existence for four months, brought about by growing public pressure in the United States. Hearings had begun in Washington in early August, and in late November the committee had departed for Haiti and the Dominican Republic, mainly for the purpose of hearing witnesses.

In the opening days of the hearings in Washington, the Dominicans had presented their case through their lawyer, Horace Knowles, while President Henríquez had submitted a supporting memorandum. Knowles outlined the history of the intervention and then made a series of charges: (1) there was no legal basis for the intervention; (2) the 1916 invasion was in violation of the U.S. Constitution, existing U.S.-Dominican treaties, international law, the purpose of the Monroe Doctrine as defined by the U.S. government, the fourteenth of Woodrow Wilson's Fourteen Points, and a U.S.-sponsored resolution adopted at the Third Conference of the Hague Tribunal; (3) "excesses, abuses, cruelties and murders" had been committed by the U.S. Marines; (4) various orders of the military government were "unreasonable, cruel, and totally un-American"; (5) both private and corporate rights and property had been violated and damaged by the military government and its agents, resulting in various losses; and (6) the military government had been "incompetent, wasteful and extravagant."[4]

Except for Knowles' introductory presentation and one on behalf of the military government, the Senate committee had devoted almost no time to the Dominican case before its arrival in Santo Domingo. The committee began hearing testimony in the National Palace on 10 December after a one-day delay caused by Dominican resentment over the site, a room next to the military governor's office in the headquarters of the military government. To no avail, Dominicans protested that this location, plus the presence of a great many fully armed marines in the corridors, intimidated the witnesses who were to appear.

The Dominicans who went before the Senate panel, coordinated by Knowles, tended to testify on one of two subjects. The first concerned the events of 1916, testimony which the Dominicans believed would establish that the occupation was from the beginning unnecessary, unjustified, and illegal. The second matter was the abuse of Dominican citizens by the marines, especially the cases arising from the guerrilla war in the east. Occasionally other matters surfaced, usually concerning military government policy, which the Dominicans alleged was often inappropriate and/or poorly implemented.[5]

The hearings continued until 15 December, when the senators abruptly suspended them and sailed for the United States. As their itinerary had called for them to depart on 20 December, the Dominican case was left in disarray. A large number of witnesses were still arriving, and a number already present had no opportunity to testify. These events, in addition to the hearings' location and the fact that the committee stayed in the republic as the official guests of the body they were supposed to investigate (receiving free transportation, food, lodging, and a cordial social reception), left the investigation somewhat discredited in the eyes of the Dominicans and their supporters.[6]

Later events tended to corroborate the views of those who saw the investigation as a whitewash. Shortly after departing from Santo Domingo, the committee issued a preliminary report which, in the nationalists' eyes, was "plainly contrary to the evidence" and "decidedly unfavorable" to the Dominican cause.[7] Furthermore, Senator Medill McCormick proposed to hear the uncalled Dominican witnesses by means of taking affidavits, which would then be accepted or rejected by the Senate committee based on a review of each by the military governor. In the end, after some months of correspondence, it became clear that McCormick was not interested in gathering more evidence. The committee took no more evidence, suspended the investigation for some months, and finally closed the hearings altogether.[8]

Throughout, nationalist activity had continued in the press and on the street. "Agitators and extremists" were working busily against the Harding Plan, intelligence officials reported, and "the press continues to attack the military government and the Forces of Occupation at every opportunity." In response to this agitation, officials of the military government restrained themselves, usually limiting their reaction to keeping careful track of each incident. There were, however, cases of outright repression. In one, several government employees who in the first wave of protest against the Harding Plan signed the "malicious and anarchistic" nationalist protest of 18 July 1921 were fired from their civil service jobs.[9] In another, military censors threatened the editor of the *Listín Diario* with dire consequences for an article by José Patín advocating that all Dominican officials renounce their offices en masse in order to cripple the military government. "No further articles of this nature will be tolerated," wrote the military governor.[10]

The general policy of restrained response to nationalist provocation reflected the renewed control of the State Department over the Dominican situation, as well as the department's concern to improve the disastrous relationship which had developed between the Dominican people and the military government under Rear Admiral Snowden. Despite his best efforts, Snowden's blunt, arbitrary, and dictatorial manner, combined with poor judgment, had alienated many. With this in mind, the Navy Department had replaced Snowden with an officer who appeared to be more perceptive and sophisticated, considerably better suited to cultivating positive relations with the Dominicans. But Military Governor Robison and his small staff could improve matters only to a point, for it was the marines who were in daily contact with most Dominicans. Thus when, in August 1921, the Department of the Navy appointed Brigadier General Harry Lee to take over the direction of the marines in the Dominican Republic, one of his principal instructions was to cultivate the best possible relations between the marines and Dominican citizens.[11]

Lee, a capable officer who took his task seriously, soon issued detailed instructions to his officers and men. Not only were harsh or abusive measures against the population totally forbidden, but the marines were to "avoid every semblance of friction" with civilians. Officers were to set up machinery to investigate all Dominican complaints and were to exercise "constant vigilance" to see that all marines stayed away from Dominican political gatherings, that they did not congregate in large groups while on liberty, that they avoided the use of harsh language or "wholesale criticism of the people," that they repaid all debts and fulfilled all other obligations to Dominicans, and that they learn enough of "local conditions and customs" to avoid violating local prejudices. Even a "mistake committed by us through ignorance is a serious dereliction," Lee wrote. He also ordered marine commanders to design programs to keep their troops occupied, content, and thus out of trouble.[12]

Lee put teeth into his effort to control marine-civilian conflict, and it apparently worked. Marine records suggest that incidents, even relatively trivial matters such as hostile verbal exchanges, were reported quickly and investigated thoroughly. It appears that marine transgressors were, more than ever before, dealt with sternly. As a result, Lee reported a year later, the marine-civilian relationship had improved remarkably despite the continuing tensions endemic to any occupation.[13]

In instituting this campaign to improve relations, the military government by no means gave up its methods of control. Marines continued their armed patrols, and intelligence officers and spies maintained their surveillance of communications, meetings, political groups, and individuals. They reported on political trends and developments and even on individual speeches, letters, and conversations. But there was an effort to avoid the obvious appearance of repression.

Impasse: The Withdrawal of the Harding Plan

By early 1922, U.S. officials had resolved to break the deadlock which had evolved. After conferences in Washington with the secretary of state and the U.S. minister to Santo Domingo, Robison received orders to issue an ultimatum to the Dominican leaders. Unless they would cooperate with the Harding Plan by moving toward elections, the United States would withdraw the proclamation of 14 June 1921, the military government would move immediately to borrow a large sum on behalf of the Dominican government to meet current obligations, and withdrawal would be postponed until after the completion of the public works program and the training of the Guardia Nacional, a date projected for 1 July 1924 at the earliest. Robison's ultimatum also contained a concession: the United States would reduce its demand for a military mission to a simple legation guard. Nevertheless, the Dominican political leaders refused to cooperate on these terms. "It is impossible to consider any point raised," they wrote to Robison on 23 February 1922. As a result, on 6 March the military governor issued a new proclamation prolonging the military government until 1 July 1924. Soon afterward occupation authorities arranged for a $10 million twenty-year loan.[14]

In the aftermath of Robison's withdrawal postponement, authorities observed that the populace was strangely quiet. The "press has been very mild and there has been less agitation than for many months," wrote the military governor. Only occasionally did a demonstration break the general tranquillity. In early March the Asociación de Jóvenes held a rally and, according to an intelligence officer, the "speeches were enthusiastically received . . . and the orators were applauded at every patriotic reference." But so quiet was the general situation that in mid March the *Listín Diario* ran an editorial calling upon the Dominican people to awaken from the stupor into which they had fallen. Even the work of the Comisión Nacionalista came to a virtual halt, with several memoranda from Tulio Cestero to foreign officials apparently constituting the whole of the effort through the spring of 1922. Lack of money forced the closing of the commission's offices in Washington, despite the scheduled reopening of the Senate hearings on Haiti and the Dominican Republic.[15]

The nationalists faced a financial crisis now that the funds from the Semana Patriótica were finally exhausted. In January President Henríquez had initiated a campaign for thirty thousand dollars, but not even sympathetic observers gave him any chance of reaching his goal. Following his futile effort, other nationalists put forward several new fund-raising schemes. But these efforts produced so little that the Dominicans' chief U.S. lobbyist, Horace Knowles, went without payment except for small amounts he received from Francisco Peynado and Peynado's friends.[16]

Adding to the nationalists' financial problems in early 1922 was the fact that their titular head, President Henríquez, was dispirited about the campaign and bogged down by personal problems after he left the Dominican Republic for Santiago de Cuba in early February. Writing to Cestero, he spoke only vaguely of continuing the Comisión Nacionalista. He was ill for most of the spring, had to attend to various personal matters, and was struggling financially, all of which caused him to leave the nationalist campaign in abeyance. Not until late May did he confide his hope to Knowles that "the activities of the nationalist committee will be resumed in the very near future." Meanwhile, Henríquez' influence in Santo Domingo had apparently declined considerably.[17]

Henríquez faced a bewilderingly complex situation in those months. Dominican unity vis-à-vis the United States had been increasingly fragmented since the signing of the pact of Puerto Plata. From the first there were strong disagreements over the meaning of the document between Horacio Vásquez and Enrique Jiménez on one side and President Henríquez on the other, with the former arguing that the pact was a charge to negotiate according to specified principles and the latter now insisting upon the no-negotiation, *pura y simple* approach. Though the political leaders still managed to agree to reject Robison's February 1922 ultimatum, from then on disunity grew. A nationalist effort to promote a restoration of the Puerto Plata agreement in late March came to nothing, as the principal political leaders were hopelessly divided. The situation, Henríquez wrote Tulio Cestero, revealed "unequivocally the debility of the Dominican people: each political group pursues its own course."[18]

The final collapse of the pact of Puerto Plata signaled not only the impossibility of preserving unity but also a severe decline over the year before of the ability of nationalists of any stripe to influence public opinion. The cause of this reversal was the nationalists' failure to adapt to the post–June 1921 situation. While a majority of politically active Dominicans and their leaders were moving toward a position of compromise, the nationalists were more and more dedicated to the inflexible formula of *pura y simple*.

A variety of forces led Dominicans in the direction of accommodation. Basic was the compelling hope of quick withdrawal which had been raised by the proclamations of 1920 and 1921. Another was the gradual realization that the Harding administration was not so desperate to withdraw that it would do so on the terms demanded by the radical nationalists, a fact brought home by Robison's March postponement. A third was the perception that the much heralded U.S. Senate investigation was controlled by senators who basically favored the intervention. Though the committee might condemn individual abuses, the senators were unlikely to (and did not) recommend an immediate or unconditional withdrawal. Concrete evidence of this position became available as early as December 1921 in the committee's preliminary report, which almost completely justified the intervention and its conduct.[19]

The growing spirit of compromise soon found its spokesmen. Velásquez and Vásquez, who as the chiefs of the two largest political parties were the most likely to benefit from a settlement, quietly approached the military governor and let it be known that, once the impending loan and other politically delicate matters were taken care of, they wanted to come to terms with Washington. Similarly, a group of influential citizens in the ayuntamiento of Santo Domingo publicly proposed a national convention of ayuntamientos to work out a withdrawal agreement.[20]

The nationalists condemned these moves toward compromise. The *Listín Diario* editorialized against those politicians "whose only desire is to clear the way for a realization of their ambition for power." Horace Knowles, writing from Washington, declared those who broke the Puerto Plata agreement as "greater enemies to the . . . Dominican people than the Military Government or the Harding administration." Similarly, Fiallo condemned the plan of the "pseudo-ayuntamiento" on the grounds that most of its members had been chosen by the military government. But, aside from their condemnations and calls to adhere to the principle of *pura y simple*, the nationalists could offer little advice but to refuse all compromises and wait for Washington to accept their terms, hardly a tonic to those who hoped for a speedy withdrawal. In an effort to remedy this matter, Fiallo proposed to add a new tactic to the *pura y simple* formula, a boycott of all imports from the United States. But the idea failed to catch the public's imagination.[21]

Although the nationalists were able to force abandonment of the ayuntamiento's withdrawal proposal, they were becoming increasingly isolated from their constituency at home, which had the secondary effect of lessening their ability to bargain with the U.S. government. They further diminished their influence by refusing to deal with Military Governor Robison on substantive matters. This they did on the advice of Knowles, who argued that Robison "is only a piece of tubing through which communications and instructions are passed to Washington."[22]

One reason for the nationalists' steady faith in the *pura y simple* approach was their belief, based in part on overly hopeful reports from Knowles, that the State Department, faced with exposing more evidence of wrongdoing by the U.S. forces of occupation in the Senate hearings, would elect to withdraw unconditionally rather than complete the investigation. Second, and more important, they placed great stock in a resolution introduced by Senator William H. King, Democrat of Utah, asking for immediate withdrawal from Haiti and Santo Domingo.[23]

The nationalists were in need of an issue to reunite the Dominican people behind them—and the marine commander in Santiago, Colonel Charles H. Lyman, nearly obliged them by reawakening the censorship issue in early 1922. Lyman suspended several newspapers and used the provost courts to imprison and fine the journalists. But Washington, anxious to avoid a blowup, acted rather quickly to force revocation of the sentences. A few months later, U.S. authorities in Santo Domingo received orders that they could no longer prosecute censorship cases or other "purely political offenses" without permission of the State Department.[24]

Breaking the Impasse: Peynado's Mission

In March 1922, the prominent Dominican Francisco Peynado traveled to Washington to explore the possibility of working out an agreement with the State Department regarding withdrawal. Peynado believed that such an accord was attainable but that the officials of the military government were incapable of negotiating it because they so misunderstood the Dominican people. Likewise, while he recognized the justice of the nationalists' *pura y simple* position, he believed that it was politically unrealistic.[25] Unlike the officials of the military government and most of the nationalists,

Peynado understood both his own people and, to an unusual degree, those of the United States. An eminent lawyer and former cabinet official, Peynado had strong ties to U.S. sugar corporations and had served as the representative of the Dominican government in Washington.

Peynado had generally maintained a position of neutrality within the heavily partisan world of Dominican politics, devoting his energy to his personal and business affairs, except during the crisis of 1916. At that time he headed the Committee of Public Safety, designed to maintain order in Santo Domingo during the first days of the U.S. invasion, and he later joined the short-lived government of Dr. Henríquez as the minister of finance.[26] Thereafter, while sometimes cooperating with the military government and avoiding open identification with the nationalists, he nevertheless maintained ties with Henríquez and his followers and contributed heavily to the retainer paid to Horace Knowles.

Peynado's journey to Washington was a success. In a series of conferences with Secretary of State Hughes and other officials, he worked out a compromise fairly rapidly. The new plan considerably revised the previous U.S. proposals, eliminating the military mission, a financial "adviser," and possible U.S. control of internal finances, and added a new feature, a provisional Dominican government to oversee elections and implement other prewithdrawal measures. This last feature seemed to remove the principal obstacle to Dominican acceptance of previous U.S. proposals.[27]

Peynado had entered the negotiations with the object of sounding out the U.S. position to determine which points might be subject to bargaining and which were inflexible. Within several weeks, he realized that Washington was adamant on some points: the acts of the military government, or at least selected laws and contracts, should be ratified before withdrawal, and the highway-building program should be completed. Similarly, the United States had determined to refuse the reestablishment of Dr. Henríquez' 1916 government or a withdrawal based on the Puerto Plata accord. Likewise, Peynado believed that there was no point in arguing against the $10 million loan. Although it was still in process and was hotly opposed by many Dominicans, including himself, he considered it inevitable, owing to the military government's desperate financial condition, and therefore not worth including in his discussions.[28]

To present the compromise agreement to the Dominican people, Peynado believed it was first necessary to obtain the backing of the republic's political leaders. To this end, Peynado and the U.S. negotiators agreed to invite party leaders Federico Valásquez, Horacio

Vásquez, and, later, Elías Brache of the Jimenista party to join in the accord. On 30 June 1922, they signed and issued a memorandum of understanding, soon published in the Dominican Republic as a "tentative Plan of Evacuation."[29]

Why was Peynado successful in obtaining this agreement, which had previously eluded negotiators on both sides? One obvious reason was that he was willing, unlike either the nationalists or the prominent political leaders, to commit himself openly to compromise. Likewise, the U.S. negotiators were ready to come to terms with the Dominicans, even at the cost of some concessions. Second, Peynado had no official connection with the nationalists, whose principal representatives, Francisco Henríquez and Horace Knowles, had long since alienated official Washington. Third, Peynado hit upon an idea, the provisional government, which satisfied the basic concerns of a majority of both parties. Fourth, the nationalist campaign of agitation and other pressure tactics continued during Peynado's talks, and it was especially successful in the United States in the spring of 1922. Fifth, Peynado was a uniquely capable person to deal with the U.S. government. His command of English, his understanding of North Americans, and his many U.S. connections all caused North Americans to like and to trust him. He quickly impressed Senators McCormick and Pomerene, heads of the Senate committee, and through them reached others. "I have been attracted toward him since the first day I met him both because of his fine personality and extraordinary ability," wrote Pomerene.[30]

Forming a constant background to Peynado's talks were the activities of Horace Knowles. Peynado "has been a guest in the fort, while I have been outside keeping up a continuous fire against the military government and the policy of Washington," wrote Knowles. Knowles himself gave widely reported speeches which aggressively attacked the military government and its policies, and he orchestrated actions by others. His propaganda masterpiece was a speech by Senator William E. Borah in Carnegie Hall attacking the occupation. The event sold out, but Knowles was careful to arrange box seats in advance for Latin American ambassadors, newspaper editors, and other influential persons. Borah's speech received widespread attention; it was "published generally by the press throughout the country" and was even broadcast nationwide on radio.[31]

Knowles also lobbied the U.S. Congress, especially the Senate. He often wrote to provide senators with information, to send them copies of articles, or to query them on their position vis-à-vis the occupation, the Senate investigation, and related matters. One result of his persistence was Borah's speech; another was the antioccupation legislation sponsored by Senator King. The latter, though hopeless politically, was useful propaganda.[32]

Knowles particularly continued to press the Senate committee on Haiti and Santo Domingo, which had practically ceased its work after returning from the Dominican Republic. He attacked the testimony of those who had favored the occupations and demanded that the committee bring to Washington those Dominican witnesses who had been denied time to testify in Santo Domingo, making it clear that he had more damning evidence. However, Senator McCormick stalled reopening his committee's investigation, in the obvious hope that a rapid settlement would avoid the airing of more unpleasant information.[33]

A special focus of Knowles' efforts in the spring of 1922 was the anticipated $10 million loan which Military Governor Robison had announced in March. The subject stirred anger and controversy in Santo Domingo, as the Dominicans rightly assumed that this new loan would hold them in financial bondage to the Customs Receivership for a longer time than provided by the original 1907 treaty. "Bankers have no right to force loans upon these people," Knowles told one audience, "and demand that the U.S. government collect them at the point of a pistol." He also claimed that the loan was needed only because of mismanagement by the military government. Writing to Senator Andrieus A. Jones, he charged that "the said loan of $10 million is the second foreign loan made by Washington, and is made necessary, like the first one, by the extravagant expenditures and wastefulness of the military government, and which expenditures were both unauthorized and opposed by the Dominican people." When, despite the protests, Washington arranged a loan of $6.7 million from the Lee Higginson Company, Knowles found the terms very attractive for the bankers and tried to get Senator King to investigate.[34]

Knowles' pressure tactics were an effective counterpoint to Peynado's quiet negotiations. Added to these were the efforts, though generally unambitious in early 1922, of nationalists in Santo Domingo and elsewhere. Most notable was Fabio Fiallo's propaganda tour of Cuba with Cayo Báez, a peasant victim of marine torture. An effort to bring Báez to the United States for similar purposes was frustrated by a barrier of red tape erected by the Immigration Service and the State Department. In Spain, former Dominican consul Enrique Deschamps used his press connections to publish photographs of the maimed Báez and verbatim reports of Senator Borah's Carnegie Hall speech.[35]

A major problem which faced Peynado in his negotiations was whether to reveal the details of his talks to other Dominicans, especially the nationalist groups around President Henríquez. He soon decided to keep complete silence, except for his full and frequent communication with Horace Knowles, whom he pledged to secrecy. Peynado had "resolved not to write to [Henríquez] or to any of the other leaders until I have something positive and firm to communicate to them." Thus, he explained to Knowles, he hoped to avoid raising false hopes, unrealistic expectations, and criticism and debate of points which were still being worked out.[36] As a result, Knowles' reports to Dominicans, including Arturo Pellerano of the *Listín Diario*, tended to be very general, suggesting the positive results of the talks but omitting details. One negative result of this policy was that the lack of specific information caused widespread circulation of rumors.

Cutting off President Henríquez presented the most difficulty. But Peynado believed him to be firmly dedicated to an unworkable principle; to divulge details to him would invite the same fate— total condemnation by the nationalists—which had helped destroy earlier attempts at negotiation. As it happened, President Henríquez made it easy for Peynado and Knowles to limit communication. Preoccupied with health and financial problems, Henríquez wrote infrequently and answered Knowles' few letters very slowly until it became clear that a settlement had been reached.[37]

Upon conclusion of an agreement, both Peynado and Knowles wrote at length to President Henríquez, describing the negotiations and the necessary compromises and asking Henríquez' support. "Peynado has obtained the most that any man or group of men, either Dominicans or Americans, could obtain from this administration," wrote Knowles. Possible flaws, he argued, could be worked out later, and their acceptance was preferable to continuation of the occupation.[38]

The Reception and Implementation of the Hughes-Peynado Agreement

The four Dominican signers of the memorandum of understanding returned home in July to find that the nationalists had mobilized public opinion against the new accord. The nationalists' initial attack relied heavily on the fact that only a summary of the original document had been published in the Dominican Republic. Claiming that there were unannounced provisions which would convert the republic into a U.S. protectorate, they were able to campaign effectively for continued adherence to the *pura y simple* formula.[39]

The wave of protest gave new life and importance to the Junta de Abstención Electoral, which had first formed in opposition to the Harding Plan of 1921. The junta took as its principal task the frustration of the Hughes-Peynado accord by a boycott of the proposed election. The new plan, announced the junta in a broadside, with its revision of the Dominican constitution under North American bayonets, would result in another Platt Amendment; its ratification would amount to acceptance of the U.S. right to intervene. It must therefore be prevented.[40]

Radical nationalist Américo Lugo, the founder and principal leader of the Junta de Abstención Electoral, soon created an argument which would serve the group until the end of the occupation. The Hughes-Peynado agreement, Lugo maintained, was the work of unrepresentative Dominicans who had made concessions to the United States which were totally unjustifiable. Under international law, he argued, the U.S. occupation and most of the acts of the military government were illegal. For this reason the U.S. government anxiously sought an agreement which would legitimize its misdeeds and, further, which would secure the future interests of its investors and bankers. It was not the Dominican people who needed a withdrawal agreement; with all the world condemning the U.S. occupation, he asserted, Dominicans could hold out successfully for withdrawal *pura y simple*. Nor would such a withdrawal create anarchy, as the U.S. government and Dominican conservatives maintained. On the contrary, ending the occupation would remove "a deep and permanent disturbance in the social order."[41]

It was to clarify and explain the Hughes-Peynado accord, as well as to counter the nationalists' propaganda, that President Harding appointed Sumner Welles as his special commissioner to the Dominican Republic. Welles, a skillful diplomat with an excellent command of Spanish, began his work by touring a dozen of the largest cities of the republic in the company of one or more of the political leaders who had signed the agreement. In this manner, he and his party were apparently able to convince a majority of politically active Dominicans that the agreement was reasonable and would soon lead to withdrawal and reestablishment of full sovereignty.[42]

Welles also immediately set up an executive board of influential Dominicans whom he hoped would facilitate communication and work out any difficulties which arose concerning the evacuation scheme. More particularly, this Comisión de Representantes or Commission of Representatives was to study, revise as necessary, and complete in greater detail the tentative withdrawal agreement of 30 June. Included on the commission were Peynado, Archbishop Nouel, and the leaders of the three large political parties. President Henríquez, for the nationalists, refused to participate. Beginning in August and for the next several months, Welles and the Dominicans debated every detail of the original proposal and, in addition, reviewed the large body of legislation produced under the military government to determine which laws should remain in force and which should be discarded. As it happened, by the time Welles' commission completed its work on 19 September, its members had made only a few modifications, mainly clarifications, to the original plan of withdrawal.[43]

That Welles was successful in his effort to undermine nationalist support is suggested by the considerable distaste with which the nationalists viewed him and his mission. They condemned him as a "judge whose decisions were beyond appeal" concerning the contents and purpose of the Hughes-Peynado Plan and belittled his politicking by claiming that he had done nothing more than convince a tiny but powerful minority of Dominicans to accept the plan. Nevertheless, intelligence reports for the month of August 1922 indicate a steady erosion of nationalist support. Both the people and the press became more friendly and had moderated their criticisms, noted marine observers. Some newspapers, most notably the *Listín Diario*, had deserted the nationalist camp and came out in support of the plan. The general public seemed "very quiet" and in keen anticipation of the final publication of the plan and the installation of the provisional government in October.[44]

The final draft of the Hughes-Peynado agreement and the plan of evacuation appeared in Dominican newspapers on 23 September 1922. The effect of publication, Welles believed, was salutary, for it dispelled both the fear that the long negotiations of the representatives might result in provisions adverse to the republic as well as the rumors that the original document contained secret provisions. Marine intelligence officers bore out Welles' observation. The press, they reported, was "as a whole for the Plan," and the attitude of the people and the press toward the military government and its troops seemed "milder and more frank." Both Dominicans and foreign property owners, they claimed, seemed content with the security the plan afforded their interests.[45]

There is little doubt that the events of the summer and fall of 1922 severely crippled the ability of the nationalists to continue their campaign against the occupation—for, in the eyes of a large number of the backers of the nationalist movement, the battle for a just settlement had been won. With the revivification of the political parties, many erstwhile nationalists followed the lead of the party heads, accepted the Hughes-Peynado accord, and began preparing for the forthcoming election. Among them were Tulio Cestero and six of the presidents of the *juntas nacionalistas*.[46] Other nationalists, believing the struggle against the United States to be over, settled back into their old mode of ignoring a political process which they had long disdained. A similar pattern occurred abroad. In the United States, virtually all those who had supported the Dominican cause, including editors, legislators, labor leaders, and Horace Knowles himself, believed the Hughes-Peynado agreement to be a just settlement. And it appears that the majority of Latin American governments accepted the proposed plan to end the occupation.[47] Thus, in a period of a few months, the nationalist leaders had become leaders without followers, both unable to affect political events at home and unable to bring to bear the outside pressures which had previously been so effective in forcing the United States to negotiate.

Francisco Henríquez and other nationalists resisted the disintegration of their forces. In late July 1922, Henríquez issued a circular decrying the Hughes-Peynado Plan and calling on the *juntas nacionalistas* to hold a national meeting to decide upon a definite policy. The resulting meeting, held in Santiago in October, attracted not only the *juntas nacionalistas*, of which only three out of twelve managed to send representatives, but also delegates from the Junta de Abstención Electoral and the Asociación de Jóvenes. The various groups issued a forceful statement condemning the plan, the proposed treaty, Welles' Comisión de Representantes, the provisional government, and "the connivance of the personalistic Dominican political parties with North American imperialism." But the nationalist blast had no effect.[48]

Regardless of the disintegration of the nationalist movement as a controlling political force, regardless of Welles' successful propaganda, certain provisions of the final document were open to legitimate question. Among these were the acceptance of most of the laws decreed by the military government, the selection of a provisional government by the U.S.-chosen Comisión de Representantes, and the presence of U.S. troops during the election of the new constitutional government. None of these items was changed, nor was the provision which compelled future governments to leave unchanged the tariff schedule of 1920, which was distinctly adverse to some Dominican interests.[49]

For entirely different reasons, the military governor and his staff were nearly as unhappy with the Hughes-Peynado agreement and its implementation as were the radical nationalists. The occupation authorities had not been consulted before its issuance, and they viewed the plan for rapid withdrawal as a case of political expedience which took into account neither the need of the military government to complete its mandate nor the eventual good of the Dominican people. In addition, Military Governor Robison soon developed a marked personal antipathy to Sumner Welles.

The dispute between Robison and Welles arose over the role of the military government in the withdrawal process. Although once he arrived in the republic, Welles took care to inform Robison of his actions, particularly those involving the Comisión de Representantes, he also made clear that he regarded his agreements with the Dominicans as *faits accomplis*.[50] This view caused a problem in the context of the continuing discussions of the details of the Hughes-Peynado Plan between Welles and the Dominicans. When Robison proposed a number of modifications of the accord, especially concerning military affairs under the provisional government, Welles balked on the grounds that the Dominicans would regard even their suggestion as a breach of faith. The resulting argument was resolved in Welles' favor by presidential intervention between the Departments of State and the Navy in Washington.[51]

The dispute established clearly the supremacy of Welles and the State Department over Dominican policy, removing the military government from effective control even before the creation of the provisional government. Robison was left clearly dissatisfied with his second-class status. "The State Department did not cast me nor the General [Brigade Commander Harry Lee] for very important roles in the new state of affairs. We are mostly to twiddle our thumbs," he complained.[52]

The Provisional Government and the Withdrawal Process

During the weeks following the publication of the final text of the withdrawal agreement, the Dominican representatives selected a provisional president and, with the nominee, a cabinet. The new president was Juan Bautista Vicini Burgos, never before active in politics and—by virtue of his family's sugar estates—one of the wealthiest men in the country. His cabinet was more or less equally divided between the main political parties, excepting the nationalists.[53]

The inauguration of the Vicini Burgos government took place

on 21 October 1922, solemnized by a Te Deum in the cathedral of Santo Domingo and applauded by a large number of Dominican onlookers. On the same afternoon Military Governor Robison and his staff departed from the country, leaving General Harry Lee as acting military governor. Lee, who became the official military governor six months later, established an excellent working relationship with Vicini Burgos and the provisional government.[54]

The essential function of the provisional government was to preside over the process of electing a new constitutional government, to take office in 1924. It also tended to the everyday matters of running and policing the country while U.S. forces completed two basic tasks preparatory to withdrawal. These were finishing the public works program and preparing the Guardia Nacional Dominicana to function without U.S. Marine supervision.[55]

Standing behind the provisional government were Welles and his Comisión de Representantes, which continued to exist as an executive council, facilitating communication between the government, the several political factions, and the U.S. military, as well as mediating the disputes which arose from time to time between members of the government. The military governor was generally uninvolved in the everyday affairs of the country, except that the provisional government needed his approval for any unbudgeted expenditures.[56]

The greatest problems of the provisional government arose not from managing the daily affairs of state but from the political controversies which marked the reawakening of partisan politics in the republic. Numerous disputes, some quite serious, occurred over appointments to the provisional government, over the setting up and staffing of the electoral boards for the 1924 national election, and over the implementation of the electoral law concerning registration and voting. These quarrels, in addition to dilatory behavior on the part of the Comisión de Representantes and the government, nearly led to the breakdown of the withdrawal process on several occasions.[57]

Greater problems faced the military government in its limited role. The public works program was plagued by cash shortages and other problems which resulted in long delays. And the seemingly simple matter of completing the long-neglected expansion and training of the Guardia Nacional and its officer corps was gravely compromised, in the eyes of U.S. officers, by the short time which the Hughes-Peynado agreement had allotted for the task. Nevertheless, after largely unsuccessful efforts to modify the withdrawal plan in this regard, the military governor and his staff labored diligently and apparently successfully to complete the Guardia's training in time. They also worked to insure that there would be no serious marine-civilian confrontations which could delay or destroy the withdrawal process. To this end, General Lee continued strict enforcement of the regulations governing marine behavior which he had issued in 1921.[58]

Aiding the program to maintain harmonious relations was the provision of the Hughes-Peynado agreement which called for the concentration of the marines in a few specified locations. After late September 1922, the marines were located in Santo Domingo, Santiago, Puerto Plata, and San Pedro de Macorís. Forces were also authorized in October 1922 for Los Chicharrones, at the center of the area dominated by guerrilla Ramón Natera until May 1922, but this contingent was withdrawn in early 1923.[59]

The concentrated marines were unable to leave the cities where they were billeted either for official duties or for personal recreation unless they had written permission. And in these cities the marines were no longer responsible for policing anyone except, in the case of the military police, other marines. This was in keeping with a new policy of divorcing "the purely military forces of the United States . . . from what normally are civil duties."[60]

The withdrawal of the marines from most of the republic presented no serious difficulties. Even the partially trained Guardia, commanded in part by preintervention Dominican officers, proved capable of policing the nation, and the public cheered this first concrete step toward withdrawal. "The concentration of the Marines has had a good effect on the people," wrote a marine intelligence officer.[61]

The Nationalists under the Provisional Government

The nationalists had reacted quickly and effectively to the announcement of the Hughes-Peynado agreement in June 1922. But the propaganda effort of Sumner Welles and the Dominican party leaders as well as the publication of the final draft of the withdrawal agreement and the proposed treaty put to rest the fears of most Dominicans. Thereafter, the nationalists were faced with an ever growing number of defections from their supporters.

In particular, the nationalist organizations in the provinces, the *juntas nacionalistas*, began to disintegrate. "They folded up their banners and collapsed into silence," wrote Federico Henríquez. Remaining, though much weakened, were the national-level director-ates, the Junta Nacionalista Dominicana and the Junta Patriótica de Damas. Left to take the lead in the nationalist movement were the Junta de Abstención Electoral and the Asociación de Jóvenes, led by Rafael Estrella Ureña. Meanwhile, the *pura y simple* doctrine became the guiding principle of all the active nationalists.[62]

After the nationalists' active campaign in mid 1922 against the newly announced Hughes-Peynado agreement, the whole movement had fallen into a period of desuetude, punctuated only occasionally by publications and speeches. In mid 1923, however, the nationalists returned to the attack, keeping up a steady fire against the withdrawal agreement through the rest of 1923 and 1924. In July 1923, for example, a marine intelligence officer noted that criticism of the occupation and of the withdrawal process was "becoming more and more severe" and constant. There were, he noted, "to be heard and found many . . . men to offer . . . extreme criticism and numerous jeering remarks daily against Americans. The newspapers make use of every available opportunity to make derogatory remarks against the American forces."[63] The active nationalists branded those who cooperated with the withdrawal plans *transaccionistas* or sellouts. Though their arguments against the withdrawal process varied, their main tactic for stopping it was to promote the boycott of the coming election.

The most noted spokesman of the nationalists continued to be Américo Lugo. A speech he delivered in Puerto Plata's Teatro Colón in September 1923 is representative of his views and much of the nationalist movement at that time. The nationalists, he argued, were not a political party. Unlike the parties, which sought political advantage and power, the nationalists were interested only in self-determination for the republic. The nationalist position was based on international law, which gave the United States no right to pass legislation in the republic, except that needed to maintain order; for this reason, Dominicans should refuse to ratify the executive orders, as called for by the Hughes-Peynado agreement (which in any case had been negotiated and signed by "pseudorepresentatives"). "The most serious abuse of the North American imperialist forces is the constitutional reform," he continued. The only solution, as it would destroy the Hughes-Peynado agreement, was electoral abstention. Only this would save the Dominicans from a settlement which promised to make them, like the Haitians, "slaves in their own country." In closing, Lugo delivered a ringing charge to Dominicans to get up off their knees, to confront head-on "the beast of Yankee imperialism."[64]

Speeches like Lugo's as well as the actions of other nationalists were followed closely by U.S. military intelligence. Many reports document newspaper articles, handbills, meetings, demonstrations, and speeches. Later in 1923, as the nationalists turned more and more of their attention to their campaign against the election, intelligence sources reported with alarm any abnormal trends in voter registration, such as the "remarkable reduction in the number of registrations of voters in certain Provinces in the Northern District," a phenomenon which turned out to be only short-lived. As the year passed, marines observed that nationalist propaganda seemed to improve and to mount in enthusiasm. Among the targets of the nationalists' "vituperation and caustic comments" were not only the election but also the participating political parties, the provisional government, the forces of occupation, and "everything American." Their behavior, remarked an intelligence officer, seemed an obsession. They saw themselves as "the saviors of the country" and, as each week passed, they seemed to become "more emboldened and energetic."[65]

In order to rally support and to educate the public, the nationalists held a series of conferences in the latter half of 1923. In Santo Domingo and Santiago, in San Pedro de Macorís and El Seibo, their fundamental message was clear: boycott the elections and force an evacuation *pura y simple*. They also sponsored demonstrations, especially in the larger cities; in October they held as many as three a week in Santo Domingo, causing "some concern to the provisional government." But the nationalist group was "exceedingly small," reported Sumner Welles in November. "I do not believe that the total number of Dominicans affiliated amounts to two per cent of the population. The leaders, however, are able speakers and the notoriety they have obtained through the public meetings . . . has created the impression that the nationalista movement is more important than it is." Underscoring Welles' point was the fact that by early 1924 only two daily newspapers continued to support the nationalist cause, *El Independiente* of Santo Domingo and *La Información* of Santiago.[66]

The nationalists also tried to keep their case before an international audience. To this end they, as well as the Haitians, sent an extraofficial representative to the Fifth Pan American Conference in Santiago, Chile. But their effectiveness was surely limited by the fact that the regular Dominican delegate was none other than the exnationalist Tulio Cestero, well known in Chile and now supporting the United States' Dominican policy. Also, the State Department, fearing outbursts by "anti-American propagandists," had carefully rehearsed the U.S. delegation on the accomplishments of the occupations.[67] In any case, the nationalists no longer found such a favorable audience in Latin America. The new Dominican policy, boasted Welles, "has done much to dispel the feeling which existed in some parts of the Continent a few years ago that the United States intended to pursue an imperialistic policy in the Caribbean by establishing virtual protectorates in all the Central American and Caribbean Republics."[68]

Although the military authorities continued to keep a tight rein on the marines during the period of the provisional government, there were many disturbances between marines and Dominicans. However, perhaps because the marine command monitored such incidents very carefully—approximately half the papers of the commanding general in this period concern these matters—none got out of hand. In some cases, because the military government had lost the right to try Dominicans in provost courts, the military authorities counted on the provisional government to punish those Dominicans whom they viewed as having exceeded certain limits.[69] For example, when *La Prensa* of San Pedro de Macorís excoriated President Harding on the occasion of his death for the continuing occupation of the Dominican Republic and Puerto Rico, the provisional government arrested and tried the writer and the editor, fining and jailing one and deporting the other for three years.[70]

Such cases of direct official cooperation between the military government and Dominican officials angered the nationalists.[71] So did the increasing social mixing between the higher officials of the military government and those Dominicans associated with the provisional government, the Comisión de Representantes, the diplomatic corps, the church, the press, and others in elite circles. Elite leaders were found not only at the office of the military governor offering their allegiance, charged Fabio Fiallo in a speech in La Vega, but "also at the country club parties, where they bring their wives and daughters to dance and amuse themselves with the same brutish sergeants who burned our little country towns to ashes."[72]

By the end of 1922, the reawakened Dominican political process had begun to overshadow all else, including the nationalists' protests, the limited work of the military government, and the activities of the Vicini Burgos administration. Politics focused on the hot competition between the republic's preintervention political factions for control of the postintervention presidency and Congress. During 1923, it became evident that two groups would dominate the coming election. The Alianza Nacional-Progresista, a combination of the two personalist parties of Horacio Vásquez and Federico Velásquez, nominated the two leaders for president and vice-president respectively. The Coalición Patriótica, composed of a variety of smaller groups, the most important of which was one branch of the personalist party of the deceased president Juan Jiménez, nominated Francisco Peynado.[73]

This narrative will not attempt to detail the politicking which led up to the 1924 election, except to note that it followed the fiercely competitive nature of pre-1916 Dominican politics. So engrossed in the contest did the competitors become that several times the electoral process came to a complete halt. According to one observer, Julio Campillo Pérez, "the intransigence, the emotionalism, and the distrust so characteristic of our politics increased with each passing moment."[74]

North Americans were similarly impressed and disturbed by what they saw as extreme factionalism, personalism, and a refusal to compromise. "Political feeling is intense," wrote Minister Russell in mid 1923, as he reported political killings and persistent rumors of arms smuggling for political purposes. The situation had not improved four months later when, in the midst of a severe political crisis, Sumner Welles noted that "the political situation is precarious in the extreme," that the electoral process had been all but destroyed by the uncontrolled "personal animosity between the opposing candidates." At times it appeared that the Dominicans were willing to continue the occupation indefinitely rather than to give up a political advantage, in the case of the personalist parties, or to compromise a principle, in the case of the nationalists. Even Horace Knowles, after struggling for Dominican sovereignty for four years, was moved to confide to Francisco Peynado that "the situation is simply beyond my comprehension. At times I am in doubt whether the Dominicans are really ready for complete independence."[75]

By early 1924, perhaps because the outcome of the election was becoming obvious, the political situation in the republic had quieted. The election of 15 March 1924 was without incident, and the Alianza party won a smashing victory, gaining not only the presidency for Horacio Vásquez but also, by a wide margin, the Senate and the Chamber of Deputies.[76] Why did Vásquez and the Alianza emerge victorious? First, as a traditional caudillo politician of national stature, Vásquez headed a large and well-organized political machine which owed its loyalty to him personally and which worked hard in his favor. In addition, through his alliance with Velásquez (whom some believed would inherit the presidency because Vásquez, an older man, would die in office),[77] Vásquez picked up the support of the second-largest political organization in the country. He was, in short, a practical politician with a widespread following.

Peynado, on the other hand, had generally remained aloof from politics. He was no caudillo; in fact, part of his appeal to the electorate was based on the claim that the republic would best avoid the extreme personalism and factionalism of caudillo rule, which, he argued, would lead only to another intervention. But Peynado thus lacked a caudillo's large and popular following. His party, in the words of one critic of the time, was "an elite of theoreticians, more thinkers than actors." Or, as Peynado's admirer Sumner Welles more kindly stated: "His appeal was primarily to the professional classes who were not strong numerically; the organization of the groups supporting him was deficient, and the Coalition party lacked the financial support which its opponents possessed."[78]

Peynado's campaign gave rise to one issue which would strike an observer of Dominican politics today as very familiar. At one point, his opponents characterized him as the candidate of the U.S. sugar companies, with which he had long worked closely, and the favorite of Washington. This charge, which Welles soon forced both Vásquez and Velásquez to disavow, had a plausible ring but was not without a certain irony.[79] Neither Vásquez nor Velásquez had raised a finger against the intervention, while Peynado had provided both money and advice to the nationalists under President Henríquez. And Velásquez in particular had been one of the first to cooperate with the military government, was a close friend of U.S. Minister Russell, and, in the words of Horace Knowles, had "always been a sellout."[80]

Vásquez' election took place with surprisingly little active opposition from the nationalists. There was a notable diminution of their activities by early 1924, probably because it had become clear that their work was doomed to have little effect on the balloting. The apparent futility of their effort might also explain an uncharacteristic but reasonably well documented action on the part of a small group of nationalists. Having lost the war of words, they began a conspiracy to assassinate the presidential candidates, Welles, and others; almost immediate discovery of the plot apparently ended it.[81]

At Bonao in September 1924, the nationalists voted to continue their struggle against the majority parties and the compromise negotiated with Washington by organizing as a political party. In this way they hoped to begin to participate in the political process and eventually to build a majority political party based on principles, among them antiimperialism, rather than personalities. The Nationalist party survived into the early 1930s and was marginally involved in the rise to power of Rafael Trujillo.[82]

The Withdrawal

As the date for withdrawal approached, the military governor and his staff carried out certain final provisions. On 4 July 1924, the last twenty-five provost prisoners, twenty-one of them followers of Vicentico who had begun ten- and fifteen-year sentences in 1917, were released by order of the military governor. Between April and August 1924, the marines stationed at San Pedro de Macorís, Puerto Plata, and Santiago turned over the fortresses and other military installations in those cities to the Guardia. They then moved to Santo Domingo, where they awaited final evacuation by ship.[83]

When the new constitutional government of Horacio Vásquez took office on 12 July 1924, U.S. forces were already engaged in a gradual embarkation from the republic. On 18 September 1924, the last marine left Dominican soil. U.S. Minister Russell reported laconically that "provisions of the Plan of the Evacuation have been completed and all of the Forces of Occupation have left the country."[84]

Epilogue

The July 1924 inauguration of President Horacio Vásquez as the new constitutional president marked the end of an eight-year national trauma. Not only had the U.S. military government attempted to refashion Dominican national life during this period, but a series of other forces had affected the island nation. Foremost among these were the lengthy guerrilla war which had disrupted large parts of the eastern region, the severe economic dislocations caused by World War I and the postwar depression, and an intense national political struggle, first to end the occupation and then to determine the terms of withdrawal and the complexion of postoccupation politics.

Despite the operation of these forces, the fundamental pattern of Dominican society remained surprisingly similar from 1916 to 1924. So too did the nature of the republic's overall relationship with the United States. This is not to deny that significant changes had taken place or to declare the reforms of the military government totally ineffective—for, while the broad contours of Dominican life remained much the same, there had been changes, caused both by the military government and by the ambient political and economic forces of the time. These alterations varied in importance from one area of Dominican life to another and often had an unpredictable quality, with the unanticipated results of change sometimes more significant than those which had been planned.

The Impact of the Military Government

Occupation officials instituted many reforms in the hope of reshaping the nature of Dominican political life. But, almost as though there had been no occupation, the Vásquez administration and the national political life of which it was a part were notable for their similarity to what had gone before. Personalist leaders and issues obscured by personalist feuds again dominated politics, while administrative standards declined and corruption reappeared. Similarly, there remained a willingness to abuse the constitutional system, as Vásquez showed in 1928 when he artificially extended his term in office by two years. The government was wealthier as the result of occupation fiscal reforms, but the increased expenses of new responsibilities meant that it was as likely as before to be insolvent and in need of foreign loans (the Vásquez administration borrowed $10 million in 1926). The increased wealth and the new nationally directed programs which occasioned this increased spending also made the government a more powerful actor in national life. This, along with the temporary spirit of political consensus which followed the withdrawal, may explain the initial absence of a rebellious opposition, one of the main differences between the Vásquez years and earlier.[1]

The overwhelmingly important new factor in Dominican politics turned out to be the Guardia Nacional, which serves as an excellent illustration of the unplanned and unpredictable nature of the occupation's legacy. Well supported by the Vásquez regime but increasingly controlled by Rafael Trujillo, this efficient new force, combined with improved roads and communications, proved eminently capable of maintaining order. After 1930 it became the tool for total control of the republic, dealing effectively with the old counterbalancing forces of regionalism and caudillismo. This became clear early in Trujillo's reign when the Guardia quickly eliminated two famous caudillos, Desiderio Arias and Cipriano Bencosme, who had risen in rebellion.[2]

In the economic field, the military government had been even more active than in the political, but the overall result of its policies was much the same. The economy in 1924 remained basically as it had been in 1916. The reason for this is obvious: the large majority of the military government's actions tended to support the existing economic arrangement. This was certainly true of its largest project, public works, which in the process of creating an infrastructure primarily advanced the fortunes of the country's existing planter and merchant elite. Likewise, the greatest number of remedial measures during World War I and the postwar depression were meant to succor the same groups and served the same purpose. Even the occasional efforts on behalf of consumers, employees, and others on the bottom of the economic ladder, though genuinely meant to protect and help those who were less fortunate, had the effect of maintaining the status quo.

The one area of economic affairs which appears to break this pattern is foreign investment. Here the military government's surprisingly negative attitude toward foreign investors brought about actions meant to control and limit outside economic penetration, especially in sugar agriculture. The military authorities ended the various concessionary giveaways set up by pre-1916 Dominican governments to attract foreign capital and enacted a number of other laws decidedly contrary to the interests of foreign investors. Yet they also passed several laws regarding landownership which proved a tremendous boon to foreign agricultural interests and all but negated their other actions. The Ley de Registro de Tierras of 1920, as much as any Dominican legislation in the first quarter of the twentieth century, confirmed the republic's place in the world as a producer of agricultural commodities for the industrially developed North Atlantic nations. It reinforced the economic status quo and in so doing reinforced the political and social status quo. The same could be said for the new tariff of 1920, one of the less defensible major acts of the occupation period.

The impact of the military government on Dominican culture, on such matters as social life, customs, behavior, and language, is more difficult to measure. Though some observers have guessed that the impact was great, no one has yet advanced many particulars.[3] It seems more likely that during the period of the occupation Dominicans merely received a greater exposure to cultural forces which were already a steady influence on their lives and which became an even greater influence thereafter. Even the concept of an accelerated North Americanization, presumably owing to the increased presence of North Americans, may be exaggerated, since the newcomers were mostly enlisted men. Though the enlisted marines certainly had a culture, it seems unlikely that it would inspire widespread emulation, in part because their behavior was often brutish by traditional Dominican standards and in part because the purpose of their presence frequently provoked a negative reaction.

Leaving aside speculation and looking to the actions of the military government, one finds fairly few legislative efforts in the social and cultural area. The major programs in this field were the educational reform and the improvement of health and sanitation. The educational program had as its goal strengthening rather than changing Dominican culture and, although the health and sanitation program did aspire to change attitudes and habits by such measures as ending prostitution and eliminating the practice of folk medicine, it appeared to make rather limited headway in these endeavors. So too, for example, the program in agriculture appeared to have little or no effect on the traditional practices of peasant farming.

While there is little evidence of significant legislated change, it is possible that ordinary person-to-person influences were more effective agents of cross-cultural change. There is some evidence of new words entering Dominican Spanish, such as *pic-nic* and *usa* (allegedly a word in the east for saddle blanket, from the letters U.S.A. on marine blankets). The celebration of Christmas may have shifted somewhat to the North American style during the occupation. The sport of baseball, which Dominican students had imported before the intervention, grew dramatically during this period, helped along by the presence of marine teams. And the Dominican Boy Scouts apparently originated in 1917.[4] On a more serious level, it is possible that the virulent racism of the occupiers aggravated to some degree the more moderate racism which existed in the republic before 1916. Finally, the status and role of women were undergoing change at this time. Military government laws and practices sometimes encouraged this phenomenon, though feminist influences were as much or more European or even Latin American (via more modern cultures, such as those of Argentina, Uruguay, and Cuba) as they were North American.

Perhaps more important than the process of North Americanization during the occupation was its obverse, the self-conscious celebration of things Dominican. There are clear indications that the U.S. presence bred a stronger Dominican nationalism. Citizens of the republic could claim with pride in 1924 to have launched a program of protest which had forced the United States to abandon the occupation. And in the process they acquired a growing consciousness of their own national culture. Illustrating this change on the lighter side was the elite's new attachment to what has become the national dance, the merengue, and the increased emphasis on such holidays as 12 October, the Día de la Raza, which celebrates the republic's Hispanic origins and cultural ties. More substantial reflections of the same phenomenon included the first interest in Dominican folklore and the publication of various literary works with consciously Dominican, sometimes anti-Yankee themes, such as the famous novel *Over* by Ramón Marrero Aristy.[5]

In summary, the military government's many programs and administrative actions in the political, economic, and social fields left the basic pattern of Dominican life relatively unchanged. That they did not have more effect is a testimony to the strength of Dominican society and culture. But this also reveals an important characteristic of the military government: military officials in most cases intended to support rather than to change the fundamental pattern of Dominican life. Occupation officials basically accepted the republican and constitutional political system, the liberal capitalist economic system, and the class-based social system which existed in the republic when they arrived in 1916. Their task, as they conceived it, was to reform and strengthen what was already in place. The same was true of the attitude of Washington officials. Thus the military administration had neither the desire nor the mandate to change the basic pattern of Dominican life. And, even if officials had tried, the evidence is overwhelming that they would have failed, either through ineptness or through massive popular opposition.

The pattern of the Dominican occupation also holds true for the other Caribbean interventions of the early twentieth century. Neither in Cuba, Haiti, nor Nicaragua did U.S. intervention change the fundamental characteristics of those societies. Though reformist programs induced changes, economic underdevelopment, social and economic inequality, and political instability remained. Even Puerto Rico in 1948, after fifty years of absolute U.S. control, displayed the same basic social and economic features which it had in 1898.

The Limits of Power: Factors Affecting the Programs of the Military Government

The power of the military government, and the ability of occupation officials to carry out their programs, was affected by a number of factors. Some of these acted to enhance power, such as the military government's reasonably efficient administrative system or—considering the time and the place—its unusually abundant technological resources. Others, such as the lack of a consistent policy, tended to detract from its ability to accomplish its goals. Still other factors cut both ways, either because, like the military government's financial base, they changed over time or because they simultaneously created advantages and disadvantages.

Two of the paramount features of the military government—the fact that it was a military dictatorship and the agent of a major world power—are examples of these favorable-unfavorable factors. On the one hand, these characteristics gave the regime the freedom to move ahead on projects which Dominican governments had had to avoid for political reasons, for it had the ability to resist both domestic and foreign pressures. On the other hand, these same features were a serious political liability, as Dominicans displayed a natural tendency to suspect and sometimes to reject occupation programs because they were the products of a nonrepresentative and often oppressive government. Undoubtedly some programs which failed under occupation patronage might have succeeded in Dominican hands.

There were, moreover, sometimes good reasons to protest military government policies. Proposals to alter long-standing Dominican social, political, and economic ways often threatened people's individual or collective personal interests, and, as a vocal minority of the educated elite correctly saw, they also menaced an independent national identity and ultimately the republic's sovereignty.

The effect on established Dominican interests was one of a number of factors which commonly helped determine the success or failure of military government programs. Generally the programs which were most likely to succeed were those which had the support of a sizable group of influential Dominicans, which harmonized well with prevailing political, economic, and social realities, or which, like the construction projects, involved primarily material concerns. Programs doomed to failure were those which provoked the resistance of large and influential groups, which ignored Dominican realities, or which depended on the transplanting of U.S. values to make them function successfully. The military government's successful new system of land registration, for instance, though imported from the other side of the globe, met a pressing Dominican need and had the support of much of the elite. It carried to completion goals for which previous Dominican governments had worked and did so within the same basic philosophic framework, that is, liberal capitalism. On the other hand, the military government's land taxation law, though abstractly a just and needed piece of legislation, had no precedent in Dominican life and found little support from influential Dominicans. As a result, it never functioned well and within a few years was abolished. The military authorities, because they governed by fiat, could create and impose any policy they wished, but experience soon demonstrated that they could not create public enthusiasm or even cooperation, nor could they insure the survival of unpopular measures after 1924.

One of the major problems of the military government was its lack of a coherent policy. With three different executive departments of the U.S. government involved in Santo Domingo and with the war in Europe absorbing most of official Washington's time and energy, the military government received little direction. As a result, naval, marine, and State Department officials, aided by interested outsiders, had to piece together a policy on a largely *ad hoc* basis. This led to a confusing and sometimes debilitating lack of consistency, as the military government's policy toward the sugar industry clearly showed. The complex process of working out a policy also caused long delays in some areas, a problem which Washington's slow approval process aggravated considerably.

Policy implementation was another problem, for the naval and marine officers running the government often lacked the training and experience necessary to develop and administer the complex programs which the situation demanded. Even more important, they lacked an understanding of Dominican society, a point which Sumner Welles made as harshly as any critic could. The reforms of the occupation "conformed solely to the customs, habits, and prejudices of the intervening power," he wrote, because the "Military Government not only failed to consider local customs and prejudices, but was actually ignorant of what they were."[6] Though Welles may exaggerate, it is true that many high-level naval and marine officials were hampered by cultural biases, xenophobia, and racial prejudices.

Military officials might have overcome this problem with more extensive use of Dominican advisers. But instead they frequently excluded Dominicans from significant high-level participation in both the planning and the execution of military government programs. Or, as in the case of Military Governor Snowden and the *junta consultiva*, they appointed Dominicans to advisory boards and then ignored their advice. This, however, was not always the case. There were a few officials, like the head of the Ministry of Justice and Public Instruction, Rufus Lane, who had a basically positive attitude toward Dominican society and who worked often and well with Dominicans.

Another basic obstacle to policy implementation was the lack of qualified personnel, particularly to staff the new or greatly expanded programs in such areas as education and health. There was a serious shortage of well-trained Dominicans in many fields, and often those who had the needed skills were reluctant to work with the occupation. Though the military government was sometimes able to recruit personnel from the United States and its colonies for higher-level positions, this did not solve the overall problem. Ultimate policy implementation often depended on Dominicans with inferior training, on Puerto Ricans who were resented as overbearing outsiders, or even on marine enlisted men and lower-ranking officers who were often unable to communicate, prejudiced, and insensitive to Dominican culture. Individuals from any of these groups had the potential to defeat the purposes of nearly any program, whatever its merits or failings.

The eastern guerrilla war is an unequaled example of both policies formulated by higher officials in ignorance of Dominican social and political realities and of remarkably poor implementation by enlisted marines. Marine officials failed to comprehend the history and the strength of the caudillo system and, once the fighting began, lacked the know-how to combat a guerrilla war. They long failed to perceive how the social circumstances of the east fed the war or how their own actions aggravated rather than improved the situation.

There were times, also, when the implementation of policy in and of itself contradicted policy goals. The development of democratic habits and institutions, for instance, a goal to which military officials paid at least lip service, was hardly encouraged by a six-year dictatorship. Perhaps recognition of this fact caused the military government to do little toward the active pursuit of democracy.

There were two factors affecting the success of the military government's programs which changed over time. One was its financial situation, which began as a very positive factor and ended as a negative one, and the other was the general level of repressiveness required to maintain the military government's authority, which followed a similar pattern.

The favorable financial situation resulted in part from the efforts of military officials to tighten up the collection of internal revenues, to diminish graft, and to create new taxes. But other circumstances (over which military officials had no control but which nevertheless reflected well on their rule) turned out to be even more important. Soaring world commodity prices sent Dominican private sector earnings rapidly upward until late 1920, resulting in considerably increased public revenues as well. These provided the military government a considerable sum with which to reform and expand former government programs and to embark on new ones. Military officials also had at their disposal millions of dollars provided by U.S. taxpayers, which paid for personnel, equipment, and supplies.[7] The benefits of this were considerable. Because these funds paid officers' salaries, for example, they met a large part of the occupation government's upper-level administrative budget, allowing money to be shifted into programs. And, because they paid the salaries and the support costs of enlisted men, the financial effect of the eastern peasant war on the military government was negligible, although a similar episode would have severely crippled and perhaps destroyed a Dominican administration.

How much the military government's record of achievement depended on favorable financial circumstances became clear after late 1920, when a depression curtailed and even destroyed many of the military government's programs. But even at this point the occupation authorities operated at an advantage over their Dominican predecessors, for they could obtain large amounts of credit at better rates, thus enabling them to continue basic government and to salvage some of their programs.

The general lack of Dominican resistance in the first years of the occupation also worked to the advantage of the occupation officials. It allowed favorably disposed Dominicans to support the military government and even, on some occasions, to work for its programs. More important, after an initial period of adjustment, it allowed authorities to rule without the appearance of severity and harshness. The one place where this was not true was, of course, the east, where the marines' involvement in the guerrilla war was often associated with brutal and repressive methods. But censorship, poor communication, and elite disdain of the peasants and the popular military forces long prevented these events from interfering with the military government's efforts to govern the rest of the republic.

The rise of an active nationalist movement throughout the republic in 1919 rapidly changed the situation, forcing the military government to act in more obviously repressive ways, beginning with the harsh treatment of journalists during the 1920 Semana Patriótica. From that point forward, until late 1922, the nationalists were able to maintain a polarized political situation, thus eliminating general support for the regime. The depression of the early 1920s aided them considerably. Its severity not only destroyed basic government programs but generally worsened the conditions of people's lives, causing widespread unemployment, bankruptcy, and other hardships. This in turn caused resentment against the military government, prompted additional resistance to some occupation programs, and generally called into question the ability of military officials to manage the country's affairs.

Patterns of Resistance to the Occupation

Resistance to the occupation was a primary factor in bringing it to an end. In different ways, this was true both of the peasants' war against the marines in the east and of the nationalists' political-intellectual campaign of protest.

The guerrilla war caused a constant drain on the military government's personnel and energy. It also sapped morale, since for over five years the marines were defeated by an enemy they did not respect, a fact they found especially difficult to explain to continually inquiring Washington officials. Worse, the marines could not establish control over an important region of the republic. This fact belied the military government's contention that one benefit of the occupation was to bring order to the country. The war also cast into grave doubt the claim of military officials that the Dominican people favored the occupation.

Furthermore, the guerrilla conflict caused diplomatic embarrassment, as the unrest was centered in an area increasingly dominated by corporate sugar interests, with connections to the mainland United States, Puerto Rico, England, and Cuba. Not only was the trouble easily seen by outsiders, but occasionally their nationals ran afoul of its violence. More important in this regard was the fact that the marines' conduct of the war led to frequent abuses and even atrocities against Dominican guerrillas and civilians alike. Despite severe censorship, information concerning these events sometimes made its way into the hands of Dominican nationalists and from them to the international press. As a result, the government of the United States was censured severely, both at home and abroad, giving Washington officials a reason to question the wisdom of continuing the occupation.

Another aspect of the resistance to the intervention was the campaign of international diplomacy and propaganda and of domestic noncooperation led by certain elements of the Dominican elite. Their efforts were responsible, more directly than those of the guerrillas, for the withdrawal of the U.S. forces from Santo Domingo. Their campaign made the military government's rule of the republic increasingly difficult, caused President Wilson's interventionist foreign policy to become a liability in U.S. domestic politics, and brought extreme embarrassment and difficulty to the United States in its international relations. Together these nationalist activities caused Washington officials to move toward withdrawal beginning in late 1920. Yet, having brought the United States to withdraw, the nationalists were not the ones who reaped the political benefits of their success when the occupation ended in 1924. What had happened?

From late 1916 to early 1920, the displaced constitutional president, Francisco Henríquez y Carvajal, and a small coterie of followers—most of them connected personally with him or with his brother, Federico—dominated the nationalist movement. Though a group with high political principles, they were vulnerable to occasional charges, usually leveled by members of the traditional Dominican political parties and by Washington, of being a personalist clique. They were also moderate, even willing to cooperate with the United States in instituting what they considered to be necessary reforms in Santo Domingo. But, because of this attitude of compromise and because of Washington's failure to negotiate in good faith with them, the moderates lost control of the movement to the radicals of the Unión Nacional Dominicana in 1920.

The radicals, following a policy of defying the military government, managed to build an effective organization within the republic —an area which the moderates' internationally oriented campaign had somewhat neglected—mobilizing a large number of Dominicans behind their no-compromise position of withdrawal *pura y simple*. At the same time they managed to capture political initiative, which they maintained until late 1922.

The radicals' more confrontational tactics provoked the military government to use draconian measures, resulting in increased agitation, further acts of defiance, and a growing polarization which made it nearly impossible for those citizens sympathetic to the occupation to continue to display their allegiance. More important, the military government's harshness, especially in regard to censorship, caused itself and Washington immense embarrassment, turning the occupation into a diplomatic and political liability which had effects far beyond the shores of the Dominican Republic.

Withdrawal negotiations were stalemated while the radicals controlled the nationalist movement, as Washington refused to consider their position. When Francisco Peynado's compromise agreement eventually broke the deadlock, it also provided an opportunity for the leaders of the three largest political parties. They could desert the nationalist position, to which they were hardly committed, yet appear responsible for a settlement and the subsequent withdrawal. The nationalists of both camps, now united behind the radical line, were left outmaneuvered. Although they protested loudly against what they saw as a sellout, they rapidly lost political influence to those who saw compromise as agreeable or necessary. Thus in 1922 the nationalists lost control of the Dominican political process, and their role was reduced to that of a gadfly. As a result, those who took power in 1924 were the same personalist leaders who had dominated Dominican politics before 1916. But there can be no doubt that the nationalist resistance was responsible for obtaining the withdrawal from which the traditional politicians had benefited. And the considerable pressure the nationalists had placed on Washington had resulted in a renewed Dominican sovereignty relatively free of U.S. fetters, unlike the Haitian or Cuban style of settlement which U.S. representatives had originally demanded.

In considering the question of the nationalist resistance to the occupation, it is instructive to make brief comparisons to the other

Caribbean occupations. Why were the Dominicans, like the Nicaraguans, successful in ending U.S. intervention when the Puerto Ricans and (for some time) the Haitians were not?

The closest parallels would appear to be with Haiti, which was occupied from 1915 to 1934. The Haitians also developed a caudillo-peasant armed resistance, the *cacos*, and an intellectual-political resistance. However, the *cacos* apparently disintegrated after several years of fighting when the marines killed its chief leader, Charlemagne Peralte, in 1919. And the Haitian intellectual resistance, centered in the Union Patriotique, remained relatively weak, failing to become an elite "mass" movement until the late 1920s. Only then did economic decline help create a political crisis, which eventually led to the reestablishment of Haitian independence in 1934. Probably the worst problem facing the Haitian nationalists was the fact that some traditional politicians had cooperated in the creation of a puppet regime and had signed the U.S.-Haitian treaty of 1915, legitimizing behind-the-scenes U.S. control. Also, the nationalists lacked the wide international audience which the Dominicans had found in Latin America and Spain. Outside of the U.S. antiimperialists, the Haitians' main potential ally was France, whose colonialism, racism, and postwar friendship with the United States made it an unlikely base for support.[8]

Racism was another factor which prejudiced the U.S. policymakers' attitude toward Haitian independence. Ferdinand Mayer, a prominent State Department official in the Division of Latin American Affairs, put the matter succinctly to Secretary of State Charles Evans Hughes in July 1921. In regard to future policy, he wrote, "it is well to distinguish at once between the Dominicans and the Haitians. The former, while in many ways not advanced far enough for the highest type of self-government, yet have a preponderance of white blood and culture. The Haitians on the other hand are negro for the most part, and, barring a very few highly educated politicians, are almost in a state of savagery and complete ignorance. The two situations thus demand different treatment. In Haiti it is necessary to have as complete a rule within a rule by Americans as possible. This sort of control will be required for a long period of time, until the general average of education and enlightenment is raised. In the Dominican Republic, on the other hand, I believe we should endeavor rather to counsel than control." The State Department's Sumner Welles undoubtedly would have agreed with this analysis, once having written that "responsibility could be borne only up to a certain point" by persons of the Negro race.[9]

Puerto Rican nationalists faced a problem similar to that of the

Haitian puppet government. After 1898, a substantial portion of politically active Puerto Ricans agreed to participate in a political system under U.S. control, thus legitimizing U.S. presence. The problem was aggravated in 1917 when Washington imposed U.S. citizenship on the population. Also, because the Puerto Ricans had never been independent, both Puerto Rican and international expectations concerning the island's political status differed considerably from expectations concerning formerly sovereign Haiti and the Dominican Republic.[10]

Unlike Puerto Rico, Nicaragua presents an instance of a successful struggle against U.S. control, although in a way quite different from the Dominican experience. Augusto César Sandino's military effort was very effective and, unlike the Dominican peasant guerrillas, he had connections with the majority Liberal party, whose political ambitions had long been frustrated by U.S. support for the minority Conservatives. Sandino also had strong international connections, especially with Mexico, and a number of supporters in the United States. Thus military and political efforts combined with international support to bring victory to his cause.[11]

The Dominican nationalists, compared to nationalists in other countries suffering U.S. intervention, had put together an unusually effective campaign against the occupation. The major elements were a broad-based protest in the Dominican Republic, a very strong lobby and propaganda system within the United States, and an influential international campaign focused on Latin America. In addition, the eastern peasant war, with no thanks owed to the elite nationalists, caused great difficulties for the military government. Combined with these four basic elements were a number of other factors and conditions, some the result of Dominican planning, some the result of ordinary luck. Among these were the Dominicans' refusal to legitimize the occupation (which forced the United States to establish a blatantly undemocratic military government), the political blunders of the military administration, and the economic depression beginning in late 1920. In the other cases noted here, the antioccupation campaigns took longer or were never successful either because some of these elements were missing or because the factors failed to combine at one time.

The Legacy of Intervention

One of the main results of the occupation was a strong anti-U.S. feeling. This immediately revealed itself in the postwithdrawal period in the form of a hard-fought political struggle in the Dominican Congress over the ratification of the new U.S.-Dominican convention of 1924. Though it eventually received the votes necessary for passage, the nationalists found considerable, if not always principled, support for their opposition.[12] There was also a continuing political sensitivity on matters relating to national sovereignty. For this reason, the Vásquez government found it impossible to accede to two U.S. requests, one for a small U.S. military mission to continue the training of the Guardia and another asking the Dominican government to continue the practice, dating from the Cáceres administration, of employing a U.S. director of public works.[13]

Another aspect of this antagonism toward the United States was the postoccupation work of the nationalists, now organized into an antiimperialist political party headed by Américo Lugo. Antiimperialism in the Dominican context meant anti-U.S. imperialism, and during the 1920s the nationalists and their supporters produced a small but steady stream of anti-Yankee articles and books. In particular, there were campaigns directed against foreign ownership of Dominican land and against the U.S.-owned sugar companies and their privileges.[14] Though this stream of anti-U.S. thinking and writing was forced underground during much of the Trujillo period, it reemerged afterward and was soon reinforced by the intervention of 1965.

The cost of the intervention of 1916 to 1924 to the Dominican people, whatever they may have gained in new laws, buildings, and nationalist enthusiasms, was great. For eight years they lost the opportunity to guide their own destiny and to work toward creating a more democratic, just, and stable society. On a personal level, those who resisted paid with long prison sentences and sometimes with their lives. In a less direct sense, the entire society would soon begin to pay a terrible political and economic price during the thirty-one years of the Trujillo regime and the decades of continued underdevelopment.

What was the cost to the United States? To begin with, the intervention required the expenditure of millions of dollars by U.S. taxpayers. Worse, some naval and marine personnel lost their lives. But the greatest cost was the damage that this and the other Caribbean interventions did to the United States' diplomacy in Latin America and to its reputation in the rest of the world. The benefits which Washington derived from eight years' control of the Dominican Republic, concluded Sumner Welles, "have been of infinitesimal importance when compared to the suspicions, fears, and hatred to which the Occupation gave rise throughout the American continent, and when compared to the lasting hostility towards the American people which the Occupation created in the hearts of a very great number of the Dominican people."[15]

A modern observer might disagree with Welles' assessment, noting that the occupation and its aftermath eventually brought thirty years of stability to the republic and further strengthened U.S. political and economic hegemony in the Caribbean area. But the stability came at the price of a repressive dictatorship and was again followed by chaos in the 1960s; likewise, the reinforcement of U.S. hegemony has led to increasing Latin American resentment and to ever greater efforts to challenge U.S. dominance. Such facts have caused this author to conclude that foreign intervention, as practiced in the Dominican Republic from 1916 to 1924, was neither wise nor just, a policy which in the long run yielded little good to either party but which, on the other hand, brought considerable harm. It was an episode which, if humans were really to learn from experience, could have saved the United States and the less powerful victims of its interventionist diplomacy incalculable waste of life and wealth in the future.

Notes

1. The most balanced Dominican account of the 1916 to 1924 period is the work of Luis F. Mejía, *De Lilís a Trujillo: Historia contemporánea de la República Dominicana*, chaps. 6–8. Other books treat individual aspects of the intervention. Max Henríquez Ureña, *Los Estados Unidos y la República Dominicana: La verdad de los hechos comprobada por datos y documentos oficiales*, documents the period up to and including the overthrow of the last Dominican government in late 1916. Henríquez Ureña's book was republished in 1929, with additional data on the occupation itself, as *Los yanquis en Santo Domingo: La verdad de los hechos comprobada por datos y documentos oficiales*. Fabio Fiallo, *La Comisión Nacionalista Dominicana en Washington, 1920–1921*, and Federico Henríquez y Carvajal, *Nacionalismo: Tópicos jurídicos e internacionales*, detail the intellectual resistance. Antonio Hoepelman and Juan A. Senior, *Documentos históricos que se refieren a la intervención armada de los Estados Unidos de Norte-América y a la implantación de un gobierno militar en la República Dominicana*, presents considerable material from the 1921 to 1922 hearings on the Dominican Republic and Haiti of the U.S. Senate, biographical sketches of the Dominicans who testified, and other documents. A number of other works might be mentioned in a more exhaustive list; all of them are cited in the following chapters.

2. Sumner Welles, *Naboth's Vineyard: The Dominican Republic, 1844–1924*, 2 vols.; Melvin M. Knight, *The Americans in Santo Domingo*.

3. Concerning the Caribbean area, the largest number of recent works treat the several Cuban interventions. On the first intervention, there are David F. Healy's policy-oriented *The United States in Cuba, 1898–1902* and James H. Hitchman's *Leonard Wood and Cuban Independence, 1898–1902*. On the second intervention, Allan R. Millett, *The Politics of Intervention: The Military Occupation of Cuba, 1906–1909*, joins David A. Lockmiller's earlier *Magoon in Cuba: A History of the Second Intervention, 1906–1909*. And Louis A. Pérez'

several books, particularly *Intervention, Revolution, and Politics in Cuba, 1913–1921,* detail the later period along with David A. Lockmiller, *Enoch H. Crowder: Soldier, Lawyer and Statesman.* On Haiti the two outstanding recent works are David F. Healy, *Gunboat Diplomacy in the Wilson Era: The U.S. Navy in Haiti, 1915–1916,* and Hans Schmidt, *The United States Occupation of Haiti, 1915–1934.* They complement earlier works by Arthur C. Millspaugh, Emily G. Balch, and Dantès Bellegarde. On Nicaragua, Neill Macaulay, *The Sandino Affair,* joins a number of less well documented books by Latin American authors on this historic figure, while Richard Millett, *Guardians of the Dynasty: A History of the U.S. Created Guardia Nacional de Nicaragua and the Somoza Family,* takes a wider view. On Mexico, Robert Freeman Smith, *The United States and Revolutionary Nationalism in Mexico, 1916–1932,* is but one particularly apt study from a large number of books by North American and Mexican scholars on the subject of U.S.-Mexican relations. Similarly, there is a large useful bibliography on the United States in Puerto Rico, although no one recent book recommends itself. Several more general works are also essential, including David F. Healy, *U.S. Expansionism: The Imperialist Urge in the 1890s;* Joseph S. Tulchin, *The Aftermath of War: World War I and the U.S. Policy toward Latin America;* and Dana Gardner Munro's excellent two-volume study, *Intervention and Dollar Diplomacy in the Caribbean, 1900–1921* and *The United States and the Caribbean Republics, 1921–1933.* Cole Blasier, *The Hovering Giant: U.S. Responses to Revolutionary Change in Latin America,* although generally treating later interventions, leads the way for further comparative analyses.

4. Wilfredo Lozano, *La dominación imperialista en la República Dominicana, 1900–1930.*

5. This overview of the Dominican Republic in 1916 is based on H. Hoetink, *El pueblo dominicano, 1850–1900: Apuntes para su sociología histórica* and "The Dominican Republic in the Nineteenth Century: Some Notes on Stratification, Immigration, and Race"; Otto Schoenrich, *Santo Domingo: A Country with a Future;* George William Lloyd, "Economic and Social Changes in Santo Domingo, 1916–1926"; Juan Bosch, *Trujillo: Causas de una tiranía sin ejemplo;* Welles, *Naboth's Vineyard;* A. Hyatt Verrill, *Porto Rico, Past and Present, and Santo Domingo of Today;* Fred R. Fairchild, "The Public Finance of Santo Domingo," *Political Science Quarterly* 33 (December 1918): 461–481; and República Dominicana, *Censo de la República Dominicana: Primer censo nacional, 1920.* For a much fuller description of the Dominican Republic in 1916, based on numerous additional sources, see Bruce J. Calder, "Some Aspects of the United States Occupation of the Dominican Republic, 1916–1924," chap. 2.

1. THE OCCUPATION BEGINS: 1916

1. This sketch of Dominican-U.S. relations to 1890 is based on Welles, *Naboth's Vineyard*, vol. 1, chaps. 1–4. For a detailed analysis, see Charles C. Tansill, *The United States and Santo Domingo, 1798–1873: A Chapter in Caribbean Diplomacy*, on the period to 1870 and David C. MacMichael, "The United States and the Dominican Republic, 1871–1940: A Cycle in Caribbean Diplomacy," on 1870 and after.

2. On post-1890 U.S.-Dominican relations, see MacMichael, "The United States," and Welles, *Naboth's Vineyard*, vol. 1, chap. 7, and vol. 2.

3. Walter LaFeber, *The New Empire: An Interpretation of American Expansion, 1860–1898*, chaps. 1–4.

4. Schmidt, *Haiti*, pp. 5–8.

5. Munro, *Intervention*, pp. 65–111. For a more Dominican view (written by a Haitian), see Antonio de la Rosa [Alexandre Poujols], *Las finanzas de Santo Domingo y el control americano*, pp. 15–162.

6. Welles, *Naboth's Vineyard*, vol. 2, pp. 680–770; Munro, *Intervention*, pp. 259–307. Munro's account is heavily based on documents found in the U.S. National Archives, record group 59, decimal file 839, *General Records of the Department of State*, also examined by myself and available on microfilm as U.S. National Archives Publication, microcopy 626 (hereafter USNA, 839, with the proper file number). For the Dominican view, see Mejía, *De Lilís*. Mejía was an active participant in Dominican affairs from 1907 through 1924. Another personal account, for 1899 to 1916, is Antonio Hoepelman, *Páginas dominicanas de historia contemporánea*.

7. Munro, *Intervention*, pp. 263–306, notes nine such occasions. The documents of USNA, 839.00/400–1000, record dozens of additional incidents.

8. Julio G. Campillo Pérez, *El grillo y el ruiseñor: Elecciones presidenciales dominicanas; contribución a su estudio*, pp. 131–146.

9. The following review of events to 1916, unless otherwise noted, is based on Welles, *Naboth's Vineyard*, vol. 2, pp. 695–766, and Munro, *Intervention*, pp. 260–305.

10. Américo Lugo, "Emiliano Tejera," *Boletín del Archivo General de la Nación* 4, no. 18 (October 1941): 304; Welles, *Naboth's Vineyard*, vol. 2, pp. 761–763.

11. Russell to Sec. St. Knox, 19 Sept. 1912, cited in Welles, *Naboth's Vineyard*, vol. 2, p. 694.

12. Welles, *Naboth's Vineyard*, vol. 2, pp. 766–768.

13. Mejía, *De Lilís*, pp. 125–127; Edwin N. McClellan, "Operations Ashore in the Dominican Republic," *United States Naval Institute Proceedings* 47, no. 216 (February 1921): 238–239; Comdr. F. B. Benton, USN, to Surg. Genl., 27 Oct. 1919, USNA, RG38, E6, B13. Most of the important documents pertaining to the seizure of Santo Domingo, in-

cluding the announcement of the first marine landing, Jiménez' resignation, and the ultimatum, are contained in Henríquez Ureña, *Los Estados Unidos,* pp. 83–91, and in United States, State Department, *Papers Relating to the Foreign Relations of the United States, 1916,* pp. 220–229 (hereafter *Foreign Relations,* with the appropriate year appended).

14. Mejía, *De Lilís,* p. 127; Bernardo Pichardo, *Resumen de historia patria,* p. 292. Pichardo was one of the remaining ministers.

15. Desiderio Arias, *Al País* (broadside), Campamento Jeneral de la Victoria, 22 May 1916, Colección Rodríguez Demorizi (hereafter this private collection of Emilio Rodríguez Demorizi will be referred to as CRD).

16. McClellan, "Operations Ashore," p. 240; Frank L. Polk, Acting Sec. St., to Sec. Nav., 29 May 1916, with enclosure, USNA, RG45, WA7, B644; J. M. Puig, Vice-Pres., et al., Ayuntamiento de la Común de Puerto Plata, *Al Pueblo* (broadside), 31 May 1916, CRD. For detailed descriptions of U.S. military actions during May and June 1916, see the cables in Office of Nav. Intel. Register No. 6598, USNA, RG45, WA7, B644.

17. Kenneth W. Condit and Edwin T. Turnbladh, *Hold High the Torch: A History of the 4th Marines,* pp. 36–37, and Russell to Sec. St., 10 May 1916, USNA, RG45, WA7, B643. Mejía, *De Lilís,* p. 129, presents some details on the defense of Puerto Plata.

18. Condit and Turnbladh, *Hold High the Torch,* pp. 50–62. For correspondence on these and subsequent actions, see Martin K. Gordon, ed., *Joseph Henry Pendleton, 1860–1942: Register of His Personal Papers,* pp. xiv–xvi, 59 ff.

19. Vetilio Alfau Durán, "Nuestros próceres: Wenceslao Báez (Laito)," *Listín Diario,* 17 Mar. 1940.

20. Two separate memoranda, both E. L. Roach, Ch. of Staff, to Adm. Pond, 20 Aug. 1916. These items are in a large file (no. 53-1) in package 27 concerning the surrender of Santiago and other important 1916 events, held with the military government papers in the Archivo General de la Nación, Santo Domingo (hereafter identified as AGN, P, with the appropriate number). See also the related documents located in the U.S. Marine Corps Historical Center, Geographical File, no. 2 (hereafter USMC, Geogr. File).

21. Condit and Turnbladh, *Hold High the Torch,* pp. 63, 65, 70.

22. McClellan, "Operations Ashore," p. 240.

23. Américo Lugo, *Listín Diario,* 2 Oct. 1916, quoted in Vetilio Alfau Durán, "Planes patrióticos de desocupación," *Ahora,* 6 Nov. 1967, p. 62; Mejía, *De Lilís,* p. 129. Gustavo Adolfo Mejía Ricart, *Acuso a Roma: Yo contra el invasor,* pp. 63–88, notes a few limited efforts to organize Dominicans against the U.S. invasion.

24. Lugo, "Emiliano Tejera," p. 313.

25. Emilio C. Joubert, *Cosas que fueron,* p. 207.

26. R. H. Dunlap, Ch. of Staff, to all CO's, U.S. Naval Forces Operating Ashore in Santo Domingo, 18 Aug. 1916, AGN, P27.

27. Munro, *Intervention*, pp. 307–308; Welles, *Naboth's Vineyard*, vol. 2, pp. 773–776; Federico Henríquez y Carvajal, *Declinatoria* (broadside), 11 June 1916, from the document collection of the Casa de Don Federico y Biblioteca del Maestro, Santo Domingo (hereafter identified as HyC). Henríquez' personal recollections of this period, and some documents, appear in his *Nacionalismo*, pp. 1–17, 53–57.

28. Lugo, "Emiliano Tejera," p. 307; Henríquez Ureña, *Los Estados Unidos*, pp. 119–120; *Junta de Defensa Nacional al Poder Ejecutivo* (broadside), undated, CRD.

29. Henríquez Ureña, *Los Estados Unidos*, pp. 109–111; typescript of speech, hand-dated 31 July 1916, HyC.

30. Russell to Sec. St., 25 July 1916, USNA, RG45, WA7, B643; Munro, *Intervention*, p. 309.

31. Henríquez Ureña, *Los Estados Unidos*, pp. 127–128; Horacio Blanco Fombona, *Crímenes del imperialismo norteamericano*, pp. 115–116.

32. Welles, *Naboth's Vineyard*, vol. 2, p. 780; Russell to Sec. St., 17 and 20 June 1916, USNA, RG45, WA7, B643.

33. MacMichael, "The United States," pp. 420–440; Munro, *Intervention*, pp. 309–311; Mejía, *De Lilís*, pp. 113–134; Russell to Lansing, 25 and 26 Aug. 1916, 5 and 14 Sept. 1916, *Foreign Relations, 1916*, pp. 234–237. Dominican eyewitness accounts of the negotiations appear in Henríquez Ureña, *Los Estados Unidos*, pp. 111–116, 133–154, and in José M. Cabral y Báez, "Resumen de las actuaciones de la Cancillería Dominicana...," in Hoepelman and Senior, *Documentos*, pp. 330–371.

34. Russell to Lansing, 25 Aug. 1916, and Lansing to Russell, 29 Aug. 1916, *Foreign Relations, 1916*, pp. 234–235; Sec. St. to Sec. Nav., 30 Aug. 1916, enclosing Russell to Sec. St., 18 Aug. 1916, USNA, RG45, WA7, B644.

35. Mejía, *De Lilís*, p. 128; Russell to Lansing, 6 June 1916, *Foreign Relations, 1916*, p. 231.

36. Tulio A. Cestero Burgos, *Entre las garras del águila*, pp. 26–28; letters, signed "La Juventud," Rafael E. Ricart and M. de J. Troncoso de la Concha, Pres. del Ayuntamiento, in *El Tiempo*, 16 May 1916, CRD.

37. Mejía, *De Lilís*, p. 127; Lugo, "Emiliano Tejera," p. 314; protests, *El Tiempo* and *Listín Diario*, 16 May 1916; Academia Colombina, *Memorial de protesta contra la arbitraria ocupación de la República Dominicana por tropas de los Estados Unidos de América*.

38. Mejía, *De Lilís*, p. 128; Pedro M. Hungría, *Apuntes para la historia de Santiago: Centro de Recreo, sociedad fundada el 16 de agosto 1894*, p. 27; Juan Gómez, "The Gallant Dominicans," *American Mercury* 17 (May 1929): 94.

39. Henríquez y Carvajal, *Nacionalismo*, p. 13; Max Henríquez Ureña, *Panorama histórico de la literatura dominicana*, vol. 2, pp. 406–407.

40. For example, Francisco Henríquez y Carvajal's program in *Las Novedades* (New York), 25 June 1916, reprinted in Henríquez Ureña, *Los*

Estados Unidos, pp. 111–116; the 1916 articles of Manuel Piña Benítez in his *Del pasado;* and the translations of Pelegrín Castillo's articles, originally published in the *Listín Diario* in August 1916, enclosed in Dir. of Nav. Intel. to Ch. of Nav. Op., 3 Mar. 1917, USNA, RG45, WA7, B643.

41. Jaime Lockward, *Teatro dominicano: Pasado y presente,* pp. 19, 50, 57, 58; Manuel de Jesús Goico Castro; "Raíz y trayectoria del teatro en la literatura nacional," *Anales* 10, nos. 37–38 (January–June 1946): 176, 179–181, 183–184; *Listín Diario,* 13 Sept. 1916.
42. Governor Juan Fco. Sánchez to various newspaper editors, 19 Sept. 1916, in Henríquez Ureña, *Los Estados Unidos,* pp. 156–157; Jacinto López in *La Nación* (Havana), reprinted in *Listín Diario,* 10 Nov. 1916; Blanco Fombona, *Crímenes,* pp. 17–18 (Blanco Fombona was the editor of *El Domingo* in 1916); reports from the newspapers *El Filorio* and *El Iris* (San Francisco de Macorís), in USNA, RG45, WA7, B643.
43. Persio C. Franco, *Algunas ideas,* p. 6; *Listín Diario,* 7 and 10 Oct. 1916; Russell to Sec. St., 6 Dec. 1916, USNA, RG45, WA7, B643.
44. CO, U.S. Landing Force Operating Ashore in Santo Domingo, to Comdr., Cruiser Squadron, U.S. Atlantic Fleet, daily reports beginning 11 June 1916, USNA, RG45, WA7, B643; Henríquez Ureña, *Los Estados Unidos,* p. 160.
45. Henríquez Ureña, *Los Estados Unidos,* pp. 155–156; Knight, *The Americans,* pp. 78–79.
46. These incidents and others are reported in various issues of the *Listín Diario* of Santo Domingo, in *La Información* and *El Diario* of Santiago, and in *La Nación* of Havana, cited in Henríquez Ureña, *Los Estados Unidos,* pp. 157–164, and in Teófilo Castro García, *Intervención yanqui, 1916–1924,* pp. 29–40.
47. Henríquez Ureña, *Los Estados Unidos,* pp. 161–164.
48. Welles, *Naboth's Vineyard,* vol. 2, pp. 783–784, 789.
49. Pichardo, *Resumen,* p. 298; Henríquez Ureña, *Los Estados Unidos,* pp. 165–171; Manuel Arturo Peña Batlle, ed., *Constitución política y reformas constitucionales, 1844–1942,* p. 635.
50. MacMichael, "The United States," pp. 428–436; Henríquez Ureña, *Los Estados Unidos,* p. 170.
51. Capt. H. S. Knapp, USN, "Proclamation," Sto. Dom., 29 Nov. 1916, *Foreign Relations, 1916,* pp. 246–247. Knapp's actions just prior to 29 November are detailed in a series of cables in Office of Nav. Intel. Register No. 6598a, USNA, RG45, WA7, B644.
52. Peña Batlle, ed., *Constitución política,* pp. 635, 668–676.
53. República Dominicana, *Colección de órdenes ejecutivas del número 1 al 116 inclusive . . . de noviembre 29, 1916 hasta diciembre 31, 1917,* pp. 6–7. (This is the first in a series of volumes which contain the laws of the military government, called executive orders. Subsequent references to this annual publication will appear as *Colección,* with the appropriate year.) Brewer, Chargé, Sto. Dom., to Lansing, 6 Dec. 1916, USNA, RG45, WA7, B643.

54. Condit and Turnbladh, *Hold High the Torch,* pp. 69–70; Frank Anderson Henry, U.S. Consul at Puerto Plata, to Sec. St., 12 Dec. 1916, USNA, RG45, WA7, B644.
55. R.D., *Colección, 1916–1917,* pp. 9–12.
56. Henríquez Ureña, *Los Estados Unidos,* pp. 182–184.
57. Brewer to Lansing, 6 Dec. 1916; Knapp to Sec. Nav., 17 Dec. 1916, USNA, RG45, WA7, B643; Executive Orders Nos. 12 and 18, 26 Dec. 1916 and 2 Jan. 1917, R.D., *Colección, 1916–1917,* pp. 17, 21.
58. Exec. Order No. 44, 20 Mar. 1917, R.D., *Colección, 1916–1917,* p. 186; Henry C. Davis, "Indoctrination of Latin-American Service," *Marine Corps Gazette* 5, no. 2 (June 1920): 158.
59. Henríquez Ureña, *Los Estados Unidos,* pp. 180–181; Condit and Turnbladh, *Hold High the Torch,* pp. 70–75; Mejía, *De Lilís,* p. 142.
60. R.D., *Colección, 1916–1917,* p. 17; Ramón Batías [pseud.?], "El patriota se llamaba Fidel Ferrer," *Renovación,* 1969, p. 5.
61. Henríquez Ureña, *Los Estados Unidos,* p. 180.
62. Armando Pérez Perdomo, E. E. y Ministro Plenipotenciario, to Lansing, 4 Dec. 1916, and J. M. Cabral y Báez, S. de E. Rel. Ext., to Lansing, 4 Dec. 1916, in ibid., pp. 185–191, 178–179.
63. Fiallo, *La Comisión Nacionalista,* pp. 69–71; Max Henríquez Ureña, ed., *Pedro Henríquez Ureña, Antología,* p. xlv, and his *Los Estados Unidos,* pp. 184, 193–206.
64. Brewer to Lansing, 4 and 6 Dec. 1916, F. A. Henry to Sec. St., 12 Dec. 1916, and F. A. Ramsey, Brig. Intel. Off., to Ch. of Staff, 2 Jan. 1917, USNA, RG45, WA7, B643–644.
65. Russell to Sec. St., 14 Dec. 1916, enclosed in Frank S. Polk to Sec. Nav., [?] Dec. 1916, USNA, RG45, WA7, B643.
66. "Censura," signed H. S. Knapp, in R.D., *Colección, 1916–1917,* pp. 6–7; Dimas Frías, Director del *Heraldo Dominicano, Al Pueblo Dominicano* (broadside), undated, CRD; Daily Reports, CO, U.S. Forces, to Brig. Comdr., 1 and 3 Dec. 1916, USNA, RG45, WA7, B643; Henríquez Ureña, *Los Estados Unidos,* p. 79.
67. Knapp, "Proclamation," 29 Nov. 1916, *Foreign Relations, 1916,* pp. 246–247.
68. The Dominican minister to the United States, Armando Pérez Perdomo, outlined the Dominican position in his protest note to Lansing, 4 Dec. 1916, in Henríquez Ureña, *Los Estados Unidos,* pp. 185–187. President Henríquez expanded on it in his memorandum of 12 August 1921, printed in United States, Senate, Inquiry into the Occupation and Administration of Haiti and Santo Domingo, *Hearings before a Select Committee on Haiti and Santo Domingo* (hereafter U.S., Senate, *Hearings*), vol. 1, pp. 53–57.
69. Munro, *Intervention,* p. 313; Carl Kelsey, "The American Intervention in Haiti and the Dominican Republic," *Annals of the American Academy of Political and Social Sciences* 100, no. 189 (March 1922): 178. Rayford W. Logan, *Haiti and the Dominican Republic,* p. 61, discusses the problem of stressing the importance of the German factor in U.S.-

Dominican policy. In my own research, I found that Germany is seldom directly mentioned in U.S. diplomatic and military papers on the Dominican Republic until *after* the military government had already been established. Another historian who has examined the German factor in U.S.-Dominican policy and, like myself, finds Germany more an important background factor than an immediate concern is Marlin D. Clausner, *Rural Santo Domingo: Settled, Unsettled, and Resettled*, pp. 165–167.

70. Arthur S. Link, *Woodrow Wilson and the Progressive Era, 1910–1917*, pp. 82, 93–94, 103.
71. See, for example, Russell to Sec. St., 14 Mar. 1916, *Foreign Relations, 1916*, p. 221. Many Dominican historians believe that the economic factor was of the utmost importance.
72. Henry Kittredge Norton, "The Ethics of Imperialism," *World's Work* 51 (January 1926): 328.
73. Kelsey, "American Intervention," p. 178.
74. McIntyre, Bur. of Insular Affairs, to Rec. Genl. of Customs, 2 Dec. 1916, *Foreign Relations, 1916*, p. 255.
75. Lansing to Russell, 20 Dec. 1916, *Foreign Relations, 1916*, p. 249. Concerning the fiction of a continuing Dominican government, see Sec. Nav. to Sec. St., 29 Nov. 1920, USNA, RG38, E6, B31.
76. Memorandum, "Conference with Rear-Admiral J. S. McKean . . . ," 27 Jan. 1919, USNA, 839.00/2124. Concerning several controversies, see Mil. Gov. to Ch. of Nav. Op., 16 Apr. 1919, and attached corres., USNA, RG38, E6, B17, and A. H. Mayo to Snowden and Snowden to Russell, 27 and 26 Dec. 1919, USNA, RG45, WA7, B646 and 645. Concerning the re-establishment of State's ascendancy, see Sec. Nav. to Sec. St., 27 Nov. 1920, USNA, RG38, E6, B31, and Richard Millett and G. Dale Gaddy, "Administering the Protectorates: The U.S. Occupation of Haiti and the Dominican Republic," *Revista/Review Interamericana* 6, no. 3 (Fall 1976): 394–398.
77. Knapp became a rear admiral on 20 March 1917. Russell to Sec. St., 11 Dec. 1916, *Foreign Relations, 1916*, p. 248.
78. Henry C. Davis, Batl. Comdr., to Brig. Comdr., 28 July 1918, USNA, RG38, E6, B23.
79. Otto Schoenrich, "The Present American Intervention in Santo Domingo and Haiti," p. 211; Rufus H. Lane, "Civil Government in Santo Domingo in the Early Days of the Military Occupation," *Marine Corps Gazette* 7, no. 2 (June 1922): 129.
80. Knapp to Sec. Nav., 17 Dec. 1916, USNA, RG45, WA7, B643.
81. Knapp to Sec. Nav., 30 Nov. 1916 and 26 Nov. 1917, USNA, RG45, WA7, B644; H. S. Knapp, "Annual Report of the Military Government of Santo Domingo . . . ," 21 July 1917, USNA, 839.00/2043.
82. See the comments of Military Governor Knapp concerning agriculture, public works, public health, and other matters in his "Annual Report of the Military Government of Santo Domingo . . . ," 21 July 1917, USNA, 839.00/2043; C. H. Baxter, Rec. Genl., to Knapp, 4 Dec. 1916,

AGN, P44; M. A. Peters, "Recommendations for the Betterment of Dominican Affairs," 1917, enclosed in A. J. Peters, U.S. Treas. Dept., to Wm. Phillips, 17 Jan. 1917, USNA, 839.00/1991.

83. Munro, *Intervention*, pp. 302–303; Russell to Sec. St., 29 May and 18 Aug. 1916, *Foreign Relations, 1916*, pp. 249–250, 252–253; Knapp to Sec. Nav., 17 Dec. 1916, USNA, RG45, WA7, B644.

84. C. C. Baughman, "United States Occupation of the Dominican Republic," *United States Naval Institute Proceedings* 51, no. 274 (December 1925): 2311–2325; Welles, *Naboth's Vineyard*, vol. 2, pp. 810–817.

85. Russell, "Confidential Memorandum," to Stabler, 12 Sept. 1917, enclosed in Lt. Comdr. Charles Belknap, Office of Nav. Op., to Knapp, [?] Oct. 1917, USNA, RG38, E6, B6; Schoenrich, "American Intervention," p. 211; Kelsey, "American Intervention," pp. 178–179, 198.

86. H. S. Knapp, "Annual Report of the Military Government of Santo Domingo . . . ," 21 July 1917, and Russell to Sec. St., 11 Sept. 1917, USNA, 839.00/2043 and 2051.

87. McIntyre to Russell, 5 Oct. 1917, USNA, RG38, E6, B3. The names of various persons with Philippine experience appear in the Genl. Corres. file, USNA, RG38, E6, B3. See also Lt. Comdr. Arthur H. Mayo, Treasury and Commerce, to Mil. Gov. Snowden, 31 Mar. 1919, USNA, RG38, E6, B14, and Knapp to Arthur Yager, Gov. of Puerto Rico, 15 Sept. 1917, USNA, RG38, E6, B5. Biographies of several transferred officials appear in Harry Alverson Franck, "Santo Domingo, the Land of Bullet-Holes," *Century Magazine* 100 (July 1920): 304, 306.

88. Genl. Pendleton, Int. and Pol., to Knapp, 17 Oct. 1917, USNA, RG38, E6, B4.

89. H. S. Knapp, Memorandum, 1 July 1918, USNA, RG38, E6, B6; Mil. Gov. Snowden to José E. Benedicto, Acting Gov. of Puerto Rico, 14 and 17 June 1920, and to Sec. Nav., 9 Aug. 1920, USNA, RG38, E6, B27 and 31.

90. Kelsey, "American Intervention," p. 179; Mejía, *De Lilís*, p. 145; Schoenrich, "American Intervention," p. 211; Arthur J. Burks, *Land of Checkerboard Families*, pp. 106, 159, 226.

91. Julian N. Frisbee, Intel., Memorandum to Col. Macker Babb, citing a report from Maj. H. M. Butler, 16 Mar. 1920, USNA, RG38, E6, B22; copy of a confidential letter, signature removed, sent to Phillips, St. Dept., 18 Aug. 1918, filed with Knapp to Russell, 2 Nov. 1918, USNA, RG45, WA7, B644.

92. Many such letters are contained in the Genl. Corres. file, USNA, RG38, E6, B1 through 3, and in AGN, P59. Among the petitioners for jobs were several men later found among the most active nationalists, Rafael Damirón and Enrique Deschamps.

93. Félix María Nolasco and Alejandro Mencía to Genl. Pendleton, 22 Feb. 1917, and Knapp to McKelvey, 18 Oct. 1917, USNA, RG38, E6, B2 and 4.

94. Mario F. Cabral to Knapp, 19 Mar. 1917, and Knapp to Haim H. López-Penha, 12 Mar. 1917, USNA, RG38, E6, B3 and 2; F. A. Herrera to J. H. Edwards, Spec. Dep. Rec. Genl., Customs Receivership, translation en-

closed in Edwards to Knapp, 27 Sept. 1917, USNA, RG45, WA7, B645;
P. A. Ricart, V. P., Cámara de Comercio, Industria, y Agricultura, to
Knapp, 2 June 1917, USNA, RG38, E6, B1; Knapp to F. J. Peynado, 7 Dec.
1917, USNA, RG38, E6, BU ("BU" indicates a box number which is unknown); Dr. A. Fiallo Cabral, Superintendente Genl. de Enseñanza
Pública, to Knapp, 16 Mar. 1917, USNA, RG38, E6, B2. Fiallo Cabral, despite his effort, was soon dismissed.

95. Velásquez to Knapp, 17 May 1917, and Knapp to Velásquez, 17 May
1917, USNA, RG38, E6, B5; Russell, Memorandum, 30 Aug. 1924, USNA,
839.00/2859.

96. Emilio Joubert, 1st V.P., National Committee of the Horacista party, to
the members of Provincial and Municipal Committees, 19 Apr. 1917,
quoted in Welles, *Naboth's Vineyard*, vol. 2, p. 821; Joubert to Knapp,
28 Apr. 1917, AGN, P23.

97. Exec. Orders Nos. 26 and 60, 22 Jan. and 26 June 1917, R.D., *Colección,
1916–1917*, pp. 55–56; Joubert to Robison, 17 May 1922, AGN, P45.

98. For example, concerning the adulteration of honey: Enrique A. Ricart,
Pres., Cámara de Comercio, to Mil. Gov., 19 Feb. 1918, and J. H. Pendleton, Acting Mil. Gov., to E. A. Ricart, 28 Feb. 1918, AGN, P49. Concerning a forestry law: Dr. Alfonseca, Pres., Convención de Ayuntamientos del Cibao, to Mil. Gov., 18 Apr. 1918, AGN, P49.

99. Exec. Orders Nos. 25, 26, 50, and 60, 19 and 22 Jan. 1917, 14 Apr. 1917,
and 26 June 1917, R.D., *Colección, 1916–1917*, pp. 28–30, 47–48,
55–56; Knapp to Col. Rufus H. Lane, 18 Oct. 1917, USNA, RG38, E6, B4;
H. S. Knapp, "Annual Report of the Military Government of Santo Domingo . . . ," 21 July 1917, USNA, 839.00/2043.

100. H. S. Knapp, "Annual Report of the Military Government of Santo Domingo . . . ," 21 July 1917, USNA, 839.00/2043.

101. Russell, "Confidential Memorandum," to Stabler, 12 Sept. 1917, enclosed in Lt. Comdr. Charles Belknap, Office of Nav. Op., to Knapp, [?]
Oct. 1917, USNA, RG38, E6, B6.

102. Russell to Sec. St., 5 Jan. 1917, *Foreign Relations, 1917*, p. 707; Knapp
to Belknap, 6 Oct. 1917, and Ch. of Nav. Op. to Sec. Nav., 11 Oct. 1921,
USNA, RG45, WA7, B644 and 647. These are but a few of many letters
which discuss the desirable length of the occupation.

2. The Political Economy of the Military Government, I

1. United States, Military Government of Santo Domingo, *Santo Domingo: Its Past and Its Present Condition*; Knight, *The Americans*, pp.
97–107.

2. Exec. Order No. 25, 19 Jan. 1917, R.D., *Colección, 1917*, pp. 28–29.
Some of the commission's papers are in AGN, P21 and 44.

3. Lane, "Civil Government," pp. 143–145; U.S. Mil. Govt., *Santo Domingo*, pp. 31–32; Clausner, *Rural Santo Domingo*, pp. 181–182.

4. Emilio Rodríguez Demorizi, ed., *Papeles de Pedro F. Bonó*, pp. 144–
150; Hoetink, *El pueblo*, pp. 233–239; Clausner, *Rural Santo Do-*

mingo, pp. 98–113, 181–182; Paul H. Muto, "The Illusory Promise: The Dominican Republic and the Process of Economic Development, 1900–1930," pp. 158–160.

5. Exec. Order No. 145, 5 Apr. 1918, R.D., *Colección, 1918*, pp. 46–87. Baughman, "U.S. Occupation," p. 2314, notes a controversy over the use of Spanish. Military Governor Knapp, quoted in Russell to Sec. St., 12 Sept. 1917, USNA, 839.041/5, advocated retention of Spanish.

6. U.S. Mil. Govt., *Santo Domingo*, pp. 34–37; Rufus H. Lane, Justice and Public Instr., to Mil. Gov., 1 Feb. 1921, AGN, P45. Lane was the officer in charge of public education from 1917 to 1921.

7. R. H. Lane, Order No. 47, 5 Mar. 1918, in República Dominicana, Servicio Nacional de Instrucción Pública, *Colección de órdenes emanadas . . .*

8. S. S. Robison, "Memorandum for Senate Committee," 6 Dec. 1921, AGN, P37. U.S. Mil. Govt., *Santo Domingo*, p. 34, claims higher salaries for 1920 than appear in the actual budget in Exec. Order No. 387, 17 Jan. 1920, R.D., *Colección, 1920*, pp. 9–77.

9. Kelsey, "American Intervention," p. 182; Lane to Mil. Gov., 1 Feb. 1921, AGN, P45; Clausner, *Rural Santo Domingo*, pp. 184–185.

10. U.S. Mil. Govt., *Santo Domingo*, pp. 35–36; A. T. Marix, Justice and Public Instr., to Mil. Gov., 14 Oct. 1920, AGN, P45. Marix became head of the ministry after Lane's departure.

11. U.S. Mil. Govt., *Santo Domingo*, pp. 35–36.

12. Pichardo, *Resumen*, p. 272; Henríquez y Carvajal, *Nacionalismo*, pp. 182–183; "Instituto Profesional de Santiago de los Caballeros, República Dominicana," *Anales* 3, no. 1 (January 1939): 150.

13. Knapp to Sec. Nav., 8 Oct. 1917, USNA, RG45, WA7, B644; R. H. Lane, Order No. 11, 3 Oct. 1917, R.D., Servicio Nacl., *Colección*; Lane to Mil. Gov., 1 Feb. 1921, AGN, P45; "Questionnaire," pp. 2–3 and 27, attached to Rear Adm. R. M. Kennedy to Surg. Genl., 7 Apr. 1921, AGN, P11 (hereafter this basic forty-page source will appear as "Questionnaire").

14. U.S. Mil. Govt., *Santo Domingo*, p. 35.

15. Marix to Mil. Gov., 14 Oct. 1920, AGN, P45; Clausner, *Rural Santo Domingo*, p. 185.

16. Knapp to Justice and Public Instr., 27 Sept. 1918, AGN, P64; Julio Peynado to Horace Knowles, 22 Apr. 1922, Papeles de la Familia Peynado (hereafter PFP). Salary reductions were made in a series of executive orders beginning with no. 607.

17. Snowden to Justice and Public Instr., 11 May 1921, and Marix to Mil. Gov., 13 and 20 June 1921, AGN, P8, 19, and 10; Fiallo, *La Comisión Nacionalista*, pp. 30, 83; Adolfo Nouel, Junta Consultiva, to Pres. Harding, 19 May 1921, USNA, 839.42/4; A. Pastoriza, Cámara de Comercio, Santiago, to Snowden, 7 June 1921, AGN, P9; Mil. Gov. Lee to Sec. Nav., 16 May 1924, USNA, RG38, E6, B74.

18. F. A. Ramsey, Justice and Public Instr., to Mil. Gov., 24 Jan. 1922, AGN, P37.

19. Luis Vallejo de la Concha, Inspector, 17th Dist., to Inspector, E. Dist., 27 Mar. 1922, USNA, RG38, E6, B48.
20. The debate on the patent tax is recorded in R. H. Lane to Mil. Gov., 5 Dec. 1919, and A. T. Marix to Robison, 13 June 1921, AGN, P19. Lane, defending the tax against Lieutenant Commander Arthur Mayo, head of Treasury and Commerce, lost the debate and was eventually forced to resign his post; see J. Peynado to Knowles, 22 Apr. 1922, PFP.
21. Exec. Order No. 758, 13 June 1922, R.D., *Colección, 1922,* pp. 106–124; Lee to Sec. Nav., 16 May 1924, USNA, RG38, E6, B74; A. T. Marix to Robison, 13 June 1921, AGN, P19.
22. Mejía, *De Lilís,* p. 215; Dominican Economic Commission, *Report,* p. 78; Great Britain, Department of Overseas Trade, *Report on Economic Conditions in the Dominican Republic . . . by Mr. John Bowering,* p. 15; Clausner, *Rural Santo Domingo,* pp. 220–221. Adult illiteracy in 1970 was 30 to 35 percent. For an example of still miserable conditions in 1980, see Joseph Ros, "Barahona," *Salesian* 26, no. 26 (Fall 1980): 25–28.
23. S. S. Robison in U.S., Senate, *Hearings,* vol. 1, p. 102; P. E. Garrison to Mil. Gov., 12 Aug. 1917, and attached memorandum, AGN, P106.
24. Exec. Order No. 6, 13 Dec. 1916, R.D., *Colección, 1917,* pp. 12–13; Garrison to Brig. Comdr., 31 Jan. 1917, USNA, RG45, WA7, B644; "Questionnaire"; U.S. Mil. Govt., *Santo Domingo,* p. 38.
25. Garrison to Brig. Surg., 23 Mar. 1918, AGN, P21.
26. Exec. Orders Nos. 196, 222, 243, and 247 of 1918 and Nos. 254 and 270 of 1919; R. Hayden to Mil. Gov., 3 Nov. 1919, AGN, P40.
27. Exec. Order No. 338, 13 Oct. 1919, R.D., *Colección, 1919,* pp. 305–349.
28. Garrison to Brig. Surg., 23 Mar. 1918, AGN, P21.
29. "Questionnaire," pp. 26, 29; Lester L. Pratt, Med. Dir., to Col. Comdt., PND Training Center, 19 Nov. 1923, USNA, RG38, E6, B69. R. Hayden to Mil. Gov., 3 Nov. 1919, AGN, P40, reveals the first of several efforts to upgrade the training of midwives.
30. Reynolds Hayden, "Review of Reorganization of Sanitary and Public Health Work in the Dominican Republic under U.S. Military Government of Santo Domingo," *U.S. Naval Medical Bulletin* 16, no. 4 (April 1922): 663.
31. Exec. Order No. 247, 27 Dec. 1918, R.D., *Colección, 1918,* pp. 267–272; R. Hayden, Sanit. and Benef., to Mil. Gov., 21 Mar. 1921, enclosing Min. of Sanit. and Benef., "Annual Report, 1920," p. 32, AGN, P77 (hereafter "Report, 1920"); Exec. Order No. 420, 5 Mar. 1920, R.D., *Colección, 1920,* pp. 107–120; Hayden, "Review," p. 664.
32. "Questionnaire," pp. 25–29; Hayden, "Review," pp. 668–669.
33. "Report, 1920," pp. 13–14; "Questionnaire," p. 36.
34. Min. of Justice and Public Instr. to Mil. Gov., 9 Oct. 1918, and Knapp to Chief Sanitary Officer, 17 Oct. 1918, AGN, P59.
35. Garrison to Mil. Gov., 12 Aug. 1917, AGN, P106; W. C. Braisted, Surg. Genl., to Snowden, 17 June 1919, USNA, RG38, E6, B17.
36. "Report, 1920," pp. 28–29; Hayden, "Review," p. 669.

37. Exec. Order No. 338, 13 Oct. 1919, R.D., *Colección, 1919*, pp. 329, 331, 336.
38. "Report, 1920," pp. 2, 4.
39. Mejía, *De Lilís*, p. 154.
40. Sec. of Sanit. and Benef. to Mil. Gov., 17 Dec. 1921, AGN, P11.
41. "Report, 1920," p. 8; Hayden, "Review," p. 664. F. Mañón to Richard Strong, U.S. Senate Committee, 30 Nov. 1921, AGN, P37, reviews the Billini case.
42. R. Hayden to Mil. Gov., 21 Mar. 1921, AGN, P77. "Questionnaire," p. 4, estimated two to three years.
43. Sec. of Sanit. and Benef., "Annual Report, 1920."
44. Quarterly Reports of the Mil. Gov. of Sto. Dom., July 1921 through Dec. 1923, USNA, 839.00/2449, 2502, 2528, 2577, 2663, 2688, 2722, 2735, 2766, and 2805.
45. República Dominicana, Secretaría de Estado de Sanidad y Beneficencia, *Informe que el Secretario de Sanidad y Beneficencia presenta al Presidente Provisional de la República*, pp. 47–48; Quarterly Report of the Mil. Gov. of Sto. Dom., 1 Oct. to 31 Dec. 1923, USNA, 839.00/2805.
46. Mejía, *De Lilís*, pp. 154, 215.
47. Speech, Juan Fco. Sánchez, 6 May 1922, USNA, RG38, E6, B56; Welles, *Naboth's Vineyard*, vol. 2, pp. 663–665; Tulio M. Cestero, *Los Estados Unidos y las Antillas*, pp. 119–120.
48. For example, William D. Boyce, *United States Colonies and Dependencies Illustrated*, p. 572, and Verrill, *Porto Rico*, pp. 251–254.
49. Genl. Frank McIntyre, Bur. of Insular Affairs, to Knapp, 28 Mar. 1917, and Knapp to McIntyre, 10 Apr. 1917, USNA, RG38, E6, BU; Russell to Sec. St., 12 Sept. 1917, USNA, 839.041/3.
50. Knapp to Sec. St., 7 Jan. 1917, USNA, RG80, CNO Planning, file C-24 to 24-19 (corres. 1917–1919); U.S. Mil. Govt., *Santo Domingo*, pp. 20–21; misc. docs., USNA, RG38, E6, B1.
51. Knapp to Sec. Nav., 12 Jan. 1918, USNA, RG38, E6, B7.
52. Baughman, "U.S. Occupation," pp. 2315–2322; Knapp to Russell, 1 Dec. 1919, and E. R. Gayler, Chief Engineer of Haiti, to Knapp, 3 Feb. 1918, USNA, RG38, E6, B13 and 9; U.S. Mil. Govt., *Santo Domingo*, pp. 20–23. Concerning the telephone nationalization, see Exec. Order No. 275, 20 Mar. 1919, R.D., *Colección, 1919*, pp. 53–54.
53. A. H. Mayo to Mil. Gov., 1 Apr. 1919, USNA, RG38, E6, B14.
54. Baughman, "U.S. Occupation," p. 2316; Kelsey, "American Intervention," p. 183; R. M. Warfield, Fomento y Comunicaciones, to Agric. e Inmigración, 20 Nov. 1919, AGN, P121.
55. Knapp to Russell, 1 Dec. 1919, USNA, RG38, E6, B13; Kelsey, "American Intervention," p. 183; Quarterly Report of the Mil. Gov. of Sto. Dom., 1 Apr. to 30 June 1921, USNA, 839.00/2445.
56. Ch. of Nav. Op. to Sec. Nav., 10-11-CD, attached to Robison, "Memorandum for Senate Committee," 6 Dec. 1921, USNA, RG38, E6, B44; Kelsey, "American Intervention," p. 183. See also the correspondence on the 1922 loan in *Foreign Relations, 1922*, vol. 2, pp. 78–79.

57. Unsigned memorandum, "Dominican Republic," Feb. 1923, USNA, 839.00/2742; Mejía, *De Lilís*, p. 210; Great Britain, Department of Overseas Trade, *Report on the Economic, Financial and Commercial Conditions in the Dominican Republic* (report dated October 1924 by Darrell Wilson), p. 19; Mil. Gov. to Sec. Nav., 16 May 1924, USNA, RG38, E6, B74.

58. Great Britain, Dept. of Overseas Trade, *Report* (October 1924), pp. 19, 24; Mejía, *De Lilís*, p. 214; Dominican Economic Commission, *Report*, p. 89; St. Dept., Memorandum, conversation between Welles and White, cited in MacMichael, "The United States," p. 628.

59. Mil. Gov. to Sec. Nav., 29 Nov. 1917, USNA, RG45, WA7, B644; D. G. Munro, Memorandum, 20 Mar. 1922, USNA, 839.00/2651. For the Dominican view, see Junta Consultiva, Memorandum, 3 Dec. 1919, AGN, P121.

60. Verrill, *Porto Rico*, p. 270; Muto, "Promise," p. 183; Great Britain, Dept. of Overseas Trade, *Report* (October 1924), pp. 19, 24.

61. Unsigned memorandum, "Dominican Republic," Feb. 1923, USNA, 839.00/2742.

62. Welles to Francis White, St. Dept., 5 Sept. 1922, USNA, 839.00/2983. Other harsh criticisms of public works appear in Russell, Memorandum, undated but stamped 25 Mar. 1919, USNA, 839.00/2123, and in Junta Consultiva to Snowden, 3 Dec. 1919, and attached corres. in file 28-227, AGN, P121.

63. Marvin Goldwert, *The Constabulary in the Dominican Republic and Nicaragua: Progeny and Legacy of U.S. Intervention*, pp. 5–6; Exec. Order No. 47, 7 Apr. 1917, R.D., *Colección, 1917*, pp. 188–189.

64. Knapp to Sec. Nav. Daniels, 14 Jan. 1917, USNA, RG45, WA7, B644; J. H. Pendleton to Maj. Genl. Comdt. Geo. Barnett, 9 Apr. 1917, USMC, Pendleton Papers, folder 18, in Gordon, ed., *Joseph Henry Pendleton*, p. 73. Snowden to Chargé Brewer, 29 June 1920, *Foreign Relations, 1920*, pp. 116–120, practically repeats Knapp's view.

65. Lane, "Civil Government," p. 136.

66. Knapp to Sec. Nav., 12 Dec. 1916, and Lansing to Sec. Nav., 14 Mar. 1917, USNA, 839.1051/8 and 11; Knapp, "Annual Report," 21 July 1917, *Foreign Relations, 1917*, p. 717.

67. Rufus Lane, Brig. Comdr., Genl. Order No. 23, 30 May 1917, USNA, RG38, E6, B1; U.S. Mil. Govt., *Santo Domingo*, p. 52.

68. "Report of Strength and Distribution of the GND . . . ," 30 Nov. 1918, and James J. McLean, Dir., S. Dist., to Comdt., GND, 6 Aug. 1919, USNA, RG38, E6, B40; C. O. Kimball, "Duty with the Medical Corps of the Policía Nacional Dominicana," *U.S. Naval Medical Bulletin*, suppl., 6, no. 4 (October 1922): 82.

69. C. F. Williams, Comdt., GND, to Int. and Pol., 23 May 1918, USNA, 839.1051/15; Charles F. Williams, "La Guardia Nacional Dominicana," *Marine Corps Gazette* 3, no. 3 (September 1918): 198; Knapp, "Annual Report," 21 July 1917, *Foreign Relations, 1917*, p. 717; McLean to Comdt., GND, 6 Aug. 1919, USNA, RG38, E6, B40.

70. Maj. F. A. Ramsey, Acting Comdt., GND, to Sec. of War and Nav., 1 June 1917, USNA, RG45, WA7, B646; Bosch, *Trujillo*, p. 122; Goldwert, *The Constabulary*, p. 16.
71. Geo. C. Reid, Comdt., GND, to Comding. Genl., 5 June 1920, AGN, P7 (this letter marks the end of any effort to recruit Dominicans until late 1921); C. F. Williams to Int. and Pol., 8 May 1919, USNA, RG38, E6, B14.
72. McLean to Comdt., GND, 6 Aug. 1919, USNA, RG38, E6, B40.
73. Kimball, "Duty," p. 84; Reid to Maj. Genl. Comdt., USMC, 19 Sept. 1919, USNA, RG38, E6, B16.
74. Williams to Int. and Pol., 8 May 1919, and McLean to Comdt., GND, 6 Aug. 1919, USNA, RG38, E6, B14 and 40.
75. Col. B. Cabral to Comdante. Asistente, 20 Dec. 1917, AGN, P22; Stephen M. Fuller and Graham A. Cosmas, *Marines in the Dominican Republic, 1916–1924*, p. 47.
76. Harry Alverson Franck, *Roaming through the West Indies*, pp. 233, 235.
77. Snowden to Brig. Comdr., 20 Feb. and 5 June 1920, USNA, RG38, E6, B23.
78. McLean to Comdt., GND, 6 Aug. 1919, USNA, RG38, E6, B40.
79. Polk to Roosevelt, 23 May 1919, and Russell to Sec. St., 8 Aug. 1919, USNA, 839.00/2133 and 2143; J. C. Dunn, L. A. Div., St. Dept., Memorandum, 8 Apr. 1919, and Russell, Memorandum, 19 Apr. 1919, USNA, 839.1051/17 and 18.
80. Mil. Gov. Harry Lee to Sec. Nav., 19 May 1924, USNA, RG38, E6, B74; Harry Lee to Mil. Gov., 2 Aug. 1922, USNA, RG45, WA7, B645. Lee himself became military governor in 1923.
81. Mil. Gov. Robison to Lejeune, 25 Oct. 1921, USNA, RG45, WA7, B646.
82. Quarterly Report of the Mil. Gov. of Sto. Dom., 1 July to 30 Sept. 1921, USNA, 839.00/2449; Edward A. Fellowes, "Training Native Troops in Santo Domingo," *Marine Corps Gazette* 8, no. 4 (December 1923): 218–222; Harry Lee to Mil. Gov., 3 Aug. 1922, USNA, RG45, WA7, B645.
83. Goldwert, *The Constabulary*, p. 19; Exec. Orders Nos. 800 and 817, 15 Sept. and 2 Oct. 1922, R.D., *Colección, 1922*, pp. 299–304, 320–321. Exec. Order No. 809, 9 Oct. 1922, attempted to prevent future Dominican politicians from using promotions and demotions to control the Guardia; instead the law backfired and served as a primary tool in Trujillo's rise to power. See Mejía, *De Lilís*, pp. 146–147.
84. Lee to Mil. Gov., 31 Dec. 1921, AGN, P26.
85. Robison to Lejeune, 20 Sept. 1922, USNA, RG45, WA7, B646; Robison to A. H. Mayo, 18 Oct. 1922, USNA, RG38, E6, B56. Copies of the extensive correspondence between Robison and Welles concerning the marines' role under the provisional government are in USNA, 839.1051/25–38.
86. Lee, Report of Operations, No. 10, 14 Nov. 1922, and Lee to Mil. Gov., 2 Aug. 1922, USNA, RG45, WA7, B646 and 645; Fellowes, "Training Native Troops," pp. 226–233.
87. Manuel Aybar, Jr., Office of the Director, S. Dist., PND, to Col. Comdt., Training Centers, 5 Feb. 1923, USNA, RG38, E6, B68.
88. Flag San Domingo to Comdt. Marcorps, 4 Aug. 1924, USNA, RG45, WA7,

B646. Based on the marine belief that more training was needed, attempts were made to persuade President Vásquez to retain marines for this purpose, but they were not successful. See USNA, 839.1051/36–46.

89. Office of Nav. Intel., Sec. C-1, to M.I.D., 4 Nov. 1918, USNA, RG165, B575, file 2012-41; Arthur H. Mayo to Mil. Gov., 2 June 1919, AGN, P26; Ley 118, 24 Dec. 1923, in República Dominicana, *Colección de leyes, decretos y resoluciones del Gobierno Provisional de la República*, pp. 324–327. These percentages are based on amounts available to the government after the deduction of loan payments by the receivership.

90. Russell to Sec. St., 12 July 1923, USNA, 839.00/2725.

91. Russell to Sec. St., 30 June 1925, USNA, 839.00/2893. Russell to Sec. St., 10 Dec. 1924, USNA, 839.1051/45, made less definite charges of a similar nature.

92. Fed. Velásquez, Memorandum, enclosed in Warden McK. Wilson to Sec. St., 7 June 1926, USNA, 839.00/2979.

93. Howard J. Wiarda, *Dictatorship and Development: The Methods of Control in Trujillo's Dominican Republic*, chap. 3.

94. J. D. Alfonseca, Pres. de la Convención de Ayuntamientos del Cibao, to Snowden, 20 Oct. 1919, and James J. McLean to Comdt., GND, 21 Mar. 1918, AGN, P121 and 50.

95. Exec. Order No. 96, 22 Nov. 1917, R.D., *Colección, 1917*, pp. 87–88.

96. "Questionnaire," p. 21.

97. Mejía, *De Lilís*, p. 154.

98. "Report, 1920," pp. 21–22, 30.

99. The Ley de Sanidad created an elite five-person board of citizens to work with the Ministry of Sanitation and Beneficence, but only after the basic legislation was in place. "Questionnaire," pp. 11–12.

3. The Political Economy of the Military Government, II

1. Schoenrich, *Santo Domingo*, pp. 150–151; Muto, "Promise," chap. 2. Muto's dissertation is the most detailed study of the Dominican economy in this period. For a more global analysis based on secondary sources, see Lozano, *La dominación imperialista*.

2. Arthur H. Mayo, *Report on Economic and Financial Conditions of the Dominican Republic*, p. 11; Verrill, *Porto Rico*, pp. 242–243; República Dominicana, Department of Promotion and Public Works, *The Dominican Republic*, pp. 67–68; Muto, "Promise," pp. 86–92.

3. Schoenrich, *Santo Domingo*, p. 377; United States, Bureau of Insular Affairs, War Department, *Report . . . Dominican Customs Receivership*, 1921 (hereafter U.S. Receivership, *Report*, with the appropriate year).

4. Schoenrich, *Santo Domingo*, pp. 232–235; Muto, "Promise," pp. 72–86.

5. Knapp to Sec. Nav., 16 Oct. 1917 and 25 June 1918, USNA, RG45, WA7, B645 and 646.

6. Knapp to Sec. Nav., 19 June 1918, José C. Ariza to Knapp, 8 June 1918,

and J. W. McClosky, War Trade Board (WTB), to Knapp, [date?] 1918, USNA, RG38, E6, B7 and 12. Arturo J. Pellerano A. to Knapp, 12 Dec. 1917, USNA, RG38, E6, BU, reports a shortage of newsprint for the *Listín Diario.*

7. Knapp to Sec. Nav., 19 June 1918, USNA, RG38, E6, B12.
8. Robt. Lansing to Knapp, 30 Aug. 1917, USNA, RG45, WA7, B645; Minutes, WTB, 29 July 1918, and Asst. Dir., Bureau of War Trade Intel., Memorandum for Mr. McCormick, 30 July 1918, USNA, RG38, E6, B12.
9. Schoenrich, *Santo Domingo,* p. 236; Robt. H. Patchin, W. R. Grace Co., to Frank J. Mitchell, WTB, 12 Aug. 1918, and WTB, license no. ET-9866, 2 Mar. 1918, issued to Theodore Harris of New York, USNA, RG38, E6, B12. Tulchin, *The Aftermath of War,* pp. 23–51, discusses the WTB, the purchases of German firms, and trade within the general context of U.S.–Latin American relations.
10. Exec. Order No. 119, 10 Jan. 1918, R.D., *Colección, 1918,* pp. 6–7; Knapp to Sec. Nav., 12 Jan. 1918, USNA, RG38, E6, B7; Memorandum, "Deliveries of Flour to the Dominican Republic by the Clyde Line on the Acct. of the Mil. Govt.," 1919, and Contract between the Mil. Govt. of Sto. Dom. and La Industrial y Comercial, S.A, 9 Aug. 1919, USNA, RG38, E6, B22 and BU.
11. R. B. Farquarson, Acting Dist. Comdr., La Vega, to Brig. Comdr., 10 Dec. 1917, USNA, RG38, E6, B1; Comding. Officer, Moca, to Brig. Comdr., 10 Dec. 1917, and Memorandum, "Prices at Sánchez," Dec. 1917, AGN, P111.
12. U.S. Mil. Govt., Press Release, 17 Dec. 1917, and Knapp to Brig. Comdr., 23 Dec. 1917, USNA, RG38, E6, B5.
13. Exec. Order No. 117, 7 Jan. 1918, R.D., *Colección, 1918,* pp. 3–5; Food Control Orders Nos. 1–5, 10 Jan. and 3 Feb. 1918, AGN, P104.
14. Arthur H. Mayo, Hacienda y Comercio, to Mil. Gov., 30 July and [?] Oct. 1919, AGN, P56 and 121; Food Control Order No. 10, 19 May 1920, AGN, P108; Lybrand Smith to Mil. Gov., 9 Dec. 1920, and attached corres., AGN, P7; proposed executive order on rent control and attached corres., file 30-101, AGN, P16; Exec. Order No. 394, 6 Feb. 1920, modified by Exec. Order No. 571, 1 Dec. 1920, R.D., *Colección, 1920,* pp. 84, 526–527.
15. U.S. Mil. Govt., Memorandum for Senate Committee, 6 Dec. 1921, AGN, P37.
16. Russell to Sec. St., 20 and 24 June 1916, and enclosures, USNA, 839.00/1754 and 1763; Exec. Order No. 9, 18 Dec. 1916, R.D., *Colección, 1917,* p. 15; Antonio Hoepelman, *Apuntes históricos documentados de la honorable Cámara de Cuentas . . . ,* p. 35.
17. Tulio M. Cestero, "Los Estados Unidos y la República Dominicana de 1903 a 1916," *La Reforma Social,* 17 Oct. 1916, pp. 88–90; Exec. Order No. 563, 20 Nov. 1920, R.D., *Colección, 1920,* pp. 505–518; Mejía, *De Lilís,* p. 148.
18. Exec. Order No. 60, 20 June 1917, R.D., *Colección, 1917,* pp. 55–56; Knapp to Rufus Lane, 27 Dec. 1917, and enclosure, USNA, RG38, E6,

B11; Comisión de Reclamaciones, "Informe final de las reclamaciones," 1920, USNA, RG38, E6, B41.

19. Knapp to Ch. of Nav. Op., 5 Jan. 1918, USNA, RG38, E6, B7; Senator Henry Cabot Lodge to Sec. Nav., 7 July 1919, and attached corres., USNA, RG45, WA7, B646; Snowden to Nouel, 3 Jan. 1920, USNA, RG38, E6, B30; Harry Lee to Wenceslao Báez, 1 Feb. 1922, and attached corres., AGN, P3.

20. Knight, *The Americans*, p. 170.

21. Mayo, *Report*, pp. 25–26; Knapp, "Annual Report," 21 July 1917, USNA, RG38, E15. (References to this series of the National Archives' record group 38 are without box numbers because I consulted a microfilm copy of the documents which did not specify their box location.)

22. Fairchild, "Public Finance," pp. 472, 476–478; Exec. Orders Nos. 158 and 197, 4 May and 19 Aug. 1918, R.D., *Colección, 1918*, pp. 100–114, 166–214; Quarterly Report of the Mil. Gov. of Sto. Dom., 1 July to 30 Sept. 1918, USNA, RG38, E15. For correspondence on the Ley de Patentes, see USNA, file 839.512/7, and AGN, P117, file 2-65.

23. Exec. Order No. 282, 10 Apr. 1919, R.D., *Colección, 1919*, pp. 60–101.

24. Lybrand Smith, Hac. y Com., to Mil. Gov., 17 Dec. 1920, AGN, P9, with enclosures marked no. 2 (a draft of the proposed law) and no. 3 (a memorandum dated 16 Dec. 1920, recommending its immediate publication).

25. Exec. Order No. 420, 5 Mar. 1920, R.D., *Colección, 1920*, pp. 107–120; Exec. Order No. 726, 18 Mar. 1922, R.D., *Colección, 1922*, pp. 54–55; Great Britain, Dept. of Overseas Trade, *Report on Economic Conditions*, pp. 8–9.

26. Concerning later graft, see Orme Wilson, Memorandum, 31 Oct. 1925, and Fed. Velásquez, Memorandum, enclosed in W. McK. Wilson to Sec. St., 7 June 1926, USNA, 839.00/2983½ and 2979; Víctor M. Medina Benet, *Los responsables: Fracaso de la tercera república*, pp. 157–165.

27. Knight, *The Americans*, pp. 163–164.

28. Russell to Sec. St., 2 June 1925, and Evan E. Young to Sec. St., 17 Nov. 1925, USNA, 839.00/2889 and 2916.

29. Exec. Order No. 280, 7 Apr. 1919, R.D., *Colección, 1919*, pp. 57–59; Snowden to Dom. Tariff Comm., "Final Instructions . . . ," 1 Aug. 1919, AGN, P5.

30. U.S. Receivership, *Report, 1919*, p. 4; U.S. Mil. Govt., Memorandum for Senate Committee, 6 Dec. 1921, AGN, P37; Francisco J. Peynado, *Informe sobre la situación económica y financiera de la República Dominicana y el modo de solucionar sus problemas* (this work was also printed in Hoepelman and Senior, *Documentos*, pp. 263–293); Mayo, *Report*, p. 29.

31. Walker M. St. Elmo, Dir. Genl., Rentas Internas, to Mil. Gov., 26 Sept. 1919, and Snowden to Sec. Nav., 31 Jan. 1920, are part of a considerable correspondence on protecting home industries in AGN, P40-A. The divided view of the Dominican elite on the protectionism is seen in Peynado, *Informe*, and Alfredo Ricart y Olives, *Refutación al informe*

del Lic. Fco. J. Peynado. On the coffee matter, see P. A. Ricart to Snowden, 1 Feb. 1921, and related correspondence, files 28-8 and 28-38, AGN, P8.

32. U.S. Receivership, *Report, 1924*, p. 8, and *Report, 1925*, pp. 8, 9; Knight, *The Americans*, pp. 126–128.

33. Mil. Gov. to Ch. of Nav. Op., 22 Nov. 1919, and attached corres., USNA, RG45, WA7, B645.

34. Frank L. Polk, Acting Sec. St., to Sec. Nav., 24 Feb. 1920, and Robison to Ch. of Nav. Op., 1 Oct. 1921, and related corres., file 43-82, USNA, RG38, E6, B44; Welles to Francis White, St. Dept., 5 Sept. 1922, USNA, 839.00/2983. Various Dominican business groups advocated reciprocity; for a summary of their view, see Peynado, *Informe*.

35. Muto, "Promise," p. 274.

36. A. H. Mayo to Snowden, 20 Dec. 1920 and Robison to [?], 25 Oct. 1921, AGN, P10 and 57-A.

37. Various papers in AGN, P7 and 8 (especially file 28-72), document the cooperation with the chambers of commerce. See also A. R. Nanita, Sec., Cámara de Com., to Robison, 1 Aug. 1921, with enclosed pamphlet, *La Crisis*, USNA, RG38, E6, B43. On the tobacco matter, see Min. of Hacienda papers in AGN, especially P3 and 9, and Quarterly Report of the Mil. Gov. of Sto. Dom., 1 July to 30 Sept. 1923, USNA, 839.00/2766. On cacao, see A. H. Mayo to Snowden, 20 Dec. 1920, AGN, P10.

38. Mayo to Flag San Domingo, 14 Jan. 1921, and Cámara de Com., San Pedro de Mac., to Robison, 1 Oct. 1921, and attached corres., USNA, RG38, E6, B33 and 44. Knight, *The Americans*, p. 105, somewhat understated the loss.

39. John Loomis, Memorandum, attached to Lybrand Smith, Hac. y Com., to P. A. Ricart, Cámara de Com., 11 Dec. 1920, and Snowden to Ricart, 5 and 13 Jan. 1921, AGN, P7 and 8.

40. Food Control Order No. 13, [?] Sept. 1920, A. H. Mayo, Food Controller, to Mil. Gov., 28 Sept. 1920, and Mil. Gov. to Mayo, enclosing the protest of the Hermandad Comunal Nacionalista, 10 Nov. 1920, USNA, RG38, E6, B31; Muto, "Promise," pp. 198 and 214, n. 43, citing the protest of José Ramón López.

41. P. A. Ricart to Mil. Gov., 22 Feb., 28 Apr., and 19 May 1921, and Richard U. Strong, Legal Adv., to Mil. Gov., 15 July 1922, AGN, P8, 9, and 12; Exec. Order No. 699, 22 Dec. 1921, R.D., *Colección, 1921*, pp. 333–372, revised as Exec. Order No. 759, 13 June 1922, R.D., *Colección, 1922*, pp. 124–185; Snowden to Min. of Justice via Hac. y Com., 25 Feb. 1921, AGN, P8.

42. Robison to [?], 25 Oct. 1921, AGN, P57-A; W. D. Durland, Univ. of P.R., Mayagüez, to Mil. Gov., 22 Apr. 1924, USNA, RG38, E6, B75; Lybrand Smith to Mil. Gov., 7 May 1921, AGN, P8. The various executive orders which adjusted government salaries can be found in R.D., *Colección, 1921* and *Colección, 1922*.

43. Quarterly Report of the Mil. Gov. of Sto. Dom., 1 Apr. to 30 June 1921, USNA, 839.00/2445.

44. Sec. Nav. to Flag San Domingo, 31 Jan. 1921, USNA, RG38, E6, B56; Exec. Orders Nos. 597 and 637, 31 Jan. and 18 June 1921, R.D., *Colección, 1921*, pp. 25–26, 192–196; Quarterly Report of the Mil. Gov. of Sto. Dom., 1 Apr. to 30 June 1921, USNA, 839.00/2445.

45. Robison to Sec. Nav., 16 Dec. 1921, USNA, RG38, E6, B44; F. U. Lake to Robison, 16 Jan. 1922, USNA, RG45, WA7, B646; Mil. Gov. to Sec. Nav., 21 Jan. 1922, and Sec. St. Hughes to Pres. W. G. Harding, 30 Mar. 1922, USNA, 839.00/2461 and 2462; Exec. Orders Nos. 713 and 735, 23 Jan. and 28 Mar. 1922, R.D., *Colección, 1922*, pp. 17–22, 68–79.

46. For example, Knight, *The Americans*, pp. 170–171, and Knowles to Senator Wm. E. Borah, 8 Apr. 1922, PFP.

47. Mil. Gov. to Sec. Nav., 9 Dec. 1921, Lt. Comdr. D. W. Rose, Aide to the Mil. Gov. in N.Y.C., to Mil. Gov., 7 Jan. 1923, and Harry Lee to Prov. Pres. Vicini Burgos, 15 June 1923, USNA, RG38, E6, B44, 56, and 67.

48. Mil. Gov. to All Depts., 6 Apr. 1922, AGN, P45; Exec. Orders Nos. 788 and 793, 30 Aug. and 8 Sept. 1922, R.D., *Colección, 1922*, pp. 281, 285–286.

49. Quarterly Reports of the Mil. Gov. of Sto. Dom. Jan.–Dec. 1923, USNA, 839.00/2722, 2735, 2766, and 2805; J. C. Ariza to Sec. St., 8 Aug. 1924, *Foreign Relations, 1924*, p. 651. There was considerable controversy within the U.S. government over the fiscal health of the provisional government. The State Department's positive view appears in *Foreign Relations, 1924*, pp. 645–649, but is refuted by Mil. Gov. Harry Lee to Sec. Nav., 16 May 1924, USNA, RG38, E6, B74.

50. Knapp, "Annual Report," 21 July 1917, USNA, RG38, E15.

51. Exec. Order No. 110, 24 Dec. 1917, R.D., *Colección, 1917*, pp. 112–113; Knapp, "Annual Report," 21 July 1917, USNA, RG38, E15, Holger Johansen, Yearly Report of the Dir. of Agric., 1 July 1919 to 30 June 1920, and R. M. Warfield, Agric. and Immig., to Mil. Gov., 11 Oct. 1920, AGN, P46.

52. Knapp, "Annual Report," 21 July 1917, USNA, RG38, E15; R. M. Warfield to Mil. Gov., 1 Oct. 1919, and Johansen, Report, 1919–1920, AGN, P5 and 46.

53. Pedro A. Bobea, "Duties of Inspectors of Agriculture," in *El Adalid* (La Vega), 21 June 1917, trans. enclosed in John H. Russell, Regt. CO, Santiago, to Mil. Gov., 6 July 1917, and attached corres., AGN, P48; Welles, *Naboth's Vineyard*, vol. 2, p. 584; Henry P. Lewis, U.S. Consul, Sto. Dom., to Sec. St., 3 Sept. 1910, USNA, 839.423; United States, Bureau of Foreign and Domestic Commerce, *The Development of the Dominican Republic* (by Charles H. Albrecht and Frank Anderson Henry), p. 13; Muto, "Promise," pp. 184–185, 212.

54. Warfield to Mil. Gov., 14 June 1921, AGN, P10.

55. Warfield to Mil. Gov., 28 Apr. 1922, AGN, P3; Exec. Order No. 756, 12 June 1922, R.D., *Colección, 1922*, pp. 103–105; Quarterly Reports of the Mil. Gov. of Sto. Dom., 1 Jan. to 31 Mar. and 1 July to 30 Sept. 1923, USNA, 839.00/2722 and 2766; Mejía, *De Lilís*, pp. 214–215; Welles, *Naboth's Vineyard*, vol. 2, p. 910.

56. W. L. Abbott, Smithsonian Inst., to H. Johansen, Dir. of Agric., 26 May 1919, and related corres., AGN, P57-C; William D. Durland, *Los bosques en la República Dominicana*; Exec. Order No. 365, 9 Dec. 1919, R.D., *Colección, 1919*, pp. 380–384; Exec. Order No. 586, 28 Dec. 1920, R.D., *Colección, 1920*, pp. 547–548; Knight, *The Americans*, pp. 151–152.

57. Exec. Order No. 207, 12 Sept. 1918, R.D., *Colección, 1918*, pp. 223–224; T. W. Vaughan et al., *A Geological Reconnaissance of the Dominican Republic*; Baughman, "U.S. Occupation," pp. 2317–2319; Exec. Order No. 471, [6–8] May 1920, R.D., *Colección, 1920*, pp. 209–239 (other relevant executive orders include nos. 133–135 [1918] and 379 [1919]); Mayo, *Report*, pp. 6–7.

58. Baughman, "U.S. Occupation," p. 2311; Exec. Order No. 286, 3 May 1919, R.D., *Colección, 1919*, pp. 103–104.

59. Baughman, "U.S. Occupation," pp. 2310–2311; Knapp to James Scott Brown, Neutrality Board, 1 June 1917, USNA, RG38, E6, B1.

60. Snowden to Sec. Nav., 3 May 1920, and Otto Schoenrich to Leo S. Rowe, St. Dept., 11 Dec. 1919, USNA, 839.00/2211 and 2447.

61. Snowden to Sec. Nav., 6 Sept. 1920, and attached corres., AGN, P13, concerning the inquiry of U.S. Senator Duncan U. Fletcher. See also USNA, RG38, E6, B30, file 41-32.

62. Ralph Whitman, Fomento y Comunic., to Mil. Gov., 2 June 1919, and Mil. Gov. to Sec. Nav., 7 June 1919, and attached corres., USNA, RG45, WA7, B646; Exec. Order No. 275, 20 May 1919, R.D., *Colección, 1919*, pp. 53–54; Dirección Genl. de Correos y Telégrafos, "Report of Progress . . . ," 1 Apr. to 30 June 1919, AGN, P63.

63. Exec. Order No. 452, 10 Apr. 1920, R.D., *Colección, 1920*, pp. 176–187.

64. Mil. Gov. to Hac. y Com., 3 Aug. 1921, AGN, P10; A. W. Paul, Dist. Intel. Officer, Daily Report, 27 Jan. 1923, USNA, RG38, E6, B63; Russell to Sec. St., 6 Aug. and 5 Sept. 1924, USNA, 839.00/2864 and 2860.

65. R.D., *Censo de la república*; Peynado, *Informe*.

66. The changes summarized here are fully explained in Rufus H. Lane, Min. of Justice, to Mil. Gov., 1 Feb. 1920 (pp. 1–26), AGN, P16. They are scarcely mentioned in published sources, except briefly in Lane, "Civil Government," pp. 141–142. Exec. Order No. 199, 27 Aug. 1918, R.D., *Colección, 1918*, pp. 215–216.

67. Pendleton to Knapp, 17 Oct. 1917, and Knapp to Lane, 18 Oct. 1917, USNA, RG38, E6, B4; Lane to Mil. Gov., 1 Feb. 1920 (pp. 12–16); and Civil Eng. Ralph Whitman to Mil. Gov., 4 Feb. 1922, AGN, P16 and 42; Exec. Order No. 258, 17 Feb. 1919, R.D., *Colección, 1919*, pp. 11–12.

68. Dr. A. Ortiz, Ozama Prison, to Provost Marshal, 22 July 1920, A. T. Marix to Snowden, 13 Nov. 1920, and F. A. Ramsey to Mil. Gov., 24 Jan. 1922, AGN, P51 and 37.

69. U.S. Mil. Govt., *Santo Domingo*, pp. 26–27; Lane to Mil. Gov., 1 Feb. 1920 (pp. 17–19), AGN, P16; Exec. Order No. 375, 26 Dec. 1919, R.D., *Colección, 1919*, pp. 403–418; Exec. Order No. 168, 13 June 1918,

R.D., *Colección, 1918*, pp. 128–129; Mejía, *De Lilís*, pp. 155–156.
70. Snowden to Abogado Consultor, 9 Dec. 1920, AGN, P51; Exec. Order No. 201, 28 Aug. 1918, R.D., *Colección, 1918*, p. 217; Exec. Order No. 338, 13 Oct. 1919, R.D., *Colección, 1919*, p. 325; Russell to Ramsey, Sec. of For. Rels., 3 Nov. 1921, and L. H. Moses, Sec. of Int. and Pol., to Mil. Gov., 17 Dec. 1921, AGN, P72.
71. Blanco Fombona, *Crímenes*, p. 79; "La Mujer," *El Dogal* (Santiago), 27 Aug. 1921; "Nueve Cosas," *El Indice* (Santiago), 1 Sept. 1921. These articles resulted in the permanent suppression of these newspapers; C. H. Lyman, CO, 4th Regt., to Comding. Genl., 20 Sept. 1921, USNA, RG38, E6, B48.
72. Norman H. Davis to Sec. Nav., 16 Dec. 1920, AGN, P8.
73. Rear Adm. R. M. Kennedy to Surg. Genl., 7 Apr. 1921 (p. 35), AGN, P11.

4. The Military Government, the Sugar Industry, and the Land Question

1. For a description, history, and analysis of the sugar industry since 1870, see Juan J. Sánchez, *La caña en Santo Domingo*; José D. Vicini, *La isla de azúcar*; República Dominicana, Presidencia, Dirección General de Información y Prensa, *Evolución de la industria azucarera en la República Dominicana: Historia y descripción de los ingenios azucareros*; Hoetink, *El pueblo*; Muto, "Promise," chaps. 2 and 9; Franc Báez Evertsz, *Azúcar y dependencia en la República Dominicana*; Lozano, *La dominación imperialista*; and Andrés Corten et al., *Azúcar y política en la República Dominicana*.
2. Samuel Hazard, *Santo Domingo, Past and Present, with a Glance at Haiti*, p. 208; Sánchez, *La caña*, pp. 35–40; R.D., *Evolución*, pp. 9–138.
3. Secretaría de Estado de Agricultura e Inmigración, "Estadística azucarera de la República Dominicana, zafra 1920–21," USNA, RG38, E6, B36; Mayo, *Report*, p. 10.
4. Mil. Gov. Harry Lee to the Editors, St. Martin's Press, 2 Aug. 1923, USNA, RG38, E6, B68; Sugar Cos. to Pres. Horacio Vásquez, 11 Nov. 1926, USNA, 839.512/35; U.S. Min. Franklin B. Frost to Sec. St., 6 Aug. 1927, USNA, 839.52/64.
5. Knight, *The Americans*, p. 134.
6. Lee to St. Martin's Press, 2 Aug. 1923, USNA, RG38, E6, B68.
7. Knight, *The Americans*, pp. 130–140; Frost to Sec. St., 6 Aug. 1927, USNA, 839.52/64.
8. Hoetink, *El pueblo*, pp. 31–35. The number of persons so affected is open to question.
9. Américo Lugo, quoted in Luis C. del Castillo, *Medios adecuados para conservar i desarrollar el nacionalismo en la república*, pp. 25–26; Franco, *Algunas ideas*, p. 14.
10. Frank Garnett, Mgr., Porvenir Sugar Co., to Knapp, 31 Jan. 1918, AGN, P59.
11. "Report of American Federation of Labor Commissioners, Peter J.

Brady and Anthony McAndrew, on Conditions in Santo Domingo," in American Federation of Labor, *Report of the Proceedings of the 40th Annual Convention of the American Federation of Labor, Held at Montreal, Quebec, Canada, June 7 to 19, Inclusive, 1920*, p. 246; Knight, *The Americans*, p. 157.

12. Speech of J. E. Kunhardt to the Congress of the Pan American Federation of Labor, N.Y., 1919, and comments of other Dominican labor leaders, reported by Dist. Comdr. Dion Williams to Mil. Gov., 18 Aug. 1919, and Luis M. Poncerrate and José Casado R., Comité Central de la Confederación Dominicana del Trabajo (CDT), to Mil. Gov. Snowden, 2 June 1920, AGN, P61; José Ramón López, "La Industria Azucarera," *Listín Diario*, 25 Feb. to 9 Apr. 1915, cited in Muto, "Promise," p. 106.

13. Hoetink, *El pueblo*, p. 36; G. C. Thorpe to Brig. Comdr., 21 Oct. 1918, USNA, RG45, WA7, B647. On the contrary, F. A. Dillingham, Pres., Central Romana, to Knapp, 29 Oct. 1918, AGN, P63, recommends legislation to establish prohibition.

14. Poncerrate and Casado R., Comité Central, CDT, to Snowden, 2 June 1920, AGN, P61; Knight, *The Americans*, pp. 158, 188 n. 6.

15. James J. Murphy, Jr., U.S. Consul, Sto. Dom., 18 May 1926, "Wages of Native Labor in the Dominican Republic," USNA, 839.5041/1. Murphy's prices are for 1926, probably for stores in Santo Domingo. The wages he quotes, from fifty to eighty cents per day, are little changed from ten years before.

16. Wm. C. Harllee, Dist. Comdr., to Comding. Genl., 24 Jan. 1922, USNA, RG38, E6, B48; Snowden to Comité Central, CDT, 29 June 1920, AGN, P61; W. Medrano, hijo, and Manuel Pazos, "Memorándum que a los miembros del Quinto Congreso de la Federación Americana del Trabajo reunido en Washington el 18 de julio de 1927, presentan los delegados obreros de la República Dominicana," p. 3, AFL-CIO Library, Washington, D.C. A number of papers concerning the military government's investigation of conditions on the sugar estates may be found in AGN, P61.

17. José del Castillo, *La inmigración de braceros azucareros en la República Dominicana, 1900–1930*, gives the most comprehensive immigration data as well as the fullest treatment to date of these workers. See also Mercedes Acosta, "Azúcar e inmigración haitiana," in Corten et al., *Azúcar*, pp. 115–154, and the immigration files in AGN, P47.

18. Patrick Bryan, "La cuestión obrera en la industria azucarera de la República Dominicana a finales del siglo XIX y principios del siglo XX," *EME EME* 7, no. 41 (March–April 1979): 57–77, supports this thesis with British consular documents. *El Confederado Nacionalista*, 20 Nov. and 2 Dec. 1916; Pan American Federation of Labor (PAFL), *Report of the Proceedings of the Second Congress of the Pan American Federation of Labor, Held at New York City, N.Y., July 7th to 10th, Inclusive, 1919*, pp. 40–41.

19. J. H. Fay, Provost Marshal, interview with J. Jolibois, Director of the *Haitian Courier*, and Alphonse Henriquex, Director of *La Défense*, re-

port to the Mil. Gov., 2 Feb. 1922, USNA, RG38, E6, B48; Knight, *The Americans*, pp. 157, 188 n. 6.

20. PAFL, *Report, 1919*, pp. 40–41; Luis Sánchez A. to Snowden, 17 Mar. 1920, USNA, RG38, E6, B23.
21. Peter J. Brady, AFL, to Snowden, 17 Mar. 1920, reprinted in Hoepelman and Senior, *Documentos*, pp. 276–277.
22. Memorandum, Col. G. C. Thorpe to Knapp, 25 Oct. 1918, USNA, RG45, WA7, B647; "Report of American Federation of Labor Commissioners, Peter J. Brady and Anthony McAndrew, on Conditions in Santo Domingo," in AFL, *Report, 1920*, p. 246.
23. Alcibiades Albuquerque, *Títulos de los terrenos comuneros de la República Dominicana*, pp. 53–57.
24. Emilio A. Morel, public letter in *Listín Diario*, 8 and 12 Aug. 1921, reported in Knight, *The Americans*, p. 118; Castro García, *Intervención*, pp. 22–24.
25. Schoenrich, *Santo Domingo*, pp. 150–151; Sánchez, *La caña*, pp. 32–34; Miguel A. Fiallo, "La Ley de Registro de Tierras: La adquisición de nuestras tierras," *Listín Diario*, 31 Aug. 1920.
26. E. L. Klock, Mgr., Central Romana, to Knapp, 22 Dec. 1917, AGN, P30. The estimate of Morales' gross profit on the first contract is based on the following calculation: in 1921–22, with a moderately good crop, Central Romana produced 22.45 tons of cane per acre. Thus Morales would have produced 15,715 tons on his 700 acres and, at $1.50 per ton, he would earn $23,572. Central Romana's production per acre is stated in Secretaría de Estado de Agricultura e Inmigración, "Estadística azucarera de la Repúbilica Dominicana, zafra 1920–1921," USNA, RG38, E6, B36.
27. Knight, *The Americans*, p. 102.
28. Knapp to Sec. Nav., 4 Aug. 1917, and Knapp to Maj. Genl. Comdt., USMC, 26 Oct. 1918, USNA, RG45, WA7, B644 and 647.
29. "Recommendations Made by P. J. Brady and A. McAndrew, Commissioners of the American Federation of Labor, Appointed by President Gompers to Investigate Working and Living Conditions in the Dominican Republic, to Admiral Snowden, Military Governor of Santo Domingo, and His Replies Thereto," in AFL, *Report, 1920*, p. 248.
30. MacMichael, "The United States," pp. 534–535; Cámara de Comercio, San Pedro de Mac., to Robison, 1 Oct. 1921, and attached corres., USNA, RG38, E6, B44.
31. See Snowden's answers to questions four, five, and eighteen in "Recommendations Made by P. J. Brady and A. McAndrew," in AFL, *Report, 1920*, pp. 247–248, 250.
32. For example, Francisco J. Peynado, a leading lawyer associated with the sugar industry and on the board of directors of the Enriquillo Lumber Co., a U.S. corporation which held 450,000 acres of Dominican timberland; see USNA, 839.52/En 7. For Peynado's views, see "Deslinde, mensura y partición de terrenos," *Revista Jurídica*, no. 4 (1919): 1–19.

33. On the State Department, see Munro, *Intervention*, p. 303 and footnotes. Knight, *The Americans*, pp. 151–152, notes N. L. Orme, a receivership official who was also president of the Orme Mahogany Co., and J. H. Edwards, deputy receiver general until 1919 and thereafter president of the Enriquillo Lumber Co. Each concern held approximately half a million acres of Dominican land. Land legislation which encouraged the sugar companies' expansion did the same, of course, for other land-extensive operations such as lumber corporations. In 1917 the Habanero Lumber Co. of Richmond, Va., reported that it had instituted judicial proceedings involving titles to more than half the land in Azua Province, as well as other land in adjacent Barahona Province; see J. Scott Parrish, Pres., Habanero Lumber Co., to St. Dept., 21 Feb. 1917, enclosed in Russell to Knapp, 27 Apr. 1917, USNA, RG38, E6, B3. Another firm, the Maryland Land and Timber Co. of Philadelphia, owned or had timber rights to over 100,000 acres of Dominican land; see L. B. Runk to Sec. St., 29 Jan. 1920, USNA, 839.52/37.

34. Clausner, *Rural Santo Domingo*, especially chaps. 6, 7, and 8; Alfonso Sosa Albuquerque, *Apuntes históricos sobre la propiedad territorial de Santo Domingo.*

35. Schoenrich, *Santo Domingo*, pp. 147–148; Fairchild, "Public Finance," pp. 478–481. For fuller descriptions, emphasizing legal aspects, see Albuquerque, *Títulos*, pp. 12–94, and Manuel Ramón Ruiz Tejada, *Estudio sobre la propiedad inmobiliaria en la República Dominicana,* especially pp. 56–60.

36. Albuquerque, *Títulos*, pp. 50–63; Sosa Albuquerque, *Apuntes*, pp. 15–18; Ley sobre División de Terrenos Comuneros, 25 Apr. 1911, República Dominicana, *Colección de leyes, decretos y resoluciones emanados de los poderes legislativos y ejecutivos de la República Dominicana*, vol. 20, pp. 182–185.

37. Ley sobre Franquicias Agrarias, 26 June 1911, R.D., *Colección de leyes,* vol. 20, pp. 224–230. The owners of Central Romana apparently helped bring about the passage of the Ley sobre Franquicias Agrarias; see Wm. L. Bass to the Hon. T. C. Dawson, ex–U.S. Minister to the D.R., 12 Dec. 1911, USNA, 839.635.

38. Albuquerque, *Títulos*, pp. 63–72; Ruiz Tejada, *Estudio*, pp. 52, 74–77; Francisco J. Peynado and Moisés García Mella, *Capacidad de los alcaldes para actuar como escribanos o como notarios.*

39. Knight, *The Americans*, pp. 132, 139.

40. Petition, signed by sixty-eight individuals, to Secretaría de Agricultura e Inmigración via Brig. Genl. B. H. Fuller, 15 Jan. 1919, and similar petitions dated 30 Oct. 1918 and 5 Feb. 1919, USNA, RG38, E6, B18. Challenging the petitions is F. L. Mitchell, Mgr., Barahona Co., to F. H. Vedder, 22 Feb. 1919, AGN, P103.

41. Report of Board of Inquiry, 23 Apr. 1919, USNA, RG38, E6, B18.

42. Anonymous "operator" to Maj. D. M. Randall, Intel., 3 June 1918, USNA, RG38, E6, B8.

43. Ruiz Tejada, *Estudio*, pp. 80–81, 101; Albuquerque, *Títulos*, pp. 56–

57; "Statement . . . by the Habanero Lumber Company. . . , Nov. 1915," pp. 25–40, USNA, 839.52/13.

44. Russell to Sec. St., 17 June 1911, Sullivan to Sec. St., 1 May 1914, and Wm. Phillips for Sec. St. to John C. White, chargé d'affaires, Sto. Dom., 8 July 1914, USNA, 839.52/1 and 9; Polk to Russell, 17 Sept. 1915, cited in Munro, *Intervention*, p. 303; Wilson to Jiménez, 24 Nov. 1915, quoted in Logan, *Haiti and the Dominican Republic*, p. 62.

45. Munro, *Intervention*, p. 303; Letter, Representatives of Sugar Estates to Poder Ejecutivo de la Nación, *Listín Diario*, no. 7728, reprinted in Peynado and García Mella, *Capacidad*, pp. 3–5.

46. Two other executive orders, nos. 48 and 85, 12 Apr. and 2 Oct. 1917, amplified the provisions of the first; see R.D., *Colección, 1917*, pp. 30, 45–56, 76–77. Russell to Stabler, 12 Sept. 1917, enclosed in Chas. Belknap, Nav. Op., to Knapp, [?] Oct. 1917, USNA, RG38, E6, B6.

47. Fairchild, "Public Finance," pp. 478, 481.

48. Exec. Orders No. 195 of 8 Aug. 1918, No. 281 of 9 Apr. 1919, No. 304 of 10 June 1919, and No. 500 of 30 June 1920, listed in Ruiz Tejada, *Estudio*, p. 81. Exec. Order No. 363, 6 Dec. 1919, was subsequently modified by Exec. Order No. 217, 20 Mar. 1920, and No. 590, 2 Jan. 1921; see Ruiz Tejada, pp. 101–106, 108 ff.

49. Exec. Order No. 511, 11 July 1920, quoted in ibid., pp. 134–135.

50. Ibid., pp. 141–142, 148, 158.

51. Russell to Sec. St., 24 July 1919, quoting Rufus H. Lane, USNA, 839.52/39; Clausner, *Rural Santo Domingo*, p. 195; Snowden to Brig. Genl. B. H. Fuller, 30 Apr. 1919, and Acting Mil. Gov. to Fuller, 21 July 1919, USNA, RG38, E6, B18 and 14.

52. U.S. Receivership, *Report, 1918*, app. E, pp. 70–71, and *Report, 1919*, app. D, pp. 78–79; Knight, *The Americans*, p. 152; Rufus H. Lane to Snowden, 1 Dec. and 26 Dec. 1919, USNA, RG38, E6, B29 and 14.

53. Memorandum, Frank Vedder to Lt. Comdr. Mayo, undated, USNA, RG38, E6, B14. Vedder's consultations with sugar company lawyers (Jacinto de Castro, Horacio V. Vicioso, and Rafael A. Sánchez) on the proposed law are documented in Jorge J. Serralles, Ingenio Puerto Rico, to Snowden, 17 July 1920, AGN, P51.

54. Russell to Sec. St., 11 Aug. 1920, and Leo S. Rowe to Snowden, 3 Feb. 1920, USNA, 839.52/42 and 45; *Who Was Who*, vol. 1, p. 922.

55. F. J. Peynado to Rufus H. Lane, Sec. de Estado de Justicia, 15 Dec. 1919, HyC. Peynado wrote his criticisms before the law was published, but the features which he criticized remained unchanged.

56. Ruiz Tejada, *Estudio*, pp. 136–137; Knight, *The Americans*, pp. 118, 140. Relatively minor modifications were made to the 1920 law by Exec. Orders Nos. 547, 553, 590, 691, 700, 741, 764, 799, 805, and 814. After 1922 the Dominican provisional government made adjustments with Decree No. 83, and the new constitutional government followed with changes in Ley 36 and Ley 959. The 1928 text of the Ley de Registro de Tierras appears in USNA, 839.52/69.

57. Albuquerque, *Títulos*, p. 94; Ruiz Tejada, *Estudio*, pp. 423–424. Both

authors express reservations on some points. Wm. H. Ford, Jefe de Agrimensores, to Secretaría de Fomento y Comunicaciones, 30 June 1922, USNA, RG38, E6, B75. Copies of several surveying contracts between the military government, the estates of Santa Fe and Barahona, and the Compañía Azucarera Dominicana are in USNA, RG38, E6, B37 and 75.

58. Ruiz Tejada, *Estudio*, p. 159; Clausner, *Rural Santo Domingo*, pp. 198–199.

59. Félix E. Mejía, *Al rededor y en contra del plan Hughes-Peynado*, pp. 125–126; "Manifiesto del nacionalismo dominicano contra la' intervención, el entendido Hughes-Peynado y las elecciones venideras," 11 Nov. 1923, typescript with two pages of signatures appended, p. 6, CRD. Protests continued, peaking in 1927; see Franklin B. Frost to Sec. St., 6 Aug. 1927, USNA, 839.52/64, and related correspondence beginning with file 839.6351.

60. Juan Fco. Mejía, Pres., Asoc. Nac. de Agrimensores, to Snowden, 24 Aug. 1920, USNA, RG38, E6, BU. Peynado to Lane, 15 Dec. 1919, HyC, noted that the new law violated the "traditional rights" of the surveyors.

61. Albuquerque, *Títulos*, pp. 53–54. See also Ruiz Tejada, *Estudio*, pp. 92–100, 114–115.

62. Snowden to J. F. Mejía, 27 Aug. 1920, J. F. Mejía to Snowden, 14 Sept. 1920 (and subsequent letters in file 41-15), and R. M. Warfield, USN, "Rules for Government Agrimensores," [date?] 1920, USNA, RG38, E6, BU.

63. Fairchild, "Public Finance"; Snowden to F. R. Fairchild, 4 Aug. 1919, USNA, RG38, E6, B16; Exec. Order No. 282, 10 Apr. 1919, R.D., *Colección, 1919*, pp. 60–101.

64. Snowden to F. R. Fairchild, 5 Aug. 1919, and Mil. Gov. to Ch. of Nav. Op., [12?] Sept. 1919, USNA, RG38, E6, B16 and 17.

65. Russell to Sec. St., 27 May 1919, USNA, 839.52/27.

66. Frank H. Vedder to Snowden, 20 May 1919, AGN, P6; Snowden to Vedder, 23 May 1919, and Sugar Assoc. of Sto. Dom. to Sec. Nav., 24 July 1919, enclosed in Vedder to Fuller, 30 Aug. 1919, USNA, RG38, E6, B17. Other correspondence related to this matter is located in USNA, 839.512/11 and 12.

67. Daniels to Snowden, 22 July 1919, USNA, RG38, E6, B17.

68. Mayo, *Report*, pp. 29–30.

69. Exec. Order No. 545, 20 Sept. 1920, R.D., *Colección, 1920*, pp. 479–480; Clausner, *Rural Santo Domingo*, p. 190. For protests by some urban landholders, see Junta Consultiva, Memorandum No. 2, 16 Dec. 1919, USNA, 839.00/2187. Vedder to the Hon. J. B. Vicini Burgos, Prov. Pres., Memorandum on Amending the School Tax Law, [date?] 1923, USNA, RG38, E6, B67.

70. P. A. Ricart, Pres., Cámara de Comercio de Santo Domingo, to Mil. Gov. S. S. Robison, 17 Oct. 1921, and Robison to Chamber of Commerce, Industry, and Agriculture of Santo Domingo, 5 Nov. 1921, USNA, RG38, E6, B44.

71. Lybrand Smith to Mil. Gov., 30 Dec. 1920, AGN, P9; Mil. Gov. to Sec. Nav., 16 Dec. 1921, and S. S. Robison to J. B. Vila Morel, Gob. Civ. de Santiago, 19 Oct. 1922, USNA, RG38, E6, B44 and 55; Exec. Order No. 758, 13 June 1922, R.D., *Colección, 1922,* pp. 106–185; Mil. Gov. to Ch. of Nav. Op., 2 Aug. 1922, USNA, RG38, E6, B56; Evan E. Young, U.S. Min., to Sec. St., 25 May 1926, USNA, 839.5122. Young notes evidence that sugar companies paid 85 percent of total land taxes in 1925 and 1926. After October 1926, the sugar companies successfully refused to pay more than a small portion of their tax bill; see MacMichael, "The United States," p. 614.

72. In 1927 the Dominican Congress added debilitating modifications to the original law, and in 1935 the tax was abolished completely. See Clausner, *Rural Santo Domingo,* p. 193.

73. Exec. Orders No. 148 of 11 Apr. 1918, No. 203 of 30 Aug. 1918, and No. 237 of 16 Dec. 1918, R.D., *Colección, 1918,* pp. 89–90, 219–221, 246–248; Logia "La Fe" No. 7, *El caso de la respetable Logia "La Fe" No. 7 con el gobierno militar: Relación documentada,* pp. 3–44.

74. Exec. Orders Nos. 286 and 287 of 3 May 1919, No. 318 of 19 July 1919, and No. 365 of 9 Dec. 1919, R.D., *Colección, 1919,* pp. 103–104, 140–145, 380–384; Mayo, *Report,* p. 25.

5. GUERRILLA WAR IN THE EAST: ORIGINS

1. Calder, "Some Aspects," pp. 5–8 and 130–135, explores the reasons for this obscurity. Only recently have two Dominican works appeared, namely, Gregorio Urbano Gilbert's autobiographical *Mi lucha contra el invasor yanqui de 1916,* which contains data on 1917, and newspaper writer Félix Servio Ducoudray's articles, based on local and provincial records, collected in *Los "gavilleros" del este: Una epopeya calumniada.*

2. Pertinent military government papers are found in the U.S. National Archives, particularly in Record Groups 38, 45, 59, 80, and 127. Others are located in the Geographical File of the U.S. Marine Corps Historical Center, Washington, D.C., and in the Archivo General de la Nación, Santo Domingo.

3. For several analyses of the Dominican caudillo system, see Francisco Henríquez y Carvajal, Memorandum, 14 Apr. 1919, enclosed in Henríquez y Carvajal to J. H. Stabler, 19 Apr. 1919, *Foreign Relations, 1919,* pp. 111–113; United States, Commission of Inquiry to Santo Domingo, *Report of the Commission of Inquiry to Santo Domingo,* pp. 8–9; and Tulio M. Cestero, *El problema dominicano,* pp. 10–13.

4. Payoffs to caudillos are cited in Welles, *Naboth's Vineyard,* vol. 2, p. 589, and in Munro, *Intervention,* pp. 82, 274–277, 311–312.

5. Welles, *Naboth's Vineyard,* vol. 2, p. 908; Harry Lee to Sec. Nav., 19 May 1924, USNA, RG38, E6, B74.

6. Chargé Johnson, Sto. Dom., to Sec. St., 15 Sept. 1915, and Russell to

Sec. St., 30 Nov. 1915, *Foreign Relations, 1915*, pp. 294, 297; Russell to Sec. St., 14 Mar. 1916, *Foreign Relations, 1916*, p. 221.

7. Knapp to Maj. Genl. Comdt., USMC, 27 Oct. 1918, USNA, RG45, WA7, B647. The analysis in this and the two following paragraphs is in part speculative, based on my study of many military government and Dominican civilian documents.

8. For a typical incident, when the *comandante de armas* of El Seibo rebelled against his civilian superior, the governor, in 1916, see Pichardo, *Resumen*, p. 297.

9. Knapp to Maj. Genl. Comdt., USMC, 27 Oct. 1918, USNA, RG45, WA7, B647.

10. Note that the notorious pre–1917 caudillos were killed or captured during the first year of fighting. Thereafter, with the war under way, new leaders appeared.

11. Several tense situations developed in the west. In Barahona Province there was unrest over land and water rights, and in neighboring Azua Province there was a messianic movement led by Dios Olivorio Mateo, whom the marines finally killed in 1922.

12. Eric J. Hobsbawm, *Bandits*, p. 23; Pérez, *Intervention, Revolution, and Politics in Cuba*, pp. 69–79. These books, and Hobsbawm's *Primitive Rebels: Studies in Archaic Forms of Social Movements in the 19th and 20th Centuries*, offer many suggestive parallels to the Dominican situation.

13. G. C. Thorpe to Brig. Comdr., 18 July 1917, AGN, P4, reporting a conversation with Capt. D. B. Roben.

14. James J. McLean, Dir., S. Dist., to Comdt., GND, 6 Aug. 1919, and Robison to Sugar Cos., 13 June 1922, USNA, RG38, E6, BU and B36.

15. Of more than one hundred men imprisoned on charges of banditry in the spring of 1922 in San Pedro de Macorís, fourteen had French names and were scheduled for deportation, probably to Haiti; Prov. Mar. to Comding. Genl., 14 Aug. 1922, USNA, RG38, E6, B50. Of about forty guerrillas who surrendered in April and May 1922, only four had Haitian-French names; Comding. Genl. Harry Lee to Mil. Gov., 22 May 1923, USNA, RG38, E6, B64. Ducoudray, *Los "gavilleros,"* pp. 89–91, discusses the limited Haitian involvement. The absence of British West Indians from guerrilla ranks can be explained by the overt hostility which the insurgents displayed toward them, probably for both economic and social reasons. Concerning guerrilla attacks on West Indians in 1918, see Frank H. Vedder to Franklin D. Roosevelt, Asst. Sec. Nav., 26 Oct. 1918, and attached corres., USNA, 839.6135/6.

16. Col. C. Gamborg-Andresen, CO, 3rd Prov. Regt., to Brig. Comdr., 27 Feb. 1919, USNA, RG45, WA7, B645.

17. Julio Peynado to Horace G. Knowles, 22 Apr. 1922, PFP; Lt. Col. G. C. Thorpe to Brig. Comdr., 8 July 1917, USNA, RG45, WA7, B646.

18. Capt. T. P. Cheatham, 114th Co., to Batl. Comdr., 22 Nov. 1918, USNA, RG45, WA7, B646.

19. Record of the Proceedings of a Superior Provost Court, Sto. Dom., convened 16 Feb. 1920, Trial of Olivorio Carela, USNA, RG38, E6, B36.
20. Capt. Robt. Yowell, El Seibo Barracks, to Batl. Comdr., 14 Sept. 1920, USNA, RG38, E6, B22.
21. Sugar Estate Mgrs. to Mil. Gov. Robison, 4 Oct. 1921, USNA, RG38, E6, B24.
22. Wm. C. Harllee, E. Dist. Comdr., 15th Regt., to Comding. Genl., 25 Jan. 1922, and R. Sánchez González, Civ. Gov., San Pedro de Macorís, to Col. P. M. Rixey, Jr., Int. and Pol., 8 Mar. 1921, USNA, RG38, E6, B48 and BU. Ducoudray, *Los "gavilleros,"* pp. 19–20, notes several similar cases. See also an interview with guerrilla leader Tolete in "Del pasado y del presente: Pedro Celestino del Rosario alias Tolete," *Listín Diario,* 26 Sept. 1926.
23. Wm. O. Rogers, 15th Regt., to Dist. Comdr., 25 Apr. 1919, USNA, RG45, WA7, B645; Maj. Watson, 9th Co., GND, to Comdt., 23 Nov. 1920, USNA, RG38, E6, BU.
24. In 1918 a regional leader of the Horacista party, Basilio Camilo, was accused of connivance with the guerrillas. One of his lawyers, Luis F. Mejía, wrote later that Camilo was sentenced to prison "despite the lack of proof against him" but was pardoned soon afterward. Mejía, *De Lilís,* p. 164.
25. Blanco Fombona, *Crímenes,* p. 122; Pres. and Members, Club Faro de Hicayagua, to Mil. Gov. Thomas Snowden, 25 May 1920, USNA, RG38, E6, B24. I wish to make it clear that the worst of the abuses cited in this chapter were committed by a small percentage of marines. This is irrelevant to the argument, however, which seeks to explain the motivation of the Dominican guerrillas.
26. Marine Corps to Flag Sto. Dom., 17 Mar. 1922, USNA, RG80, CNO Planning, file 159-9; Horace Knowles to U.S. Senator Medill McCormick, 17 Mar. 1922, PFP.
27. Colonel George C. Thorpe notes that Dominican peasants feared the marines' very appearance. See his "American Achievements in Santo Domingo, Haiti and the Virgin Islands," *Journal of International Relations* 11, no. 1 (July 1920): 63–64.
28. Mil. Gov. to Bur. of Navig., 9 Sept. 1920, USNA, RG38, E6, B32, estimates that the majority of naval enlisted men in Santo Domingo had not completed grade school and only a few had begun high school; the figure is probably no higher for the marines. Franck, *Roaming,* pp. 245–246, and Schoenrich, "American Intervention," p. 211, both note the marines' lack of Spanish. Knapp to Sec. Nav., 17 Dec. 1916, USNA, RG45, WA7, B643, reveals his inability to read Spanish. Condit and Turnbladh, in *Hold High the Torch,* note the marines' general unpreparedness for their occupation duties.
29. Snowden to Josephus Daniels, Sec. Nav., 2 June 1920, USNA, RG38, E6, B31.
30. Knapp to Arthur T. Hadley, Pres., Yale Univ., 20 Sept. 1917, USNA,

RG38, E6, BU. A Dominican, Mejía, *De Lilís*, p. 157, noted U.S. racial prejudices. For a fuller description, see Franck, *Roaming*, pp. 239–240. See also Rubin Francis Weston, *Racism in U.S. Imperialism: The Influence of Racial Assumptions on American Foreign Policy, 1893–1946*, especially pp. 209–256.

31. Herbert S. Goold to Phillips, State Dept., 18 Aug. 1918, USNA, 839.00/1051/16; Knapp to Russell, 2 Nov. 1918, USNA, RG45, WA7, B644; Mrs. Helen Leschorn to U.S. Senator Atlee Pomerene, 24 Jan. 1922, enclosed in W. C. MacCrone, Regtl. Intel. Officer, to Brig. Intel. Officer, 25 Mar. 1922, USNA, RG38, E6, B48; Franck, *Roaming*, p. 239. Goold's letter also contained a number of even more serious accusations.

32. J. I. Bowman to Mil. Gov., 21 Dec. 1921, and G. M. Kincade, Prov. Mar., to Mil. Gov., 11 Jan. 1922, USNA, RG38, E6, B37.

33. Finding of Facts, Opinion, and Recommendations of Court of Inquiry convened at Marine Barracks, San Francisco de Macorís, 24 Feb. 1920, USNA, RG38, E6, B38.

34. News Release, 29 Oct. 1921, USNA, RG38, E6, B37, issued by HQ, E. Dist., San Pedro de Macorís, citing the problem of guerrillas "appearing like any other citizen." Franck, *Roaming*, p. 236, also notes this problem.

35. Various documents in the first file of USNA, RG45, WA7, B646.

36. Geo. C. Thorpe, Ch. of Staff, to Brig. Comdr., 29 May 1917, USNA, RG45, WA7, B645, orders house burnings to end. But in Thorpe to 2nd Lt. Wm. A. Buckley, 7 Oct. 1918, USNA, RG45, WA7, B646, Thorpe denounces two subsequent burnings. J. H. Williamson to CO, 15th Regt., 5 July 1919, USMC, Geogr. File, no. 5, openly reports burning houses. Concerning hidden settlements of twenty and thirty to thirty-five houses, one of which was burned, see Capt. R. S. Hunter to Batl. Comdr., 20 Sept. 1918, and H. L. Jones, 33rd Co., to Batl. Comdr., 24 Sept. 1918, USMC, Geogr. File, no. 4.

37. Harllee to Comding. Genl., 25 Jan. 1922, USNA, RG38, E6, B48.

38. Sgt. Morris A. Stout, Jr., 113th Co., to Senior Officer, 16 Oct. 1918, Brig. Comdr. B. H. Fuller to Col. Geo. C. Thorpe, 31 Oct. 1918, and operations report, unsigned, 4 Mar. 1919, filed in "Marine Operations in Santo Domingo, 1919–1924," USNA, RG45, WA7, B645.

39. Record of the Proceedings of a Superior Provost Court, Sto. Dom., convened 16 Feb. 1920, Trial of Olivorio Carela, USNA, RG38, E6, B36; "Ramón Batía dice . . . ," *Listín Diario*, 18 May 1922.

40. U.S., Senate, *Hearings*, vol. 1, pp. 1106–1155, documents a large number of incidents of marine violence against captured guerrillas, suspected guerrillas, and *pacíficos*. Franck, a journalist who spent some time with the marines in the Dominican Republic circa 1920, gives a sketch of marine abuses and suggests some possible motivations for them in *Roaming*, pp. 234–235. "Summary of Exceptional Military Courts in the Dominican Republic from November 29, 1916, to De-

cember 29, 1919," USNA, RG38, E6, B13, shows that military courts tried eighty-five persons during the first three years of the occupation for allegedly concealing information regarding guerrillas or arms.

41. Wm. C. Harllee to Comding. Genl., 25 Jan. 1922, USNA, RG38, E6, B48.
42. Findings of a Court of Inquiry held at El Seibo, 27 Mar. 1918, USNA, RG38, E6, B9.
43. Brig. Genl. B. H. Fuller to CO, 15th Regt., [?] Mar. 1919, USNA, RG38, E6, B19. J. C. Breckinridge, E. Dist. Comdr., to Comding. Genl., 8 June 1920, USMC, Geogr. File, no. 6, notes two such cases in one report.
44. CO, 2nd Batl., 15th Regt., to Dist. Comdr., 28 Sept. 1921, USNA, RG38, E6, B36; Wm. C. Harllee to Comding. Genl., 2 Jan. 1922, USNA, 839.00/2502.
45. 1st Lt. Allan S. Heaton, 2nd Batl., 15th Regt., to Brig. Comdr., 11 June 1919, USNA, RG45, WA7, B645.
46. Julio Peynado to Horace Knowles, 22 Apr. 1922, PFP.
47. Lt. Col. Henry C. Davis, Dist. Comdr., "Public Notice," 10 May 1921, USNA, RG38, E6, B36.
48. Schoenrich, "American Intervention," p. 212.
49. Blanco Fombona, *Crímenes*, pp. 123–124.
50. Finding of Facts, Opinion, and Recommendations of Court of Inquiry convened at Marine Barracks, San Francisco de Macorís, 24 Feb. 1920, USNA, RG38, E6, B38.
51. Col. C. M. Perkins, Brig. Law Officer, to Brig. Comdr. Logan Feland, 1 May 1920, USNA, RG38, E6, B38. Mejía, one of Pelegrín Castillo's lawyers, describes the case in *De Lilís*, p. 172. A provost court eventually acquitted Castillo; Logan Feland to Sec. Nav., 24 July 1920, and Perkins to Lt. Col. C. B. Taylor, 4 Mar. 1921, USNA, RG38, E6, B27 and 38.
52. José María Hernández to Genl. Head of the Marines and Internal Revenue [*sic*], [?] Jan. 1921, attached to Mil. Gov. to Comding. Genl., 4 Feb. 1921, and Report of Investigation concerning José María Hernández, Feliz, La Romana Section, 26 Feb. 1921, USNA, RG38, E6, B34 and 35. See also the affidavit of Luis Bautista, Hato Mayor, 14 Dec. 1921, AGN, P37.
53. Officer Walter J. Sheard to Comdt., GND, 8 June 1918, USNA, RG38, E6, BU.
54. Sworn and notarized statement concerning the case of José Cepeda, signed and witnessed, 31 May 1920, HyC.
55. Comding. Genl. Charles G. Long to Mil. Gov., 11 Jan. 1921, USNA, RG38, E6, B38.
56. Knapp to CO, 2nd Prov. Brig., 14 June 1918, and Josephus Daniels to Brig. Comdr. Pendleton, 9 July 1917, USNA, RG38, E6, B6 and 4.
57. Henry C. Davis, S. Dist. Comdr., to Mil. Gov., 13 May 1922, USNA, RG38, E6, B49.
58. Wm. C. Harllee, E. Dist. Comdr., 25 Jan. 1922, USNA, RG38, E6, B48.
59. Knapp to Brig. Comdr., Confidential, 17 Oct. 1918, USNA, RG38, E6, B6.
60. G. C. Thorpe, Batl. Comdr., to Regtl. Comdr., 9 Oct. 1918, USNA, RG45, WA7, B646; Snowden to Josephus Daniels, 2 June 1920, USNA, RG38, E6,

B31. Merkel's crimes are documented in U.S., Senate, *Hearings*, vol. 1, pp. 1117–1147.
61. F. A. Ramsey, 2nd Prov. Brig., to Mil. Gov., 4 Sept. 1917, USNA, RG38, E6, B1.
62. Knapp to Brig. Comdr., 21 Oct. 1921, USNA, RG45, WA7, B646.
63. C. M. Ledger, HBM Chargé d'Affaires, to Mil. Gov., Note No. 79, 4 Nov. 1921, and attached letters and Report of Investigation, USNA, RG38, E6, B37.
64. U.S., Senate, *Hearings*, vols. 1 and 2.

6. GUERRILLA WAR IN THE EAST: THE FIRST YEARS

1. Flag Olympia to Sec. Nav., 11 Jan. 1917, USNA, 839.00/1978. Urbano Gilbert was later tried and convicted of murder by a military commission and sentenced to be hanged. Upon review, his penalty was reduced to life imprisonment. Judge Advocate Genl. to CO, 2nd Prov. Brig., 2 Aug. 1918, USNA, RG38, E6, B7. Urbano Gilbert later wrote of the attack, his flight, arrest, and imprisonment in *Mi lucha*.
2. Flag Olympia to Sec. Nav., 11 Jan. 1917, USNA, 839.00/1978; Bearss to USS *New Hampshire*, 11 Jan. 1917, USNA, RG45, WA7, B647.
3. USS *New Hampshire* to USS *Olympia*, 13 Jan. 1917, USNA, RG45, WA7, B647; Flag Olympia to Sec. Nav., 12 Jan. 1917, USNA, 839.00/1979.
4. USS *New Hampshire* to USS *Olympia*, 13 and 15 Jan. 1917, USNA, RG45, WA7, B647.
5. Flag New Hampshire to Sec. Nav., 25 Jan. 1917, USNA, 839.00/1988. Bearss to Brig. Comdr., 2 Feb. 1917, USMC, Geogr. File, no. 3, reports talks with "Mrs. Chachá" leading to Chachá's surrender, trial, and release on suspended sentence.
6. Lt. Col. George C. Thorpe, CO, 3rd Prov. Regt., to Brig. Comdr., 8 July 1917, USNA, RG45, WA7, B646. Thorpe's claims are corroborated by the Dominican historian Mejía, *De Lilís*, p. 115. 2nd Lt. Nimmo Old to Dist. Comdr., 30 Mar. 1917, AGN, P23, is one of the first reports on Natera.
7. USS *New Hampshire* to Sec. Nav., 28 Jan. 1917, USNA, 839.00/1990; Bearss to Brig. Comdr., 2 Feb. 1917, USMC, Geogr. File, no. 3; Thorpe to Brig. Comdr., 8 July 1917, USNA, RG45, WA7, B646; McClellan, "Operations Ashore," p. 244.
8. Thorpe to Mil. Gov., 2 Apr. 1917, USNA, RG45, WA7, B645. At the time of Chachá's surrender, Vicentico had only eleven active followers according to Urbano Gilbert, *Mi lucha*, p. 65.
9. Thorpe to Brig. Comdr., 29 May 1917, USNA, RG45, WA7, B645.
10. Sworn declaration of Livio H. Sánchez and seven others in National Popular Government League, *Bulletin*, no. 73, PFP; Thad T. Taylor to CO, 11 Mar. 1917, USMC, Geogr. File, no. 3. Col. Rufus H. Lane to Brig. Comdr., 6 July 1917, and attached corres., USNA, RG38, E6, B1, reveals that these activities soon resulted in serious accusations against U.S. officers, but a marine investigation found all the charges without merit.

11. H. C. Davis, CO, 1st Batl., to Regtl. Comdr., 1 June 1917, USNA, RG45, WA7, B646; D. B. Roben, CO, 1st Co., to CO, 3rd Regt., 2 Feb. 1917, and H. I. Bearss to Brig. Comdr., 2 Feb. 1917, USMC, Geogr. File, no. 3.

12. D. B. Roben, CO, 44th Co., to Regtl. Comdr., 30 July 1917, USNA, RG45, WA7, B646. Guerrilla attacks on two local officials are noted in Thorpe to Brig. Comdr., 29 May 1917, USNA, RG45, WA7, B645. Vicentico burned the houses of two others; Gov. Civ. Octavio Beras, El Seibo, to Dept. of Int. and Pol., 21 Mar. 1917, USMC, Geogr. File, no. 3. Ducoudray, *Los "gavilleros,"* pp. 29–33 and 55–59, notes instances of cooperation between local officials and the marines.

13. Thorpe to Brig. Comdr., 8 July 1917, USNA, RG45, WA7, B646; Knapp, Memorandum, 22 May 1918, AGN, P119.

14. Thorpe to Brig. Comdr., 18 July 1917, AGN, P4; Thomas K. Debevoise of Rounds, Hatch, Dillingham, and Debevoise, N.Y.C., to Frank L. Polk, St. Dept., 17 May 1917, and Memorial, Ann Bradshaw Miller to Sec. St., 30 July 1917, USNA, RG38, E6, B1 and 7.

15. Roben, CO, 44th Co., to Regtl. Comdr., 30 July 1917, and Davis, CO, 1st Batl., to Regtl. Comdr., 1 June 1917, USNA, RG45, WA7, B646; Knapp to Ch. of Nav. Op., 16 June 1917, USNA, RG38, E6, B1.

16. 2nd Lt. Harold S. Fassett, 44th Co., to Regtl. Comdr., 11 June 1917, USNA, RG38, E6, B1.

17. Davis to Regtl. Comdr., 1 June 1917, USNA, RG45, WA7, B646.

18. Roben to Regtl. Comdr., 30 July 1917, USNA, RG45, WA7, B646.

19. Knapp to Ch. of Nav. Op., 16 June 1917, USNA, RG38, E6, B1; Thorpe to Brig. Comdr., 8 July 1917, USNA, RG45, WA7, B646; E. L. Klock, Mgr., Central Romana, to Mil. Gov., 17 May 1918, AGN, P30.

20. Davis to Regtl. Comdr., 1 June 1917, USNA, RG45, WA7, B646.

21. Thorpe to Brig. Comdr., 8 July 1917, USNA, RG45, WA7, B646.

22. Thorpe to Brig. Comdr., 29 May 1917, and Lorenzo Semple of Coudert Bros., Counsellors at Law, to Genl. C. H. Lauchheimer, USMC, Washington, 17 Sept. 1918, USNA, RG45, WA7, B646 and 647; Marion Landais, Mgr., Santa Fe Plantation and Sugar Co., to Frank H. Vedder, 19 June 1917, and Frank Garnett, Mgr., Porvenir Sugar Co., to Vedder, 19 June 1917, USNA, RG38, E6, B1.

23. Thorpe to Brig. Comdr., 29 May 1917, USNA, RG45, WA7, B645.

24. Thorpe to Brig. Comdr., 8 July 1917, USNA, RG45, WA7, B646. On the total failure to control units in the field, see Henry C. Davis to Comding. Genl., 30 Dec. 1921, USMC, Geogr. File, no. 10.

25. Antonio Draiby to Knapp, 20 and 22 Aug. 1917, and attached corres., AGN, P30. In 1918 marines commanded by Merkel and Taylor imprisoned and murdered Agapito José. Attachment to Mil. Gov. S. S. Robison to Sen. Medill McCormick, USMC, Geogr. File, no. 10.

26. Knapp to Sec. Nav., 14 July 1917, USNA, RG45, WA7, B646.

27. Knapp to Sec. Nav., 14 July 1917, USNA, RG45, WA7, B646.

28. Statement of Henry C. Davis, USMC, contained in U.S. Senate, *Hearings*, vol. 1, p. 1109; Thorpe to Brig. Comdr., 8 July 1917, USNA, RG45, WA7, B646.

29. Thorpe to Brig. Comdr., 8 July 1917, USNA, RG45, WA7, B646; Arturo Logroño to Robison, 11 Aug. 1922, AGN, P109; Rufino Martínez, *Diccionario biográfico-histórico dominicano, 1821–1930*, p. 439.
30. Franck, *Roaming*, p. 236.
31. Record of Proceedings of a Board of Investigation convened at Marine Barracks, San Pedro de Macorís, D.R., to inquire into the circumstances connected with the killing of Vicentico Evangelista, 7 July 1917, USNA, RG38, E6, B4. The journalist Franck, who befriended various marines, presents two possible versions of the murder; see *Roaming*, p. 237. Blanco Fombona, *Crímenes*, p. 38, reports still another version. See also MacMichael, "The United States," p. 462.
32. J. H. Pendleton, Brig. Comdr., to Mil. Gov., 5 Jan. 1918, and Knapp to Judge Advocate Genl. of the Navy, 10 Jan. 1918, USNA, RG45, WA7, B644.
33. Quarterly Report of Provost Prisoners confined at the Cárcel Pública, Sto. Dom. City, D.R., during the Quarter ending 31 Mar. 1924, and Mil. Gov. Harry Lee to CO, Cárcel Pública, Fort Ozama, Sto. Dom. City, 1 July 1924, USNA, RG38, E6, B74.
34. Franck, *Roaming*, pp. 237–238.
35. Col. Carl Gamborg-Andresen, CO, 3rd Prov. Regt., to Brig. Comdr., 27 Feb. 1919, USNA, RG45, WA7, B645; Rounds, Hatch, Dillingham, and Debevoise, N.Y.C., to State Dept., 17 July 1917, USNA, RG38, E6, B1; Thorpe to Brig. Comdr., 18 July 1917, AGN, P4.
36. Thorpe to Brig. Comdr., 8 July 1917, USNA, RG45, WA7, B646; Herbert S. Goold, Chargé, American Legation, Sto. Dom., to Sec. St., 27 July 1917, *Foreign Relations, 1917*, p. 709. For documents detailing marine pursuit of these individuals, see USMC, Geogr. File, no. 2, especially "Synopsis—Santo Domingo, 15 May 1916."
37. Thorpe to Brig. Comdr., 18 July 1917, AGN, P4; Wm. N. McKelvey, Brig. Comdr., to Mil. Gov., 24 Sept. 1917, and Acting Capt. W. H. West, GND, to Acting Comdt., GND, 17 Aug. 1917, USNA, RG38, E6, B1.
38. Knapp to Sec. Nav., 26 Sept. 1917, USNA, RG38, E6, BU.
39. 2nd Lt. F. D. Harbaugh, 32nd Co. Det., Sánchez, 30 May 1918, and anonymous "operator" to Maj. D. M. Randall, Intel., 3 June 1918, USNA, RG38, E6, B6 and 8. Many 1918 reports of operations are found in USMC, Geogr. File, no. 4, and a few are found in AGN, P25 and 119.
40. Thad T. Taylor, Inspector, to Dir., GND, 19 Mar. 1918, AGN, P119. Bartolo Cabrera and Francisco Fulgencio operated with Trinidad.
41. Quarterly Report of the Mil. Gov. to Sec. Nav., 6 Apr. 1918, USNA, RG38, E15; Wm. N. McKelvey, CO, 4th Prov. Regt., to Brig. Comdr., 10 June 1918, USNA, RG38, E6, B6.
42. Confidential Report, Brig. Comdr. Pendleton to Maj. Genl. Comdt., 3 June 1918, USNA, RG45, WA7, B646. Concerning Taylor's atrocities and transfer, see Mil. Gov. to Brig. Comdr., 17 May 1918, AGN, P22 and a file on him in P119.
43. Thorpe to Regtl. Comdr., 25 July 1918, USNA, RG45, WA7, B646; James J. McLean, Dir., S. Dist., GND, Report, 6 Oct. 1919, USNA, RG38, E6, B40.

44. Thorpe to Regtl. Comdr., 9 Aug. 1918, USNA, RG45, WA7, B646; Vetilio Alfau Durán, *Marcial Guerrero, héroe y mártir, 1888–1918*, pp. 7–8.
45. James J. McLean, Dir., S. Dist., GND, Report, 6 Oct. 1918, USNA, RG38, E6, B40; Lorenzo Semple to Maj. Genl. George Barnett, 3 Oct. 1918, USNA, RG45, WA7, B647.
46. [Alvin B. Kemp], "Private Kemp Reports on Our War in Santo Domingo," *Literary Digest*, 22 Feb. 1919, pp. 105–108.
47. Thorpe to Regtl. Comdr., 8 Sept. 1918, USNA, RG38, E6, B6; Lorenzo Semple, quoting H. W. Turner, to Maj. Genl. George Barnett, 3 Oct. 1918, USNA, RG45, WA7, B647.
48. 1st Lt. C. C. Simmons to Batl. Comdr., 1st Batl., 14 Aug. 1918, USNA, RG45, WA7, B646.
49. Asst. Surg. Herbert L. Shinn, USN, to CO, 33rd Co., 11 Sept. 1918, USNA, RG38, E6, BU.
50. C. A. Broadelus, Regtl. Surg., 3rd Regt., to Bur. of Medicine and Surgery, Dept. Nav., 29 Jan 1919, USNA, RG38, E6, B13.
51. Russell to Sec. St., 24 Aug. 1918, USNA, RG45, WA7, B644.
52. Consuelo Sugar Co. to A. T. Bass, Bartram Bros., 12 Aug. 1918, USNA, RG45, WA7, B647.
53. Confid. Report, Pendleton to Maj. Genl. Comdt., 3 June 1918, and Thorpe to Regtl. Comdr., 9 Aug. 1918, USNA, RG45, WA7, B646.
54. Thorpe to Regtl. Comdr., 9 Aug. and 4 Sept. 1918, and Thorpe, "Secret Instructions for Troops in the Field against Bandits," issued for the campaign of 24 Aug. 1918, USNA, RG45, WA7, B646.
55. Thorpe, Campaign Order No. 1, HQ, 1st Batl., 3rd Prov. Regt., n.d. but received by 33rd Co., Las Pajas, 20 Aug. 1918, USNA, RG45, WA7, B646.
56. Thorpe, Campaign Order No. 2, 4 Sept. 1918, USNA, RG45, WA7, B644. Franck, *Roaming*, p. 236, claims that "those who were shot were chiefly honest, simple peasants" unaware of the marines' operation.
57. Thorpe to P. M. Bannon, Regtl. Comdr., 3 Oct. 1918, and Pendleton, by R. S. Kingsbury, to Mil. Gov., 9 Oct. 1918, USNA, RG45, WA7, B644; *Términos para entregarse los bandidos en la República Dominicana* (broadside), hand-dated 12 Sept. 1918, CRD.
58. Thorpe to Regtl. Comdr., 4 Sept. 1918, USNA, RG45, WA7, B646.
59. Lorenzo Semple to Maj. Genl. Comdt. George Barnett, 20 Sept. and 3 Oct. 1918, USNA, RG45, WA7, B647; R. Sánchez González, Gob. Civ., 31 Aug. 1918, cited in Ducoudray, *Los "gavilleros,"* p. 28.
60. Antonio Sarmiento to Gobernador Militar S. S. Robison, 11 Sept. 1922, USNA, RG38, E6, B50; Julio Peynado to Horace Knowles, 22 Apr. 1922, PFP.
61. The cedula system and its pitfalls are discussed in Thorpe to Regtl. Comdr., 3 Oct. 1918, USNA, RG45, WA7, B644. Its complete failure is pronounced by Col. C. Gamborg-Andresen, CO, 3rd Prov. Regt., to Brig. Comdr., 27 Feb. 1919, USNA, RG45, WA7, B646. See also Ducoudray, *Los "gavilleros,"* pp. 29–33.
62. For example, see Vedder to Roosevelt, 14 Oct. 1918, Ch. of Nav. Op. to Mil. Gov., 19 Oct. 1918, and Knapp to Ch. of Nav. Op., 19 Oct. 1918,

USNA, RG80, CNO Planning, file 24 to 24-19 (corres. 1917–1919); Thorpe to Brig. Comdr., 21 Oct. 1918, USNA, RG45, WA7, B647. See also the extensive related material in USNA, 839.6135/6.

63. Reports of Operations for 19 Oct. and 21 Nov. 1918, Mil. Gov. Knapp to Ch. of Nav. Op., USNA, RG80, CNO Planning, file 24 to 24-19 (corres. 1917–1919).

64. Exec. Order No. 226, 15 Nov. 1918, R.D., *Colección, 1918*, pp. 236–237; Exec. Order No. 268, 25 Feb. 1919, R.D., *Colección, 1919*, p. 23.

65. Knapp to Maj. Genl. Comdt., USMC, 27 Jan. 1919, USNA, RG38, E6, B19.

66. Fuller and Cosmas, *Marines*, p. 28. Mil. Gov. Harry Lee to Sec. Nav., 19 May 1924, USNA, RG38, E6, B74, reports a greatly exaggerated "estimate" of 350 guerrillas killed or wounded by the Third Provisional Regiment. He also reports lower strength levels for the Fifteenth Regiment.

67. Col. C. Gamborg-Andresen to Brig. Comdr., 27 Feb. 1919, USNA, RG45, WA7, B645.

68. Col. J. C. Breckinridge, Dist. Comdr., to Brig. Comdr., 2 May 1919, USNA, RG45, WA7, B645.

69. Wm. O. Rogers, CO, 182nd Co., to Dist. Comdr., 2 May 1919, USNA, RG45, WA7, B645.

70. 2nd Lt. F. C. Biebush, Report, 24 Apr. 1919, and related reports filed in "Marine Operations in Santo Domingo, 1919–1924," USNA, RG45, WA7, B645. In the Quarterly Report of the Military Governor, 1 Apr. to 30 June 1919, USNA, RG38, E15, Snowden claimed that "several subchiefs and their followers" surrendered, although no other documents record such incidents.

71. 1st Lt. John C. Wishon, GND, to Dist. Comdr., 25 Apr. 1919, USNA, RG45, WA7, B645.

72. Breckinridge to Brig. Comdr., 2 May 1919, USNA, RG45, WA7, B645.

73. Josephus Daniels to Snowden, 11 May and 23 Dec. 1920, and Snowden to Sec. Nav., 2 June 1920 and 5 Feb. 1921, USNA, RG38, E6, B21, 31, and 43.

74. Breckinridge to Brig. Comdr., 2 and 12 May 1919, USNA, RG45, WA7, B645; Quarterly Report of the Military Governor, 1 Apr. to 30 June 1919, USNA, RG38, E15.

75. Wm. O. Rogers, CO, 182nd Co., 15th Regt., to Dist. Comdr., 24 Apr. 1919, USNA, RG45, WA7, B645.

7. GUERRILLA WAR IN THE EAST: STALEMATE AND RESOLUTION

1. V. E. Stack, Acting Regtl. Comdr., 4th Regt., Santiago, to Brig. Comdr., 24 May 1919, USNA, RG38, E6, B20.

2. Brig. Spec. Order No. 13 by B. H. Fuller, 12 June 1919, USNA, RG38, E6, BU.

3. Mil. Gov. Snowden to Sec. Nav., 8 May 1919, USNA, RG80, CNO Planning, file C24 to 24-19 (corres. 1917–1919); 2nd Lt. Warren F. Hamet, 182nd Co., to Dist. Comdr., 15 June 1919, USMC, Geogr. File, no. 5.

4. Brig. Comdr. B. H. Fuller to Mil. Gov., Report for Quarter Ending 30 June 1919, USNA, RG45, WA7, B645. Various reports of 1919 operations are found in USMC, Geogr. File, no. 5.

5. 2nd Lt. F. C. Biebush to Comdr., Las Pajas, 20 May 1919, USNA, RG45, WA7, B645.

6. Fuller to Mil. Gov., Report for Quarter Ending 30 June 1919, USNA, RG45, WA7, B645.

7. Co. report, sender unidentified, in file entitled "Marine Operations, 1916–1918," USNA, RG45, WA7, B646.

8. Maj. T. E. Watson to Batl. Comdr., 24 Mar. 1919, USNA, RG45, WA7, B645.

9. Miguel Angel Paulino to Mil. Gov. Snowden, 12 Apr. 1919, and accompanying corres. in file 9, USNA, RG38, E6, B13; Wm. C. Harllee to Comding. Genl., 8 Dec. 1921, AGN, P116. See also Arthur J. Burks' autobiographical *Land of Checkerboard Families*. Burks, a marine second lieutenant, organized a spy network.

10. The report concerning Cibahuete, dated 5 Mar. 1919, and others are in the file entitled "Marine Operations in Santo Domingo, 1919–1924," USNA, RG45, WA7, B645.

11. See various reports in the file entitled "Marine Operations in Santo Domingo, 1919–1924," USNA, RG45, WA7, B645.

12. See various reports in the file entitled "Marine Operations in Santo Domingo, 1919–1924," USNA, RG45, WA7, B645.

13. Antonio Sarmiento to Gobernador Militar S. S. Robison, 11 Sept. 1922, USNA, RG38, E6, B50.

14. P. J. Lapais, Central Quisqueya, to Snowden, 1 July 1919, AGN, P101. About the same time guerrillas kidnapped a planter and a judge, later releasing them; Russell to Sec. St., 14 June and 3 July 1919, USNA, 839.00/2139 and 2141.

15. G. Goicoechea, Vice-Pres., Junta de Agric., to Adm. Snowden, 14 Jan. 1920, and Capt. C. M. Marshall, Office of the Dist. Prov. Mar., to Dist. Comdr., 8 Nov. 1920, USNA, RG38, E6, B23.

16. Ducoudray, *Los "gavilleros,"* argues the latter thesis throughout his essays; see especially pp. 15–16, 51–54, and 61–64.

17. Co. reports, 1918, file, USNA, RG45, WA7, B646. The marines explained the incidents of citizens joining the guerrillas as forced recruiting.

18. Description of Juan José José, reported by Wm. C. Harllee in Information Memorandum, 15th Regt., 2nd Brig., 26 Jan. [1922], USNA, RG38, E6, B48. This document is misdated 1921.

19. Record of the Proceedings of a Superior Provost Court, Sto. Dom., convened 16 Feb. 1920, Trial of Olivorio Carela, and F. A. Ramsey, GND, to Brig. Intel. Officer, 17 Dec. 1920, USNA, RG38, E6, B36 and 40.

20. 1st Lt. John C. Wishon, GND, to Dist. Comdr., 25 Apr. 1919, and report of an unnamed informer, 23 Apr. 1919, in file entitled "Marine Operations in Santo Domingo, 1919–1924," USNA, RG45, WA7, B645.

21. 2nd Lt. Manson C. Carpenter to CO, 1st Marine Aviation Force, Squad-

ron D, Consuelo, 25 July 1919, USNA, RG45, WA7, B645. See also 2nd Lt. H. N. Miller to CO, 11 June 1919, USMC, Geogr. File, no. 5.

22. V. E. Stack, Acting Regtl. Comdr., 4th Regt., Santiago, to Brig. Comdr., 24 May 1919, USNA, RG38, E6, B20. Report on the 1st Air Squadron, Marine Aviation Force, [1921?], USMC, Geogr. File, no. 7.

23. Mil. Gov. to C. P. Comerford Co., Lowell, Mass., 30 Jan. 1920, and Snowden to Brig. Comdr., 30 Jan. 1920, USNA, RG38, E6, B23; Mil. Gov. to Ch. of Nav. Op., 17 Jan. and 2 July 1920, and R. E. Coontz, Ch. of Nav. Op., to Mil. Gov., 21 July 1920, USNA, RG45, WA7, B645. Various reports of 1920 marine operations are found in USMC, Geogr. File, no. 6, including Comding. Genl. Logan Feland to Maj. Genl. Comdt., USMC, 19 Oct. 1920, who recorded forty-two marine-guerrilla engagements from January to September 1920.

24. Mil. Gov. to Comding Genl. Feland, 24 Mar. 1920, and B. H. Fuller, Int. and Pol., 25 Mar. 1920, USNA, RG38, E6, B23; Ley sobre Guardas Campestres, 26 June 1907, R.D., *Gaceta Oficial*, 1 Mar. 1911. Concerning the Central Romana force, see Exec. Order No. 107, 17 Dec. 1917, R.D., *Colección, 1917*, pp. 110–111; E. L. Klock, Mgr., Central Romana, Inc., to Mil. Gov., 17 May 1918, and Genl. Pendleton, Brig. Comdr., to Mil. Gov., 12 Dec. 1917, AGN, P30.

25. E. Dist. Comdr. Harllee to Comding. Genl., 2 Jan. 1922, USNA, 839.00/2502, estimated yearly payments at about one thousand dollars per estate. Concerning the military government's acquiescence, see S. R. Ginsberg, Banco Territorial y Agrícola de Puerto Rico, to R. U. Strong, Legal Officer, Mil. Govt., 19 Apr. 1922, and Mil. Gov. Samuel S. Robison to Comding. Genl., 2nd Brig., 26 Apr. 1922, USNA, RG38, E6, B49. See also Comding. Genl. to Mil. Gov., 7 Oct. 1922, USNA, RG38, E6, B24.

26. *Listín Diario*, 20 Dec. 1920.

27. Report of U.S. Legation, Sto. Dom., 9 Oct. 1921, quoted in Sec. St. to British Chargé Brooks, 7 July 1924, *Foreign Relations, 1924*, vol. 1, p. 688. See also 1st Lt. Allan S. Heaton, 2nd Batl., 15th Regt., to Brig. Comdr., 11 June 1919, and Lt. Col. Breckinridge, Dist. Comdr., to Brig. Comdr., 18 June 1919, USNA, RG45, WA7, B645.

28. Mil. Gov. to C. M. Mendenhall, N.Y.C., 10 Sept. 1920, and Capt. Robt. Yowell, El Seibo Barracks, to Batl. Comdr., 14 Sept. 1920, USNA, RG38, E6, B22.

29. Wm. C. Harllee, E. Dist. Comdr., to Comding. Genl., 25 Jan. 1922, USNA, RG38, E6, B48; Franck, *Roaming*, p. 244.

30. Report on Municipalities, 1920, p. 50, AGN, P69; Maj. Watson, 9th Co., GND, to Comdt., 23 Nov. 1920, USNA, RG38, E6, BU.

31. Quarterly Report of the Military Governor, 1 Apr. to 30 June 1919. USNA, RG38, E15; J. C. Breckinridge, Comdt., GND, to Comding. Genl., 13 Dec. 1920, USNA, RG45, WA7, B646.

32. Memorandum on Public Works, attached to Mil. Gov. Robison to Sec. Nav., 27 Dec. 1921, USNA, RG38, E6, B44. Robison, the former com-

mander of the Boston Navy Yard, assumed the duties of military governor on 3 June 1921.

33. Sec. Nav. Curtis D. Wilbur to Mil. Gov., 22 Apr. 1924, Comding. Genl. Harry Lee to Mil. Gov., 7 Oct. 1921, and Gob. Civ. de Samaná to Int. and Pol., 7 Apr. 1921, USNA, RG38, E6, B74, 24, and 55.

34. Col. Comdt., GND, to Comding. Genl., [?] Mar. 1921, and Lt. Comdr. R. M. Warfield to Mil. Gov., 4 Apr. 1921, USNA, RG38, E6, B35.

35. G. Lewis, Dir. Genl. of Internal Rev., to Sec. of Finance, Memorandum, n.d. but circa 1 Sept. 1921, and CO, 2nd Batl., to Dist. Comdr., 28 Sept. 1921, USNA, RG38, E6, B36.

36. Gov. R. Sánchez González to Col. P. M. Rixey, Int. and Pol. 8 Mar. 1921, and F. H. Vedder to Rixey, 25 Jan. 1921, USNA, RG38, E6, BU and B34.

37. A. T. Marix, Sec. St. for Justice and Public Instr., to Mil. Gov., 9 Feb. 1921, USNA, RG38, E6, B34.

38. A. C. Geddes, Ambassador of Gt. Brit., to Sec. St., 21 Dec. 1921, *Foreign Relations, 1922,* vol. 2, p. 95. Knight, *The Americans,* p. 117, reports another kidnapping, that of Ramón Reyes of the Las Pajas estate on 27 August 1921, but no military government papers on this incident have been found.

39. Natera to Sugar Estate Mgrs. (translated copy), 30 Sept. 1921, and Sugar Estate Mgrs. to Robison, 4 Oct. 1921, AGN, P37; Sugar Estate Mgrs. to Ramón Natera, 4 Oct. 1921, USNA, RG38, E6, B24.

40. Lee to Sec. Nav., 19 May 1924, USNA, RG38, E6, B74.

41. Comding. Genl. to Mil. Gov., 7 Oct. 1921, quoting Orders of the Comding. Genl., 29 Sept. 1921, USNA, RG38, E6, B24.

42. Lee to Maj. Genl. Comdt., 24 Aug. 1922, USNA, RG45, WA7, B645; News Release, HQ, E. Dist., San Pedro de Macorís, 29 Oct. 1921, USNA, RG38, E6, B37.

43. James Maguire, Brig. Intel. Off., to Comding. Genl., 17 Oct. 1921, and list of intelligence vouchers enclosed in 1st Lt. Julian N. Frisbee, Brig. Intel. Off., to Mil. Gov., 20 May 1920, USNA, RG38, E6, B48 and 22. Burks, *Land of Checkerboard Families,* p. 159, notes that he paid only one of his agents more than fifteen dollars per month.

44. C. J. Miller, Brig. Intel. Off., to Lt. Comdr. Lake, 14 Oct. 1921, and News Releases, HQ, E. Dist., San Pedro de Macorís, 29 Oct. and 3 Nov. 1921, USNA, RG38, E6, B37.

45. P. M. Santana F., Síndico Municipal, and fourteen other citizens of Los Llanos to Robison, 7 Nov. 1921, and C. C. Riner, GND, to Robison, 1 Nov. 1921, AGN, P72. Harllee was eventually court-martialed and acquitted for his failure to report and/or investigate several cases of abuse during the 1921 to 1922 campaign. See "Case of Lt. Col. Wm. C. Harllee," 11 Sept. 1922, USNA, RG38, E6, B52.

46. Fabio Fiallo to Robison, 2 Nov. 1921, AGN, P72; Harllee to Comding. Genl., 16 Nov. 1921, USNA, RG38, E6, BU; Harllee to Comding. Genl., 2 Jan. 1922, USNA, 839.00/2502.

47. Memorandum, Mil. Gov. to Comding. Genl., 2 Nov. 1921, USNA, RG38, E6, B37.
48. News Release, HQ, E. Dist., 3 Nov. 1921, USNA, RG38, E6, B37.
49. Robison to Maj. Genl. Comdt. John A. Lejeune, 25 Oct. 1921, and Confid. Report, L. McNamee, Dir. of Nav. Intel., to Mr. Hurley, St. Dept., Mil. Intel. Div., 8 Feb. 1922, USNA, RG45, WA7, B646.
50. C. J. Miller to Lt. Comdr. Lake, 14 Oct. 1921, and James Maguire, Brig. Intel. Off., to Sec. St. for Justice and Public Instr., 15 Oct. 1921, USNA, RG38, E6, B37.
51. L. H. Moses, Int. and Pol., to Mil. Gov., 24 Oct. 1921, and C. H. Lyman, CO, 4th Regt., to Comding. Genl., 10 Dec. 1921, USNA, RG38, E6, B37 and 48.
52. Maj. Kincade, Intel. Off., 15th Regt., to Comding. Genl., n.d. but text of letter indicates circa 1 Nov. 1921, USNA, RG38, E6, B37.
53. Information Memorandum, HQ, 15th Regt., to Comding. Genl., 12 Oct. 1921, USNA, RG38, E6, B37; L. McNamee to Hurley, 8 Feb. 1922, USNA, RG45, WA7, B646. Guerrillas apparently manufactured much of their own ammunition.
54. Harllee to Comding. Genl., 2 Jan. 1922, USNA, 839.00/2502; Harllee to Comding. Genl., 25 Jan. 1922, USNA, RG38, E6, B48.
55. Information Memorandum, Wm. C. Harllee, HQ, 15th Regt., 26 Jan. [1922], USNA, RG38, E6, B48. Document misdated 1921.
56. Civ. Gov. of Sto. Dom. to Int. and Pol., 11 Jan. 1922, Gob. Civ. de San Pedro de Macorís to Int. and Pol., 30 Jan. 1922, and Augusto Percy, Pres. of Ayunt., Sabana de la Mar, to Int. and Pol., 14 Feb. 1922, USNA, RG38, E6, B48. Wm. H. Ford, Jefe de Agrimensores, to Fomento y Comunicaciones, Quarterly Reports, 31 Mar. and 30 June 1922, USNA, RG38, E6, B75.
57. Confid. Report of Op., no. 1, 15 Feb. 1922, USNA, RG38, E6, B48. Harllee to Comding. Genl., 12 Mar. 1922, AGN, P69, reports at length on Draiby's services to the marines. Guerrillas under Martín Peguero finally killed Draiby on 22 April 1922; Mil. Gov. to Comding. Genl., 15 May 1922, and attached corres., USNA, RG38, E6, B49.
58. Confid. Report of Op., no. 1, 15 Feb. 1922, USNA, RG38, E6, B48.
59. Lee to Maj. Genl. Comdt., 24 Aug. 1922, USNA, RG45, WA7, B645.
60. Harllee to Comding. Genl., 25 Jan. 1922, USNA, RG38, E6, B48.
61. Condit and Turnbladh, *Hold High the Torch*, p. 92.
62. Juan Francisco Sánchez to L. H. Moses, Int. and Pol., 18 Oct. 1921, USNA, RG38, E6, B37.
63. Lee to Mil. Gov., 4 Nov. 1921, USNA, RG38, E6, B37.
64. Lyman to Comding. Genl., 10 Dec. 1921, USNA, RG38, E6, B48.
65. Carlos V. de León to Robison, 19 Oct. 1921, USNA, RG38, E6, BU.
66. Memorandum, Mil. Gov. to Comding. Genl., 2 Nov. 1921, and Lee to Mil. Gov., 8 Nov. 1921, USNA, RG38, E6, B37.
67. Lee to Mil. Gov., 14 Nov. 1921, and Robison to Comding. Genl., 28 Nov. 1921, USNA, RG38, E6, B37.

68. "Exposición que hace el Congreso Nacionalista del Seybo al país y al gobierno interventor," Ligas Patrióticas and the Juntas Nacionalistas of El Seibo, San Pedro de Macorís, El Jovero, Hato Mayor, Ramón Santana, Higüey, and La Romana, 23 Nov. 1921, USNA, RG38, E6, B40.
69. Information Memorandum, Wm. C. Harllee, HQ, 15th Regt., 26 Jan. [1922], USNA, RG38, E6, B48. Document misdated 1921.
70. Lee to Maj. Genl. Comdt., 24 Aug. 1922, USNA, RG45, WA7, B645.
71. L. McNamee to Hurley, Confid. Summary of Intel., Sto. Dom., 1–20 Apr. 1922, USNA, RG38, E6, BU.
72. Lee to Maj. Genl. Comdt., 24 Aug. 1922, USNA, RG45, WA7, B645.
73. Lee to Mil. Gov., 22 May 1923, USNA, RG38, E6, B64; Cable, 15th [Regt.], Macorís, to Sec. Brig., 9 Apr. 1922, USNA, RG45, WA7, B645.
74. Lee to Robison, 5 May 1922, USNA, RG45, WA7, B645; Lee to Mil. Gov., 22 May 1923, and Confid. Report of Op., no. 5, for May 1922, by Comding. Genl. Harry Lee, 19 June 1922, USNA, RG38, E6, B64 and 48.
75. Lee to Mil. Gov., 22 May 1923, USNA, RG38, E6, B64.
76. Lee to Mil. Gov., 22 May 1923, USNA, RG38, E6, B64.
77. Arzobispo Nouel and Sebastián Leite de Vasconcellos, Apostolic Delegate, to Mil. Gov., 12 Aug. 1922, and A. D. Rorex, Justice and Public Instr., 3 Oct. 1922, USNA, RG38, E6, B51.
78. Lee to S. Dist. Comdr., 25 Aug. 1922, and copies to Civil Guards at Higüey, El Seibo, Hato Mayor, Las Pajas, Consuelo, and Santa Fe, USNA, RG45, WA7, B645.
79. Robison to the Administrators of all Sugar Estates, 26 May 1922, and Robison to E. I. Kilbourne, 12 June 1922, USNA, RG38, E6, B36 and 50.
80. Robison to all sugar cos., by name of each, 13 June 1922, and Mil. Gov. to all sugar cos., by name of each, 27 Mar. 1922, USNA, RG38, E6, B36. Various replies are attached.
81. Manuel de Jesús Gómez, Ayunt. de Sto. Dom., to Mil. Gov., 7 Apr. 1921, and Mil. Gov. to all sugar cos., by name of each, 13 June 1922, USNA, RG38, E6, B36.
82. C. C. Carpenter, E. Dist. Comdr., to Comding Genl., 14 July 1922, AGN, P109; Robison to Sumner Welles, 6 Aug. 1922, USNA, RG45, WA7, B646.
83. Report of Op., no. 9, for Sept., by Harry Lee, 1 Oct. 1922, USNA, RG45, WA7, B646; Lee to Mil. Gov., 11 Apr. 1924, USNA, RG38, E6, B74.
84. Goico to Gob. Civ. Antonio Ramírez, 22 June 1922, USNA, RG38, E6, B50; Ducoudray, *Los "gavilleros,"* pp. 68–71. Concerning abuse of Natera, see Harry Lee to Mil. Gov., 11 Aug. 1922, and attached corres., AGN, P57. Also L. H. Moses to Mil. Gov., 9 Aug. 1922, and attached corres., AGN, P109.
85. *Listín Diario,* 26 and 27 Nov. 1923 and 29 Jan. 1924; Paul R. Cowley, Summary of Intel. for Nov., 15 Dec. 1923, USNA, RG45, WA7, B646.
86. Juan Félix Peguero, Gob. Civ. de San Pedro de Macorís, to Int. and Pol., 7 July 1922, USNA, RG38, E6, BU; Summary of Intel., 2nd Brig., Jan. through Dec. 1923, USNA, RG45, WA7, B646.
87. William E. Pulliam, Rec. Genl. of Dom. Customs, to Mil. Gov., 10 Oct. 1922, USNA, RG38, E6, B54.

88. Lee to Sec. Nav., 19 May 1924, USNA, RG38, E6, B74. McClellan, "Operations Ashore," p. 245, cautions that the statistics are likely to be inaccurate. Concerning the 116 officially recognized clashes between 1916 and 1919, when he was on duty in the Dominican Republic, he writes: "There have been a great many skirmishes and contacts with Dominicans which have not been officially reported."

89. Luis Fuentes, Síndico, to Prosec., Judic. Dist. of El Seibo, 21 May 1923, USNA, RG38, E6, B64. Tolete was killed by local police officials in 1930; see Martínez, *Diccionario*, p. 440.

8. THE NATIONALIST CAMPAIGN FOR WITHDRAWAL: 1917–1921

1. Federico Henríquez y Carvajal in Fiallo, *La Comisión Nacionalista*, pp. 68–69.

2. Francisco Henríquez y Carvajal, Memorandum, 12 Jan. 1917, in Lansing to Sec. Nav., 24 Jan. 1917, USNA, RG38, E6, B9. Knapp [with Russell] to Ch. of Nav. Op., 17 Feb. 1917, USNA, RG45, WA7, BU, rejects many of Henríquez' suggestions. Henríquez' memo, like many of the documents cited in this and the next chapter, is held in two or more archival collections, which include the U.S. National Archives and several Dominican archives. In most such cases, only one source is cited.

3. Fco. Henríquez to Hatuey Robiou, 4 Jan. 1917, HyC.

4. Fed. Henríquez in Fiallo, *La Comisión Nacionalista*, p. 69; Exec. Order No. 21, 16 Jan. 1917, R.D., *Colección, 1916–1917*, p. 170.

5. Manuel M. Morillo to Capt. L. H. Chandler, 4 Jan. 1917, trans. in Knapp to Sec. Nav., 31 Jan. 1917, and translation of "portions of letters written by Francisco Henríquez y Carvajal to prominent Dominicans," enclosed in Russell to Sec. St., 9 Mar. 1917, USNA, RG38, E6, B1; H. Stimson to Sec. St., 22 Mar. 1917, USNA, 839.00/2021; Knapp to Snowden, 20 Oct. 1919, and Rear Adm. J. H. Oliver, Gov. of the Virgin Islands, to Knapp, 15 Nov. 1917, USNA, RG38, E6, BU; Exec. Orders Nos. 20 and 21, 8 and 16 Jan. 1917, R.D., *Colección, 1916–1917*, pp. 169–170.

6. Fed. Henríquez in Fiallo, *La Comisión Nacionalista*, p. 71.

7. Fed. Henríquez y Carvajal, *Nacionalismo*, pp. 18–19.

8. Enrique Jiménez to Tulio M. Cestero, 23 Aug. 1918, Archivo Cestero (hereafter AC).

9. Fed. Henríquez in Fiallo, *La Comisión Nacionalista*, pp. 71–73; Fed. Henríquez y Carvajal, *Nacionalismo*, p. 21; Clement S. Edwards, U.S. Consul, Sto. Dom., to Sec. St., 23 Mar. 1919, and Buck, U.S. Vice-Consul, Antilla, Cuba, to Sec. St., USNA, 839.00/2126 and 2140. James J. McLean to Comdt., GND, 5 Mar. 1919, AGN, P26, reveals that the U.S. government spied on the Henríquez brothers and their followers in Cuba and was fully aware of these activities.

10. For example, Fco. Henríquez to Burgos, Min. of Panama at the Versailles Conference, 24 Apr. 1919, with attached memorandum, 20 Apr. 1919, USNA, 839.00/2523; Cestero to Francisco J. Peynado, 19 June 1919, AC; *Foreign Relations, 1919*, vol. 2, pp. 106–118; Fco. Henrí-

quez, Memorandum, 12 May 1919, USNA, 839.00/2176; Fiallo, *La Comisión Nacionalista*, pp. 16–23, 74.

11. Cestero to Peynado, 19 June 1919, and attached letters of invitation and refusal. Memorandum, "Resumen de la reunión del 6 de agosto de 1919," and Fco. Henríquez, Memorandum, "Bases objectivas de los Comités pro–Santo Domingo," Washington, 12 Sept. 1919, AC.

12. Mayo to Snowden, 27 Aug. 1919, USNA, RG45, WA7, B646; Fed. Henríquez y Carvajal, *Nacionalismo*, pp. 23–24.

13. Fco. Henríquez, "Nota preliminar aclarativa (presentada al Departamento de Estado)," 22 Aug. 1919, AC. Copies of Henríquez' memos and letters to the State Dept. are located in the Henríquez and Cestero archives and in USNA microcopy 626. Many are reprinted, with commentary by U.S. officials, in *Foreign Relations*.

14. Fco. Henríquez to Horace G. Knowles, 20 Nov. 1919, AC.

15. Fco. Henríquez to Cestero, 9 Oct. and 3 Dec. 1919, Fco. Henríquez, Memorandum, "A Confidential Comment . . . ," 16 Nov. 1920, and Cestero to Fco. Henríquez, 20 Dec. 1919, AC.

16. Cestero to Fco. Henríquez, 20 Dec. 1919, AC; Fiallo, *La Comisión Nacionalista*, pp. 24–25; Fed. Henríquez y Carvajal, *Nacionalismo*, pp. 24–25; Joseph Robert Juárez, "United States Withdrawal from Santo Domingo," *Hispanic American Historical Review* 42, no. 2 (May 1962): 152–190; Gompers to Wilson, 29 Nov. 1919, USNA, 839.00/2172; Welles, *Naboth's Vineyard*, vol. 2, pp. 823–824.

17. Knowles, quoted in Edward B. McConnell, *Chains of Gold: A Story and a Study of Imperialism*, pp. 118–123.

18. Enrique Deschamps, *El espíritu de España en la liberación de la República Dominicana, 1916–1924*, pp. 5–25; Senador Rafael Altamira, Madrid, to Wilson, 14 Aug. 1919, USNA, 839.00/2153.

19. Emilio Roíg de Leuchenring, *La ocupación de la República Dominicana por los Estados Unidos y el derecho de las pequeñas nacionalidades de América*; Eduardo Santos to Roíg de Leuchenring, 12 Sept. and 18 Oct. 1920, HyC.

20. Welles, *Naboth's Vineyard*, vol. 2, p. 823.

21. Snowden to Russell, 27 Dec. 1919, USNA, RG38, E6, B13.

22. For example, see two broadsides, *Al pueblo dominicano*, [?] Aug. and 20 Nov. 1919, and a form letter, "Distinguido compatriota," 21 Nov. 1919, HyC. The Henríquez and Cestero archives hold a large number of these epistolaries. Snowden to Russell, 2 Dec. 1919, USNA, RG38, E6, B13.

23. Peynado to Fco. Henríquez, 28 Nov. 1919, Max Henríquez Ureña to Cestero, 12 Dec. 1919, Fco. Henríquez to Cestero, [?] Dec. 1919, and Cestero to Fco. Henríquez, 20 Dec. 1919, AC; Fco. Henríquez, "Carta Pública," to Osvaldo Bazil, 28 Sept. 1919, HyC. Another attack on Henríquez' policy in *El Tiempo* is noted in Russell to Sec. St., 10 Oct. 1919, USNA, 839.00/2160.

24. On money matters, including a list of some Cuban donors, see Cestero

to Fco. Henríquez, 30 Oct. 1919, Fco. Henríquez to Cestero, 7 Nov. 1919, and Peynado to Fco. Henríquez, 28 Nov. 1919, AC.

25. Alicia G. de Cestero, Treas., to Tulio M. Cestero, 1 Feb. 1920, AC; Fed. Henríquez y Carvajal, *Nacionalismo*, pp. 22, 25.

26. Peynado to Fco. Henríquez, 28 Nov. 1919, AC; Russell to Sec. St., 10 Oct. 1919, and Snowden to Opnav., 22 and 23 Aug. 1919, USNA, 839.00/2160, 2144, and 2145; Cestero to Fco. Henríquez, 30 Oct. 1919, AC.

27. Snowden's original remarks are reported in Antonio Hoepelman, "Fabio Fiallo y la intervención norte americana en Santo Domingo," *Bahoruco*, 16 July 1932, p. 12. The protest, dated 31 July 1919, was reprinted in *La Vanguardia* (Barcelona), 22 Aug. 1919. For the internal State Department debate, see J. C. Dunn, Memorandum, 11 Sept. 1919, USNA, 839.00/2150, and Snowden to Russell, 2 Dec. 1919, USNA, RG38, E6, B13. Snowden's retraction, given in a New Year's address, appears in *El Tiempo*, 30 Dec. 1919.

28. Lugo, "Emiliano Tejera," p. 314; Dion Williams to Brig. Comdr., 12 Feb. 1920, USNA, RG38, E6, B30.

29. Snowden to Ch. of Nav. Op., 1 Nov. 1919, USNA, RG45, WA7, B645. The four acceptances, as well as Enrique Jiménez' refusal, are in AGN, P27.

30. Fco. Henríquez to Cestero, 7 Nov. 1919, AC.

31. Memoranda 1, 2, and 3, 12 Nov., 3 Dec., and 16 Dec. 1919, USNA, RG38, E6, B31.

32. *Listín Diario*, 4 Nov. 1919; Snowden to Ch. of Nav. Op., 7 Nov. 1919, USNA, RG45, WA7, B645; Lugo, "Emiliano Tejera," p. 312; Hoepelman, "Fabio Fiallo," p. 12.

33. Exec. Order No. 385, 15 Jan. 1920, R.D., *Colección, 1920*, pp. 7–9; Snowden to Russell, 2 Dec. 1919, USNA, RG38, E6, B13. Several files concerning the junta are in AGN, P27 and 121.

34. Fco. Henríquez to Cestero, 9 Nov. 1919 and 13 Jan. 1920, AC; Junta to Snowden, 7 Jan. 1920, HyC; Snowden to Sec. Nav., 17 Jan. 1920, USNA, RG38, E6, B31.

35. *Credo nacional, bases de la Unión Dominicana, Santo Domingo* (broadside), 8 Feb. 1920, and *Mensaje de adhesión de la mujer dominicana* (broadside), 27 Feb. 1920, Sto. Dom., HyC; Unión Nacional Dominicana, *Reglamento interior de la sociedad patriótica Unión Nacional Dominicana*; Lugo, "Emiliano Tejera," pp. 316–318; Hoepelman, "Fabio Fiallo," pp. 12–14.

36. Snowden to Jorge J. Serralles, 13 Mar. 1920, USNA, RG38, E6, B30. For the radical view, see Lugo, "Emiliano Tejera," pp. 317–318. James J. McLean to Comdt., GND, 27 Apr. 1920, USNA, RG38, E6, B24; Welles, *Naboth's Vineyard*, vol. 2, p. 828.

37. Dion Williams, N. Dist. Comdr., to Brig. Comdr. Feland, 15 Mar. 1920, USNA, RG38, E6, B23. The article was signed with a pseudonym, "Trinitario."

38. H. T. Ariza, T. Castellanos, E. T. de Castro, M. F. Cabral, M. Febles, R.

Guzmán R., Senadores de la Rep., to Snowden, 29 Apr. 1920, and Snowden to Cabral et al., 12 May 1920, HyC.

39. Broadside, Junta Nac., San Fran. de Macorís, enclosed in Snowden to Brig. Comdr., 3 May 1920, USNA, RG38, E6, B24; Brewer to Sec. St., 19 Apr. 1920, USNA, 839.00/2204.

40. Congreso Masónico Dominicano, *Exposición del Congreso Dominicano a los Supremos Consejos 33 de los Estados Unidos de Norte América . . .* , pp. 3–10.

41. Hoepelman, "Fabio Fiallo," pp. 11–12; Fed. Henríquez y Carvajal, *Nacionalismo*, p. 27; Junta Patriótica de Damas, *Al pueblo dominicano*, pp. 4–22; Unión Nac. Dom., "Resolución," 18 June 1920, CRD; R. K. Christenberry, Vice-Consul, Sto. Dom., to Sec. St., 15 June 1920, USNA, 839.00/2215.

42. Snowden to Dr. John M. Swan, 23 June 1920, USNA, RG38, E6, B30; Hoepelman, "Fabio Fiallo," p. 12.

43. Extensive correspondence regarding the trials is found in USNA, RG38, E6, B25 (file 17), B27 (file 31), and B31, 34, and 35. See also *Foreign Relations, 1920*, vol. 2, pp. 160–173.

44. Snowden to Ch. of Nav. Op., 3 July 1920, with enclosed memorandum, Logan Feland to Snowden, 1 July 1920, and R. E. Coontz, Acting Sec. Nav., to Sec. St., 20 July 1920, and attached corres., USNA, 839.00/2217. On the investigations, see USNA, 839.00/2227 and 2237.

45. Memorandum, Wm. A. Sherwell to Leo Rowe, 23 Aug. 1920, HyC. Many of the imprisoned journalists are noted in Hoepelman, "Fabio Fiallo," pp. 12–13.

46. Sweet to Lugo, 20 Aug. 1920, and Snowden to Sweet, 8 Sept. 1920, USNA, RG38, E6, B30.

47. File 17 of USNA, RG38, E6, B25 contains hundreds of pages of trial documents for Fiallo, Flores Cabrera, and other defendants.

48. For example, Lugo's statement to the provost court, undated transcript, CRD; Blanco Fombona, *Crímenes*, pp. 129–130.

49. Lybrand P. Smith, Justice and Public Instr., to Mil. Gov., 15 Apr. 1920, and Enrique Henríquez to Mil. Gov., 6 July 1920, USNA, RG38, E6, B24 and 23. Concerning a courtroom speech by lawyer Rafael Estrella Ureña, see Mil. Gov. to Justice and Public Instr., 30 Sept. 1920, and attached corres., USNA, RG38, E6, B22.

50. Sec. Nav. Daniels to Snowden, 5 Jan. 1921, USNA, RG38, E6, B35. Actions setting aside the convictions of Sanabia, Lugo, del Castillo, Flores Cabrera, Delanoy, and others are found in USNA, RG38, E6, B34 and 35.

51. Russell to Sec. St., 9 Dec. 1920, and Norman H. Davis, Under Sec. St., to Sec. Nav., 13 Dec. 1920, USNA, 839.00/2285 and 2276a; Exec. Orders Nos. 572 and 573, 6 Dec. 1920, R.D., *Colección, 1920*, pp. 527–530. Concerning the trial of Blanco Fombona, see Snowden to Sec. Nav., 19 Nov. 1920, and related documents in AGN, P17. See also USNA, RG38, E6, B43. The military government argued that Guardia members rather than their marine commander had done the actual torturing of Báez but could not produce a culprit.

52. Hoepelman, "Fabio Fiallo," p. 14; Franco, "Insinuaciones al Congreso de la Prensa," *Algunas ideas*, pp. 13–15.

53. Snowden to Judge Willis Sweet, 8 Sept. 1920, and Report of Operations, GND, 17 July to 31 Aug. 1920, USNA, RG38, E6, B30 and 40.

54. Fiallo, *La Comisión Nacionalista*, pp. 29–30, 79–82; Juárez, "U.S. Withdrawal," pp. 156–157; Fed. Henríquez y Carvajal, *Nacionalismo*, pp. 167–170.

55. Cestero to Fco. Henríquez, 20 Dec. 1919, AC. Cestero's correspondence with President Wilson, the State Department, U.S. congressmen, diplomats of various Latin American nations, leaders of the AFL, and persons in the private sector is in the Cestero archive.

56. Cestero to Fco. Henríquez, 6 Mar. 1920, and related corres., AC. The closed door which Cestero encountered at the White House resulted in part from President Wilson's grave illness at that time.

57. Cestero to Sec. St., 27 Mar. 1920, and N. P. Hibbs, St. Dept., to Cestero, 27 Mar. 1920, AC.

58. Nouel to Russell, 29 Dec. 1919, and Cestero to Dear Sir [members of the U.S. Senate], 3 Apr. 1920, with enclosed memorandum of 2 Apr. 1920, AC. The military government's explanations comprise a thick file, 42-22, in USNA, RG38, E6, B31. See also USNA, microcopy 626, roll 19.

59. C. H. Baxter, Rec. Genl., to L. S. Rowe, 19 May 1920, USNA, 839.00/2265.

60. John W. Blassingame, "The Press and American Intervention in Haiti and the Dominican Republic, 1904–1920," *Caribbean Studies* 9, no. 2 (July 1969): 27–43.

61. Cestero to Cordero Dávila, 22 Apr. 1920, and U.S. House Resol. 513, enclosed in Cestero to Fco. Henríquez, 8 Apr. 1920, AC; W. E. Mason to Cestero, 27 Apr. 1920, HyC; Juárez, "U.S. Withdrawal," p. 159.

62. Martín Gaudier to Snowden, 6 July 1920, enclosing news clippings from London and Madrid, and Col. Geo. C. Thorpe to Mil. Gov., 24 June 1920, USNA, RG38, E6, B30 and 29; George H. Blakeslee, ed., *Mexico and the Caribbean*, gives the published proceedings of the conference.

63. Peter J. Brady and Anthony McAndrew, AFL, to Cestero, 19 Feb. 1920, Cestero to Brady and McAndrew, 7 Apr. 1920, and Cestero to Fco. Henríquez, 8 Apr. 1920, AC. Brady and McAndrew's report appears in AFL, *Report, 1920*, p. 246.

64. Gompers to Wilson, 29 Nov. 1919, Lansing to Gompers, 31 Dec. 1919, Cestero to Gompers, [?] Apr. 1920, Daniels to Gompers, 10 June 1920, and Canuto Vargas, Sec., PAFL, to Cestero, 3 Aug. 1920, AC.

65. Julius W. Pratt, *America's Colonial Experiment*, pp. 313–314; Juárez, "U.S. Withdrawal," pp. 157–158.

66. Canuto Vargas to Cestero, 21 Oct. 1920, and Circular, Fco. Henríquez to Pres. de la Junta Nac., 9 Nov. 1920, AC.

67. U.S. Mil. Govt., *Santo Domingo*, Norman H. Davis, Under Sec. St., to

300 Notes to Pages 203–205

Diplomatic Officers of the U.S. in Latin Amer., 2 Oct. 1920, and Davis
to Sec. St., 4 Sept. 1920, USNA, 839.00/2248a and 2254b.

68. Fco. Henríquez to Cestero, 13 Sept. 1920, AC; Fed. Henríquez y Carvajal, *Nacionalismo*, p. 27; Fiallo, *La Comisión Nacionalista*, pp. 75–
78. The press releases of the Dominican Republic Information Bureau
are collected in a booklet by Manuel F. Cestero and Manuel Flores
Cabrera, *Circulares de la Oficina de Información en los Estados
Unidos*.

69. Eduardo Santos to Cestero, 18 Oct. 1920, and Enriquillo Henríquez
García and Cestero to E. Santos, 15 Nov. 1920, AC; Hoffman Phillip,
U.S. Legation, Bogotá, to Sec. St., 18 Aug. and 18 Oct. 1920, USNA,
839.00/2228 and 2256; Welles, *Naboth's Vineyard*, vol. 2, p. 829.

70. Fed. Henríquez to Junta Nac. Dom., 28 Nov. 1920, HyC; Fco. Henríquez, "Instrucciones dictadas al Señor Doctor Don Tulio M. Cestero,
con motivo de la misión que se le confía en las Repúblicas de América
Latina," 29 Nov. 1920, AC; Fiallo, *La Comisión Nacionalista*, p. 36.

71. Fed. Henríquez y Carvajal, *Nacionalismo*, pp. 29–43, 205–225; Fiallo,
La Comisión Nacionalista, p. 76. The Cestero archive houses an extensive collection of letters, documents, and memorabilia from this
trip. See particularly Cestero's confidential and comprehensive fifty-
three-page "Memoria" to Fco. Henríquez, 7 July 1921, AC. The Henríquez y Carvajal archive also houses a large number of related materials.
Especially useful is Enriquillo Henríquez García, Memorandum, "Notas para el poeta-patriota Fabio Fiallo," 12 Apr. 1938, HyC.

72. Text of the Wilson Plan, Welles, *Naboth's Vineyard*, vol. 2, pp. 830–
831. Welles wrote the Wilson Plan in mid November 1920; it was in
Snowden's hands by late November. Colby to Wilson, 27 Nov. 1920,
and Daniels to Colby, 30 Nov. 1920, USNA, 839.00/2416a and 2479.

73. Departmental and interdepartmental discussions of Dominican policy
are found in literally thousands of State Department documents; particularly enlightening are 839.00/2114, 2121, 2133, 2159, 2214½,
2214a, 2244, 2245, and 2250, plus many on the actual preparation of
the plan itself. Commentaries by outside experts, including General
Enoch Crowder, Otto Schoenrich, William G. McAdoo, Abram F.
Lindberg, John T. Vance, Jr., and Clarence H. Baxter, are located in files
839.00/2159, 2223, 2247, 2248½, 2251, 2265, and 2353. A few of these
are discussed in MacMichael, "The United States," pp. 473–476,
499–500.

74. Cestero to Norman Davis, St. Dept., 1 Aug. 1920, Cestero to J. Daniels,
2 Aug. 1920, Cestero to B. Colby, 8 Sept. 1920, Cestero to Welles,
15 Oct. 1920, Fco. Henríquez, Memorandum, "A Confidential Comment on the Memorandum Presented to Mr. Wm. G. McAdoo,"
16 Nov. 1920, Fco. Henríquez to Cestero, 10 Dec. 1920, Cestero to
Welles, 18 Dec. 1920, and Cestero to Welles, 26 Dec. 1920, AC. N.
Davis, Acting. Sec. St., to Knowles, 18 Jan. 1921, USNA, 839.00/2321,
claims that President Henríquez previewed and approved "the entire

proposed program in detail"; most of the evidence belies this statement.

75. Russell to Sec. St., 27 Dec. 1920, USNA, 839.00/2284; *Las Noticias,* 23 Dec. 1920; Protesta de la Unión Nac. Dom., 24 Dec. 1920, and Fco. Henríquez to Welles, 6 Jan. 1921, HyC.

76. Junta to Snowden, 29 Dec. 1920, Snowden to Sec. Nav., 29 Dec. 1920, and Russell to Sec. St., 6 Jan. 1921, USNA, 839.00/2286, 2290, and 2294; Fco. Henríquez to Fosalba, 11 Jan. and 25 Feb. 1921, HyC; *Las Noticias,* 3 Jan. 1921. Emilio Prud'homme to Snowden, 26 Jan. 1921,' in Prud'homme's *Mi libro azul,* pp. 111–112, presents his refusal.

77. Fco. Henríquez to Peynado, 12 Jan. 1921, HyC.

78. Fco. Henríquez to Fosalba, 11 Jan. and 25 Feb. 1921, HyC.

79. Fco. Henríquez to Knowles, 20 Nov. 1920, HyC. Fco. Henríquez to Peynado, 12 Jan. 1921, AC, explains his turnabout. A public correspondence between Francisco Peynado and radical leader Enrique Apolinar Henríquez concerning President Henríquez' vacillations is enclosed in Russell to Sec. St., 5 Feb. 1921, USNA, 839.00/2343. See also Rafael Damirón, "Notas del pasado," *Listín Diario,* 17–30 Aug. 1922.

80. Damirón, "Notas del pasado," *Listín Diario,* 28 and 30 Aug. 1922; Alfau Durán, "Planes patrióticos," p. 63.

81. Knowles to Tumulty, 20 [Jan.] 1921 [misdated Feb.], Knowles to Daniels, 24 Jan. 1921; Knowles to Davis, 13, 20, 27, 28, 29, and 30 Jan. 1921, and Knowles to Colby, 30 Jan. and 24 Feb. 1921, USNA, 839.00/2324, 2378, 2321, 2314, 2325, 2326, and 2348. Primarily negative news articles from Latin America and a number of protests, all from early 1921, are in USNA, microcopy 626, rolls 21 and 34.

82. Munro, *U.S. and the Caribbean,* pp. 45–46. The negotiations, 4 Mar. to 2 June 1921, are reported in Fiallo, *La Comisión Nacionalista,* pp. 41–65, and in circulars, R. César Tolentino to Pres., Junta Nac., 8 Mar. 1921, and Fco. Henríquez to Pres., Junta Nac., 25 Mar., 21 Apr., 29 Apr., 6 May, and 27 May 1921, HyC and AC. Fco. Henríquez, Memoranda, 10, 11, and 13 Apr. 1921, state the Dominican position, HyC and AC. See also Fco. Henríquez to Hughes, 10 and 25 Apr., 22 and 26 May 1921, as well as "Memento," concerning an interview with Sumner Welles, 9 May 1921, HyC and AC. Many of these papers are also in St. Dept. file 839.00 (USNA, microcopy 626, rolls 21 and 23), which also includes Fco. Henríquez to Harding, 10–11 Apr. 1921, and Memorandum, "Argumentación jurídica acerca la situación actual . . . ," USNA, 839.00/2377 and 2389. Some of President Henríquez' correspondence to the State Department was both in Spanish and in English; sometimes the two copies bear different dates, usually one day apart.

83. Telegrams and letters to Harding from *juntas nacionalistas,* the Dominican Masonic movement, towns, and individuals are in USNA, 839.00/2357, 2361, and 2362 and 839.00/P81. The Brazilian and Argentine queries are in USNA, 839.00/2300 and 2382. The labor protests in-

clude Gompers, PAFL, to Hughes, 28 May 1921, and Emma Steghagen, Natl. Women's Trade Union League, to Hughes, 13 June 1921, USNA, 839.00/2403 and 839.00/P81/14.

84. Junta Pat. de Damas, "Al Secretario de la Marina de los E. U. de América," n.d., and "La protesta de la Liga Nacional de Estudiantes ante el Secretario de la Marina Americana," 29 Mar. 1921, HyC.

85. Samuel S. Robison, Proclamation [Harding Plan], 14 June 1921, AGN, P108; Comisión Nac. Dom., "Memorándum presentado por el señor Tulio Cestero a Mr. Sumner Welles," 18 June 1921, AC; Welles to Sec. St., 22 June and 19 Aug. 1921, USNA, 839.00/2490 and 2550. Welles again claimed Dominican approval of the plan before it was issued, and once again there is considerable evidence against his claim.

86. Fco. Henríquez to Ulises Espaillat, 9 June 1921, and Telegram to Rafael Estrella Ureña, 15 June 1921, HyC. Fiallo, *La Comisión Nacionalista,* pp. 46–50, presents a very different and unsubstantiated view, perhaps to protect Francisco Henríquez or himself against radical charges of compromise.

87. Russell to Sec. St., 14 June 1921, USNA, 839.00/2399. The protest's severity brought about a military alert, detailed in a series of orders and memos, all signed by Henry C. Davis, 18 June 1921, USNA, RG38, E6, B35. A. Pellerano Sardá, *Listín Diario,* and Rafael Brache, *El Tiempo,* to Robison, 18 June 1921 [two letters], USNA, RG38, E6, B40; Robison to Pellerano Sardá and Brache, 20 June 1921, USNA, RG45, WA7, B646.

88. *A los extranjeros residentes en el Territorio Nacional* (broadside), 19 June 1921, in Fiallo, *La Comisión Nacionalista,* pp. 49, 102–104; broadsides, Congreso Masónico and Asociación de la Prensa (announcing the demonstration at Robison's residence on 19 June 1921), HyC; copies of protests sent to Washington, dated 16 June 1921, HyC; Russell to Sec. St., 20 June 1921, USNA, 839.00/2404; translated copy, Teófilo Cordero Bidó, Gob. Civ. de La Vega, to Int. and Pol., 20 June 1921, citizens of Barahona to Robison, 16 June 1921, and citizens of Sánchez to Robison, 21 June 1921, USNA, RG45, WA7, B646.

89. Junta de Abstención Electoral de la Provincia de Santo Domingo, *Constitución de la Junta de Abstención Electoral de la Provincia de Santo Domingo;* Asociación de Jóvenes Dominicanos, *A la juventud del país.* Fed. Henríquez y Carvajal, *Nacionalismo,* pp. 45 and 134, describes the origins of the two Jóvenes groups and notes that they soon joined forces as the Asociación Independiente de Jóvenes Dominicanos. José Rafael Bordas, *Frente al imperialismo,* a collection of newspaper articles by a member of the Asociación de Jóvenes during 1921 and 1922, presents views typical of the groups.

90. M. de J. Lluveres, Sub–Sec. St., Int. and Pol., to Sec., 11 July 1921, USNA, RG45, WA7, B646.

91. A *Listín Diario* editorial of 29 June 1921 called for President Henríquez' replacement as head of the nationalist movement for his initial failure to condemn the plan. Fco. Henríquez, "Memorándum contra el

Plan Harding presentado al Departamento de Estado en Wash.," 14 July 1921, AC.

92. Robison, "Order of Convocation," 14 July 1921, AGN, P108; Mil. Gov. to Comding. Genl., n.d., item 14-317, USNA, RG38, E6, B36. A series of undated, unsigned memos in the last file of USNA, RG45, WA7, B646, discuss preparations for withdrawal. The official record of the advisory panel for 16 July 1921, USNA, RG45, WA7, B646, shows the members to be Arch. Nouel, R. J. Castillo, M. de J. González Marrero, F. J. Peynado, J. R. de Castro, F. Velásquez, P. A. Pérez, and M. de J. Camarena Perdomo, the same personnel as the second *junta consultiva* except for Camarena.

93. Robison, "To the Dominican People," 6 July 1921, AGN, P108; Robison to Comding. Genl., 6 July 1921, USNA, RG38, E6, B36; "Entrevista de hoy," *Listín Diario*, 12 July 1921; H. Vásquez, F. Velásquez, and R. Báez to Robison, 13 July 1921, L. F. Vidal to Robison, 14 July 1921, and Robison to Sec. Nav., 3 Aug. 1921, USNA, RG45, WA7, B646. Robison's papers on these conferences are in USNA, RG38, E6, B43. Enrique Jiménez to Pres. Henríquez (in code), 29 July 1921, and other moderate nationalists favoring the Harding Plan are quoted in Cestero to Fco. Henríquez, 30 July 1921, AC.

94. Lugo, speech delivered in San Pedro de Macorís, 1921, excerpted in Lugo, "Emiliano Tejera," pp. 309–313. Junta Nac. to Pres. Henríquez, 6 Aug. 1921, HyC, defended Henríquez.

95. Robison, Proclamation, 27 July 1921, AGN, P108; Fco. Henríquez, Circulars, 22 July, 5 Aug., 30 Aug., and 27 Sept. 1921, HyC, CRD, and AC. Fco. Henríquez to Cestero, 5 Oct. 1921, and other letters concerning the fruitless talks of August through October are in AC.

96. Robison to Sec. Nav., 3 Aug. 1921, USNA, RG45, WA7, B646.

97. Fco. Henríquez, Circulars, 5 Aug. and 27 Sept. 1921, HyC; Fco. Henríquez, "Memorandum presented to the Committee of the Senate of the U.S. . . . ," 12 Aug. 1921, AC.

98. Millett and Gaddy, "Administering the Protectorates," pp. 393–399; Mayo to Snowden, 7 May 1921, USNA, RG38, E6, B43.

9. The Nationalist Campaign, the Hughes-Peynado Accord, and Withdrawal: 1921–1924

1. Circular, Adán Creales Morcelo and Miguel E. Castro V., La Romana, 28 Sept. 1921, HyC.

2. "Compromiso político solemne de Puerto Plata," in Hoepelman and Senior, *Documentos*, pp. 312–316. The signers were Dr. Henríquez, Horacio Vásquez (Horacistas), L. F. Vidal (Legalistas), and Enrique Jiménez (Jimenistas).

3. Mil. Gov. to Sec. Nav., 30 Dec. 1921, USNA, RG38, E6, B44; Peynado to Knowles, 23 Jan. 1922, PFP.

4. Knowles, "Memorandum of Charges against the U.S. Govt.," 12 Aug. 1921, and Fco. Henríquez, Memorandum, 12 Aug. 1921, U.S., Senate, *Hearings*, vol. 1, pp. 48–60.

5. U.S., Senate, *Hearings*, vol. 2.
6. Knowles to Senator Medill McCormick, 5 [Jan.] 1922 [mistyped as 5 Dec. 1922], PFP; Interview, Senator Ernest Gruening, 25 May 1969, Wash., D.C.; Interview, Knowles, quoted in McConnell, *Chains of Gold*, pp. 120–123. Military government papers concerning the Senate committee are in USNA, RG38, E6, B37, and in AGN, P37; they show that the military government spied on nationalist witnesses and their lawyers, had complete access to documents submitted to the committee, and investigated all Dominicans involved after the committee's departure.
7. Knowles to Peynado, 28 Dec. 1921, PFP.
8. Knowles to McCormick, 5 Jan. 1922, PFP. Copies of letters, December 1921 to June 1922, between Knowles and McCormick concerning witnesses, the continuation of the hearings, and other matters are in the Peynado papers.
9. Summary of Intel. for Nov., [?] Dec. 1921, USNA, RG45, WA7, B646; C. L. Lang, Pres., Civil Service Commission, to Mil. Gov., 29 Nov. 1921, USNA, RG38, E6, B40. See also corres. in file 28-243, AGN, PIO.
10. Mil. Gov. to Comding, Genl., 1 July 1921, and attached corres., USNA, RG38, E6, B36. See also file 43-45, "Libels and Calumnies of the Santo Domingo Press," in B43 and other items in B37 and 40.
11. Comding. Genl. Harry Lee to Mil. Gov., 3 Aug. 1922, USNA, RG45, WA7, B645.
12. Lee to Mil. Gov., 3 Aug. 1922, and Lee to All Officers of the Brig., 31 July, 19 Aug., and 15 Nov. 1921, USNA, RG45, WA7, B645 and 646.
13. Lee to Mil. Gov., 3 Aug. 1922, USNA, RG45, WA7, B645. Monthly intelligence reports to Lee included a section labeled "Psychological Situation," which noted the general tenor of marine-Dominican relations and reported all "cases of friction."
14. Robison to Sec. St., 30 Jan. 1922, Hughes to Sec. Nav., 10 Feb. 1922, Robison and Russell to Dominican Leaders, 20–21 Feb. 1922, and Dominican Leaders (J. M. Cabral y Báez, H. Vásquez, F. Velásquez, M. de J. Troncoso de la Concha, E. Jiménez, J. F. Sánchez, R. J. Castillo, M. de J. Lluveres, F. J. Peynado, J. R. de Castro, and T. Cestero) to Robison, 23 Feb. 1922, and attached memorandum by Robison, USNA, RG45, WA7, B646; "Proclamation to Provide for Continuing Military Occupation until approximately 1 July 1924," 6 Mar. 1922, USNA, 839.00/2496, and AGN, P108.
15. Robison, Memorandum, attached to Robison to Sec. St., 30 Jan. 1922, and other letters, USNA, RG45, WA7, B646; Regt. Intel. Officer to Brig. Intel. Officer, 15 Mar. 1922, USNA, RG38, E6, B48; *Listín Diario*, 15 Mar. 1922; Cestero to Chargé d'Affaires de Belgique, 22 Apr. 1922, and Cestero to Pres. A. Zayas, Cuba, 27 May 1922, AC.
16. Peynado to Knowles, 23 Jan. 1922, "Proyecto de Lotería Patriótica," undated, "Protest of the Assembly of Directors of the Patriotic Organizations of the Capital," trans. enclosed in Knowles to Peynado, 5 Apr. 1922, and trans. editorial, "Hopes, Blasted Hopes," *Listín Dia-*

rio, 29 Mar. 1922, PFP. Knowles to Peynado, 12 July 1922, PFP, relates that Knowles received $2,900 through Peynado between January and July 1922, while apparently incurring much greater expenses.

17. Fco. Henríquez to Cestero, 14 May 1922, AC; Fco. Henríquez to Knowles, 20 May and 28 June 1922, PFP; Robison, Memorandum, attached to Robison to Sec. St., 30 Jan. 1922, and other letters, USNA, RG45, WA7, B646.

18. Peynado to Knowles, 23 Jan. 1922, PFP; Robison, Memorandum, attached to Robison to Sec. St., 30 Jan. 1922, USNA, RG45, WA7, B646; *Listín Diario*, 22 Mar. 1922; Fco. Henríquez to Cestero, 14 May 1922, AC.

19. U.S. Senate Committee, Preliminary Report, [? Dec.] 1921, AGN, P103. Knowles to Peynado, 28 Dec. 1921, PFP, notes its contents.

20. Russell to Sec. St., 27 Mar. 1922, USNA, 839.00/2499; Robison to M. de J. Gómez, Ayunt. of Sto. Dom., 10 Mar. 1922, AGN, P3.

21. *Listín Diario*, 22 Mar. 1922; Knowles to Peynado, 18 Feb. 1922, PFP; Fabio Fiallo, *Plan de acción y liberación del pueblo dominicano . . .*, pp. xxviii–xxix.

22. M. de J. Gómez to Robison, 12 Apr. 1922, AGN, P45; *Listín Diario*, 13 Mar. 1922; Knowles to W. E. Pulliam, 14 Jan. 1922, PFP.

23. Knowles to Fco. Henríquez, 3 Apr. 1922, and Peynado to Knowles, 4 Apr. 1922, PFP.

24. Mil. Gov. to Sec. Nav., 27 May 1922, and Sec. Nav. to Flag San Domingo, 6 Oct. 1922, USNA, RG80, CNO Planning, file 159-16; Hughes to Sec. Nav., 13 July 1922, USNA, 839.00/2541. See also file 43 of USNA, RG38, E6, B56, especially Wm. Phillips, Acting Sec. St., to Acting Sec. Nav., 31 Aug. 1922. *"La Información" frente a la ocupación de la República Dominicana por las fuerzas armadas de los Estados Unidos de América* describes the position of the newspaper which was the primary focus of Lyman's censorship.

25. Welles, *Naboth's Vineyard*, vol. 2, p. 855; Peynado to Knowles, 4 Apr. 1922, PFP.

26. Martínez, *Diccionario*, p. 392.

27. Peynado met with Hughes, Welles, and Dana Munro of State, with Denby of Navy, and with Senators McCormick and Pomerene of the Senate committee on Haiti and Santo Domingo. Peynado's letters to Knowles, 18 Mar. and 6, 7, 10, and 19 Apr. 1922, PFP, describe his conferences. Peynado's communications to Hughes, from mid March to late May 1922, are in the Cestero archive. State Department papers on the talks are in USNA, 839.009/2650–2686.

28. Peynado to Hughes, 28 Mar., 10 Apr., and n.d. 1922, AC; Peynado to Knowles, 6, 7, and 10 Apr. 1922, PFP.

29. Peynado to Cestero, 29 May 1922, AC; Mil. Gov. to Sec. Nav., 16 June 1922, and Memorandum, 15 July 1922, USNA, RG45, WA7, B646; Welles, *Naboth's Vineyard*, vol. 2, pp. 855–859.

30. Munro, *U.S. and the Caribbean*, pp. 53–54. Tulio Cestero to Peynado, 19 June 1919, AC, had suggested the idea of a provisional government;

Peynado's achievement was to combine this idea with other features which made it acceptable to the State Department. Pomerene to Knowles, 6 Apr. 1922, PFP.

31. Knowles to Fco. Henríquez, 26 May 1922, and Knowles to Peynado, 5 May 1922, PFP. Copies of Knowles' letters to Borah, to editors, diplomats, and others, dated mid April to early May, are in the Peynado papers.

32. Senate Resol. 219, 19 Jan. 1922, in USNA, RG39, B39 (country file); Knowles to Peynado, 18 Feb. 1922, Knowles to Fco. Henríquez, 3 Apr. and 29 June 1922, and Knowles to King, 14 June 1922, PFP.

33. Knowles to McCormick, 5 Jan., 24 Mar., 12, 17, 20, and 28 Apr., 7 June, and 18 July 1922, and McCormick to Knowles, 17 Apr. 1922, PFP.

34. *Protesta* (broadside), Sto. Dom., [date?] 1922, PFP; Knowles, Speech to the Natl. Popular Govt. League, in NPGL, *Bulletin*, 28 Feb. 1922; Knowles to Jones, 5 Apr. 1922, Knowles to Borah, 8 Apr. 1922, and Knowles to Peynado, 3 Apr. 1922, PFP. Munro, *U.S. and the Caribbean*, pp. 50–53, presents a more favorable view of the loan. The loan's authorized amount was $10 million, but $3.3 million was held back as a carrot so that the new Dominican government would endorse it.

35. Knowles to Peynado, 22 June 1922, and Fco. Henríquez to Knowles, 28 June 1922, PFP; *Listín Diario*, 26 June 1922; B. Spencer, Chargé, Madrid, to Sec. St., 4 July 1922, USNA, 839.00/2547.

36. Peynado to Knowles, 4 and 11 Apr. 1922, PFP.

37. Knowles reviewed all events between January and April in a long letter, 3 Apr. 1922, PFP, to which Henríquez failed to reply until 20 May 1922. Henríquez' next letter, 28 June 1922, asked Knowles for the details of the agreement.

38. Knowles to Fco. Henríquez, 29 June 1922, PFP. Knowles described Peynado's letter to Henríquez in Knowles to McCormick, 25 July 1922, PFP. Knowles' Dominican work ended at this time. MacMichael, "The United States," pp. 597–599, notes that Knowles never received his long-promised retainer from the Dominicans, in part because of State Department pressure on the Dominican government after 1924.

39. Circular, Fco. Henríquez to Pres., Junta Nac., 27 July 1922, USNA, 839.00/2585.

40. *Protesta de la Junta de Abstención Electoral*, Sto. Dom., 18 July 1921, AGN, PIO, and *Protesta de la Junta de Abstención de Santo Domingo . . .*, 7 Aug. 1922 (broadsides), HyC.

41. Américo Lugo, *Conferencia . . .*, pp. 15–16. For other versions of the argument see Américo Lugo, *El plan de validación Hughes-Peynado*, and Mejía, *Al rededor y en contra del plan Hughes-Peynado*.

42. Welles to Sec. St., 7 Aug. 1922, USNA, 839.00/2561.

43. Welles, *Naboth's Vineyard*, vol. 2, pp. 863–871. Welles' papers and other State Department documents concerning the commission are in USNA, microcopy 626, especially rolls 24 and 25.

44. Broadsides, José A. Lemos, Pres., Ayunt. of Barahona, and others, *Protesta*, [?] Aug. 1922, and *Protesta de la Junta de Abstención de Santo Domingo* . . . , 7 Aug. 1922, HyC; Capt. Gerald A. Johnson, Confid. Report of Intel., no. 8, 1–31 Aug. 1922, USNA, RG38, E6, B50; Welles to Sec. St., 1 Aug. 1922, USNA 839.00/2552.

45. Welles to Director, *Ecos del Norte*, Puerto Plata, 21 Sept. 1922, CRD; Welles to Sec. St., 12 Oct. 1922, USNA, 839.00/2646; Maj. Gerald A. Johnson, Confid. Summary of Intel., no. 9, 1–30 Sept. 1922, USNA, RG45, WA7, B646. Some U.S. investors had voiced concern over the withdrawal before they knew the details of the plan; for example, see USNA, 839.00/2538 and 2539.

46. Welles to Sec. St., 1 and 29 Aug. 1922, USNA, 839.00/2553 and 2590.

47. Cestero, "Gestiones complementarias en Wash., D.C.," in "Memoria" to Fco. Henríquez, 7 July 1921, AC, reported that many Latin American diplomats had even counseled him to accept the Harding Plan. A. A. Alvarez, Pres., Senate of Cuba, to Pres. of the U.S., 4 Oct. 1922, USNA, 839.00/2620, reports a vote lauding the United States for the Hughes-Peynado withdrawal plan.

48. Circular, Fco. Henríquez to Pres., Junta Nac., 27 July 1922, AC; Welles to Sec. St., 1 Aug. 1922, USNA, 839.00/2553; *Protesta del Congreso Nacionalista de la R.D., contra el "Entendido" o Plan Hughes-Peynado* (broadside), Santiago, 6 Oct. 1922, enclosed in Welles to Sec. St., 17 Oct. 1922, USNA, 839.00/2643.

49. Orme Wilson, Memorandum, 31 Oct. 1925, USNA, 839.00/2983½, notes that the treaty, as signed later, allowed the Dominicans some freedom to adjust tariffs.

50. For example, Welles to Robison, 26 Sept. 1922, USNA, RG80, CNO Planning, file 159-22, and many letters between Robison and Welles in USNA, RG45, WA7, B646.

51. Mil. Gov. to Ch. of Nav. Op., 29 Oct. 1922, USNA, RG38, E6, B56; Hughes to Denby, 4 Oct. 1922, and Denby to Flag San Dom., 6 Oct. 1922, USNA, RG80, CNO Planning, file 159-22. Welles' essential correspondence on this matter appears in *Foreign Relations, 1922*, vol. 2, pp. 39–43, 64, and 68 and in USNA, microcopy 626, roll 24. Kenneth J. Grieb, "Warren G. Harding and the Dominican Republic: U.S. Withdrawal, 1921–1923," *Journal of Inter-American Studies* 11, no. 3 (July 1969): 434–438, studies the dispute from the State Department's point of view.

52. Robison to Genl. John A. Lejeune, 26 Aug. 1922, USNA, RG45, WA7, B645.

53. Welles to Sec. St., 23 and 30 Oct. 1922, USNA, 839.00/2654 and 2624.

54. Welles to Sec. St., 5 Apr. 1923 [two letters], USNA, 839.00/2692 and 2694; Welles, *Naboth's Vineyard*, vol. 2, pp. 876–878.

55. "Condiciones para el funcionamiento del gobierno provisional," in Welles to Sec. St., 26 Sept. 1922, USNA, 839.00/2618.

56. Welles, *Naboth's Vineyard*, vol. 2, pp. 867–873, 880–881. For a strong

critique of Welles' views and actions in this period, see [Julio Ortega Frier?], *Memorándum relativo a la intervención de Sumner Welles en la República Dominicana*, [1 Aug. 1945], pp. 1–69.

57. These disputes are detailed in Welles, *Naboth's Vineyard*, vol. 2, pp. 879–899, in *Foreign Relations, 1923*, vol. 1, pp. 893–894 and 899–917, and more extensively in USNA, microcopy 626, especially rolls 26–31.

58. Harry Lee, "Indoctrination anent Proper Attitude of Forces of Occupation toward Dominican Government and People," 30 Oct. 1922, USNA, 839.00/2688; Fuller and Cosmas, *Marines*, p. 65.

59. Harry Lee, Report of Operations for Sept., 1 Oct. 1922, and for Mar., 1 Apr. 1923, USNA, RG45, WA7, B646.

60. G. A. Johnson to Mil. Gov., 11 Dec. 1922, and file 14-386, USNA, RG38, E6, B51; Acting Sec. Nav. to Mil. Gov., 23 May 1922, USNA, 839.00/ 2525; Lee, Brig. Order No. 2, 31 May 1922, USNA, RG38, E6, B51.

61. G. A. Johnson, Confid. Summary of Intel., 1 Oct. 1922, USNA, RG45, WA7, B646.

62. Fed. Henríquez y Carvajal, *Nacionalismo*, pp. 49, 177.

63. Summaries of Intel., Feb.–July 1923, USNA, RG45, WA7, B646.

64. Américo Lugo, *El nacionalismo dominicano*, pp. 3–30. See also "Manifiesto del nacionalismo dominicano contra la intervención, el Entendido Hughes-Peynado y las elecciones venideras," 11 Nov. 1923, CRD.

65. Summaries of Intel., Feb.–Dec. 1923, USNA, RG45, WA7, B646.

66. Fed. Henríquez y Carvajal, *Nacionalismo*, pp. 225–244; Russell to Sec. St., 24 July 1923, Lee, Quarterly Report of the Mil. Gov., Oct.–Dec. 1923, Welles to Sec. St., 19 Nov. 1923, and Russell to Sec. St., 24 Mar. 1924, USNA, 839.00/2727, 2805, 2762, and 2820.

67. Blanco Fombona, *Crímenes*, pp. 49–53; Junta de Abstención Electoral de la Provincia de Santo Domingo, *Protesta contra la sentencia que condena al Dr. Federico Ellis Cambiaso*; Francis White, St. Dept., to Welles, 17 Feb. 1923, USNA, 839.00/2686a. The Cestero archive contains many papers from this conference.

68. Welles to Sec. St., 1 June 1923, USNA, 839.00/2717.

69. Lee, Reports of Operations, Jan.–Dec. 1923, USNA, RG45, WA7, B646; Papers of the Comdng. Genl., 1923, and Lee to Russell, 20 Dec. 1922, USNA, RG38, E6, B67 and 51.

70. Lee to Prov. Pres., 15 Aug. 1923, and Vicini Burgos to Lee, 6 Oct. 1923, USNA, RG38, E6, B67.

71. *Protesta de la Junta de Abstención Electoral de la Provincia de Santo Domingo, contra la sentencia que condena al patriota dominicano Dr. Federico Ellis Cambiaso* (broadside), HyC, protested the trial and sentence of the author of *Los cuatro monstruos de anexión*, an attack on the Hughes-Peynado Plan. Russell to Sec. St., 31 Jan. 1923, USNA, 839.00/2676. Mil. Gov. to Vicini Burgos, 16 May 1924, USNA, RG38, E6, B75, documents a 1924 case.

72. Fabio Fiallo, *Presentación del mártir Cayo Báez . . .* , p. 9. The social

correspondence of the military governor and his staff is in USNA, RG38, E6, B60–68.

73. Peynado resigned from the Comisión de Representantes in January 1923 and was replaced by M. de J. Troncoso de la Concha; Russell to Sec. St., 9 Jan. 1923, USNA, 839.00/2669.

74. On prewithdrawal politicking from a Dominican point of view, see Rafael Damirón, *Memorias y comentarios*, pp. 155–190; Campillo Pérez, *El grillo*, pp. 151–158; and Mejía, *De Lilís*, pp. 190–197. The U.S. view is given by two State Department officials in Welles, *Naboth's Vineyard*, vol. 2, pp. 879–898, and in Munro, *U.S. and the Caribbean*, pp. 60–64. Also see the documents in *Foreign Relations, 1923*, pp. 892–917, and *1924*, pp. 618–624.

75. Russell to Sec. St., 12 July 1923, and Welles to Sec. St., 5 Nov. 1923, USNA, 839.00/2725 and 2758; Knowles to Peynado, 5 Sept. 1923, PFP.

76. Welles to Sec. St., 22 Mar. 1924, USNA, 839.00/2825.

77. Knowles to Peynado, 5 Sept. 1923, PFP.

78. Francisco J. Peynado, *El sol sale para todos: Manifiesto que al pueblo dominicano dirije el Lic. Francisco J. Peynado*, 6 Jan. 1923; Damirón, *Memorias*, p. 172; Welles, *Naboth's Vineyard*, vol. 2, p. 892. [Ortega Frier?], *Memorándum*, pp. 63–69, blames Welles in part for Peynado's defeat, accusing him of politicking on Vásquez' behalf.

79. Welles to Sec. St., 30 Apr. 1923 and 17 Jan. 1924, USNA, 839.00/2709 and 2786; Munro, *U.S. and the Caribbean*, p. 61.

80. Knowles to Peynado, 5 Sept. 1923, PFP.

81. Welles to Sec. St., 19 and 21 Nov. 1923, and Lee, Quarterly Report of the Mil. Gov., Oct.–Dec. 1923, USNA, 839.00/2762, 2771, and 2805.

82. Fed. Henríquez y Carvajal, *Nacionalismo*, pp. 245–250; Russell to Sec. St., 18 Sept. 1924, USNA, 839.00/2863; Campillo Pérez, *El grillo*, pp. 161, 166.

83. Quarterly Report of Provost Prisoners, Sto. Dom., quarter ending 31 Mar. 1924, and Harry Lee to CO, Cárcel Pública, 1 July 1924, USNA, RG38, E6, B74; Comding. Genl. to Mil. Gov., 11 Apr. 1924, USNA, RG45, WA7, B646.

84. Russell to Sec. St., 18 Sept. 1924, USNA, 839.00/2861; Condit and Turnbladh, *Hold High the Torch*, pp. 96–99.

EPILOGUE

1. The basic thesis of Medina Benet, *Los responsables*, is that the Vásquez government followed pre-1916 patterns almost exactly, missing a golden opportunity to renew Dominican political life.

2. Campillo Pérez, *El grillo*, p. 170.

3. For example, Hoetink, *El pueblo*, p. 338.

4. Muto, "Promise," pp. 154–155.

5. Warden McK. Wilson, Chargé, Sto. Dom., to Sec. St., 6 Oct. 1924, USNA, 839.00/2910; Muto, "Promise," pp. 155–156. Ramón Emilio Jiménez' two-volume work on Dominican folklore, *Al amor de bohío:*

Tradiciones y costumbres dominicanas, and Ramón Marrero Aristy's *Over* illustrate the latter trend.

6. Welles, *Naboth's Vineyard*, vol. 2, pp. 927–928.
7. Knight, *The Americans*, p. 101, cites minimum costs to the U.S. taxpayer of $12 million between 1916 and 1922.
8. Schmidt, *Haiti*.
9. Mayer to Sec. St., 30 July 1921, USNA, 839.00/2451; Welles, *Naboth's Vineyard*, vol. 2, p. 514.
10. Gordon K. Lewis, *Puerto Rico: Freedom and Power in the Caribbean*, chap. 3.
11. Macaulay, *Sandino Affair*.
12. Mejía, *De Lilís*, pp. 211–212; Medina Benet, *Los responsables*, pp. 55–73.
13. Welles to Francis [White], 22 July 1925, USNA, 839.00/2938; Mejía, *De Lilís*, p. 212.
14. Evan E. Young to Sec. St., 19 and 29 Dec. 1925, 12 Jan., and 8 Feb. 1926, USNA, 839.00/2929, 2930, 2931, and 2935; Franklin B. Frost to Sec. St., 6 Aug. 1927, USNA, 839.52/64, and related corres., beginning with file 839.6351; Mejía, *De Lilís*, p. 215.
15. Welles, *Naboth's Vineyard*, vol. 2, pp. 928–929.

Bibliography

BOOKS AND ARTICLES

Academia Colombina. *Memorial de protesta contra la arbitraria ocupación de la República Dominicana por tropas de los Estados Unidos de América.* Santo Domingo: Imprenta del Listín Diario, 1916.

Albuquerque, Alcibiades. *Títulos de los terrenos comuneros de la República Dominicana.* Ciudad Trujillo: Impresora Dominicana, 1961.

Alfau Durán, Vetilio. *Marcial Guerrero, héroe y mártir, 1888–1918.* Extra of *El Progreso.* La Vega: Tipografía El Progreso, [November 1937].

———. "Planes patrióticos de desocupación." *Ahora,* 6 November 1967, pp. 62–63.

American Federation of Labor. *Report of the Proceedings of the 40th Annual Convention of the American Federation of Labor, Held at Montreal, Quebec, Canada, June 7 to 19, Inclusive, 1920.* Washington, D.C.: Law Reporter Printing Company, 1920.

Arzeno, Julio V. *Sumario explicativo de los actos del gobierno militar que valida el plan Hughes-Peynado.* San Pedro de Macorís: Imprenta La Provincia, 1923.

Asociación de Jóvenes Dominicanos. *A la juventud del país.* Santo Domingo: Imprenta Montalvo, 1922.

Báez Evertsz, Franc. *Azúcar y dependencia en la República Dominicana.* Santo Domingo: Alfa y Omega, 1978.

Batías, Ramón [pseud.?]. "El patriota se llamaba Fidel Ferrer." *Renovación,* 1969, p. 5.

Baughman, C. C. "United States Occupation of the Dominican Republic." *United States Naval Institute Proceedings* 51, no. 274 (December 1925): 2306–2327.

Blakeslee, George H., ed. *Mexico and the Caribbean.* New York: Stechert and Company, 1920.

Blanco Fombona, Horacio. *Crímenes del imperialismo norteamericano.* Mexico City: Editorial Churubusco, 1927.

Blasier, Cole. *The Hovering Giant: U.S. Responses to Revolutionary Change in Latin America.* Pittsburgh: University of Pittsburgh Press, 1976.

Blassingame, John W. "The Press and American Intervention in Haiti and the Dominican Republic, 1904–1920." *Caribbean Studies* 9, no. 2 (July 1969): 27–43.

Bordas, José Rafael. *Frente al imperialismo.* Santo Domingo: Imprenta de E. M. Casanova N., 1923.

Bosch, Juan. *Trujillo: Causas de una tiranía sin ejemplo.* 2d ed. Caracas, 1961.

Boyce, William D. *United States Colonies and Dependencies Illustrated.* Chicago: Rand McNally and Company, 1914.

Bryan, Patrick. "La cuestión obrera en la industria azucarera de la República Dominicana a finales del siglo XIX y principios del siglo XX." *EME EME* 7, no. 41 (March–April 1979): 57–77.

Burks, Arthur J. *Land of Checkerboard Families.* New York: Coward McCann, 1932.

Calder, Bruce J. "Some Aspects of the United States Occupation of the Dominican Republic, 1916–1924." Ph.D. dissertation, University of Texas, Austin, 1974.

Campillo Pérez, Julio G. *El grillo y el ruiseñor: Elecciones presidenciales dominicanas; contribución a su estudio.* Santo Domingo: Editora del Caribe, 1966.

Castillo, Pelegrín. *La intervención americana.* Santo Domingo: Imprenta del Listín Diario, 1916.

Castro García, Teófilo. *Intervención yanqui, 1916–1924.* Santo Domingo: Editora Taller, 1978.

Cestero, Manuel F., and Manuel Flores Cabrera. *Circulares de la Oficina de Información en los Estados Unidos.* [Washington, D.C.?], 1921.

Cestero, Tulio M. "Los Estados Unidos y la República Dominicana de 1903 a 1916." *La Reforma Social,* 17 October 1916, pp. 88–90.

———. *Los Estados Unidos y las Antillas.* Madrid: Ibero-Americana, 1931.

———. *El problema dominicano.* New York, 1919.

Cestero Burgos, Tulio A. *Entre las garras del águila.* Santo Domingo, 1922.

Clausner, Marlin D. *Rural Santo Domingo: Settled, Unsettled, and Resettled.* Philadelphia: Temple University Press, 1973.

Condit, Kenneth W., and Edwin T. Turnbladh. *Hold High the Torch: A History of the 4th Marines.* Washington, D.C.: U.S. Marine Corps, 1960.

Congreso Masónico Dominicano. *Exposición del Congreso Dominicano a los Supremos Consejos 33 de los Estados Unidos de Norte América . . .* Santo Domingo: Imprenta del Listín Diario, 1920.

Corten, Andrés, et al. *Azúcar y política en la República Dominicana.* Santo Domingo: Editora Taller, 1976.

Damirón, Rafael. *Memorias y comentarios.* Ciudad Trujillo: Stella, 1953.

Davis, Henry C. "Indoctrination of Latin-American Service." *Marine Corps Gazette* 5, no. 2 (June 1920): 154–161.

de la Rosa, Antonio [Alexandre Poujols]. *Las finanzas de Santo Domingo y el control americano.* Santo Domingo: Editora Nacional, 1969. A translated edition of *Les finances de Saint Domingue et le control américaine.* Paris: A. Pedrone Ed., 1915.

del Castillo, José. *La inmigración de braceros azucareros en la República Dominicana, 1900–1930.* Vol. 262, no. 7. Santo Domingo: Centro Dominicano de Investigaciones Antropológicas, 1978.

del Castillo, Luis C. *Medios adecuados para conservar i desarrollar el nacionalismo en la república.* [Santo Domingo]: Imprenta La Cuña de América, 1920.

Deschamps, Enrique. *El espíritu de España en la liberación de la República Dominicana, 1916–1924.* Caracas: Tipografía Universal, 1928.

Dominican Economic Commission. *Report.* Chicago: Lakeside Press, 1929.

Ducoudray, Félix Servio. *Los "gavilleros" del este: Una epopeya calumniada.* Santo Domingo: Universidad Autónoma de Santo Domingo, 1976.

Durland, William D. *Los bosques en la República Dominicana.* Santo Domingo, 1925.

Ellis Cambiaso, Federico. *Los cuatro monstruos de anexión.* Santo Domingo: Imprenta Montalvo, 1922.

Fairchild, Fred R. "The Public Finance of Santo Domingo." *Political Science Quarterly* 33 (December 1918): 461–481.

Fellowes, Edward A. "Training Native Troops in Santo Domingo." *Marine Corps Gazette* 8, no. 4 (December 1923): 215–233.

Fiallo, Fabio. *La Comisión Nacionalista Dominicana en Washington, 1920–1921.* Ciudad Trujillo: Imprenta La Opinión, 1939.

———. *Plan de acción y liberación del pueblo dominicano* . . . Santo Domingo: Imprenta Montalvo, 1922.

———. *Presentación del mártir Cayo Báez.* La Vega: Tipografía El Progreso, 1923.

Franck, Harry Alverson. *Roaming through the West Indies.* New York: Century Company, 1920.

———. "Santo Domingo, the Land of Bullet-Holes." *Century Magazine* 100 (July 1920): 300–311.

Franco, Persio C. *Algunas ideas.* Santiago, 1926.

Fuller, Stephen M., and Graham A. Cosmas. *Marines in the Dominican Republic, 1916–1924.* Washington, D.C.: U.S. Marine Corps, 1974.

Goico Castro, Manuel de Jesús. "Raíz y trayectoria del teatro en la literatura nacional." *Anales* 10, nos. 37–38 (January–June 1946): 155–202. Universidad Autónoma de Santo Domingo.

Goldwert, Marvin. *The Constabulary in the Dominican Republic and Nicaragua: Progeny and Legacy of U.S. Intervention.* Gainesville: University of Florida Press, 1962.

Gómez, Juan. "The Gallant Dominicans." *American Mercury* 17 (May 1929): 89–95.

Gordon, Martin K., ed. *Joseph Henry Pendleton, 1860–1942: Register of His Personal Papers.* Washington, D.C.: U.S. Marine Corps, 1975.

Grieb, Kenneth J. "Warren G. Harding and the Dominican Republic: U.S. Withdrawal, 1921–1923." *Journal of Inter-American Studies* 11, no. 3 (July 1969): 425–440.

Hayden, Reynolds. "Review of Reorganization of Sanitary and Public Health Work in the Dominican Republic under U.S. Military Government of Santo Domingo." *U.S. Naval Medical Bulletin* 16, no. 4 (April 1922): 657–671.

Hazard, Samuel. *Santo Domingo, Past and Present, with a Glance at Haiti.* New York: Harper and Brothers, 1873.

Healy, David F. *Gunboat Diplomacy in the Wilson Era: The U.S. Navy in Haiti, 1915–1916.* Madison: University of Wisconsin Press, 1976.

———. *The United States in Cuba, 1898–1902.* Madison: University of Wisconsin Press, 1963.

———. *U.S. Expansionism: The Imperialist Urge in the 1890s.* Madison: University of Wisconsin Press, 1970.

Henríquez Ureña, Max. *Los Estados Unidos y la República Dominicana: La verdad de los hechos comprobada por datos y documentos oficiales.* Havana: Imprenta El Siglo XX, 1919.

———. *Panorama histórico de la literatura dominicana.* 2 vols. 1945; reprint Santo Domingo: Librería Dominicana, 1965–1966.

———, ed. *Pedro Henríquez Ureña, Antología.* Ciudad Trujillo: Librería Dominicana, 1950.

———. *Los yanquis en Santo Domingo: La verdad de los hechos comprobada por datos y documentos oficiales.* Madrid: M. Aguilar, 1929.

Henríquez y Carvajal, Federico. *Nacionalismo: Tópicos jurídicos e internacionales.* Santo Domingo: Imprenta de J. R. Viuda García, 1925.

Hitchman, James H. *Leonard Wood and Cuban Independence, 1898–1902.* The Hague: M. Nijhoff, 1971.

Hobsbawm, Eric J. *Bandits.* Middlesex, Eng.: Penguin, 1969.

———. *Primitive Rebels: Studies in Archaic Forms of Social Movements in the 19th and 20th Centuries.* New York: Norton, 1959.

Hoepelman, Antonio. *Apuntes históricos documentados de la honorable Cámara de Cuentas de la República Dominicana.* Ciudad Trujillo, 1943.

———. "Fabio Fiallo y la intervención norte americana en Santo Domingo." *Bahoruco,* 16 July 1932.

———. *Páginas dominicanas de historia contemporánea.* Ciudad Trujillo: Impresora Dominicana, 1951.

——— and Juan A. Senior. *Documentos históricos que se refieren a la intervención armada de los Estados Unidos de Norte-América y a la implantación de un gobierno militar en la República Dominicana.* 1922; reprint Santo Domingo: Librería Dominicana, 1973.

Hoetink, H. "The Dominican Republic in the Nineteenth Century: Some Notes on Stratification, Immigration, and Race." In Magnus Mörner, ed., *Race and Class in Latin America.* New York: Columbia University Press, 1970.

———. *El pueblo dominicano, 1850–1900: Apuntes para su sociología histórica.* Santiago: Universidad Católica Madre y Maestra, 1971.

Hungría, Pedro M. *Apuntes para la historia de Santiago: Centro de Recreo, sociedad fundada el 16 de agosto 1894.* Santiago, 1946.

"La Información" frente a la ocupación de la República Dominicana por las fuerzas armadas de los Estados Unidos de América. Santiago: Franco Hermanos y Compañía, 1922.

"Instituto Profesional de Santiago de los Caballeros, República Dominicana." *Anales* 3, no. 1 (January 1939): 150–152. Universidad de Santo Domingo.

Jiménez, Ramón Emilio. *Al amor de bohío: Tradiciones y costumbres dominicanas.* 2 vols. Santiago: Editora La Información, 1927–1929.

Joubert, Emilio C. *Cosas que fueron.* Santo Domingo: Imprenta de J. R. Viuda García, 1936.

Juárez, Joseph Robert. "United States Withdrawal from Santo Domingo." *Hispanic American Historical Review* 42, no. 2 (May 1962): 152–190.

Junta de Abstención Electoral de la Provincia de Santo Domingo. *Constitución de la Junta de Abstención Electoral de la Provincia de Santo Domingo.* Santo Domingo: Imprenta Montalvo, 1921.

———. *Protesta contra la sentencia que condena al Dr. Federico Ellis Cambiaso.* Santo Domingo: Imprenta La Cuña de América, 1923.

Junta Patriótica de Damas. *Al pueblo dominicano.* Santo Domingo: Imprenta La Cuña de América, 1922.

Kelsey, Carl. "The American Intervention in Haiti and the Dominican Republic." *Annals of the American Academy of Political and Social Sciences* 100, no. 189 (March 1922): 110–202.

[Kemp, Alvin B.] "Private Kemp Reports on Our War in Santo Domingo." *Literary Digest,* 22 February 1919, pp. 105–108.

Kimball, C. O. "Duty with the Medical Corps of the Policía Nacional Dominicana." *U.S. Naval Medical Bulletin,* supp., 6, no. 4 (October 1922): 80–86.

Knight, Melvin M. *The Americans in Santo Domingo.* New York: Vanguard Press, 1928.

LaFeber, Walter. *The New Empire: An Interpretation of American Expansion, 1860–1898.* Ithaca, N.Y.: Cornell University Press, 1963.

Lane, Rufus H. "Civil Government in Santo Domingo in the Early Days of the Military Occupation." *Marine Corps Gazette* 7, no. 2 (June 1922): 127–146.

Lewis, Gordon K. *Puerto Rico: Freedom and Power in the Caribbean.* New York: Harper and Row, 1968.

Link, Arthur S. *Woodrow Wilson and the Progressive Era, 1910–1917.* 1954; reprint New York: Harper and Row, 1963.

Listín Diario. Santo Domingo, 1916–1924.

Lloyd, George William. "Economic and Social Changes in Santo Domingo, 1916–1926." M.A. thesis, Clark University, Worcester, Mass., 1928.

Lockmiller, David A. *Enoch H. Crowder: Soldier, Lawyer and Statesman.* Columbia: University of Missouri Press, 1955.

———. *Magoon in Cuba: A History of the Second Intervention, 1906–1909.* Chapel Hill: University of North Carolina Press, 1938.

Lockward, Jaime. *Teatro dominicano: Pasado y presente.* Ciudad Trujillo: Editorial La Nación, 1959.

Logan, Rayford W. *Haiti and the Dominican Republic.* New York and London: Oxford University Press under the Auspices of the Royal Institute of International Affairs, 1968.

Logia "La Fe" No. 7. *El caso de la respetable Logia "La Fe" No. 7 con el gobierno militar: Relación documentada.* Santo Domingo: Imprenta de J. R. Viuda García, 1926.

Lozano, Wilfredo. *La dominación imperialista en la República Dominicana, 1900–1930.* Santo Domingo: Universidad Autónoma de Santo Domingo, 1976.

Lugo, Américo. *Conferencia dictada por el Dr. Américo Lugo en el Teatro Colón de Santiago de los Caballeros el día 25 de junio de 1922.* Santo Domingo: Imprenta Montalvo, 1922.

———. "Emiliano Tejera." *Boletín del Archivo General de la Nación* 4, no. 18 (October 1941): 283–318.

———. *El nacionalismo dominicano.* Santiago: Tipografía La Información, 1923.

———. *El plan de validación Hughes-Peynado.* Santo Domingo: Imprenta La Cuña de América, 1922.

Macaulay, Neill. *The Sandino Affair.* Chicago: Quadrangle, 1967.

MacMichael, David C. "The United States and the Dominican Republic, 1871–1940: A Cycle in Caribbean Diplomacy." Ph.D. dissertation, University of Oregon, Eugene, 1964.

Marrero Aristy, Ramón. *Over.* Ciudad Trujillo: Imprenta La Opinión, 1939.

Martínez, Rufino. *Diccionario biográfico-histórico dominicano, 1821–1930.* Santo Domingo: Universidad Autónoma de Santo Domingo, 1971.

Marvin, George. "Watchful Acting in Santo Domingo." *World's Work* 34 (June 1917): 205–218.

Mayo, Arthur H. *Report on Economic and Financial Conditions of the Dominican Republic.* Santo Domingo: Imprenta de J. R. Viuda García, 1920.

McClellan, Edwin N. "Operations Ashore in the Dominican Republic." *United States Naval Institute Proceedings* 47, no. 216 (February 1921): 235–245.

McConnell, Edward B. *Chains of Gold: A Story and a Study of Imperialism.* Philadelphia: Dorrance, 1929.

Medina Benet, Víctor M. *Los responsables: Fracaso de la tercera república.* [Dominican Republic, 1974.]

Mejía, Félix E. *Al rededor y en contra del plan Hughes-Peynado.* Santo Domingo: Imprenta de Gran Librería Selecta, 1922.

Mejía, Luis F. *De Lilís a Trujillo: Historia contemporánea de la República Dominicana.* Caracas: Editorial Elite, 1944.

Mejía Ricart, Gustavo Adolfo. *Acuso a Roma: Yo contra el invasor.* Havana: Imprenta El Fígaro, 1920.

Millett, Allan R. *The Politics of Intervention: The Military Occupation of Cuba, 1906–1909.* Columbus: Ohio State University Press, 1968.

Millett, Richard. *Guardians of the Dynasty: A History of the U.S. Created*

Guardia Nacional de Nicaragua and the Somoza Family. Maryknoll, N.Y.: Orbis Books, 1977.

—— and G. Dale Gaddy. "Administering the Protectorates: The U.S. Occupation of Haiti and the Dominican Republic." *Revista/Review Interamericana* 6, no. 3 (Fall 1976): 383–402.

Moscoso Puello, F. E. *Cañas y bueyes.* Santo Domingo: Editorial La Nación, n.d. [ca. 1935].

Munro, Dana Gardner. *Intervention and Dollar Diplomacy in the Caribbean, 1900–1921.* Princeton, N.J.: Princeton University Press, 1964.

——. *The United States and the Caribbean Republics, 1921–1933.* Princeton, N.J.: Princeton University Press, 1974.

Muto, Paul H. "The Illusory Promise: The Dominican Republic and the Process of Economic Development, 1900–1930." Ph.D. dissertation, University of Washington, Seattle, 1976.

Nanita, Abelardo R. *La crisis.* Santo Domingo: Imprenta Boletín Oficial, 1921.

Norton, Henry Kittredge, "The Ethics of Imperialism." *World's Work* 51 (January 1926): 321–328.

[Ortega Frier, Julio?] *Memorándum relativo a la intervención de Sumner Welles en la República Dominicana.* [1 August 1945.] Santo Domingo: Editora Taller, 1973.

Pan American Federation of Labor. *Report of the Proceedings of the Second Congress of the Pan American Federation of Labor, Held at New York City, N.Y., July 7th to 10th, Inclusive, 1919.* Washington, D.C., n.d.

Peña Batlle, Manuel Arturo, ed. *Constitución política y reformas constitucionales, 1844–1942.* Santiago: Editorial El Diario, Edición del Gobierno Dominicano, 1944.

Pérez, Louis A., Jr. *Intervention, Revolution, and Politics in Cuba, 1913–1921.* Pittsburgh: University of Pittsburgh Press, 1978.

Peynado, Francisco J. "Deslinde, mensura y partición de terrenos." *Revista Jurídica,* no. 4 (1919): 1–19. Santo Domingo.

——. *Informe sobre la situación económica y financiera de la República Dominicana y el modo de solucionar sus problemas.* Santo Domingo: Imprenta de J. R. Viuda García, 1922.

——. *El sol sale para todos: Manifiesto que al pueblo dominicano dirije el Lic. Francisco J. Peynado.* Santiago: Lepervanche, 1923.

—— and Moisés García Mella. *Capacidad de los alcaldes para actuar como escribanos o como notarios.* [Santo Domingo], 1919.

Pichardo, Bernardo. *Resumen de historia patria.* 3d ed. 1st ed., 1921. Buenos Aires: Talleros Gráficos Americalée, 1947.

Piña Benítez, Manuel. *Del pasado.* Santo Domingo: Imprenta La Cuña de América, 1925.

Pratt, Julius W. *America's Colonial Experiment.* New York: Prentice-Hall, 1950.

Prud'homme, Emilio. *Mi libro azul.* Ciudad Trujillo: Impresora Dominicana, 1949.

Ricart y Olives, Alfredo. *Refutación al informe del Lic. Fco. J. Peynado.* Santo Domingo: Tipografía Listín Diarió, 1922.

Rodríguez Demorizi, Emilio, ed. *Papeles de Pedro F. Bonó.* Santo Domingo: Editora del Caribe, 1964.

Roíg de Leuchenring, Emilio. *La ocupación de la República Dominicana por los Estados Unidos y el derecho de las pequeñas nacionalidades de América.* Havana: Imprenta El Siglo XX, 1919.

Ros, Joseph. "Barahona." *Salesian* 26, no. 26 (Fall 1980): 25–28.

Ruiz Tejada, Manuel Ramón. *Estudio sobre la propiedad inmobiliaria en la República Dominicana.* Ciudad Trujillo: Editora del Caribe, 1952.

Sánchez, Juan J. *La caña en Santo Domingo.* 1893; reprint Santo Domingo: Editora Taller, 1972.

Schmidt, Hans. *The United States Occupation of Haiti, 1915–1934.* New Brunswick, N.J.: Rutgers University Press, 1971.

Schoenrich, Otto. "The Present American Intervention in Santo Domingo and Haiti." In George H. Blakeslee, ed., *Mexico and the Caribbean.* New York: Stechert and Company, 1920.

———. *Santo Domingo: A Country with a Future.* New York: Macmillan Company, 1918.

Smith, Robert Freeman. *The United States and Revolutionary Nationalism in Mexico, 1916–1932.* Chicago: University of Chicago Press, 1972.

Sosa Albuquerque, Alfonso. *Apuntes históricos sobre la propiedad territorial de Santo Domingo.* Santo Domingo: Imprenta Montalvo, 1920.

Tansill, Charles C. *The United States and Santo Domingo, 1798–1873: A Chapter in Caribbean Diplomacy.* Baltimore: Johns Hopkins University Press, 1938.

Thorpe, George C. "American Achievements in Santo Domingo, Haiti and the Virgin Islands." *Journal of International Relations* 11, no. 1 (July 1920): 63–86.

Tulchin, Joseph S. *The Aftermath of War: World War I and the U.S. Policy toward Latin America.* New York: New York University Press, 1971.

Unión Nacional Dominicana. *Reglamento interior de la sociedad patriótica Unión Nacional Dominicana.* Santo Domingo: Tipografía El Progreso, 1919.

Universidad de Santo Domingo. *Anales de la Universidad de Santo Domingo.* January 1939.

Urbano Gilbert, Gregorio. *Mi lucha contra el invasor yanqui de 1916.* Santo Domingo: Universidad Autónoma de Santo Domingo, 1975.

Vaughan, T. W., et al. *A Geological Reconnaissance of the Dominican Republic.* Washington, D.C., 1921.

Verrill, A. Hyatt. *Porto Rico, Past and Present, and Santo Domingo of To-day.* New York: Dodd, Mead and Company, 1914.

Vicini, José D. *La isla de azúcar.* Ciudad Trujillo: Editorial Pol Hermanos, 1957.

Welles, Sumner. *Naboth's Vineyard: The Dominican Republic, 1844–1924.* 2 vols. New York: Payson and Clarke, Ltd., 1928.

Weston, Rubin Francis. *Racism in U.S. Imperialism: The Influence of Ra-*

cial Assumptions on American Foreign Policy, 1893–1946. Columbia, S.C.: University of South Carolina Press, 1972.

Who Was Who, Vol. 1. Chicago: Marquis Publishers, 1942.

Wiarda, Howard J. *Dictatorship and Development: The Methods of Control in Trujillo's Dominican Republic.* Gainesville: University of Florida Press, 1968.

Williams, Charles F. "La Guardia Nacional Dominicana." *Marine Corps Gazette* 3, no. 3 (September 1918): 195–199.

GOVERNMENT PUBLICATIONS

Great Britain. Department of Overseas Trade. *Report on Economic Conditions in the Dominican Republic . . . by Mr. John Bowering.* London: Her Majesty's Stationery Office, 1926.

———. Department of Overseas Trade. *Report on the Economic, Financial and Commercial Conditions in the Dominican Republic.* Report dated October 1924 by Darrell Wilson. London: Her Majesty's Stationery Office, 1925.

República Dominicana. *Censo de la República Dominicana: Primer censo nacional, 1920.* Santo Domingo, 1920.

———. *Colección de leyes, decretos y resoluciones del Gobierno Provisional de la República.* 2 vols., 1923–1924. Santo Domingo: Imprenta de J. R. Viuda García, 1924.

———. *Colección de leyes, decretos y resoluciones emanados de los poderes legislativos y ejecutivos de la República Dominicana.* Vol. 20, 1910–1911. Santo Domingo: Imprenta del Listín Diario, 1929.

———. *Colección de órdenes ejecutivas del número 1 al 116 inclusive . . . de noviembre 29, 1916 hasta diciembre 31, 1917.* 6 vols., 1917–1922. Santo Domingo: Imprenta de J. R. Viuda García, 1918–1923.

———. Department of Promotion and Public Works (Secretaría de Estado de Fomento y Obras Públicas). *The Dominican Republic.* Washington, D.C.: Published by Direction of the Department of Promotion and Public Works for the Jamestown Tercentennial Exposition, Press of Byron S. Adams, 1907.

———. Presidencia, Dirección General de Información y Prensa. *Evolución de la industria azucarera en la República Dominicana: Historia y descripción de los ingenios azucareros.* Santo Domingo: Editora del Caribe, 1968.

———. Secretaría de Estado de lo Interior y Policía. *A los habitantes de la República Dominicana.* Santo Domingo: Imprenta de J. R. Viuda García, 1919.

———. Secretaría de Estado de Sanidad y Beneficencia. *Informe que el Secretario de Sanidad y Beneficencia presenta al Presidente Provisional de la República.* Santo Domingo: Imprenta de J. R. Viuda García, 1923.

———. Servicio Nacional de Instrucción Pública. *Colección de órdenes emanadas de la Secretaría de Estado de Justicia e Instrucción Pública . . . de 12 de septiembre, 1917, al 31 de diciembre, 1918.* Santo Domingo: Imprenta de J. R. Viuda García, 1919.

United States. Bureau of Foreign and Domestic Commerce. *The Development of the Dominican Republic.* Special Consular Report 65 by Charles H. Albrecht and Frank Anderson Henry. Washington, D.C.: Government Printing Office, 1914.

———. Bureau of Insular Affairs. War Department. *Report . . . Dominican Customs Receivership.* Washington, D.C.: Government Printing Office, 1908–1940.

———. Bureau of Labor Statistics. "Wages and Prices in the Dominican Republic." *Monthly Labor Review* 23, no. 2 (August 1926): 119–120.

———. Bureau of Labor Statistics. "Wages in the Dominican Republic." *Monthly Review of the Bureau of Labor Statistics* 6, no. 1 (January 1918): 109.

———. Commission of Inquiry to Santo Domingo. *Report of the Commission of Inquiry to Santo Domingo.* Washington, D.C.: Government Printing Office, 1871.

———. Military Government of Santo Domingo. *Informe final de la Comisión Dominicana de Reclamaciones de 1917 presentado al honorable gobernador militar de Santo Domingo.* Santo Domingo: Imprenta de J. R. Viuda García, 1920.

———. Military Government of Santo Domingo. *Santo Domingo: Its Past and Its Present Condition.* Santo Domingo, 1920.

———. Navy Department. "Information on Living Conditions in Santo Domingo and Haiti, 6 April 1921." In *Haiti and Santo Domingo,* a specially bound volume of pamphlets in the U.S. Naval Library, Washington, D.C.

———. Senate. Inquiry into the Occupation and Administration of Haiti and Santo Domingo. *Hearings before a Select Committee on Haiti and Santo Domingo,* 2 vols. 67th Cong., 1st and 2d sess., 1922.

———. State Department. *Papers Relating to the Foreign Relations of the United States.* Washington, D.C.: Government Printing Office, 1909–1940.

DOCUMENT COLLECTIONS

American Federation of Labor–Congress of Industrial Organizations. Vertical file: "Pan American Federation of Labor." AFL-CIO Library, Washington, D.C.

Archivo Cestero. Correspondence of Tulio M. Cestero and assorted nationalist documents. Library of the Universidad Autónoma de Santo Domingo, Santo Domingo. Cited as AC.

Archivo del Gobierno Militar de Santo Domingo. Papers of the military government, especially of the ministries. Archivo General de la Nación, Santo Domingo. Cited as AGN.

Colección Rodríguez Demorizi. Various historical documents collected and held by Emilio Rodríguez Demorizi, Santo Domingo. Cited as CRD.

Papeles de la Familia Henríquez y Carvajal. Correspondence and other materials of Federico and Francisco Henríquez y Carvajal. Casa de Don Federico y Biblioteca del Maestro, Santo Domingo. Cited as HyC.

Papeles de la Familia Peynado. Correspondence of Francisco J. Peynado held by the Peynado family and by the Archivo General de la Nación, Santo Domingo. Cited as PFP.

United States. Marine Corps. *Archives of the United States Marine Corps.* Geographical File. Marine Corps Historical Center, Washington, D.C.

———. Navy Department. *General Records of the Department of the Navy.* Record group 80. National Archives, Washington, D.C.

———. Navy Department. *Naval Records Collection of the Office of Naval Records and Library.* Record group 45. National Archives, Washington, D.C.

———. Navy Department. *Records of the Military Government of Santo Domingo, 1916–1924.* Record group 38. National Archives, Washington, D.C.

———. Navy Department. *Records of the United States Marines.* Record group 127. National Archives, Washington, D.C.

———. State Department. *General Records of the Department of State.* Record group 59, decimal file 839. U.S. National Archives Publication, microcopy 626. National Archives, Washington, D.C.

———. Treasury Department. *Records of the Bureau of Accounts.* Record group 39. National Archives, Washington, D.C.

———. War Department. *Records of the War Department General and Special Staffs.* Record group 165. National Archives, Washington, D.C.

Index